ILLUSTRATED DICTIONARY OF THE MUSLIM WORLD

❖ MUSLIM WORLD ❖

ILLUSTRATED DICTIONARY OF THE MUSLIM WORLD

Marshall Cavendish
Reference
New York

Website: www.marshallcavendish.us

This publication represents the opinions and views of the authors based on personal experience, knowledge, and research. The information in this book serves as a general guide only. The authors and publisher have used their best efforts in preparing this book and disclaim liability rising directly and indirectly from the use and application of this book.

Other Marshall Cavendish Offices:
Marshall Cavendish International (Asia) Private Limited, 1 New Industrial Road, Singapore 536196 • Marshall Cavendish International (Thailand) Co Ltd. 253 Asoke, 12th Flr, Sukhumvit 21 Road, Klongtoey Nua, Wattana, Bangkok 10110, Thailand • Marshall Cavendish (Malaysia) Sdn Bhd, Times Subang, Lot 46, Subang Hi-Tech Industrial Park, Batu Tiga, 40000 Shah Alam, Selangor Darul Ehsan, Malaysia

Marshall Cavendish is a trademark of Times Publishing Limited

All websites were available and accurate when this book was sent to press.

Library of Congress Cataloging-in-Publication Data

Illustrated dictionary of the Muslim world.
    p. cm.
  ISBN 978-0-7614-7929-1
  1. Islam--Dictionaries. 2. Islamic civilization--Dictionaries. I.
Marshall Cavendish Reference.
  BP40.I45 2010
  297.03--dc22
                                    2010008613

Printed in Malaysia
14 13 12 11 10 1 2 3 4 5 6

Marshall Cavendish
Publisher: Paul Bernabeo
Production Manager: Michael Esposito

The Brown Reference Group Ltd.
Editors: Felicity Crowe, Jolyon Goddard, Ben Hollingum, Sally MacEachern, Henry Russell
Development Editor: Tom Jackson
Designer: Joan Curtis
Picture Researchers: Sophie Mortimer, Andrew Webb
Indexer: Christine Michaud
Senior Managing Editor: Tim Cooke
Editorial Director: Lindsey Lowe

CONSULTANTS

Shainool Jiwa, Institute of Ismaili Studies, London

Omar Khalidi, Collections Librarian, Aga Khan Program for Islamic Architecture, Massachusetts Institute of Technology, Cambridge, Mass.

Dona J. Stewart, Associate Professor, Department of Anthropology and Geography, Georgia State University, Atlanta

CONTENTS

FOREWORD

Understanding the Muslim world is a challenging task. Hardly any corner of the world has not been touched by Islam in some manner. The presence of a Muslim minority, the Uighur, in China and the existence of the Islamic Community Center of Anchorage Alaska attest to the spread of Islam from its heartland on the Arabian Peninsula.

The story of the "Muslim" world is recorded in the scores of languages spoken and written by the global Muslim population. To distill this global experience into a single narrative inevitably loses richness and detail. Yet consolidation in some form is necessary to make the rich heritage of the Muslim world more accessible.

This volume contains a number of tools to guide study of the Muslim world. Here, fundamental concepts, key events, and significant people and places can be referenced quickly.

GLOSSARY

The glossary explains essential concepts and words fundamental to the Muslim experience. Many entries are derived from Islamic theological concepts or the civilizations that developed from Islam. For example, words such as *minaret* and *minbar* describe key architectural features of mosques. *Caliph*, *caliphate*, and *sultan* are all based on Muslim religious-political institutions and reflect a time when large Islamic empires ruled western Asia, North Africa, and parts of southern Europe.

It is important to note that some terms, often used in English, such as *jihad* and *sharia* can have very different connotations among Muslims from those they have among non-Muslims. *Jihad* in recent years has been translated into English primarily as "holy war," usually with reference to violent Islamic militants. More accurately, however, *jihad* means "struggle" and also refers to the nonviolent struggle of an individual to be a good Muslim. The conditions under which violent jihad is acceptable today is a hotly debated topic in the modern Muslim community.

Likewise, discussion of Sharia—Muslim law—often focuses on extreme cases such as the Taliban in Afghanistan. But directly translated *sharia* means simply "path." There is no one Sharia because Islam is practiced in many ways around the world; law derived from Islam is extremely varied. Many concepts, such as freedom of speech and the right to privacy, are common in both Sharia and Western legal codes.

TIME LINE

The Muslim experience spans over 1,500 years. In its early years in Arabia, Islam was feared by existing elites. As elsewhere in the world, warfare and force were the primary mechanisms for resolving conflict; the early history of Islam is dredged in violence. Soon Islam created vast empires, many of which promoted a scientific and intellectual flowering. The Islamic civilization that helped spark the European Renaissance was shattered by the arrival of Mongols from the east. After sacking Baghdad, the Mongols converted to Islam. Ultimately the Mongol invasion led to further expansion of the Muslim world.

The fall of the Ottoman Empire at the end of World War I had a profound impact on the political structures of many Muslim majority countries and often ushered in rule by largely secular leaders. However, populations retained their Muslim identity. In many places this Muslim identity was a major unifying force for resisting European imperial rule as it expanded into traditional Muslim regions in the 19th and 20th centuries. Colonialism, largely under the British and French, ended after World War II, with many Muslim majority countries attaining true independence for the first time. Today these countries face enormous economic and political challenges.

BIOGRAPHICAL AND GEOGRAPHICAL DICTIONARIES

While the Prophet Muhammad is likely the best-known person associated with Islam, many individuals have influenced not only the Muslim world but also global society. Sadly, Osama bin Laden is today the most familiar "famous Muslim" for much of the world. His heinous acts are far more familiar than the positive achievements of Benazir Bhutto, the first woman elected to lead a Muslim country (Pakistan), or Anwar Sadat, the Egyptian president who made peace with Israel only to be killed by Islamic extremists.

In addition to important historical and political leaders, this dictionary also reports on the cultural contributions of great Muslim thinkers such as the Persian philosopher and scientist Ibn Sina, known in European thought as Avicenna, as well as popular modern musicians like Yusuf Islam, or Cat Stevens. This dictionary also provides a handy gazetteer of the most important places in Muslim history and culture.

COUNTRY FACT FILES

Many, but not all, majority Muslim countries are in close proximity to Islam's cultural hearth on the Arabian Peninsula. Trade, along sea and land routes, dispersed Islam throughout much of Asia and Africa. Islam arrived in the Indonesian archipelago during the 11th century; today Indonesia is the most populous Muslim country.

Although there is much diversity among Muslim majority countries, many of them face considerable demographic and economic challenges. Youth compose a very large proportion of the population in many such countries. Young people often have few educational opportunities or job prospects, creating anger and deep societal tension. Country fact files in this work expose the socioeconomic realities of the Muslim world.

SUGGESTIONS FOR FURTHER READING

No one resource can adequately capture the diversity of the Muslim world in significant depth. Guidance can be provided, however, to ever-expanding resources for further reading and research, including online sources and broadcast networks as well as the more traditional media such as newspapers and books in print that record both the official positions of governments and religious institutions as well as the singular ideas of courageous thinkers. There are over one billion Muslims in the world, living diverse lives in varied places; it takes many voices to tell their story.

Dona J. Stewart
Center for Middle East Peace, Culture, and
Development; and Department of Anthropology
and Geography; Georgia State University

GLOSSARY

Abbasids a dynasty of caliphs formed by descendants of Muhammad's uncle Abbas; ruled from Baghdad (750–1258) until the city was sacked by Mongols. Accorded a purely religious function in Egypt, the Abbasids held power there from 1261 to 1517.

adab originally meaning "good manners," this Arabic word was later applied to a literary genre that developed in the ninth century under the Abbasid dynasty. By the 21st century, *adab* had become a general term meaning "literature."

adhan (Arabic: "announcement") the call to Friday public worship and to the five daily prayers. The *adhan* is proclaimed by the muezzin. The exact form of words varies from sect to sect, but the *adhan* most widely used in majority Sunni tradition is: "Allah is most great. I testify that there is no god but Allah. I testify that Muhammad is the prophet of Allah. Come to prayer. Come to salvation. Allah is most great. There is no god but Allah." The first phrase is proclaimed four times, the final phrase once, and the others twice each; worshippers make set responses to each phrase.

adl Arabic term for "justice," divine or legal.

Aghlabids Arab Muslim dynasty that ruled parts of northern Africa (modern Tunisia and eastern Algeria) from 800 to 909. The Aghlabids were nominally subject to the Abbasid caliphs of Baghdad.

ahd covenant with Allah. Particularly important in Sufism, the *ahd* is a ceremonial oath by which the *murid* (student) swears formal allegiance to a *murshid* (teacher) or *pir* (saint).

ahkam (singular: *hukm*) Islamic legal commandments, derived from interpretations of the Koran; the rulings of a Sharia court.

A muezzin performs the **adhan**—*call to prayer—at the Aqsunuqar Mosque in Cairo, Egypt.*

Ahl al-Kitab (Arabic: "People of the Book") members of religions whose faith is founded on divinely inspired works of literature. The main Peoples of the Book are Jews, Christians, and Zoroastrians, whose faiths are based on, respectively, the Torah, the Gospel, and the Avesta. Muslim men may marry women from Ahl al-Kitab even if the latter choose to remain in their religion, but men from Ahl al-Kitab must convert to Islam before they may marry a Muslim woman.

akhira the spiritual world. The temporal world is known as *dunya*. Figuratively, the terms may be used to mean good and evil, respectively.

al- in Arabic, the definite article.

Alawi a minority Shiite Muslim sect. Alawites venerate and take their name from Ali, who was the cousin and son-in-law of the Prophet Muhammad and the fourth of the "rightly guided" (*rashidun*) caliphs (ruled 656–661). They do not observe the Five Pillars of Islam. In spite of being regarded as heretics by some orthodox Muslims, the Alawites are powerful in Syria because their membership includes the ruling Assad family.

Alevi an Islamic sect in Turkey. Members worship in assembly houses rather than in conventional mosques and pray in Turkish or Kurdish rather than in Arabic.

Alf Laylah wa Laylah the Arabic title of the collection of 480 stories known in English as *The Thousand and One Nights* or *The Arabian Nights*. The authorship of the work is unknown and so, too, is the date of its composition, although the earliest reference to it is in a fragment from the ninth century. The basic plot—which is the framework for all the tales—concerns Shahryar, the king of an unnamed country in Central Asia, who, because of his hatred of women, marries a new wife every day and has her executed on the following morning. He eventually meets his match in the vizier's daughter, Shahrazad (Scheherazade), who every night tells him the first part of a story that he finds so enthralling that he spares her in order to hear how it ends. After listening to a host of adventures, featuring characters such as Aladdin, Ali Baba and the Forty Thieves, and Sindbad the Sailor, Shahryar realizes he has found true love.

algebra the branch of mathematics that uses letters to solve numerical problems. The English word comes from the Arabic *al-jabr* (literally, "reunion"), the title of a text by al-Khwarizmi (780–850).

Although al-Khwarizmi is sometimes described as "the father of algebra," the methods described in his work were in use long before his lifetime.

alim (Arabic: "scholar"; plural *ulama*, "the learned") a person who possesses *ilm* (learning) in the widest sense. The term may be applied to theologians (*mutakallimun*), high state religious officials, religious lawyers (muftis), judges (*qadis*), and professors.

Allah (Arabic: "God") Muslims believe that the god of Islam is unique (*wahid*), omnipotent, and omniscient. Allah has 99 names that are known to humans and a 100th name that will be revealed when the world ends on the Day of Judgment. Allah—who is neither male nor female—loves humanity and is infinitely merciful. It is therefore the duty of all believers to abandon themselves to Allah. The word *Islam* means "submission." One of the most commonly heard colloquial expressions—not only in Arabic-speaking countries but throughout the Muslim world—is *insha'a Allah* ("if Allah wills"), a constant reminder that nothing happens unless it is by the will or commandment of Allah.

Allahu akbar (Arabic: "God is great") an expression used widely in religious ceremonies and in colloquial speech. The phrase is sometimes known as the *takbir*.

Almohads a confederation of Muslim Berbers who succeeded the Almoravids as rulers of the Islamic empire in northern Africa and Spain (ruled 1130–1269).

Almoravids a confederation of Muslim Berbers who established an Islamic empire in northwestern Africa and Spain in the 11th and 12th centuries.

ansars (literally, "helpers") a term applied to the citizens of Yathrib (later Medina) who helped Muhammad and his followers on their arrival from Mecca at the end of the *hijra*.

aqida the Islamic creed, which conventionally comprises six articles of faith: in god (Allah), in the prophets (*nabi*) and messengers (*rusul*), in the angels (*malaika*), in the Koran and other holy books, in the Day of Judgment (*qiyama*), and in destiny (*qadar*).

aqiqah a ritual performed by Muslims, traditionally on the seventh day after the birth of a child, to welcome the new arrival into the world. The word is also applied to the food—customarily lamb or mutton—that is cooked for the guests on such an occasion.

aql human intellect or knowledge.

Arabic see box.

ARABIC

Arabic is a language spoken by about 170 million people in Algeria, Bahrain, Egypt, Eritrea, Iraq, Jordan, Kuwait, Lebanon, Libya, Mauritania, Morocco, Oman, Qatar, Saudi Arabia, Somalia, Sudan, Syria, Tunisia, and Yemen. Elsewhere, it is spoken by exiled and emigré Arabs and in every country in which Islam is one of the religions. Arabic is the most widely spoken of the Semitic languages—a group that also includes Amharic and Hebrew. Arabic is important because it is the language of the Koran. This holy text must be read and recited in the original language, and thus there is some knowledge of Arabic throughout the Muslim world.

Today, Arabic is the liturgical language of Muslims in Afghanistan, Indonesia, Iran, Kazakhstan, Kyrgyzstan, Pakistan, parts of sub-Saharan Africa, Tajikistan, Turkey, Turkmenistan, and Uzbekistan. These are all countries in which the national language is something other than Arabic. Although the Koran must be recited in classical Arabic, almost every Arabic-speaking nation has a local variation of the language. These vernaculars differ widely. The diverse colloquial dialects of Arabic are interrelated, but differ both from standard Arabic and from each other in grammar, pronunciation, and vocabulary. They are usually labeled according to major geographic areas, such as North African Arabic, Egyptian Arabic, and Gulf Arabic. Within these broad classifications, the daily speech of urban, rural, and nomadic speakers is very different. Uneducated speakers from widely separated parts of the Arab world may not understand each other at all, even though they are speaking the same language—Moroccan Arabic, for example, may be virtually unintelligible in Iraq.

Arabic has 28 consonants, including all the Semitic guttural sounds produced far back in the mouth and throat. Three of these consonants—*alif, waw,* and *ya*—also represent long vowels. Each of the three vowels in standard Arabic occurs in a long and a short form, creating the long and short syllables so important to the meter of Arabic poetry. Normal sentence word order in standard Arabic is verb-subject-object. In poetry and in some prose styles, this word order can be altered; when that happens, subject and object can be distinguished by their case endings. Arabic script, which is derived from that of Aramaic, is written from right to left. The Arabic alphabet has been adopted by non-Semitic languages such as modern Persian (Farsi), Urdu, Malay, and some West African languages, such as Hausa.

Ashura Muslim holy day that falls on the 10th day of Muharram, the first month of the Islamic year. It was originally designated by the Prophet Muhammad as a day of compulsory fasting but, after Ramadan took over as the month of abstinence, Ashura became the occasion of a voluntary fast. Ashura's principal modern significance is as a Shiite day of mourning to commemorate the death of Husayn, the son of Ali and the grandson of Muhammad, on the 10th of Muharram in the year 680. In some countries—including Bahrain, Iran, Iraq, Lebanon, and Pakistan—Ashura has become a national holiday.

asr the third of the five prayers (*salat*) recited daily before sunset by devout Muslims; also the name of a short chapter (sura) in the Koran.

atabat (Arabic: "thresholds") Shiite holy places in Iraq, at Karbala, Najaf, Qadimayn, and Samarra, containing the tombs of six of the imams revered in Twelver Shiism. *Atabat*s are pilgrimage destinations and centers of learning.

aya a verse in the Koran. The Koran is divided into 114 suras, each of which contains between 3 and 286 *aya*s. The word *aya* may also be used to mean "miracle" because that is what the holy book of Islam is considered by Muslims to be.

ayatollah a high-ranking Shiite Muslim cleric. Holders of the title are experts in various aspects of Islam, particularly law, ethics, and philosophy. The ayatollah best known in the West, Ruhollah Khomeini (ruler of Iran, 1979–1989), was a leading authority on all three subjects.

Ayyubids a mainly Kurdish dynasty of Sunni Muslims. Founded by Salah ad-Din (Saladin; 1138–1193), the Ayyubids ruled Egypt, the greater part of modern Iraq and Syria, and Yemen for more than a century before they were gradually displaced by the Mamluks.

Ba'ath (also known as the Arab Socialist Renaissance Party) a secular political party advocating the formation of a single Arab socialist nation. It has been in power in Syria since 1963 and was the ruling party in Iraq from 1968 to 2003.

Badw (Bedouin) nomadic, pastoral, Arabic-speaking peoples of western Asia, particularly the Arabian Peninsula, Iraq, Jordan, and Syria, and northern Africa. The traditional occupations of the Bedouin—herding camels, sheep, goats, and cattle—were severely disrupted in the 20th century by Western colonial powers that erected national borders across lands over which the indigenous tribes had previously had free rein. Since then, many Bedouin have adopted sedentary lifestyles. Many of those who remain nomadic have become embroiled in internecine territorial rivalries.

Baha'i a non-Islamic religion founded in Iran in the mid-19th century by Baha' Ullah. The essence of the Baha'i faith is the oneness of humanity and all religions. Baha'i has increased its membership worldwide since the 1960s but has been persecuted in Iran since the Islamic Revolution of 1979.

Barelvi Islam a liberal Sunni Muslim movement, informed by the tenets of Sufism, that originated in the 19th century in southern India and spread during the 20th century to Bangladesh, Britain, Pakistan, and South Africa.

barakah any blessing, particularly of divine providence or spiritual gifts. The first name of U.S. president Barack Obama is a Swahili form of this Arabic word.

basmalah literally, "in the name of god." This word derives from the phrase "*bism Allah ar-rahman ar-rahim*" (in the name of God, the Merciful, the Compassionate), which begins all but one of the suras in the Koran and is used at the start of most formal documents, especially those that are legally binding.

Bayt al-Hikma ("house of wisdom") a scientific institution

Bedouin are sometimes classified according to the animals they keep. Camel nomads roam vast territories. Other Bedouin, such as sheep, goat, and cattle herders, are more localized.

founded in Baghdad, Iraq, by al-Ma'mun, the seventh Abbasid caliph (ruled 813–833). There are no reliable records of its detailed workings, but the Bayt al-Hikma is known to have been the main palace library and the center of a vibrant copying industry that transcribed major works from Persian into Arabic.

Bayt al-Mal (Arabic: "house of money" or "house of wealth") a treasury that collected taxes and controlled expenditure in caliphates and sultanates. The Bayt al-Mal was also responsible for the distribution of *zakat* revenues for public works.

bazaar originally the Persian for "market," the term was quickly adopted throughout the Arab world. The equivalent word in Arabic is *suq*.

Bedouin see **Badw**.

Berbers a mainly white non-Semitic people who ruled much of northern Africa until the seventh century, when the Arab conquest of the region reduced their status. Today, most Berbers are sedentary farmers living in scattered communities across Algeria, Egypt, Libya, Morocco, and Tunisia; there are also Berber communities in Mali, Mauritania, and Niger. They are nearly all Muslims, although some of their religious practices retain vestiges of the pre-Islamic period.

bida any innovation in the practice of Islam that is not derived from the traditional Sunna of the Muslim community. Some fundamentalist Muslims, such as the Wahhabis of Saudi Arabia, reject any form of *bida* as heretical on the grounds that the Sunna was established by the Prophet Muhammad and no ordinary mortal has the authority to alter it in any way.

bint part of an Arabic personal name meaning "daughter of." The word is followed by the forename of the father—for example, Muhammad's wife Hafsah bint Umar was the daughter of Umar ibn al-Khattab.

Black Stone known in Arabic as al-Hajar-ul-Aswad, the Black Stone is embedded in the eastern corner of the Kaaba of Al-Masjid al-Haram (the Great Mosque) in Mecca, Saudi Arabia. It is said to have been given to Adam when he was expelled from Paradise. Its geological origin is uncertain, but it may be a meteorite or a tektite (rock formed from molten glass). It stands about 5 feet (1.5 m) aboveground—held in a silver frame—and has a diameter of about 12 inches (30 cm). When hajj pilgrims circle the Kaaba, they try to kiss the Black Stone as the Prophet Muhammad is said to have done. Because of the vast numbers of Muslims who crowd the Great Mosque, that is not always possible—those who cannot get within reach of the stone point to it on each of their seven ritual revolutions around it.

Bohora an Ismaili Muslim sect that originated in western India. Bohoras are predominantly Shiites, but there is also a Sunni minority. As a result of a schism in

This ancient caravansary in Kyrgyzstan was built to shelter travelers and their animals on the Silk Road, a trade route linking Asia to the Mediterranean world.

in 1588, there are now two major groups—the Daudis, whose principal center is in Mumbai, India, and the Sulaymani, who reside mainly in Yemen.

burqa see *hijab*.

Buyyids a native dynasty that ruled in western Iran and Iraq in the period between the Arab and Turkish conquests (945–1055).

caliph (from *khalifah*, Arabic: "successor") a religious and political leader of Islam; successor to Muhammad. Rival caliphs divided the Islamic states.

caliphate the office and realm held by a caliph.

caravansary a public building, usually outside the walls of a town or village, used for sheltering caravans and other travelers. Most caravansaries had only one entrance, a heavy door large enough to allow the passage of laden camel trains. The ground floor of the interior of a typical caravansary took the form of a quadrilateral outdoor courtyard with feeding and watering facilities for the camels. Around its perimeter were cloistered arcades. Above the arcades, accessed from the ground floor by open stone staircases, was a second story comprising sleeping quarters for the guests.

chador see *hijab*.

Chishtiyah a Muslim Sufi order, named for Chisht, the village in which the founder of the order, Abu Ishaq of Syria, took up residence on his arrival in India. Chishtiyah has been one of the most popular forms of Sufism since the 12th century. Members are pacifists who cut themselves off as far as possible from worldly concerns. The order has an extensive series of monasteries (*khanqahs*) in India and Pakistan.

dai someone who practices *dawah*, the act of increasing another's understanding of Islam or encouraging him or her to join the faith; a Muslim missionary.

Dajjal (Arabic: "Deceiver") the Antichrist who, Muslims believe, will appear on earth shortly before the end of time and claim to be God. He will be destroyed by Jesus Christ, by the Mahdi ("rightly guided one"), or by both of them; after Dajjal's death, the world will submit eternally to the will of Allah.

Dar al-Hikma the Cairo equivalent of the Bayt al-Hikma in Baghdad. The Dar al-Hikma center of learning was founded in 1004 by the Fatimid caliph al-Hakim.

Dar al-Islam (Arabic: "House of Islam") a political term for the region in which Islam has ascendancy; its obverse is Dar al-Harb ("House of War"), any non-Muslim region into which the faith could—and, in the view of the ideologues who use the expression, should—expand.

deen (or *din*) Arabic word usually rendered in English as "religion" but which may mean, more generally, "the Islamic way of life." Arab Christians also use it to refer to their faith. There are three essential components of *deen*—*iman* (faith), *islam* (in this context, submission), and *ihsan* (broadly, good deeds).

Deobandis members of the Deoband school, the ultra-puritanical and orthodox Muslim theological madrassa in Uttar Pradesh, India. The program of studies at the Deoband school is highly traditional and prepares its annual intake of about 1,500 students for leadership of the Islamic community. The core curriculum is study of the Koran and the Hadiths, together with jurisprudence (*fiqh*), theology (*kalam*), and philosophy (*falsafah*).

dervish any member of a *tariqa* (Sufi fraternity). Student dervishes are taught by their sheikhs, or masters, the devotional formula in praise of Allah that they must recite in order to attain oneness with God. Dervishes often live in communities similar to monasteries. An itinerant or a mendicant dervish is known as a *faqr* (fakir).

devshirme in the Ottoman Empire, the conscription of Christian boys, who were taken from their families, converted to Islam, and trained as Janissary soldiers. The term was also applied to the conscripts themselves.

dhikr (Arabic: "remembrance of Allah") an act of solitary or communal religious devotion that may involve the recital of the 99 names of Allah and of quotations from the Koran and the Hadiths. The *dhikr* that involves the repeated recitation of a devotional formula in praise of Allah is the main ritual practiced by dervishes as a means of attaining an ecstatic experience.

dhimmi (literally, "protection") any non-Muslim living in a state governed by Sharia law. *Dhimmi* status afforded holders various rights, such as the freedom to practice their own religions, but also imposed several restrictions—for example, *dhimmi*s were not permitted to bear arms. *Dhimmi* status was originally availed only to Christians and Jews, but it was later extended to Buddhists, Hindus, Sikhs, Zoroastrians, and other religionists.

Dhu'l-Hijja the 12th month of the Muslim lunar calendar.

Dhu'l-Qa'dah the 11th month of the Muslim lunar calendar.

diwan generally, lyric poetry; specifically, *Diwan* is the title of a celebrated collection of verse by the Persian poet Mohammad Shams od-Din Hafez (1325–1390).

Druze a religious sect founded in Cairo, Egypt, in the 11th century. Druze believe in reincarnation and in the divinity of the Fatimid caliph al-Hakim (996–1021). Members class themselves as Muslims, but they are not universally acknowledged as such by mainstream followers of Islam. The Druze forbid conversions, either to or from their faith, and marriages to non-Druze. They became well-known during the Lebanese civil war (1975–1990) when their militia was one of the three main combatant factions, along with the Shiites and the Christian Maronites. In spite of their international fame, the Druze are a small group—estimates of the exact number vary between 300,000 and one million worldwide. About one-half of that number lives in Syria; Lebanon is home to between 30 percent and 40 percent; the remaining Druze are scattered throughout Israel and Jordan, as well as in various countries of Europe and in the United States. The uncertainty about the exact number of Druze is largely attributable to the clandestine nature of their faith. Their doctrines are kept secret, even from many members. They are permitted to deny that they are Druze whenever it suits them to do so, probably as a response to the persecution that they have suffered from time to time throughout their history.

dua a supplication or an entreaty directly to Allah. A *dua* may be directed only to Allah; a direct appeal of a similar nature to any other divinity or holy person would be categorized as *shirk*.

duhr the third of the five daily Muslim prayers, performed about the middle of the day.

dunya the temporal world. The spiritual world is known as *akhira*. Figuratively, the terms may be used to mean evil and good, respectively.

durud an incantation or a formulaic prayer that is spoken typically by a Muslim in response to another's mention of Allah.

Eid al-Adha ("Festival of Sacrifice") the second of the two great Muslim festivals, the other being Eid al-Fitr. Eid al-Adha lasts for three days, starting on the 10th of Dhu'l-Hijja, the last month of the Islamic calendar. Celebrated by Muslims throughout the world, Eid al-Adha commemorates Abraham's son Ishmael (Ismail, reputedly an ancestor of the Prophet Muhammad) and marks the culmination of the hajj (pilgrimage to Mecca).

Eid al-Fitr ("Festival of Breaking Fast") the first of the two great Muslim festivals. Eid al-Fitr is held on the first three days of Shawwal, the 10th month of the Islamic calendar. It celebrates the end of Ramadan, the previous month, throughout which Muslims fast during the hours of daylight.

emir a military commander, governor of a province, or a high military official. The title was first adopted by Umar, the second caliph (ruled 634–644). In spite of its name, the modern United Arab Emirates (UAE) is ruled not by emirs but by sheikhs.

fajr (Arabic: "dawn") the morning prayer, the first of the five daily prayers (*salat*) recited by devout Muslims. During the month of Ramadan, the call to *fajr* marks the beginning of the daily fasting (*sawm*), which ends at the call to the fourth prayer of the day, the *maghrib*.

fana in Sufism (Islamic mysticism), the stage of the spiritual journey to union with God that involves complete denial of the self. *Fana* is usually attained through meditation and the deliberate rejection of human attributes. After achieving *fana*, Sufis revert to full consciousness and begin their preparation for the next stage, *baqa* (direct sight of God).

faqr renunciation of wealth. *Faqr* is a *maqam* (spiritual stage) on the path of Sufis (Islamic mystics) to union with God. It represents transcendence of the need for worldly possessions. The word *faqr* is the root of the anglicized *fakir* (mendicant dervish).

fard religious duty. There are two types of *fard*. *Fard al-ayn* is obligatory—it comprises the tasks that all Muslims are required to perform as a matter of routine, such as praying five times a day. *Fard al-kifaya* is any duty required of the whole Muslim community (*ummah*). Other types of *fard* are *mustahabb* (recommended but not required); these include *sadaqah*—donations to charity over and above the compulsory *zakat* (almsgiving).

Fatah (Palestine National Liberation Movement) Arab political and military organization, founded in the late 1950s with the aim of freeing Palestine from Israeli control. By the end of the 1960s, Fatah had taken over effective control of the Palestine Liberation Organization (PLO). Fatah carried out numerous terrorist attacks, most notoriously in 1972, when a splinter group, Black September, murdered Israeli athletes at the Olympic Games in Munich, West Germany. In 1982, Fatah and the PLO were driven out of their headquarters in southern Lebanon by an Israeli invasion. In 1993, the PLO—which was now officially led by Fatah—signed a peace agreement (the Oslo Accords) with Israel. However, the treaty was opposed by Hamas, a rival Islamic group. Hamas boycotted the 1996 elections in which Fatah won a majority of the seats in the newly established Palestinian Legislative Council (PLC). In 2006, Fatah lost its majority to Hamas, which had participated in that year's elections to the PLC.

fatiha (Arabic: "opening") the first sura (chapter) of the Koran. It consists of only seven *aya* (verses).

Fatimids a Shiite dynasty of caliphs in northern Africa (909–1177); its rulers were descended from Muhammad's daughter Fatima. The Fatimids conquered Egypt and founded Cairo in the year 950.

fatwa a legal opinion. In the West, the term has been widely taken to mean "a death sentence." This inaccurate translation is obtained by reference to the fatwa of 1989 in which Ayatollah Ruhollah Khomeini (ruler of Iran, 1979–1989) publicly condemned *The Satanic Verses*, a book by the Indian British author Salman Rushdie (born 1947). A bounty was offered to anyone who would execute Rushdie, who consequently went into hiding for several years.

fiqh Islamic jurisprudence. *Fiqh* expands and develops Sharia law

on the basis of the continuing judgments and rulings of Muslim jurists. The term is used particularly with reference to judgments concerning the observance of rituals and morals, and with social legislation. A person trained in *fiqh* is known as a *faqih* (plural: *fuqaha*).

fitna generally, any trial, test, or religious-based uprising, particularly the major schism between Shiites and Sunnis that occurred in the seventh century. *Fitna* is also the title of a controversial short movie, made in 2008 by Geert Wilders, the leader of the right-wing Dutch Party for Freedom, which was strongly critical of Muslim influence in the Netherlands.

fitrah innate human nature; the knowledge that there is one god only, which Muslims believe is inherent in all people from birth. It is because of *fitrah* that Muslims refer to people who adopt Islam as "reverts" rather than as "converts"—in their view, espousing Islam is a return to the pure state of being.

Fulani a predominantly Muslim people of sub-Saharan Africa. Thought to number more than 20 million, the Fulani are found in significant numbers in almost every country of the region and are most numerous in Mali, Niger, Nigeria, and Senegal. They are linked by their common language, Fula. They generally practice endogamy (marriage within their own group). Most male Fulani are polygynous (having more than one wife at a time). A typical household comprises the husband, his wives, and all their unmarried children. Most modern Fulani maintain their traditional nomadic, pastoral existence, and these herders have the highest status within their society. However, since the 19th century, many Fulani have moved into urban life or have become sedentary farmers. Such developments have been occasioned by economic necessity, notably by the periodic depletion of their herds through drought and food shortages. The consequent loss of social standing in their original communities led to their cultural absorption into their new surroundings. Nowhere was this effect more evident than in northern Nigeria, where the Fulani were fully assimilated by the Hausa people, adopting their language and culture and, indeed, after a series of holy wars (1804–1810), becoming their ruling elite. While nomadic Fulani are often Muslims in name only, many urban and sedentary Fulani practice Islam in some of its strictest and most austere forms.

futuwwat (Arabic for "spiritual chivalry") a term applied to the lifestyle of Muslims who combined military service with commercial activity. *Futuwwat* involved the duties of a knight and the business activities of a trade guildsman. Those who practiced *futuwwat* took as their model Ali, the cousin and son-in-law of the Prophet Muhammad and the fourth of the "rightly guided" (*rashidun*) caliphs (ruled 656–661).

ghayba (Arabic: "absence" or "concealment") originally, the disappearance from view in the year 878 of the 12th and last imam (leader), Muhammad al-Mahdi al-Hujjah. The term is now also applied to similar occultations of people who are believed to have withdrawn from the world, rather than died, and who continue to exist out of the sight of humans. Shiites believe that their imams, though unseen, still live and return when needed to direct human affairs. The ultimate Shiite *ghayba* is the Mahdi (the divinely guided one), who will reveal himself as the world approaches its end. Sufis (Muslim mystics) define *ghayba* differently, as the advanced stage of enlightenment in which the faithful banish all thoughts other than those of God.

ghazal a short love poem. The earliest examples of the *ghazal* form emerged in the Arabian Peninsula in the seventh century.

Ghaznavid a Turkish Muslim dynasty that ruled Afghanistan, most of Iran, and parts of Pakistan, Uzbekistan, and Tajikistan (977–1186).

HADITH

A Hadith—Arabic for "report"—is the record of the sayings of Muhammad. The Hadith is the second most important source of religious law and moral guidance in Islam, after the Koran. The first part of each Hadith includes a record of the person who initially reported the words or deeds of the Prophet. Those who passed on the message are listed as well in this prefatory section, which is known as the *isnad* (chain of transmission). The second part of the Hadith format is known as the *matn* (body), and it is reached only after the names of the transmitters have been listed. Commentators often treat the *matn* as the content of the Hadith, but it is important to note that the chain of transmission conveys valuable information as well. It is particularly important in establishing the authenticity of any statement attributed to Muhammad.

Over time, a large number of sayings attributed to the Prophet accumulated, and scholars needed to be able to evaluate the authority of one statement in relation to another. To do so, they began to categorize the Hadiths in a way that made comparative evaluation easier. Determining the authority of any particular Hadith quickly became a complex undertaking. Ultimately, evaluating the Hadiths required an investigation into the character, talents, personalities, and affiliations of the transmitters. Was a particular source known for his faulty memory or for passing on paraphrased statements? Perhaps a transmitter was renowned for an excellent memory but was also a known member of a particular sect. Then again, investigators had to consider the question of historical plausibility. When and where did the transmitters live? With whom did they associate? Could each of the transmitters actually have met each other? The answers to such questions demanded the development of an advanced historical tradition. The discipline that was developed to record the biographies of transmitters and scholars became known as "the science of men." The theological implications of the body of a Hadith had also to be taken into account in establishing the authenticity of any particular saying. For instance, a statement attributed to Muhammad that obviously contradicted a basic message of the Koran could be considered inauthentic even if the statement otherwise boasted an impeccable chain of transmission. Even so, the main focus of traditional scholarship was on the chain of transmitters rather than on the body of the Hadiths. In fact, a wide variety of material was conscientiously maintained within the Hadith corpus, even though some of its elements could appear to contradict each other.

Ghurids rulers of a kingdom centered in Ghur, Afghanistan, from the mid-12th century to around 1215. Although the Ghurid Empire was soon ousted, it laid the foundations of subsequent Muslim rule of large parts of South Asia.

Grameen Bank a Bangladeshi bank founded in 1976 to provide small loans to poor individuals. It advances money to borrowers in the expectation that they will repay the debt because of their sense of honor and in response to peer pressure. In this, the Grameen Bank differs from Western-style banks, which normally require security for any loan.

Hadith see box.

hafiz an honorary title incorporated into the name of any Muslim who has memorized the entire Koran.

hajj see box.

halal generally, anything sanctioned by Islamic law. The adjective is applied particularly to foods that have been specially prepared so that they may be eaten by Muslims in accordance with religious requirements—for instance, the animals from which meat is obtained have to be slaughtered by a prescribed method, known as *dhabiha*, that involves a swift, deep incision

HAJJ

The hajj is a pilgrimage to Mecca and the Fifth Pillar of Islam. The pilgrimage provides Muslims with the opportunity to come into direct contact with the faith's preeminent shrine, the place toward which they have been directing their prayers throughout their lives. The pilgrimage takes the form of a reenactment of parts of the experiences of Hagar, Ishmael, and Abraham, who are supposed to be the original builders of the Kaaba in Mecca and so the first people to establish a site of worship to the one God. The hajj is an obligatory act (*fard al-ayn*) that all Muslims are expected to perform at least once in their lifetimes, unless exempted by reason of physical incapacity or poverty. The hajj to Mecca is the world's largest annual pilgrimage; by the start of the 21st century, the number of annual participants exceeded 2 million.

The pilgrimage period in Islam begins in Dhu'l-Hijja, the last month of the Islamic year. The rituals of the hajj take only a few days, but many pilgrims come early and stay late to perform supplementary rites and rituals during their stay in Mecca. Mecca and the surrounding sites are sacred for all Muslims. The focus of activities in Mecca itself is the Great Mosque (Al-Masjid al-Haram), an open space that houses the Kaaba, Islam's holiest sanctuary. After completing their prayers there, pilgrims perform *sai*, which involves proceeding seven times back and forth between the two hills of Safa and Marwah, located near the Kaaba. *Sai* recalls Hagar's desperate search for water when Ishmael was a child. Pilgrims used to run between the hills, which are around 500 yards (450 m) apart, but now the size of the crowds usually reduces the pace to a trot.

Following the *sai*, Muslims spend the night in the tent city at Mina. On the morning of the ninth day of the month, the pilgrims travel to Mount Arafat, 9 miles (14 km) from Mecca, where Muhammad gave his last sermon. Pilgrims stand there from noon until sundown in reflection, meditating or praying for forgiveness, a ritual known as *wuquf*. Failure to perform *wuquf* is a violation of the required hajj rites; without it, the whole pilgrimage is invalid. Toward the end of the day, pilgrims set off from the Plain of Arafat, in front of the mount, to Muzdalifa, a resting area on the road back to Mina. In Muzdalifa, prayers are offered and pilgrims set about collecting 49 pebbles. The following day, they use the pebbles—the number corresponds with the number of days on which Muhammad was tempted by the devil—to pelt three stone pillars, which symbolize Satan. After the stoning of the pillars, pilgrims begin the Feast of Sacrifice (Eid al-Adha). Those pilgrims who can afford to do so slaughter a goat, sheep, cow, or camel in memory of the ram offered up by Abraham in place of his son Ishmael. When the sacrifice has been completed, pilgrims usually have their heads shaved or at least some hair removed. The sacrifice marks the end of the major rituals of the hajj.

The final three days of the pilgrimage are spent in prayer and contemplation and in travel between Mecca and Mina. During this phase, pilgrims may repeat many of the rites performed earlier. Following the hajj, many pilgrims follow in Muhammad's footsteps by traveling north to Medina to see the Prophet's resting place and to pray in his mosque.

Some pilgrims—such as these women praying at the Mosque of the Prophet—include a trip to Medina during their hajj.

with a sharp knife on the neck, cutting the jugular veins and carotid arteries of both sides but leaving the spinal cord intact.

Hamas (Arabic: "zeal") a militant Palestinian movement that aims to destroy Israel and create an Islamic state in Palestine. Founded in 1987 at the beginning of the Palestinian intifada (Arabic: "shaking off") movement against Israeli occupation, Hamas opposed the 1993 peace accords between Israel and the Palestine Liberation Organization (PLO). Hostility between Hamas and the forces of Israel and the PLO escalated until, in 2005, a cease-fire was agreed. In the 2006 elections for the Palestinian Legislative Council, Hamas won the majority of seats and formed a coalition with the PLO. There was then sporadic fighting between Israel and Hamas in the Gaza Strip. After a six-month truce in 2008, Hamas resumed rocket attacks on Israel, which responded with three weeks of sustained air strikes on Gaza in which more than 1,000 people were killed and many more made homeless. At the start of 2009, in response to international pressure, both sides called a halt to the fighting.

hammam a steam bath. Also known in English as a Turkish bath, a hammam is a public place of ritual cleansing where users also socialize with each other. The layout of a hammam is similar to that of a sauna, with a room filled with hot, dry air and an adjacent plunge pool or other source of cold water.

hanif an Arabic designation for true monotheists who were not Jews, Christians, or idol-worshippers. The word may be used as a form of respectful address or as a personal name.

haram in Arabic, a sacred place or territory that is the focus of pilgrimage and a place where divine blessings are bestowed. The principal *haram*s are in Mecca, Medina, Jerusalem, and, for Shiites, in Karbala (Iraq). The Arabic word for "forbidden" derives from the same root and can be transliterated as both *haram* and *haraam*.

harem in Muslim countries, the part of a house set apart for the women of the family. There is no insistence in the Koran that women should be separated from their male relatives in this way, but harems became widespread in imitation of accounts of the life of the Prophet Muhammad, who lived in homes that had harems.

Hashemite an Arab family that claims descent from the Prophet Muhammad. The Hashemites became hereditary rulers of Mecca, a position they retained even under the Ottoman Empire. Two of the sons of Husayn ibn Ali—the Hashemite emir of Mecca (ruled 1908–1916) and king of Hejaz (ruled 1916–1924)

—became kings of Iraq and Transjordan (modern Jordan). Although the Hashemites were overthrown in Iraq, they remained in power in Jordan. King Abdullah I (ruled 1946–1951) was succeeded by his sons Talal (ruled 1951–1953) and Hussein (ruled 1953–1999), and then by Hussein's son Abdullah II.

Hausa Muslim people of sub-Saharan Africa who form the largest ethnic group in northwestern Nigeria and southern Niger. Hausa society is hierarchical and ruled by emirs. Although the people speak Hausa, their official records are kept in Arabic. Divorce is governed by Muslim law.

Hezbollah (Party of God) a Shiite militant group in Lebanon with links to Iran. Founded in the 1970s, Hezbollah attracted much popular support after Israel invaded Lebanon in 1982. In July 2006 Hezbollah carried out an attack inside Israel, kidnapping two Israeli soldiers. In response, Israel launched a massive bombing campaign, causing extensive damage to Lebanon's infrastructure, including Beirut's international airport. The death toll reached almost 1,000, nearly all of whom were Lebanese civilians. The conflict ended after 34 days with a United Nations–sponsored cease-fire. The incident increased support for Hezbollah inside Lebanon and a greater role for the organization in the government.

hidayah literally, "present" or "gift"; figuratively, in a religious context, guidance from Allah.

hijab a veil that covers the hair and usually the neck of Muslim women. The term is used generally for any form of modest Islamic dress, including the burqa (which covers the entire face and body) and the chador (an outer garment or open cloak thrown over the head and held closed in front). The *jilbab*—a long, loose-fitting coat that covers the entire body, except for hands, feet, face, and head—may be complemented by the *khimar* (a wraparound scarf) and the *niqab* (a veil). There are also veils and veil styles that reflect particular cultures and social milieus. The notion, common in the West, that Islam requires believers to cover their bodies almost completely has no basis in the Koran, which requires only the wearing of the *khimar* (head scarf), a sensible precaution for both sexes in the heat of the Arabian Desert.

hijra also Anglicized as Hejira, the flight or migration of the Prophet Muhammad in the year 622 to Medina in order to escape persecution in Mecca. The *hijra* is the event that was used to mark the start of the Islamic calendar.

hijri the Muslim calendar. The Islamic year is either 354 or 355 days long and consists of 12 lunar months, each of which begins at the appearance of the new moon. Eleven of the months consistently have either 29 or 30 days. The 12th month is 29 days long in 19 out of every 30 years; in the other 11 years of the cycle, the 12th month has 30 days. While the months of the Gregorian calendar always fall in the same season of any given year, the months of the *hijri* calendar come at different stages of every year in a cycle of 32.5 solar years. Thus, when Ramadan occurs during the winter, the task of fasting during the hours

The age at which Muslim girls first start to wear **hijab**, *or modest dress, varies among Muslim cultures; however, it is most often at about the age of puberty. These high-school girls from Esfahan, Iran, wear* **khimars**, *or head scarves.*

of daylight is less onerous than when the month occurs during the long summer days.

hikma wisdom, knowledge.

Hizb-ut-Tahrir (Party of Liberation) founded in 1953, an international pan-Islamist, Sunni political party that aims to unite all Muslim countries into a caliphate—a single Muslim state, ruled by Islamic law.

houri a soulless heavenly sexual partner; conventionally, but not exclusively, a beautiful maiden who awaits the devout Muslim in Paradise. According to tradition, houris greet new arrivals in heaven and may cohabit with them as a reward for good deeds performed on earth. However, such depictions have no basis in the Koran, where the repeated references to houris describe them only as "purified wives" and "spotless virgins."

hudud part of a *fiqh* (judgment) that describes the traditional punishments for various offenses under Sharia law. *Hudud* is the plural of the Arabic *hadd*, which means "prevention" or "prohibition," and, by extension, a restrictive ordinance of God that defines what is lawful or unlawful. In Sharia, punishments are of two classes—*hadd*, in which they are laid down by the Koran and Sunna; and *tazir*, in which case the court has more

discretion in the form of punishment. *Hadd* punishments include death by stoning; flogging by 80 or 100 strokes; and amputation of a limb or limbs. The punishments apply to such crimes as adultery, theft, drunkenness, or slander against women. Although *hudud* are often controversial to Western observers and to many Muslims because they are seen to clash with the values enshrined in contemporary Islamic legal codes, supporters believe that they are validated by the traditions of the Koran and the Sunna.

Husaynid the ruling dynasty of Tunisia from 1705 until the establishment of the Republic of Tunisia in 1957.

ibadat an Arabic term that means, literally, to enslave oneself to God; by extension, *ibadat* is any action related to the faithful practice of Islam.

Ibadi a branch of Islam that is similar to the mainstream Sunni group but has elected, rather than hereditary, imams, who are both spiritual and temporal leaders of the community. Believers—known as *Ibadiyyah*—form the majority in Oman and are also influential in northern Africa and Zanzibar.

Iblis the Islamic counterpart of the Jewish and Christian Satan. Among the names for Iblis are

aduw (enemy), *aduw Allah* (enemy of God), and *ash-Shaytan* (demon). In Christian doctrine, Satan is a fallen angel, but in Muslim ideas of salvation Iblis is a more problematic figure because he cannot be both an angel, which is incapable of sin, and a jinn, which may perform evil.

ibn part of an Arabic personal name meaning "son of." The word is followed by the given name of the father—for example, the general who led the Muslim conquest of Spain in the eighth century was Tarik ibn Zeyad—Tarik, son of Zeyad.

iddah the cooling off period before the finalization of a divorce. A Muslim husband may end his marriage simply by saying "*Talaq*" (I divorce you) three times to his wife. No religious or judicial process is involved. Between the first and the final *talaq*, the man may revoke his pronouncement at any time during the *iddah*, the waiting period during which he must still maintain his wife. If, in the meantime, the wife discovers that she is pregnant, the *iddah* is extended until the birth of the child.

ihram a sacred state into which Muslims must enter in order to perform the major pilgrimage (hajj) or any minor one (*umrah*). Muslims perform *ihram* at designated locations where males shave their heads, cut

their nails, trim their beards, and then put on white clothing. Females also wear white at these times. The term may also be used to describe a worshipper while he or she is performing the *salat* (the five prescribed daily prayers).

ihsan perfection or excellence, particularly in a religious context, where it relates to deeds rather than thoughts and motivations. *Ihsan* cannot be achieved without the assistance of Allah.

ijaz al-Quran the inimitability of the Koran. This is the idea that any attempt to paraphrase the sacred text or to translate it into a language other than the original Arabic will inevitably alter, and therefore betray, some of the intended meaning. The concept partly explains why, throughout the world, Muslims worship in Arabic, even if they understand nothing of the language other than the words of the Koran.

ijma the scholarly consensus; based on Muhammad's reported statement in a Hadith that "My people will never agree in an error." *Ijma* is used strictly to refer not to recent rulings but to long-established traditions. In popular usage, the term has lost some of its original meaning and may now be used to refer to any principle of tolerance that allows the coexistence of different traditions in the four legal schools (*madhhabs*).

ijtihad the use of rational principles to deal with religious matters that are not explicitly covered in the Koran or the Hadith or by *ijma* (scholarly consensus). When Islam was first established, all jurists had the right to exercise *ijtihad*; such people were known as *mujtahids*. Shiite Muslims still recognize their leading jurists as *mujtahids*, but the majority Sunnis have maintained since the 13th century that scholars could no longer use *ijtihad* and had to be bound in all cases by established precedents.

ilhad (literally, "to deviate") any form of heresy; the word is sometimes used as a synonym for "atheism."

Illiyun in Paradise, the register of souls in which people's good deeds on earth are recorded.

ilm (Arabic: "knowledge") investigations to determine the authenticity and validity of the Hadiths. During the seventh century and the eighth century, scholars of Hadith were not at liberty to question the Hadiths that had been narrated by the companions of the Prophet Muhammad, as these people were automatically considered trustworthy. Instead, scholars focused on the Hadiths that were indirect reports, or reports of reports, and scrutinized the *isnads* (chains of communication) from which they developed.

imam the head of a Muslim community, typically the leader of prayers in a mosque. The two main divisions of Islam view the imam's function in different ways. To the Sunnis, the imam is a caliph, a successor to Muhammad in the Prophet's temporal role but not in his spiritual role. He is appointed by men. To the Shiites, the imam is a spiritual authority of paramount importance.

iman a Muslim's strength of faith, particularly in the unseen. *Iman* is one of the six articles of faith and one of the three essential components of *deen*. The other two components of *deen* are *islam* (in this context, submission) and *ihsan* (broadly, good deeds).

Ingush the mountain-dwelling Muslim people of the Caucasus, which was incorporated into Russia in 1810. In 1936, as part of the communist Soviet Union, the Ingush territory was amalgamated with that of the Chechens—also Muslims—into the autonomous republic of Checheno-Ingushetia. During World War II (1939–1945), Checheno-Ingushetia was abolished, and its ethnic inhabitants were deported to Soviet Asia. The republic was reestablished in 1957 and the exiles allowed to return. In 1992, after the breakup of the Soviet Union, Checheno-Ingushetia was divided into two separate

republics—Chechnya and Ingushetiya. However, both republics remained under Russian rule, the harshness of which inspired an insurgency by Islamic militants in the first decade of the 21st century.

Injil the Christian Gospels of the New Testament. Muslims believe that the Injil is one of the five holy books revealed by God—the others are the Koran, the Suhuf Ibrahim (the Scrolls of Abraham), the Tawrat, and the Zabur (roughly equivalent to the Old Testament Book of Psalms). However, they also believe that the original Injil was corrupted over time; some Muslims even take the view that the entire New Testament is a substitute for the original, authentic work, which is lost.

insha'Allah (Arabic: "if Allah permits"; "God willing") probably the most frequently used phrase in the Islamic world, this expression, which is applied to any possible future occurrence, has been adopted in almost every language in the world and is employed by Muslims and non-Muslims alike. When used by the latter, Allah merely means "God" or even "fate" rather than the god of Islam.

isha the last of the five daily prayers that comprise the *salat*. The *isha* is recited after sunset, at any time between the conclusion of the *maghrib*, the fourth prayer of the day, and dawn the following morning.

Islam a major world monotheistic religion founded in Arabia in the seventh century by the Prophet Muhammad. In Arabic, *Islam* means, literally, "surrender," and that definition encapsulates the central tenet of the religion, that the believer—who is known as a Muslim, from a part of the Arabic verb "to surrender"—submits himself or herself completely to the will of Allah. God's commandments are contained in the holy books, principally the Koran, the text of which was revealed by the deity to the Prophet. Muslims regard Muhammad as the last in a series of prophets that also includes Adam, Noah, Abraham, Moses, Jesus, and others. The revelations made by Allah to the Prophet are regarded as definitive.

Islamist an ideologue who seeks to create a society based in Muslim values. The term encompasses a wide spectrum of political views and is loosely applied. It first entered common English usage to describe Muslim fundamentalists during the Iranian Revolution in 1979. It gained wider currency after the terrorist attacks on the United States by members of al-Qaeda on September 11, 2001. However, the word is not synonymous with "terrorist"; an Islamist may work for change through legitimate political channels.

Islamophobia literally, fear of believers in the faith founded by the Prophet Muhammad; by extension, it also refers to prejudice against Muslims.

Ismailis members of the most important Shiite sect. Unlike mainstream Shiites, who regard Musa al-Kadhim (ruled 765–799) as the seventh imam, most Ismailis support the claims to that title of Musa's brother, Ismail. Ismailis who believe that Musa was the last imam are known as Seveners. Established in the ninth century in northern Africa, Ismaili doctrines spread eastward across the Muslim world as far as India. The caliphs of the Fatimid dynasty in Egypt (ruled 909–1177) were Ismailis. Today there are two main groups of Ismailis—the Nizaris, headed by the Aga Khan, and the Mustalis in Mumbai, India. They worship in *jamat khana*s (gathering houses) rather than in mosques.

isnad (from the Arabic *sanad*, "support") a list of the authorities who have transmitted reports (Hadiths) of the words or deeds of Muhammad, his companions, or later religious authorities. Every Hadith is preceded by an *isnad*, which takes the form: "It has been related to me by A on the authority of B on the authority of C on the authority of D (usually a companion of the Prophet) that Muhammad said. . . ." The validity of any Hadith is

determined by the supposed reliability of the persons named.

Isra the Night Journey during which, according to tradition, Muhammad flew on Buraq, a mythical winged creature, from Mecca to Jerusalem in the company of Jibril (the Archangel Gabriel). On the same night, the Prophet is reputed to have ascended by ladder into heaven, where he met Abraham, Moses, and Jesus. This miraculous event is known as Miraj.

Invented by the ancient Persians and adopted by Muslim architects, iwans—*vaulted halls opening onto courtyards—became a trademark of mosques and other Islamic buildings.*

Israfil the archangel who will blow the trumpet from a holy rock in Jerusalem to announce the Day of Resurrection. He is constantly at the ready, with the instrument on his lips. According to tradition, Israfil prepared Muhammad for the revelation of the Koran by teaching him for three years about the duties of a prophet.

istihsan (Arabic: "to approve," or "to sanction") in Islam, a method of tackling theological problems that can be resolved neither by reference to the sacred texts nor by the other usual methods of analogy (*qiyas*) and consensus (*ijma*). In practice, *istihsan* often amounts to personal judgments, which are disapproved by some Muslim theologians because they are made without the light of true knowledge. Others take the view that, because *istihsan* involves consideration of precedents and a range of

other possible courses of action, it is no more than a variant form of *qiyas*.

ithim a bad deed and the negative consequences thereof; the negative points that a person clocks up when he or she commits a sin. See also *thawab*.

itikaf the Muslim practice of withdrawing for three days during any fasting period—usually the last 10 days of Ramadan—into a mosque for prayer and contemplation.

iwan an architectural term for a vaulted hall opening onto a courtyard.

jahiliyya the ignorance of God that preceded the coming of Islam. The term is sometimes used today to describe the attitudes of perceived or actual opponents of Islam and has

been applied by radical Muslims to the West.

Jamaat-e-Islami (Arabic: "Islamic Society") a Muslim religious organization founded in 1941 in that part of British India that is now Pakistan. Its main objective has always been the revival of Islam and, as such, it has never been a political party in the conventional sense. However, it has from time to time been drawn into politics, as for example in 1977, when it supported the Islamization program of Pakistan president Zia ul-Haq (though it later opposed his plan to outlaw student unions). In 1991, Jamaat-e-Islami supported Saddam Hussein, the ruler of Iraq, during the first Gulf War.

jamat khana a communal place reserved for the worship, education, and social contact of Ismaili Shiite Muslims.

jami a congregational mosque or any Islamic public place of prayer.

janazah the prayer (*salat*) recited by Muslims before the burial of the body at a funeral. The opening words are taken from the *fatiha* (the first sura of the Koran). Mourners then pray for forgiveness for the deceased and for all dead Muslims. The *janazah* is a *fard al-kifaya*—a duty required of the whole community (*ummah*).

janissaries an army of slaves and Christian prisoners of war who were indoctrinated with Turkish culture and military discipline. Janissaries formed the basis for Turkish military successes between 1360 and 1826. Regular janissary revolts took place from the 17th century onward. The janissaries' power ended in 1826, when Sultan Mahmud II (ruled 1808–1839) had them massacred.

Janna (Arabic: "garden") the Islamic conception of paradise. The Koran and the Hadiths describe Janna as a place whose inhabitants want for nothing and enjoy every imaginable delight. The highest level of Janna, known as *firdawsi*, is the abode of the prophets and the most righteous; this place is analogous with the Garden of Eden in the Judeo-Christian Bible.

Jemaah Islamiyah (Arabic: "Islamic Congregation") a Southeast Asian militant Muslim organization dedicated to the establishment of a Daulah Islamiyah (Islamic State) incorporating Brunei, Indonesia, Malaysia, the Philippines, and Singapore. The Jemaah Islamiyah was responsible for the Bali nightclub bombings in 2002, in which 202 people were killed.

Jibril (Gabriel) the archangel who conveyed the word of Allah to the prophets, who, in turn, disseminated the divine message among all Muslims. Jibril helped Muhammad at critical moments, notably at the Battle of Badr in the year 624. Jibril is sometimes depicted as a man with a turban dressed in green and riding on a camel, horse, or mule.

jihad usually translated as "to strive" or "to struggle," the term has often been misapplied by non-Muslims who have taken it to be synonymous with holy war. While it is true that, through the centuries, the word has become connected with the notion that it is Muslims' duty to strive or struggle against people wishing to destroy Islam, this is nevertheless, technically, the "lesser jihad." The "greater jihad" is the mental and spiritual struggle every Muslim faces in trying to pray five times every day, to fast during Ramadan, to be honest and fair with all people, and to display forgiveness.

The greater jihad is a true Muslim's constant striving to do what is right.

jihadist someone who undertakes jihad.

jinn a supernatural spirit; the Arabic word is the root of the English word *genie*. Jinn are less powerful than angels and devils but nevertheless have a wide range of capabilities that may be used for good or for evil. Beneficent jinns may provide inspiration to artists and help to individuals. Malevolent jinns (*ifrit*) can spread diseases and cause accidents and other misfortunes to humans. Some jinns always appear in the same form—these are known as *sila*s. Other jinns are treacherous shape-shifters, known as *ghul*s, which may take on the appearance of any human, animal, object, or elemental force. In spite of their considerable powers, they may be controlled by humans in possession of the right magic. Jinns are hugely popular in folklore and literature, most famously in *The Thousand and One Nights*.

jirga a great assembly of key individuals or spokesmen within each Pashtun (Afghan) tribe. A *loya jirga* is a meeting of the numerous Pashtun tribes; such conventions are infrequent.

Jumad al-Thani the sixth month of the Muslim calendar.

25

Jumad al-Ula the fifth month of the Muslim lunar calendar.

jumah a communal prayer (*salat*) recited by Muslims every Friday, soon after midday.

Kaaba see box.

kalam reflections on religious life; speculative theology. The term is a contraction of the phrase *kalam Allah* (Arabic: "word of God"), which refers to the Koran. Those who practice *kalam* are known as *mutakallimun*. There are several schools of *kalam*, including, from the eighth century, the Mutazilah—rationalists who championed reasoned faith above traditional faith—and, from the 10th century, the Ashariyah, who adopted a philosophical position between the Mutazilah and the traditionalists.

kalimah (Arabic: "the phrase") the defining statement of the Muslim faith. In practice, the *kalimah* is the *shahada*, the Islamic creed, which avers: "There is no god but Allah and Muhammad is his messenger."

khanqa a house dedicated to any Sufi community. Every room in a *khanqa* should have an altar; one room should be set aside for guests, another is devoted to silent prayer. The purpose of a *khanqa* is to demonstrate the presence of Allah in every aspect of existence—the oneness of god.

kharaj land tax levied on non-Muslims and recent converts to Islam in conquered lands during the seventh and eighth centuries. Deeply unpopular, the *kharaj* provoked opposition from those on whom it was imposed, and it was abandoned during the Abbasid caliphate (750–1258).

Kharijites (Arabic: "separatists") the earliest Islamic sect. The Kharijites emerged when they assassinated Ali (ruled 656–661), the cousin and son-in-law of the Prophet Muhammad. They maintained their opposition to subsequent caliphs, especially those of the Umayyad dynasty (ruled 661–750), because they believed that the leader of Islam should be chosen by the *ummah* (the whole Muslim community). The most prominent modern Kharijites are the Ibadiyyah.

khatib the man who delivers the sermon at Friday prayers in a mosque. The preacher is usually the imam (prayer leader) but may be another person. No particular qualifications are required for *khatib*s.

khatmi Koran a ceremony to mark a child's first complete reading of the Koran.

khul a divorce initiated by a woman.

KAABA

Muslims see the Kaaba shrine in Al-Masjid al-Haram (the Great Mosque) in Mecca as the holiest place on earth. They bow toward it during their prayers five times each day, and they are expected to visit it on pilgrimage at least once during their lifetime. Made of marble and gray stone, it is shaped like a cube—its name means "cube" in Arabic—and its corners are aligned with the points of the compass. Inside the Kaaba are three roof pillars and a number of suspended silver and gold lamps. Outside, embedded in its eastern corner, is the Black Stone. Religious tradition reports that the Kaaba was built by the ancient Jewish patriarch Abraham and his son Ishmael, using the foundations of an even older structure raised by Adam—the first man created by God. The Kaaba was a religious shrine for Arabs in the days before Islam, when it housed more than 300 statues of idols; pilgrims came from all over the Arabian Peninsula to worship there. The Prophet Muhammad cleansed the Kaaba and cleared it of idols on his triumphant return to Mecca from Medina in the year 630.

khums literally, "one-fifth," a tax paid by Shiites in addition to the *zakat*. Traditionally 20 percent of net income, the money is given to travelers, to those in need, or to orphans. The assets that are taxed by *khums* differ slightly from those under the *zakat*. However, in their purpose and intent, the *khums* and the *zakat* are one and the same.

khutba the sermon delivered by the *khatib*.

kiramen katibeen (Arabic: "noble writers") two angels that dwell alongside all human beings, recording their thoughts and actions. The angel on the right notes all the good things they think and their good deeds, while the angel on the left records all their unworthy thoughts and bad deeds. The latter angel starts writing later, to give the sinner time to repent and make amends. On the Day of Judgment, the two angels report their findings to god.

kiswah the ceremonial cloth that is used to cover the Kaaba in Mecca during the month of Dhu'l-Hijjah.

Koran the sacred scripture of Islam. Muslims regard the Koran as the infallible word of Allah, revealed to the Prophet Muhammad, and believe that the work is the completion of the earlier, imperfect texts of the Jewish Torah and the Christian Gospels. The text of the Koran, which may at first have been transmitted orally, was written down in authoritative form in the seventh century. It consists of 114 suras (chapters) of varying length. The early suras contain instructions on the moral conduct required to ensure salvation on the Day of Judgment. Later sections describe Paradise and Hell. The overall premise is that the only way to godliness and salvation is through complete submission (*islam*) to the will of Allah. The Koran forms the basis of Islamic law. It was originally written in Arabic, and translations are discouraged because they are thought to dilute the word of God. (Published foreign-language versions of the text are usually described as "renditions" of the original.) Many Muslims learn large parts of the Koran by heart. Those who memorize the whole work are awarded the honorary title *hafiz*.

kufr (Arabic: "ungrateful") nonbelief or a nonbeliever. A *kufr* is a non-Muslim who does not recognize Allah or the prophethood of Muhammad. The term is also used to describe anyone who denies or attempts to conceal the fact that he or she is Muslim. In a broader, pejorative sense, a *kufr* may be a general insult applied by Muslims of one sect to those of another.

Kurds an ethnic and linguistic group native to parts of modern Armenia, Iran, Iraq, Syria, and Turkey. Most Kurds are Sunni Muslims. After the dissolution of the Ottoman Empire, they were promised their own independent state—Kurdistan—but that never materialized and they have since been persecuted by many of the regimes under which they have been forced to live.

Layla and Majnun the eponymous lovers in a celebrated work, based on Islamic folklore, by the Persian poet Nezami (1141–1209).

Laylah al-Qadr (Night of Power) the anniversary of the night on which the first verses of the Koran were revealed to the Prophet Muhammad.

loya jirga see **jirga**.

madhhab an Islamic school of law or *fiqh* (religious jurisprudence). Sunni Muslims have four main *madhhabs*—the Hanafi, the Hanbali, the Maliki, and the Shafi'i. Based on the teachings of the theologian Imam Abu Hanifah (700–767), the Hanafi *madhhab* was the system of legal interpretation employed by the Abbasids, the Seljuks, and the Ottomans. It is used today in Central Asia, India, Pakistan, Turkey, and the countries of the former Ottoman Empire. Hanbali is the most fundamentalist of the four main *madhhab*s. It is founded on the teachings of Ahmad ibn Hanbal

(780–855), a literalist who rejected personal opinion, analogy (*qiyas*), and Mutazilah rationalism on the grounds that they were liable to cause sinful *bida* (innovations). The Hanafi *madhhab* is the official legal school of modern Saudi Arabia. The Maliki *madhhab* is based on the teachings of the imam Malik ibn Anas (715–795). It stresses the Hadiths (sayings of Muhammad), the traditional practices of the local community (Sunna), and analogical reasoning (*qiyas*) as the bases of judgment. Maliki law is practiced today in northern and western Africa, in Sudan, and in some of the Persian Gulf states. The Shafi'i *madhhab* was founded by Abu Abd Allah ash-Shafi'i (767–820), who favored the use of *qiyas* (analogical reasoning) when no valid precedents for the case under consideration could be found in the Koran or in the Hadiths. This school of law operates today in eastern Africa and Indonesia.

madrassa in the Islamic world, any school, college, or university, regardless of whether it is religious or secular.

Mahdi (Arabic: "divinely guided one") a messiah who, in the last nine years before the end of the world, will restore the true religion and bring universal truth and justice. The Koran makes no mention of the Mahdi, and the concept has become one of the differences between the Shiites, who believe in the messiah, and the Sunnis, who do not. Reports of sightings of the Mahdi generally increase in times of crisis. Several political leaders have styled themselves as the Mahdi, including Ubayd Allah, the founder of the Fatimid dynasty (909), and Muhammad Ahmad who, in 1881, led a revolt against the Egyptian rulers of Sudan.

mahr a gift given by the groom to the bride upon marriage. It may be of any value—some *mahr*s take the form of substantial endowments, other *mahr*s are of merely sentimental significance. The *mahr* is often divided into two parts—one part is given on the occasion of the wedding, the other may be withheld until the marriage ends in divorce or the death of the husband. In such cases, the *mahr* is a form of insurance for the bride.

majlis a term used specifically for a gathering in remembrance of Husayn ibn Ali, the son of Ali and the grandson of the Prophet Muhammad; also used for assemblies of religious leaders and for the legislatures of Islamic countries, including Azerbaijan, Kazakhstan, Kuwait, Oman, Pakistan, and Turkmenistan.

Majlis-i-Shura the federal legislature of the Republic of Pakistan. The Majlis-i-Shura is a bicameral assembly, consisting of the National Assembly (lower house) and the Senate (upper house).

Malamatiyah a Sufi group that flourished in Iran in the eighth century. Their core belief was that oneness with God was achieved through tolerance of others and harsh, constant self-reproach. While many Sufis made public displays of *ahwal* (states of ecstasy), the Malamatiyah worshipped privately and even concealed their beliefs.

Mamluks originally slaves hired as mercenaries by caliphs in Cairo to maintain order in the 12th century. The Mamluks gained power in 1260 and then dominated Egypt until the start of the 19th century.

Al-Manar an influential reformist Arabic journal set up in 1898 in Cairo, Egypt. The journal examined Muslim political institutions, which its publishers regarded as decadent, the influence of European colonial powers in the region, which the publishers believed were malign, and sought to convince readers that Islam was compatible with modernity and reason. *Al-Manar* is now the name of a Hezbollah satellite television station based in Beirut, Lebanon.

Mandingo (also Malinke) a West African people living in parts of Ivory Coast (Côte d'Ivoire), Gambia, Guinea,

Guinea-Bissau, Mali, and Senegal. Most Mandingo families have been Muslim since about the 12th century.

Mantiq al Tayr Attar (The conference of the birds) one of the best known and most widely read Sufi texts in the world today. It is one of the early works of Farid ud-Din Attar, a 13th-century pharmacist from northern Iran. It tells the story of 30 birds who embark on a great journey to meet Simurgh, the king of the birds. On their way, they cross seven perilous valleys, which symbolize the stages of awareness through which a Sufi must pass in order to understand fully the true nature of God. Each bird is symbolic of a moral weakness and each one, at a specific stage of the journey, refuses to go on, citing some worldly distraction as an excuse. The leader of the birds is the hoopoe and, at the journey's end, he realizes that Simurgh is actually *si murgh*—the Persian for "30 birds." Hence the birds themselves are the king they seek.

Mappila the Muslims of Kerala, southern India, where they comprise around one-quarter of the regional population and are the second-largest religious group after the Hindus.

maqam (Arabic: "place of residence") any of the stages passed through by Sufis (Muslim mystics) on their spiritual journey toward union with God. Sufism is a highly heterogeneous form of Islam, and there are many different doctrines. However, most Sufis agree that there are seven major *maqams*—*tawbah* (repenting and atoning for sins); *wara* (recognizing the horror of living cut off from God); *zuhd* (transcending the need for worldly possessions); *faqr* (living in poverty); *sabr* (patience); *tawakkul* (trust in God that enables believers to find joy in everything, even their own pain and sorrow); and *rida* (the contentment that comes from the knowledge that union with God is imminent).

marthiya an elegiac poem in Arabic or Persian.

mashrabiyya an architectural term for the lattice-wood panels or grates that cover the windows or balconies in buildings in the Islamic world.

maslaha (Arabic: "public interest") the concept in Islamic law of the common good. Invoked from time to time throughout history, it has been used most recently in attempts to reconcile traditional Muslim values with modern culture.

matn the body of the text of a Hadith. The *matn* is distinct from the *isnad*, the preamble to each Hadith that details the chain of communication linking the text in its present form to the original utterance of Muhammad.

Maturidiyyah a Muslim school of theology named for its founder, Abu Mansur Muhammad al-Maturidi (died 944 in Samarkand, a city in present-day Uzbekistan). While conventional orthodox Muslims believe that only Allah can determine a person's actions and whether he or she deserves a place in Paradise, Maturidiyyah doctrine states that humans have free will and that people who perform to the letter the religious duties prescribed in the Koran are guaranteed entry into heaven when they die.

mawlid in Islam, the birthday of any holy figure. The most important such date is the birthday of the Prophet Muhammad (Mawlid an-Nabi), which is arbitrarily fixed as the 12th day of the month of Rabi al-Awwal. Other *mawlid* celebrations mark the anniversaries of Muslim saints and the founders of Sufi brotherhoods.

mehndi henna tattoos used as temporary skin decorations.

Mevlevi a Sufi order founded in Konya (a city in present-day Turkey) by admirers and followers of the poet Rumi (1207–1273). Because of their distinctive gyrations in time to a musical accompaniment as a form of *dhikr* (remembrance of God), Mevlevis are commonly known in the West as "whirling dervishes."

mihrab the focal point of the concourse of any mosque; the place from which the imam leads prayers. The rear of the mihrab faces toward Mecca, a direction indicated by a *gibla* (pointer).

Mikail the weather angel; the Islamic counterpart of the biblical Archangel Michael.

minaret (from Arabic *madhanah*, "beacon") a tower that forms a part of, or is immediately adjacent to, a mosque. It is from the minaret that the muezzin (crier) traditionally summons the faithful to prayer five times daily. There is a wide variety of designs, but a typical minaret has a square base beneath a round tower with several floors, each of which has its own projecting balcony. Minarets are commonly topped off with bulbous domes, but they may instead have metal-covered cones or open pavilions at the highest level.

minbar in a mosque, a raised seat from which the *khatib* (preacher) addresses the congregation. A *minbar* is similar to the pulpit in a church.

Miraj (Arabic: "ladder") the ascent by ladder from Jerusalem into heaven undertaken during the Isra (Night Journey) by the Prophet Muhammad in the company of Jibril (the Archangel Gabriel). They visit all seven levels of Paradise, where they meet many of the Old Testament prophets, as well as Isa (Jesus). Eventually, Muhammad enters the presence of Allah, who tells him that he must recite the *salat* 50 times a day. Musa (Moses) then advises Muhammad that such an obligation is too onerous for humans. Muhammad intercedes with Allah, who allows a reduction of the number of daily prayers to five. The Miraj is celebrated annually on Laylah al-Miraj ("Night of the Ascension"), which falls on the 27th day of the month of Rajab.

Moors originally, a Moroccan, and any Muslim inhabitant of the Iberian Peninsula (modern Portugal and Spain). By extension, the term may be used for any follower of Islam—the Muslims of the Philippines and Sri Lanka are sometimes known as Moors. The term has been used in English to refer to any black person—the subtitle of William Shakespeare's play *Othello* is "The Moor of Venice." When used to describe individuals, the word may be pejorative, but when used for styles of art and architecture it is neutral.

Moriscos (Spanish: "little Moors") Spanish Muslims (or their descendants) who were baptized as Christians in order to avoid persecution in their native land after its recapture by Christian forces at the end of the Reconquista (Christian reconquest).

mosque see box.

Mudejars Muslims who remained in Spain during the Reconquista of the Iberian Peninsula (modern Portugal and Spain). In the early part of the Reconquista, which began in the 11th century, the Mudejars were taxed but were granted privileges in return. However, after the completion of the Reconquista in 1492, the

Minarets first began to appear as a feature of mosques in the eighth century. Al-Masjid an-Nabawi (left), the Prophet's Mosque, in Medina, has a total of ten minarets.

Mudejars were faced with a choice between converting to Christianity and leaving the region. By 1614, most of the 3 million Muslims in Portugal and Spain had been forced to emigrate, although some accepted baptism while remaining faithful to Islam in secret. These clandestine Muslims were known as Moriscos (Spanish: "little Moors"). The Mudejar style of art made a substantial contribution to architecture, ceramics, metalwork, pottery, and textiles.

muezzin (crier) a mosque official who calls the faithful to prayer five times a day. Traditionally, the muezzin performs his duties standing either on the top of a minaret or at the door of the mosque. Facing the four cardinal points of the compass—east, west, north, and south—in turn, he repeats the call in Arabic that may be translated as: "Allah is most great. I testify that there is no God but Allah. I testify that Muhammad is the prophet of Allah. Come to prayer. Come to salvation. Allah is most great. There is no God but Allah." Today, in many mosques, the functions of the muezzin have been taken over by recordings that are broadcast through loudspeakers mounted on the minarets.

mufti an Islamic legal authority who can deliver fatwas (formal legal opinions). Historically, muftis were often the highest-ranking authorities, with wide-ranging jurisdiction in spiritual and temporal disputes. However, the development of civil codes in most modern Muslim countries has limited the power of the muftis to matters of marriage, divorce, and inheritance, and not even all of those.

Mughals a Muslim dynasty that ruled India (1526–1857); founded by Babur (ruled 1526–1530), a descendant of the Mongol emperor Genghis Khan.

muhajirun any of the companions of Muhammad who accompanied the Prophet on his *hijra* (migration) from Mecca to Medina in the year 622. The term is now also used for any

MOSQUE

Throughout the Muslim world, the focal point of worship—and hence the holiest place in any locale—is the mosque. The word *mosque* is an English rendition of the Arabic *masjid*, which, in strict etymological terms, means any space—enclosed or in the open air—where believers may pray. The earliest mosques were modeled on the courtyard of Muhammad's house in Medina—open plots that became sacred because people worshipped on them—but later buildings became more ambitious in their scope. However, in spite of numerous embellishments, the mosque remains basically an open space, often but not invariably enclosed beneath an overall roof. No statues, ritual objects, or pictures are permitted in a mosque; the only decorations that are allowed are inscriptions of verses from the Koran and the names of Muhammad and his original companions.

The floor of any mosque is normally covered with mats or carpets for the comfort of worshippers who kneel while performing the ritual prayer (*salat*). Attached to the main concourse of a mosque is often a minaret (Arabic: *madhanah*, "beacon"), from which a muezzin (crier) calls the faithful to prayer, but the minaret is not an essential feature. A mosque may also contain a washroom, which Muslims traditionally use before they pray, but the ablution facilities may be separate from the religious building, although easily accessible from it. Although the main purpose of mosques is collective worship, many of them also function as educational centers—an outstanding example is Al-Azhar Mosque in Cairo, Egypt, which nurtured the development within its expanding precincts of a school, a university, and a vast library.

Muslim who has moved to a non-Muslim land.

Muharram the first month of the Muslim lunar calendar.

mujahid (Arabic: "one engaged in jihad") although the term has long been used for anyone who is struggling, either internally or externally, for the Muslim faith, the use of the plural—*mujahideen*, meaning "holy warriors"—was not widespread until the 18th century in India. The word gained much broader currency through its adoption by several guerrilla groups fighting the Soviet occupation of Afghanistan (1979–1989).

mujtahid any Islamic jurist who is entitled to use *ijtihad* (personal judgment based on rational principles) when dealing with religious matters that are not explicitly covered in the Koran or the Hadith or by *ijma* (scholarly consensus).

mullah Muslim honorific roughly equivalent to the English lord. The term is most commonly applied to religious leaders, such as imams, but may also be used for kings, sultans, and other temporal rulers, as well as for academics and scholars. No particular qualification is required to be a mullah—the title may be applied merely as a courtesy.

munafiq a religious hypocrite; one who outwardly practices

Islam, while he or she is, in reality, a *kufr* (an unbeliever), perhaps without knowing it.

munazara any debate on Islamic legal or theological matters.

muqarnas in traditional Islamic and Persian architecture, an ornate form of corbel (a load-bearing projection from a wall).

Murjiah Islamic sect established in the seventh century. Members were among the first Muslims to believe that Allah alone may decide who has been virtuous and who has strayed from the true path of Islam. Judgment of sinners is therefore reserved until they die—this theological concept of postponement is known as *irja*.

musallah a Muslim place of prayer that, unlike a mosque (*masjid*), is not consecrated because it is temporary or rented.

musharaka a legal contract that is used to provide funds to a partnership. Every party to a *musharaka* provides capital, and any or all of the investors may take an active role in managing the project. The distribution of any profits is determined from the outset by negotiation. If the venture fails, the losses are borne proportionately according to the relative sizes of the initial investments.

Muslim Brotherhood an Islamic organization founded in

Egypt in 1928 by Hasan al-Banna (1906–1949) to promote the Koran and the Hadiths as the proper basis for a just and decent society. The work of the Muslim Brotherhood to improve social conditions won it a wide following throughout northern Africa and West Asia. After 1938, it became radically politicized, rejecting secularism and Western values. Suppressed in Egypt after 1954, the Muslim Brotherhood operated under cover until the 1980s, when it reemerged as a mainstream political grouping, although its candidates habitually stood in elections under different parties' names.

mustahabb a type of *fard* (religious duty) that is recommended but not required. An example is the use of the greeting *salam alaykum* (peace be upon you), which is considered polite but not indispensable.

Mustali an Ismaili sect based in Mumbai, India. Also known as Bohras, the Mustali split from their coreligionists in 1094. Most of its original members were converts from Hinduism.

Mutazilah Islamic rationalists who champion reasoned faith above traditional, unquestioning worship. The first Mutazilah were Muslims who refused to take sides in the dispute over the legitimacy of Ali, who took over leadership of the *ummah* after the

murder in the year 656 of the third caliph, Uthman. Mutazilah beliefs were later accepted by Shiites, but Sunni Muslims maintained their opposition to them.

nafs strictly, "the soul," but commonly used as a term for selfish, worldly preoccupation.

Nar literally, "fire"; figuratively, in Islamic eschatology, "Hell."

Nation of Islam a 20th-century African American religious movement that combined black nationalism with some of the tenets of Islam. Founded in 1930 by Wallace D. Fard, the Nation of Islam preached traditional Muslim values—such as the importance of a strong family life—and upheld traditional Muslim

prohibitions—such as those on drinking alcohol, eating pork, using tobacco, and taking illicit drugs. Elijah Muhammad became leader in 1934. The organization captured the hearts and minds of many African Americans at the temples and the parochial schools that it set up in major population centers across the United States. After World War II (1939–1945), the movement achieved great prominence through the work of Malcolm X. After the death of Elijah Muhammad in 1975, the Nation of Islam renounced its former racial and nationalist attitudes and gradually disbanded. However, the organization was later reestablished as a national movement by Louis Farrakhan.

nikah in Islamic marriage, the contract between the bride and the groom.

Members of the Nation of Islam gather outside the United States Capitol in October 2005 to mark the 10th anniversary of the Million Man March, an event organized by the Nation of Islam to highlight the social and economic problems facing African American communities.

nikah mut'a in Shia Islam, a form of temporary marriage in which the material compensation that the man owes the woman is agreed before the signing of the contract. This type of marriage was originally intended to regulate the actions of men who were forced to spend long periods away from their wives and families fighting in Muhammad's army.

ninety-nine names of God on the basis of the Koran and the Hadiths (sayings) of the Prophet Muhammad, medieval Muslim scholars compiled a list of 99 divine attributes that has since become popular throughout the Muslim world. Today, it is not uncommon to find pendants, posters, and decorative plates that list all the names of God, and they are often memorized and even sung. It is believed by some Muslims that the 100th name of Allah will be revealed on the Day of Judgment.

Nizaris an Ismaili sect, headed by their imam (spiritual and temporal leader), the Aga Khan. At the start of the 21st century, there were an estimated 12 million Nizaris, widely distributed in 25 countries worldwide.

nubuwwa prophecy and the prophets. There are two kinds of both—local and universal. There were only five universal prophets—Noah, Abraham, Moses, Jesus, and Muhammad.

In Islam, the prophets and their utterances are regarded as infallible.

nur a symbol of divine light and the name given to the 24th sura of the Koran.

Organization of the Islamic Conference (OIC) an international organization established in 1971 to promote the common interests of Muslims throughout the world. Member nations include Afghanistan, Algeria, Bahrain, Bangladesh, Benin, Brunei, Burkina Faso, Cameroon, Chad, Comoros, Djibouti, Egypt, Gabon, Gambia, Guinea, Guinea-Bissau, Indonesia, Iran, Iraq, Jordan, Kuwait, Lebanon, Libya, Malaysia, Maldives, Mali, Mauritania, Morocco, Niger, Oman, Pakistan, Qatar, Saudi Arabia, Senegal, Sierra Leone, Somalia, Sudan, Syria, Tunisia, Turkey, Uganda, United Arab Emirates, and Yemen.

Panj Tan-I Pak (Arabic: "Five Pure Ones") the five most venerated humans in the history of Islam. They are the Prophet Muhammad; his uncle, Abu Talib; Muhammad's only daughter, Fatima; and her sons, Hassan and Husayn.

pasha a title given to high-ranking soldiers and civil officials in the Ottoman Empire. It was rarely applied to women and was hereditary in 19th-century Egypt.

Pashtuns Sunni Muslim people whose settlements range across the Durand Line—the modern border between Afghanistan and Pakistan that was drawn by the British in 1893. Pashtun society is divided into numerous microcommunities by the region's mountainous terrain. It is strongly tribal, and blood feuds may be carried on from generation to generation. The main code of conduct—known as Pashtunwali—is essentially nonreligious but operates in tandem with Islamic practices. The rise of the Pashtuns in the 18th century brought a semblance of order and stability to Afghanistan. Since 1947, when India gained independence from Britain, and Pakistan emerged from India, many Pashtuns have sought to create an independent nation, known as Pashtunistan, in the territory that is currently southeast Afghanistan and the North-West Frontier province of Pakistan.

pesantren Islamic boarding schools in Indonesia. They are similar to madrassas in other parts of the Muslim world but also have some of the characteristics of a seminary (an institute for training priests) and a monastery or a nunnery (establishments for people who have taken religious vows).

Pillars of Islam the five duties incumbent on every Muslim— *shahada* (the profession of faith); *salat* (the five daily prayers); *zakat* (almsgiving); *sawm* (fasting during the month of Ramadan); and hajj (pilgrimage to Mecca).

pir a title for a Sufi master, who guides disciples along the path to oneness with God.

Pomaks Muslims in southern Bulgaria and neighboring parts of Greece and Turkey who claim descent from Bulgarians who converted to Islam while they were ruled by the Ottomans.

Qadariyah (from Arabic *qadar*, "destiny") an Islamic theological school and a blanket term for Muslims who believe in free will. Among the leading Qadariyah are the Mutazilah (rationalists who champion reasoned faith above traditional faith).

qadi a Muslim judge who follows Sharia law. The *qadi* hears a wide range of cases, including those that involve inheritance, pious bequests (*waqf*), marriage, and divorce. His decision in any matter is final. The first *qadi* was appointed by Umar I (ruled 634–644) when the number of cases became too numerous for the caliph to adjudicate them all personally.

Al-Qaeda see box.

Qajars the ruling dynasty of Iran from 1794 to 1925. Having ousted the Zand dynasty, the Qajars increased diplomatic

AL-QAEDA

Arabic for "the base," Al-Qaeda is an Islamist organization founded in 1988 by Saudi millionaire Osama bin Laden. The original purpose of Al-Qaeda was to provide logistical support for Afghans—particularly the Taliban—in their war against the Soviet Union. When the Soviets withdrew from Afghanistan in 1989, Al-Qaeda dispersed throughout the Muslim world and turned against Islamic states that it regarded as corrupt and Western powers that it regarded as interfering in the Muslim world. In 1998, bin Laden declared war on the United States for its support of Israel and Saudi Arabia. There followed numerous terrorist attacks, including the destruction of the U.S. embassies in Nairobi, Kenya, and Dar es Salaam, Tanzania (1998), and a suicide bomb attack against the USS Cole in Aden,

Yemen (2000). On September 11, 2001, terrorists carried out a suicide attack on the United States that resulted in the deaths of more than 3,000 people and the destruction of the World Trade Center in New York City. The U.S. government responded by invading Afghanistan with the intention of destroying Al-Qaeda and the Taliban. Some of Al-Qaeda's leaders were captured or killed, but others went into hiding. Thereafter, Al-Qaeda changed from a relatively cohesive organization into a protean entity whose members worked in isolated cells. It became difficult for security forces to tell whether subsequent acts of terrorism were the work of Al-Qaeda itself or of independent operatives with a common goal or even of entirely unrelated criminals who claimed—or who were said—to be part of the organization.

---

contact with the West under their first shah, Agha Mohammad Khan (ruled 1779–1797). Although this initiative increased Iranian influence and prosperity, it also made Iran the goal of rival European colonial powers. Iran was steadily weakened by external pressure and eventually, during World War I (1914–1918), occupied by British, Ottoman, and Russian troops. This humiliation was a mortal blow to the last Qajar ruler, Ahmad Shah, who was deposed in 1925 in favor of Reza Khan (Reza Shah Pahlavi).

qiblah the direction of the sacred shrine of the Kaaba in Mecca, Saudi Arabia, toward which Muslims turn five times each day when performing the *salat* (daily ritual prayer). The *qiblah* is used not only for prayer

but also for burial; the dead, including slaughtered animals, are interred facing Mecca. In a mosque, the *qiblah* is indicated by the mihrab, a niche in the mosque's interior wall. When Islam was first established, Jerusalem was the Muslims' *qiblah*—the place toward which they turned when they were at prayer—but that city was superseded as the focus of worship by Mecca in the year 624, only two years after the *hijra*. The Masjid al-Haram is the only mosque in the world that has no *qiblah* because, there, the Kaaba shrine is in plain view.

qiyas analogical reasoning in Islamic law, where it replaced *ijtihad* (rational principle), which was regarded as too arbitrary in many cases. *Qiyas* is based on the

principles set out in the Koran and the Sunna and applied to matters about which neither contains specific instructions. In jurisprudence (*fiqh*), *qiyas* is complemented by *ijma* (scholarly consensus).

Quraysh the ruling tribe of Mecca at the time of the birth of the Prophet Muhammad in the year 570.

Rabi al-Awwal the third month of the Muslim lunar calendar.

Rabi al-Thani the fourth month of the Muslim lunar calendar.

Rajab the seventh month of the Muslim lunar calendar.

Ramadan the ninth month of the Muslim lunar calendar,

throughout which believers fast and abstain from sinful thoughts and deeds between dawn and dusk. The end of the fast is marked by Eid al-Fitr, one of the two major religious holidays of the year.

rashidun (Arabic: "rightly guided" or "perfect") the first four caliphs of Islam—Abu Bakr (ruled 632–634), Umar (ruled 634–644), Uthman (ruled 644–656), and Ali (ruled 656–661).

rasul a messenger from God who receives a scripture. A *rasul* is greater than a *nabi* (an ordinary messenger). The most important *rasul* was Muhammad, the final link in a chain of messengers that began with Noah.

riba the Islamic ban on usury (lending money in return for interest—usually exorbitant interest—on the loan). *Riba* is strictly the doctrine that prohibits any speculative transaction in which the material gains or losses cannot be accurately forecast. It does not, by definition, preclude banking in its Western form.

ridda in doctrinal terms, *ridda* means "rejection of faith." More generally, it is applied to a series of uprisings after the death of the Prophet Muhammad by Bedouin who refused to recognize the authority of the caliph Abu Bakr (ruled 632–634). By 634, the first *ridda* had been defeated and Islam had spread from the Arabian

The Shah Mosque in Esfahan, Iran, was built during the time of the Safavid dynasty.

Peninsula to Iraq, Syria, and Egypt.

Rifaiyya Sufis (Muslim mystics) in Egypt, Syria, and Turkey from whose best-known practice—that of whirling around on the right heel while screaming ecstatically— led them to be called "howling dervishes" and "whirling dervishes" in the West. Established in Iraq by Ahmad ar-Rifai (died 1187) and possibly influenced by the Mongols during their 13th-century occupation of Iraq, the Rifaiyya have never been accepted by orthodox Muslims.

sadaqah donations to charity other than those made as *zakat* (almsgiving), which is obligatory charity. *Sadaqah* takes numerous forms—financial assistance, public service, or even a kind word or gesture.

Safar the second month of the Muslim lunar calendar.

Safavids an Iranian dynasty (ruled 1502–1736) that established Shiite Islam as the state religion. The Safavids faced opposition from Sunnis both at home—where they formed the majority of the population— and in neighboring countries. Protracted wars against the Ottomans in the west and the Uzbeks in the northeast forced the Safavids to relocate their capital from Tehran to Esfahan. The golden period of the Safavids occurred during the reign of Shah Abbas (ruled 1588–1629), who defeated the Ottomans and captured Baghdad.

sahaba the companions of Muhammad; anyone who had

any contact with the Prophet, no matter how small, and, indeed, anyone who lived at the same time as the founder of Islam. Among those commonly agreed to be *sahaba* are the *muhajirun* (those who accompanied the Prophet on the *hijra* from Mecca to Medina), the *ansars* (citizens of Medina who helped Muhammad and his followers on their arrival), those who fought at the Battle of Badr (624), and the first four caliphs. Today, the term *sahaba* is also used for any Muslim who has moved to a non-Muslim land.

Salafi Sunni Muslims who base their moral and religious codes on the practices of their ancestors (*salaf*).

salam alaykum (Arabic: "Peace be upon you") greeting used by Muslims as well as by Arab Christians and Jews. The traditional response is "*Wa alaykum as-salam*" ("And upon you be peace").

salat a strictly defined set of actions and phrases that are performed and recited in a specific order at designated times. Personal prayer (*dua*) is also permitted, but most images of Muslims praying show the *salat*, which is the preferred form of worship. Muslims observe the following five prayers on a daily basis: the *fajr*, performed after the break of day but before sunrise; the *duhr*, performed around the middle of the day; the *asr*, which

must be performed sometime before sunset; the *maghrib*, performed after sunset but before dark; and the *isha*, performed after the *maghrib*, which must be completed before dawn. Muslims must attempt to undertake each prayer at the appropriate time, but if a prayer is missed it is always permissible to perform it later. Believers also say additional prayers for special occasions, and supplementary prayers are added after the normal ones at weddings, religious festivals, and on similar occasions. Only the five daily prayers, however, are regarded as compulsory (*fard*).

sama in Sufism (Islamic mysticism), the practice of listening to music and chanting to reinforce ecstasy and induce trances in which believers approach or attain oneness with God. Strictly orthodox Muslims denounce *sama* as un-Islamic because of its apparent self-indulgence, but Sufis defend it as consistent with the precepts of the Prophet Muhammad, who permitted the Koran to be chanted.

Samanids (ruled 819–999) Iran's first native dynasty after the Muslim Arab conquest. The Samanid dynasty presided over a great flowering of Persian culture, especially pottery and literature. The outstanding poets of the period were Rudaki (849–941) and Ferdowsi (935–1020).

Saracen Western term for any Muslim.

sawm (Arabic: "fasting") in Islam, any religious fast, but particularly the fast during the month of Ramadan, which is the fourth of the Five Pillars of Islam. Through *sawm* and general abstinence, Muslims strive to become more in tune with Allah.

sayyid a title given to any person descended from the Prophet Muhammad.

Seljuks Muslim Turkmen tribes that invaded southwestern Asia in the 11th century and eventually established an empire based in Anatolia (part of modern Turkey) that included Iran, Mesopotamia (modern Iraq), Palestine, and Syria. The Seljuk dynasty ended in the 13th century but sowed the seeds of the Ottoman Empire.

Seveners Ismaili Shiite Muslims who believe that the seventh imam, Musa al-Kazim, was the last, and that his son, Muhammad ibn Ismail al-Maktum, will return in the future as the Mahdi.

Seven Sleepers legendary heroes who, having been imprisoned in a cave, were discovered after many years not dead but sleeping. They awoke, made sure that their experience became widely known, and then died. This story—which is taken to affirm the resurrection of the dead—became popular

SHAHADA

Shahada, Arabic for "testimony," is the statement of the belief that there is only one God and that Muhammad is the messenger of God. The *shahada* is the first pillar of Islam. It must be spoken in Arabic, the first language of Islam and the language of the Koran. It must be said twice in order to authenticate the truth of the belief. Most scholars agree that the pronouncement must be made in the presence of at least one person already of the Muslim faith who can verify the convert's commitment to Islam. Simply mouthing the words is not enough, for uttering the phrase is regarded as genuine only if it is spoken with the proper motivation. Intention (*niyya*) is a major aspect of Islam, for actions, even if carried out correctly, ultimately mean nothing to God if they are not accompanied by proper intent. Every action that a Muslim performs must have *niyya* if it is to be meaningful in the sight of God. The *shahada* is simultaneously an action demonstrating attachment to the religion of Islam and a proclamation of the basic beliefs required of a Muslim. For that reason, most people categorize the *shahada* as both a practice and a belief. The formula is used frequently in daily life as one of the prime statements recited by Muslims during prayers. The *shahada*'s importance is primary, for even though Muslims are required to follow the four other Pillars of the faith, some scholars believe that simply reciting the *shahada* is enough in itself to become a Muslim.

in Christianity and Islam. In Christianity, the heroes are known as the Seven Sleepers of Ephesus, who refused to worship pagan gods. In the Koran, they are described as persecuted Muslims who slept for over 300 years and were accompanied by a dog.

Shaaban the eighth month of the Muslim lunar calendar.

shah king of Iran or Persia. The title was also adopted elsewhere, most notably by the rulers of Afghanistan before the overthrow of the monarchy in 1973 and by the leaders of some Sufi orders.

shahada see box.

shahid the Muslim equivalent of the Judaeo-Christian "martyr." There are two categories of

shahid: those killed performing a jihad, and those killed unjustly. The paramount shahid for Shiites is al-Husayn ibn Ali (626–680), whose death at the hands of the Sunnis is commemorated annually during the first 10 days of the month of Muharram.

Shah-nameh (Book of kings) an epic poem by the Persian author Firdawsi (935–1020). Consisting of 50,000 rhyming couplets, *Shah-nameh* is a history of ancient Persia. Its heroes, who include the prince Rustam and the king Jamshyd, face adversity; their experiences contain ethical lessons for them and for those listening to their adventures.

Sharia (Arabic: literally, "the path leading to the watering place") the religious law of Islam, originally codified in the eighth

century. Some scholars argue that Sharia is Islamic law generally and that *fiqh* is the principles developed from the primary sources of Islamic law (the Koran and the Sunna). Other scholars argue that Sharia refers to the experiences of Muslims at large, legal and otherwise, whereas *fiqh* is the correct name for Islamic law. The latter believe that, without the interpretation of scholars, primary sources alone do not constitute law. Many scholars, however, use Sharia and *fiqh* interchangeably and do not recognize a significant difference between the two terms. There is no one Islamic law—rather there are several different schools of Islamic law. The main division is between the Sunni and Shiite branches of Islam, which have further divisions within them. These

numerous differences make it difficult to speak in terms of one Islamic law.

sharif (Arabic: "noble" or "high-born"; plural *ashraf*) a respectful title, originally applied only to Hashim (members of the same tribe as the Prophet Muhammad), but later given to the head of any prominent family.

shatranj an ancient board game in which two opponents vie to eliminate all the other's pieces apart from the king. *Shatranj* represents a developmental stage between *chaturanga*—a four-player war game played in northwestern India from the seventh century— and modern chess.

Shawwal the 10th month of the Muslim lunar calendar.

sheikh an honorific title that predated Islam in the Arabian Peninsula and was later applied by Muslims, first to any male older than 50 years, and later to heads of state, religious leaders and theologians, college principals, and learned men. It may also be applied, like the honorific *hafiz*, to anyone who has memorized the entire Koran.

Shiite a member of the smaller of the two main branches of Islam; the larger branch is the Sunni. The schism between the two groups was caused by a dispute in the seventh century about who should succeed the Prophet Muhammad. The Shiites believe that the founder of Islam ordained al-Husayn ibn Ali (626–680)—the son of Ali ibn Abi Talib and the grandson of the Prophet Muhammad. The Sunni believe that the legitimate heir was Abu Bakr, Muhammad's father-in-law.

shirk originally, idolatry or the sacrilegious association of Allah with other deities (polytheism). In *fiqh* (Islamic jurisprudence), *shirk* became legally equivalent to *kufr* (nonbelief) and those found guilty of it were denounced as heretics and cast out of the religious community. However, the meaning of *shirk* has been extended and may now be applied by Muslims of any sect as a term of disparagement for any other sect of whose religious practices they disapprove.

shura consultation on legal and political matters. The original *shura* was convened by the second caliph, Umar I (ruled 634–644), to elect his successor. The term may now be used for any council of state or a parliament. It is also applied to a law court dealing with claims by citizens against the government.

Sijjin according to the Koran, the register of souls in Hell. The word may also mean any part of Hell or a deep pit.

sira any story of the life of the Prophet Muhammad.

sirat in Islamic eschatology, the bridge that Muslims must cross on the Day of Judgment to enter Paradise. The walkway is no wider than a single human hair and as sharp as a knife. Beneath

*Members of Saudi Arabia's **shura** council attend a session in Riyadh. They recommend legislation that is ultimately approved or rejected by the king and his ministers.*

SUFISM

Sufism is Islamic mysticism. Followers of Sufism, Sufis, may be either Sunni or Shiite. There is some debate as to the origin of the term. One theory is that it comes from the Arabic word *suf* (wool), in reference to the woolen garments worn by ascetics who renounced the pleasures of the flesh. Although it is common to translate *Sufism* as "Islamic mysticism," the term encompasses only one of three principal orientations within the Sufi movement, the other two being love and asceticism. The main goal of all of them is self-purification through identification with God. The ascetic Sufi aims to live a simple life so as to avoid any distractions that may take him or her away from the path to God. The concept of love emphasizes unconditional devotion to God above everything else in the universe. Indeed, the mystical Sufi seeks union with God. Sufi masters are able to control the ego as they draw closer to God, not through fear of punishment or desire for reward but for the sake of God alone. That state, many Muslims believe, represents the epitome of *ihsan* (perfection or excellence). Those who attain it find pleasure simply in being in the presence of God's light, a condition best illustrated by the classic "verse of light" passage from the Koran, which states: "God is the light of the heavens and the earth. The parable of his light is like a niche within which is a lamp; the lamp is in glass; the glass is like a shining star; lit from a blessed tree—an olive tree that is neither of the east nor of the west, whose oil virtually illuminates even though no fire touches it—light upon light. God guides to his light whom he wills."

it burn the fires of Hell. The speed with which people cross the *sirat* is determined by their conduct on earth—the greater their sins, the slower their progress, and hence the greater their chances of falling off. Those who make it all the way across the bridge reach the Hauzul-Kausar (lake of abundance).

Sufism see box.

Sulyahids a Muslim dynasty (ruled 1047–1138). Originally from Yemen, the Sulyahids spread through the Arabian Peninsula as far as Mecca. Although the holiest city of Islam remained in the hands of their appointed governors until the 20th century, the Sulyahids were quickly supplanted in their Yemeni heartland by the Zurayids.

sultan a title conferred on Muslim temporal rulers by the caliph (the spiritual head of the Islamic community). The first sultan is generally agreed to have been the Afghan Mahmud of Ghazni (ruled 998–1030); the term then became widely used throughout the Muslim world.

Sunna (Arabic: "custom") the record of the Prophet's deeds. The Sunna is second in authority only to the Koran in shaping Muslim worldviews and behavior. As a result, the literature recording it, while not technically scripture, functions in much the same way as holy writ. The Sunna is articulated in the Hadiths (the sayings or deeds of Muhammad). The authenticity of each Hadith is subjected to close scrutiny by Muslim scholars, who apply *tafsir* (exegesis) to distinguish true accounts of the Prophet from fabrications that were interpolated in order to advance a particular doctrine or point of view.

Sunni a member of the larger of the two main branches of Islam; the smaller branch is the Shia. The schism between the two groups was caused by a dispute in the seventh century about who should succeed the Prophet Muhammad. The Sunni believe that the legitimate heir was Abu Bakr, Muhammad's father-in-law. The Shiites believe that the founder of Islam ordained his grandson al-Husayn (626–680).

sura any of the 114 chapters in standard editions of the Koran. All but one of the suras are arranged in descending order

of length. The exception is the first sura, the *fatiha*, which is only seven *aya* (verses) long. Every sura but the ninth begins with the *basmalah*—the phrase "*bism Allah ar-rahman ar-rahim*" (in the name of God, the Merciful, the Compassionate). Some Muslims divide the Koran not into 114 suras but into 30 equal sections, known as *juz*, so that the entire work can be read in a single lunar month.

tafsir the science of explanation of the Koran. During the lifetime of Muhammad, the Prophet was the only authority qualified to interpret the will of Allah but, after his death in the year 632, commentaries were required on both the Koran and, increasingly, the Hadiths. In its earliest form, *tafsir* consisted of establishing the authentic text of the Koran. Later, several branches of the science developed as various branches of Islam sought to justify their own positions with reference to the holy texts. One of the most influential schools was that of the Mutazilah, who argued that *tawil* (exegesis) must be strictly rational rather than speculative. That approach was at odds with the tenets of Sufism, which preferred allegorical and mystical interpretations. Today, Muslim scholars use the principles of *tafsir* to reconcile traditional Islam with the modern world.

talaq a husband-initiated unilateral divorce. In the Koran,

sura 65, entitled *Al-Talaq*, gives considerable detail on the legal requirements and the behavior expected in unilateral divorce. The exercise of the unilateral divorce takes different forms: *talaq hasan* (good divorce), *talaq ahsan* (best divorce), and *talaq al-bid'a* (nontraditional divorce).

Taliban Islamic fundamentalist political grouping that emerged in 1994 in Afghanistan. Originally a student movement drawn from religious schools, and essentially Pashtun in makeup, the Taliban attracted support from all areas of Afghan society. In 1996, it took over most of the country, apart from the northeastern region, and reconstituted Afghanistan as an Islamic emirate with assistance from Pakistan and some of the oil-rich Arab states. Taliban rule confirmed the Pashtuns as the premier ethnic group and replaced Afghanistan's liberal Muslim traditions with a highly conservative interpretation of Islam. At first, the United States was sympathetic to the Taliban's stated determination to stop the opium trade, and so turned a blind eye to its barbarity, which became notorious. Yet, once the Taliban had taken more or less total control, it started to profit from opium and proved incapable of creating peace. The Taliban interpretation of Islamic law was oppressively strict: criminals had their hands or feet amputated; women were forbidden to work; girls were excluded from schools;

the burqa was made compulsory; and all music, sports, and television were barred. In 2001, in response to that year's 9/11 attacks on New York City and Washington, D.C., the United States invaded Afghanistan in a bid to topple the regime. The Taliban fled to the hills but remained a potent force of opposition to the occupying forces.

taqiyya in Islam, the practice of concealing one's faith when under threat. *Taqiyya* has been employed by the Shiites, the largest minority sect of Islam, during periods of persecution by the Sunni majority.

taqwa consciousness of God, the ideal Muslim state of awareness. *Taqwa* is achieved through obedience to the will of Allah. It is particularly associated with abstinence, although it is sometimes used to refer to positive actions.

tawba repentance. *Tawba nasuh* is heartfelt repentance through which the sinner is reformed and which sets an example to others.

tawhid the oneness of God. In mainstream Islam, this theological concept is codified in the *shahada* —the assertion that there is only one God and that Muhammad is the messenger of God—and involves the acceptance that Allah is a unity, rather than, like any being or thing in creation, an assemblage of parts. However, Sufis

apply to *tawhid* an opposite sense —that all of creation, as the work of God, is divine and that there is therefore no existence beside or apart from Allah.

tawil allegorical interpretation of the Koran.

Tawrat a holy book given to Musa (Moses) by Allah. The Tawrat is generally regarded as identical to the Hebrew Torah, which comprises the first five books (Genesis, Exodus, Leviticus, Numbers, and Deuteronomy) of the Old Testament of the Bible.

taziyas traditional Shiite passion plays commemorating the death of al-Husayn ibn Ali in 680.

thanbi (Arabic: "sin") any deed that contravenes the will of Allah. According to the Koran, only actions are sinful; thoughts are not. The holy book of Islam also asserts that all humans—even the prophets—are susceptible to *thanbi* unless Allah shows them mercy.

thawab the credits earned by humans for every one of their good deeds or acts of worship. At the end of a lifetime, people with more *thawab* than *ithim* (bad deeds) go to heaven. People with more *ithim* than *thawab* go to Hell. Those whose *thawab* and *ithim* are equal go into limbo.

tiraz embroidered fabric or textile bands with inscriptions; also the workshops in which they were made.

Tuareg Berber-speaking pastoralists of sub-Saharan Africa. The Tuareg—who are thought to number about one million—are sparsely distributed across Algeria, Burkina Faso, Chad, Libya, Mali, Mauritania, Nigeria, and Senegal.

Tulunids an Islamic dynasty of Egypt and Syria (ruled 868–905). The Tulunids were the first rulers of the region to operate independently from the Abbasid caliphate in Baghdad.

Twelvers Shiite Muslims who believe in the divine ordination of the first twelve imams. Most Shiites are Twelvers and form the majority of the total population in Azerbaijan, Bahrain, Iran, and Iraq. Twelvers are also substantial minorities in Kuwait, Lebanon, Pakistan, and Saudi Arabia.

ulama Muslim legal scholars. Most ulama are experts in jurisprudence but some are specialists in other fields. Among the groups who comprise the ulama are the mufti (Islamic legal authorities entitled to deliver fatwas), the *qadi* (judges), and the *faqih* (those who expand and develop Sharia law on the basis of the continuing judgments and rulings of Muslim jurists).

Umayyads the first great Muslim dynasty (ruled 661–750).

The founder, Muawiyah I (ruled 661–680), moved the capital from Medina to Damascus, where he began a period of expansion that eventually saw Umayyad territory extend from Spain to Central Asia and India. The Umayyads' decline began with a defeat by the Byzantine Empire in 717; they were finally overthrown by the Abbasid dynasty.

ummah the Muslim community. The term is commonly used to mean either all the Islamic nations or all the Arab world, regardless of the constitution of the countries in which the members reside.

umrah any pilgrimage made by Muslims that is of less spiritual significance than the hajj to Mecca. Unlike the hajj, *umrah* is not compulsory but it is highly recommended.

Wahhabism an ultraconservative interpretation of Sunni Islam characterized by a very strict adherence to Islamic law as well as to the practices of the early Islamic *ummah* (religious community). Its restrictions include the mandatory covering of women in full-length black cloaks. The ruling royal family of Saudi Arabia is Wahhabi.

wahy divine inspiration. The most important example and product of *wahy* is the Koran, which was revealed by Allah to the Prophet Muhammad.

ZAKAT

*Z*akat—Arabic for "growth" or "purity"—are donations to charity (almsgiving), the third of the Five Pillars of Islam. Muslims believe that wealth can be corrupting, so giving away at least a portion of one's worldly goods can help make the rest of one's wealth pure. The Koran provides a basic definition of *zakat,* but the details of what alms must be given and to whom have been further elaborated by Muslim legal scholars. Each school of law has its own distinct rulings and opinions, but certain general principles are commonly accepted, including that *zakat* becomes payable only if the donor is earning more than a certain amount. *Zakat* can be paid only from money that has been earned legally or from handling permissible products.

Before giving *zakat* to the needy, a Muslim must first pay all outstanding debts, giving alms only from the sum that remains. Finally, a Muslim must have the proper intention (*niyya*) when giving alms. *Zakat* is supposed to be offered in a spirit of charity and purely for the benefit of those in need, not to build up an individual's status by a public display of generosity. *Zakat* is applied to several different categories of income. In the traditional societies in which Islam developed, crops and livestock were the principal sources of wealth. Many of the laws

relating to *zakat* focus on assets, such as dates and camels, that were common currency in Muhammad's lifetime. Such injunctions may seem out of place in the modern world but, in fact, many Muslims today still live off the land and continue to apply the *zakat* provisions to their crops and livestock. As a rule, around 10 percent of the yearly yield goes in alms. In addition to crops and livestock, cash and other assets are also subject to *zakat*. Muslims are expected to put aside two-and-a-half percent of their annual earnings to this end.

People can either give their *zakat* directly to worthy recipients or else they can hand it over to their local mosque, which will pass it on to the needy. In Muslim countries, too, both of these options generally apply, but there may also be state-run institutions that collect and allocate the tax. *Zakat* serves a twofold purpose— it provides for those people in need and helps strengthen bonds linking a community as a whole, creating a balance between those with little money and those with much. Among those to whom *zakat* should be given are the poor, reverts to Islam who have lost their possessions, charitable causes, people in debt, travelers in need, and then any other worthy recipients, including non-Muslims.

wali (Arabic: "trusted one") a regional governor in the Ottoman Empire, or a chaperone.

walima a banquet held after the *nikah* (the traditional Muslim marriage ceremony).

whirling dervishes see Mevlevi.

wudu ritual purification before prayer, traditionally performed in a bathhouse adjacent to a mosque. The ceremony involves washing the hands three times, rinsing out the mouth and putting water into the nostrils three times, and then washing the whole head, from the chin to the nape of the neck. The feet must also be washed. At the end of this process, Muslims recite a pledge to Allah and the Prophet Muhammad and then make their way into the mosque.

Youmud Deen the Day of Judgment.

Young Turks college students and soldiers who formed a political alliance in 1908 to force the Ottoman rulers to modernize and industrialize Turkish society.

zakat see box.

ziyara the pilgrim journey from Mecca to Medina along the path taken by the Prophet Muhammad on the *hijra*. Muslims commonly make the *ziyara* immediately after the hajj.

TIME LINE

c. 570 The founder of Islam, the Prophet Muhammad, is born in Mecca (in present-day Saudi Arabia).

❖ 600 ❖

c. 610 The Archangel Gabriel appears to Muhammad for the first time and his divine mission begins.

622 Muhammad and his followers leave Mecca for Medina. This migration, known as the *hijra*, is the start of the Muslim calendar.

624 Muslim forces defeat the Meccans at the Battle of Badr.

625 Muhammad's forces suffer a defeat at Uhud.

627 Muslim forces in Medina repel the Meccan army at the Battle of the Ditch. Afterward, Muhammad attacks the chief Jewish tribe in Medina because they are suspected of conspiring with the Meccans.

630 Meccans give up their city and the Kaaba—a sacred shrine—to Muhammad's forces. A Muslim army marches northward to raid the borders of Byzantine Syria.

632 Muhammad dies. His father-in-law, Abu Bakr, is elected as *khalifah*, or caliph (leader of the Islamic world), rather than his cousin and son-in-law Ali. This decision will have far-reaching consequences for the history of Islam.

633 Muslim forces invade territories held by the Sassanian Persian Empire.

634 Muslims defeat Byzantine forces at the the Battle of Ajnadyn in Syria.

634 Umar Ibn al-Khattab becomes second caliph.

635 Muslims capture Damascus from the Byzantines.

636 Byzantine forces are routed by Muslim forces at the Battle of Yarmuk in Jordan.

637 Muslim forces end Sassanian power at the Battle of Qadisiya. Soon after, the Sassanian's capital at Ctesiphon (Iraq) falls.

638 Muslims conquer Jerusalem.

641 Muslims take Egypt and build Fustat as its capital; the following year, the Mediterranean port of Alexandria falls.

643 A Muslim victory at Nehavend, in the Zagros Mountains, puts an end to Sassanian resistance in Persia.

644 Uthman becomes third caliph after the assassination of Umar.

c. 650 Maritime trade spreads Islamic influences down the coast of eastern Africa.

651 Uthman compiles the Koran, the holy book of Muslims.

651 Muslim forces in Egypt begin their first foray against the Christian Nubian kingdoms of Alwa and Makurra.

651 Islam reaches China by way of Arab traders.

651 Muslims take Merv (in present-day Turkmenistan) and bring Islam to central Asia.

A 450-year-old tile from a mosque in Istanbul depicts the Kaaba at its center— the sacred Islamic shrine in Mecca.

■ **Africa**   ■ **Americas**   ■ **East Asia**   ■ **Europe**   ■ **South and Central Asia**   ■ **Western Asia**

654 Muslim forces turn westward into Anatolia (Turkey) after having taken Armenia from Byzantium.

656 The third caliph, Uthman, is assassinated at his home by rebels.

656 Muhammad's cousin and son-in-law Ali becomes caliph, but his succession is disputed. Conflicts with members of the Meccan aristocracy culminate in civil war against Muawiyah, cousin of the third caliph and governor of Syria. Ali makes Kufa the capital of his administration.

658 A section of Ali's army, known as the Kharijites, reject Ali's leadership after he agrees to negotiations with Muawiyah. Ali defeats the Kharijites at the Battle of Nahrawan.

661 A Kharijite assassinates Ali during the morning prayer. Ali's son al-Hasan is appointed successor. After arbitration, al-Hasan agrees to a peace settlement with Muawiyah, governor of Syria. Muawiyah is recognized as caliph. His Umayyad descendants will rule the Islamic world for 90 years.

661 Muawiyah establishes Damascus as the capital city of his caliphate.

664 Muslim forces reach Kabul (in present-day Afghanistan).

670 Uqba ibn Nafi leads Muslim forces into present-day Tunisia, founding a new campaign in northwestern Africa, known as the Maghreb.

675 Kairouan, in present-day Tunisia, is established as a base for the conquest of the Maghreb.

678 "Greek fire"—a mixture of sulfur, naphtha, and quicklime fired from metal tubes—is used by Byzantine forces to end a five-year siege of Constantinople. It marks the first major setback for Muslim forces.

680 Muawiyah dies and his son, Yazid, is named as his successor. Husayn, the son of Ali and grandson of the Prophet Muhammad, protests this decision. Husayn leaves Mecca to rally his supporters but is intercepted by forces loyal to Yazid. Husayn and many of his supporters are massacred at the Battle of Karbala, in Iraq.

683 On Yazid's death, a second civil war breaks out. Abd al-Malik eventually takes control. He restores Umayyad power, but his ruthlessness alienates the Shiites for several generations.

685 A treaty is negotiated between the Byzantine emperor Constantine IV and the Muslims, establishing a border between the Byzantine and Muslim empires.

692 The Dome of the Rock is completed in Jerusalem. It is built on the spot from which Muhammad is believed to have ascended to heaven.

692 Abd al-Malik introduces coins inscribed with Koranic verses for use throughout the Muslim world.

698 Muslim forces take the ancient city of Carthage after several years' intermittent assault.

❖ *700* ❖

702 Resistance to Muslim rule in northern Africa ends when the Berbers' rebel leader, Kahina, is defeated. She commits suicide.

705 Islamic rule extends into central Asia (Bukhara, Samarkand, and Ferghana), the Indus Valley, and part of the Punjab in northwestern India (−715).

706 Egypt adopts Arabic as its official language.

706 Work begins on the construction of the Umayyad Mosque in Damascus, which still stands today.

709 Muslim forces take Tangier.

711 A Muslim army invades and conquers Spain, as far north as the Pyrenees.

c. 715 The Islamic caliphate is now the largest empire the world has yet seen. It extends from the Indus region to northern Africa and Spain.

715 The Muslim conquest of the Iberian Peninsula (Spain and Portugal) is completed.

718 Muslim forces fail to take Constantinople.

718 Muslim forces are defeated by a Christian army at Covadonga in the mountains of northern Spain.

720–724 Tribal feuds between Yemenites (southern Arabs) and Modharites (northern Arabs) spread through the Islamic world.

725 Christian Copts in Egypt rise in unsuccessful revolt against their Islamic rulers.

732 A Muslim army from Spain pushes into France but is repelled at Tours by Charles Martel's Frankish army.

739 An uprising of Berbers, led by Maisara, and followers of the Kharijite sect of Islam occurs against Arab rule in Morocco.

c. 740 Much of northern India is united under Nagabhak I, a ruler of the Gurjara-Pratihara dynasty. The unification stems the Muslim advance into northwestern India.

747 New converts to Islam join a rebellion in the province of Khurasan because they are not entitled to the same tax privileges as Arab Muslims.

750 Rebels proclaim Abu al-Abbas Abdullah caliph. He is a member of the Abbasid family, who are descended from Muhammad's uncle, Abbas.

c. 750 The first paper mill is built by Muslims.

c. 750 Islamic merchants establish trade routes across the Sahara. Salt, glass, and horses are exchanged for gold, ivory, and slaves.

750 The Abbasid Dynasty defeats its Umayyad rival and takes control of Egypt.

751 The ruler of Tashkent (present-day Uzbekistan) asks Muslims for protection from the Chinese; a Muslim army defeats Chinese forces at the Battle of the Talas River.

756 Abd ar-Rahman escapes the Abbasids and establishes an independent Umayyad Muslim state (emirate) at Córdoba in Spain.

c. 760 Muslims adopt Indian numerals, which are the "Arabic" numerals in general use today.

762 Caliph al-Mansur establishes Baghdad in Iraq as the new Abbasid capital. Baghdad soon becomes a thriving center of commerce, especially maritime trade with China and eastern Africa.

c. 776 Jabir ibn Hayyan describes techniques such as the refining of metals and glassmaking in a scientific treatise.

786 Harun al-Rashid becomes Abbasid caliph (until 809).

789 The Idrisid dynasty, followers of the Shiite branch of Islam, establishes a caliphate in Morocco.

791 War breaks out once again between Muslim forces and the Byzantine Empire in Asia Minor (–809).

❖ *800* ❖

800 The Aghlabid Dynasty governs Ifriqiya (present-day Algeria and Tunisia) but recognizes the Abbasid ruler of Baghdad as its caliph.

c. 800 Muslim merchants establish trading towns on the coast of eastern Africa, including Kilwa Kisiwani (in present-day Tanzania).

809 Caliph Harun al-Rashid dies while putting down an uprising in Samarkand.

813 Al-Mamun becomes caliph in Baghdad. His 20-year reign is remembered as the most glorious in the history of the caliphate.

c. 820 Al-Mamun founds the House of Wisdom, an academy that makes and studies translations of key Greek and Indian scientific and philosophical works.

825 Muslims expelled from Spain conquer Crete.

827 The *Megale Syntaxis*, a work by the Greek astronomer Claudius Ptolemy, is translated into Arabic and entitled *al-Majisti*, or *Almagest*.

827 Sicily is conquered by the Aghlabid rulers of northern Africa.

c. 830 The Persian mathematician al-Khwarizmi makes advances in algebra.

831 The final uprising by Coptic Christians is put down by Egypt's Islamic rulers; a period of rapid conversion to Islam follows.

836 Caliph al-Mutasim transfers the capital of the caliphate from Baghdad to Samarra.

837 Christians and Jews make an unsuccessful revolt against their Muslim rulers in Córdoba, Spain.

838 Al-Mutasim defeats the Byzantine army at the Iris River. He abandons an attack on Constantinople when his fleet is destroyed by a storm.

c. 840 The Muslim astronomer Abu al Fadl Jafar records sunspots.

846 An Aghlabid fleet makes a raid on Rome.

861 Caliph al-Mutawakkil is murdered by his Turkish bodyguards—the real power in the Abbasid realm.

862 The Karaouine Mosque is built at Fez in Morocco.

868 The Tulunid dynasty is founded in Egypt (–905).

869 African slaves known as the Zenj begin an uprising that will devastate lower regions of Iraq (–883).

870 The power of the Turkish guards is temporarily checked by Caliph al-Mutamid.

871 Muslims in present-day southeastern Iran and Pakistan establish their independence from the Abbasid caliphs of Baghdad under the Saffarid dynasty, which eventually conquers all Persia.

■ **Africa**   ■ **Americas**   ■ **East Asia**   ■ **Europe**   ■ **South and Central Asia**   ■ **Western Asia**

Modern algebra is shaped by advances made in the ninth century by Islamic Persian mathematician al-Khwarizmi.

930 Mecca is sacked by rebels, confirming a gradual weakening of Abbasid power. The dynasty's difficulties increase as Seljuk Turks from central Asia advance westward.

935 The city of Algiers is founded by Muslims.

939 Persian poet Firdawsi is born. He will become known as author of the epic *Shah-nameh* (Book of kings).

945 The Buyids establish themselves in Baghdad and rule in the name of the Abbasids.

c. 871 Ibn Abd al-Hakam writes a history of the Muslim conquest of Egypt.

872 Eastern Africa is described by the historian and geographer al-Yaqubi.

873 The twelfth imam of the Shiite Imami sect, Muhammad al-Muntazar, disappears; his return is still awaited by his followers, who are known as Twelvers.

876 Egypt's Tulunids build a hospital, racecourse, and the Ibn Tulun Mosque in Cairo (–879).

c. 890 The Muslim astronomer al-Battani calculates the precise length of the year and the precession of the equinoxes.

❖ *900* ❖

c. 900 The Persian scholar ar-Razi (Rhazes) classifies matter as animal, vegetable, or mineral. He also describes various infectious diseases.

c. 900 Byzantine power resurges in Anatolia.

901 Saminid rule spreads in Persia (present-day Iran).

909 The Fatimid dynasty is established by the leaders of the Ismaili branch of Shia Islam in Tunisia.

913 Persia is overrun by the Buyids, nomadic peoples from the southern shores of the Caspian Sea.

929 Emir of Córdoba Abdurrahman III proclaims himself caliph.

962 A Turkic Islamic kingdom in Afghanistan, with its capital at Ghazni, is founded by Alptigin. The Ghaznavid Dynasty will rule the region for two hundred years.

963 Muslim astronomer al-Sufi writes *The Book of Fixed Stars*, which mentions nebulae—clouds of interstellar gas and dust.

965 Birth of Abu Ali al-Hasan, Muslim scientist. His *Book of Optics* remains the most authoritative treatment of optics for centuries.

969 The Fatimids seize power in Egypt.

972 The Fatimids establish Al-Azhar University in Cairo, which operates to this day.

973 Arab mathematician and traveler al-Biruni is born. His *History of India* spreads the knowledge of Indian numerals.

977 A hospital established in Baghdad employs 24 physicians and contains a surgery and a department for disorders of the eye.

980 Philosopher and physician Avicenna (Ibn Sina) is born near Bukhara, in present-day Uzbekistan.

984 The earliest surviving dated astrolabe is made by Ahmad and Mahmud, two brothers from Isfahan (Persia).

c. 985 Islam penetrates the Christian kingdoms of Nubia.

998 Mahmud of Ghazni becomes the Ghaznavid ruler. He vows to conquer Hindu India.

Monument commemorating Spanish hero Rodrigo Díaz de Vivar, more popularly known as El Cid, a military leader who fought against Muslim forces on behalf of Alfonso VI, king of Castile.

❖ 1000 ❖

1004 Muslim raiders sack Pisa.

1005 A science library called the House of Knowledge is established in Cairo, Egypt.

c. 1005 Avicenna writes his five-volume *Canon of Medicine*. The work becomes the standard Islamic work on medicine.

1007 The city of Qalat Bani Hammad is founded by the Hammadids, a Berber dynasty. It has one of the largest mosques in northern Africa, in the Algerian highlands.

1007 The 166-foot (51-m) Gunbad-i Qabus is built in northeastern Persia to house the body of an Islamic prince.

1008 Firdawsi completes the *Shah-nameh* (Book of kings). It is dedicated to the Ghaznavid ruler Mahmud.

1008 Mahmud of Ghazni defeats an alliance of northern Indian Hindu rulers at Peshawar (in present-day Pakistan).

1009 The Church of the Holy Sepulcher in Jerusalem is destroyed on the orders of Caliph al-Hakim.

c. 1010 Arab astronomer Ibn-Yunis finishes compiling the *Large Astronomical Tables of al-Hakim*. The most accurate yet compiled, the tables are named for the caliph in Cairo.

1013 Al-Hakim Mosque is constructed in Cairo for Caliph al-Hakim. The Druze Islamic sect will later revere al-Hakim as an incarnation of God.

1018 The forces of Mahmud of Ghazni ransack the city of Mathura in northern India.

1020 Persian poet Firdawsi dies.

1023 Mahmud of Ghazni razes and pillages the opulent Hindu temple of Somnath on the Gujarat coast. His army returns to Afghanistan with about six tons of gold.

1028 King Sancho of Navarre captures Castile from the Muslims.

1030 Mahmud of Ghazni dies.

c. 1030 Avicenna writes a medical encyclopedia called *The Book of Healing*.

1031 The caliphate of Córdoba breaks up into a number of small states.

1037 Avicenna dies.

1037 The Ghaznavid-controlled Persian cities of Nishapur and Merv are seized by Seljuk Turks.

c. 1038 Muslim physician and pioneer of the science of optics al-Hazen designs a room-size camera obscura.

1039 Al-Hasan dies in Cairo.

1040 The Ghaznavids are defeated by the Seljuks at Dandanqan.

1043 Seljuk Turks take the Persian city of Isfahan.

1048 A Berber clan called the Almoravids launch their first campaign. They will eventually rule much of northern Africa.

1048 Persian poet, mathematician, and astronomer Omar Khayyam is born in Nishapur, Persia.

1048 Muslim mathematician, geographer, and physicist al-Biruni dies.

c. 1050 Tall cylindrical minarets replace the earlier style of square, stepped structures in Persia.

c. 1050 Designs on lusterware—a type of pottery developed in Iraq in the ninth century—depict courtly life in Fatimid Egypt.

■ **Africa**   ■ **Americas**   ■ **East Asia**   ■ **Europe**   ■ **South and Central Asia**   ■ **Western Asia**

c. 1050 The Mossi peoples of present-day Burkina Faso in western Africa resist the spread of Islam.

1052 The Italian city-state of Pisa takes Sardinia from its Muslim rulers.

1055 The Sunni Seljuk Turks take Baghdad from the Shiite Buyids and restore the caliphate.

1056 The Almoravid dynasty begins its conquest of Morocco and part of Algeria.

1058 The Islamic theologian al-Ghazali is born at Tus in eastern Persia.

1062 The Almoravids found Marrakech in Morocco as their capital.

1064 Ani in Armenia is occupied by invading Seljuk Turks.

1067 The Muslim traveler al-Bakri writes his *Description of North Africa*, in which he describes life in the region around the middle reaches of the Niger River.

1067 The Nizamiya madrassa (religious college) is founded in Baghdad by the Seljuk vizier (chief minister) Nizam al-Mulk.

1071 The Byzantines are routed by Seljuk Turks under the leadership of Alp Arslan at the Battle of Manzikert in eastern Anatolia.

1072 Malik Shah succeeds his father Alp Arslan. The title *shah* means "king" in both Arabic and Persian, indicating Malik's ambition to unite the Islamic world.

1074 Omar Khayyam begins work on an accurate solar calendar and astronomical observatory in Persia.

1076 Islam reaches the western African empire of Ghana following a defeat by an Almoravid army.

1080 Malik Shah takes Nicaea from the Byzantines.

1083 By this time, the Almoravids have taken all of northern Africa west of Algiers from the Fatimids.

1085 King Alfonso VI of Castile takes the city of Toledo, in Spain, from Muslim rulers.

1086 Muslim rulers in southern Spain invite the Almoravids from Morocco to fight Alfonso VI. They defeat his forces near Badajoz and establish their dominion over much of Spain (–1091).

1086 Malik Shah attacks Palestine and expels the ruling Egyptian Fatimids.

1090 The Nizari Ismaili Shia (commonly known as the Assassins), who are strongly opposed to the Seljuk rulers, establish a stronghold in the Elburz Mountains of Persia.

1091 Sycacuse in Sicily is taken from the Muslims by the Norman adventurer Roger de Hauteville.

1092 Malik Shah's vizier Nizam al-Mulk is murdered by the Assassins.

1092 Malik Shah dies and the Seljuk sultanate begins to break up.

1095 The Byzantine emperor Alexius I asks the Christians of Europe for help to fight the Seljuk Turks.

1095 The First Crusade is proclaimed by Pope Urban II at Clermont, central France.

1097 An army of crusaders from western Europe and Greek soldiers take the Seljuk capital Nicaea.

1098 The Fatimids recapture Palestine from the Seljuks.

1098 The crusaders take Antioch in Syria from the Seljuk Turks.

1099 The crusaders capture Jerusalem.

1099 Spanish soldier Rodrigo Díaz de Vivar, nicknamed El Cid, who fought against the Muslims in Spain, dies.

❖ **1100** ❖

c. 1100 As new trade routes are created farther east, the Empire of Ghana falls into decline.

c. 1100 About this time, Islam has spread to a kingdom called Kanem-Bornu on the southern edge of the Sahara.

c. 1100 The Ghaznavids lose control of northwestern Afghanistan to the Ghurid dynasty.

c. 1100 Free hostels for travelers, called caravansaries, are built along major trade routes in Asia Minor.

1103 Tughtigin becomes the independent *atabeg*, or governor, of Damascus. A former Seljuk official, Tughtigin will go on to found the Burid dynasty.

1106 Ruler Yusuf Ibn Tashfin dies and the Almoravid Empire in northern Africa begins to fragment.

1107 Construction of the Friday Mosque at Kizimkazi on the island of Zanzibar is completed.

1109 The crusaders have now founded several states—called the Latin kingdoms—in Palestine and Syria.

1111 Muslim jurist and theologian al-Ghazali (born 1058) dies. He taught at Baghdad and Nishapur (Persia).

1118 King Alfonso I of Aragon takes Saragossa from the Muslims, extending his realm to the Mediterranean Sea.

1120 Religious reformer Ibn Tumert founds a Berber state in the Atlas Mountains of Morocco. Tumert's followers are known as the Almohads.

1122 Persian astronomer, mathematician, and poet Omar Khayyam dies.

1124 The crusaders take Tyre. Almost all of the coast of Palestine is now part of the Latin Kingdom of Jerusalem.

c. 1125 Mosques throughout the Islamic world now feature minarets.

1126 Zangi is appointed governor, or *atabeg*, of Mosul. He creates an independent principality for himself in northern Syria.

1130 The Egyptian Fatimid caliph al-Amir is murdered by the Assassins.

c. 1130 Leader of the Almohads, Ibn Tumart, dies and is succeeded by Abd al-Mumin.

1143 The Norman ruler of Sicily, Roger II, pillages the coast of northern Africa.

1144 Zangi takes Edessa from the crusaders; this defeat prompts the Second Crusade.

c. 1145 Astronomer and mathematician Jabir ibn Aflah dies. He designed a portable celestial sphere that explained the movement of celestial bodies.

1146 Zangi dies and is succeeded by his son Nur ad-Din.

1146 The Second Crusade is launched by Bernard of Clairvaux.

1147 Lisbon, Portugal, is taken from Muslim rule by crusaders from England and the Low Countries en route to the Holy Land.

1147 The Almohads seize the Almoravid capital of Marrakech to become the chief power in northern Africa.

1148 The Second Crusade fails to capture Damascus.

1149 Nur ad-Din reestablishes Muslim dominance in Syria after defeating Raymond of Antioch.

c. 1150 Islamic philosopher Averroës (Ibn Rushd) is active in Córdoba; his works, translated into Latin, reintroduce Greek philosopher Aristotle to western Europe.

c. 1150 By this time, the Seljuk Sultanate of Rum (named for Rome) extends far into Byzantine territory in what will become present-day Turkey.

c. 1150 The Khwarazmian Turks from central Asia attack small Seljuk sultanates in northern Persia.

c. 1150 Normans living in southern Italy and Sicily found fortified trading posts along the coast of northern Africa from Tripoli to Tunis.

1151 The Almohad dynasty extends its power as Abd al-Mumin takes Algiers and Morocco from the Almoravids.

1151 Ala ad-Din, leader of the Turks from Ghur, Persia, earns the title "the World-Burner" after razing Ghazni in Afghanistan, capital of the waning Ghaznavid dynasty.

1157 Sultan Sanjar dies, marking the decline of the power of the Seljuk Turks.

1157 Islamic Spain is invaded by Abd al-Mumin's armies. Almería and Granada fall under Almohad rule.

1159 The Byzantine emperor Manuel I marches through Antioch in triumph, asserting his authority. However, his army is attacked by Turks on its way home.

1166 Ahmad ibn Ibrahim al-Yasavi dies. A wandering Sufi, or mystic, al-Yasavi spreads Islam among the Turkic nomads living in central Asia.

1167 Cairo is taken by Amalric, the Christian king of Jerusalem. However, Muslims recapture the city the following year.

1169 Saladin becomes vizier of Egypt under the authority of the Fatimid sultans.

1171 Saladin ends Fatimid rule by making himself Egypt's first Ayyubid sultan.

1173 Muhammad Ghuri is made Ghurid governor of Ghazni in Afghanistan.

1174 Saladin takes Syria from the crusaders.

1175 With Ghazni as his base, Muhammad Ghuri attacks northern India. His army captures the city of Multan on the Indus River the following year.

1176 Turks defeat Byzantine forces at Myriokephalon.

1177 The forces of Baldwin IV of Jerusalem defeat Saladin at the Battle of Montgisard.

■ **Africa**   ■ **Americas**   ■ **East Asia**   ■ **Europe**   ■ **South and Central Asia**   ■ **Western Asia**

1179 Tyre is besieged by Saladin.

1180 A truce is agreed by Baldwin IV and Saladin.

1180 In Baghdad, Caliph al-Nasir tries to restore the authority of the Abbasid dynasty.

1184 Almohad caliph Abu Yaqub Yusuf dies in northern Africa. He is succeeded by his son Yaqub al-Mansur, whose reign sees the zenith of Almohad power.

1186 A Muslim power base is established in northern India when Muhammad Ghuri occupies the Punjab.

1187 The crusaders are defeated by Saladin at the Battle of Hattin. Saladin then captures Jerusalem.

1189 The Third Crusade is launched by the joint forces of English king Richard I, French king Philip II, and Holy Roman Emperor Frederick I Barbarossa.

1190 The Third Crusade takes Acre but fails to recapture Jerusalem.

1190 Frederick I drowns en route to the Holy Land.

1191 Despite taking Cyprus and Acre, the Third Crusade ends in failure.

1193 Sultan Saladin dies in Damascus.

1193 As the Ghurids capture Delhi, Islamic rule extends into central India.

1194 Khurasan, in eastern Persia, falls to the Khwarazmian Turks. They eventually take Iraq, killing Tughril, the last Seljuk sultan.

1195 Muslim forces defeat a Christian army at Alarcos, Spain.

During the Crusades, the Christian forces built many castles, including this one—Crak des Chevaliers—in Syria.

1197 Ghurid forces attack monasteries in an attempt to replace Indian Buddhism with Islam.

1199 Ala ad-Din Muhammad, ruler of the Turkish kingdom of Khwarezm—based in lands south of the Aral Sea—attempts to extend his realm eastward into India.

❖ **1200** ❖

c. 1200 The sultan of Kilwa in eastern Africa orders coins to be minted.

1203 Sumanguru becomes the ruler of the Kingdom of Soso on the Niger River, a vestige of the Empire of Ghana; Muslims move northward.

1203 Northern India is now under the Muslim rule of Muhammad Ghuri.

1203 Almohad forces in Spain take the Balearic Islands.

1206 After Muhammad Ghuri's murder, the Delhi Sultanate is founded in northern India by former slave and general Qutbuddin Aibak.

1212 The Christian reconquest of Spain gathers steam as Muslim forces are defeated at the battle of Las Navas de Tolosa. The Almohad dynasty collapses.

1212 The Children's Crusade ends in failure.

1218 The Mongols, led by Genghis Khan, sweep westward, conquering Khwarezm and overcoming eastern Persia (–1225). They leave total devastation in their wake.

1219 The Fifth Crusade captures the Egyptian port of Damietta—which is lost in 1221—but fails to capture Cairo.

1222 The Mongols take Afghanistan and make inroads into northern India.

1228 Under the rule of Abu Zakaria Yahya I, Ifriqiya becomes independent with its capital at Tunis.

1229 In the Sixth Crusade, Frederick II gains Jerusalem using diplomacy.

1230 The Mongols capture western Persia from the Khwarezmian Turks, whose last sultan is killed while fleeing.

1232 The construction of the Kutb Minar minaret is finished in Delhi.

1236 Ferdinand III of Castile sets out to conquer the Moorish Kingdom of Andalusia in southern Spain (–1246).

1236 Raziya succeeds to the Delhi Sultanate on the death of her father, Altamsh. She is the only Muslim woman ever to rule in India (–1240).

1240 The Malinke ruler of Mali, Sundiata Keita, razes Kumbe, capital of the Kingdom of Soso.

1243 Mongol forces defeat the Seljuks of Rum at the Battle of Kosedagh. Rum becomes a vassal state.

1244 A Muslim army, led by the Egyptian pasha Khwarazmi, retakes Jerusalem from the crusaders.

1249 Louis IX (Saint Louis) of France takes Damietta in Egypt during the Seventh Crusade.

1250 Egypt's Ayyubid dynasty ends and is replaced by the Turkish Mamluk dynasty.

c. 1250 Mali becomes the major power in western Africa.

1250 The Seventh Crusade is interrupted when Louis IX is taken and held for ransom in Egypt.

1254 The Seventh Crusade ends with mixed results—it made some gains in Palestine but fails to recapture the Christian holy places.

1256 Led by Hulagu, a Mongol army occupies Persia and founds the Ilkhan dynasty, which later converts to Islam.

1258 Hulagu sacks Baghdad, bringing the Abbasid caliphate to an end.

1258 The Persian poet Sadi writes *Gulistan* (The rose garden).

1260 Mamluk forces halt the advance of the Mongols at the Battle of Ayn Jalut in Palestine.

1260 Baibars seizes the Mamluk sultanate after murdering Qutuz.

1266 The last of the great "slave sultans," Ghiasuddin Balban, inherits the Delhi Sultanate.

1268 The Christian-ruled cities of Jaffa, Beirut, and Antioch fall to the Mamluks.

1269 Almohad rule in Morocco ends when Abbu Dabbas is overthrown by Abu Yaqub—the first ruler of the Berber Marinid Dynasty.

1270 Louis IX of France dies at Tunis during a new crusade.

1271 Balban's assistant governor in Bengal, Tughril Khan, pushes Muslim rule far into eastern Bengal.

1273 Persian mystic and poet Jalal ad-Din ar-Rumi dies.

1278 Tughril Khan establishes himself as a ruler independent of the Delhi sultan.

1280 The Mongol Ilkhan ruler of Persia, Teguder Ahmed, converts to Islam. His followers do likewise a decade or two later.

1280 Al-Mansur Qalawun becomes the Mamluk sultan of Egypt.

1281 Qalawun gains victory over the Mongol Ilkhans at the Battle of Homs.

1281 The Ottoman dynasty is born when Osman takes control of the area around Bursa in Anatolia.

1282 Tughril Khan is defeated, captured, and executed.

1284 Cairo's Mansuri Maristan, the best medical facility of its time, is built on the orders of Qalawun.

1287 Balban dies and the Delhi Sultanate is plunged into a period of instability.

1289 Tripoli in Lebanon is taken from the Latins by the Mamluks.

1290 The Khalji dynasty is established in Delhi when Jalal-ud-Din Firuz Khalji, an Afghan Turk, overthrows the last slave sultan.

1290 Sultan Qalawun dies and is succeeded by Khalil, who continues plans to take Acre from the Christians.

1291 The last Christian stronghold in western Asia, Acre, falls to the Mamluks.

1295 Mahmud Ghazan becomes the Ilkhanid ruler. During his reign, Islam spreads widely among his Mongol subjects.

1296 The Dehli Sultanate enters a golden age with the beginning of Ala ud-Din Khalji's 20-year reign.

1297 Ala ud-Din's army thwarts an attempted invasion by the Mongols.

1299 The Berber Marinids begin a nine-year siege of the Zianid capital of Tlemcen (modern Algeria).

❖ 1300 ❖

c. 1300 Muslim Queen Amina of Zazzau is now believed by historians to have lived around this time. During her reign the Emirate of Zaria dominated the Hausa states (in present-day Nigeria).

1302 The Ottoman Turks defeat Byzantine forces at the Battle of Bapheus, outside Nicomedia (in present-day Turkey).

1303 The Mongols reinvade Syria but are repelled outside Damascus by the Mamluk army.

1304 Mahmud Ghazan dies. His successor to the Ilkhan throne, Mahmud Uljaytu, is best remembered for his tomb in Sultaniyya, Persia.

1308 The Ottomans cross the Bosporus and invade Europe.

1311 Malik Kafur captures the Pandyan capital Madurai for the Delhi Sultanate.

1312 Mansa ("King") Abubakar II of Mali is never seen again after sailing west into the Atlantic with his fleet.

1313 A treatise on Turkish grammar is written by Abu Hayan.

1316 Abu Said becomes the ruler of the Ilkhans.

1320 The Tuareg lose Timbuktu to Mansa Musa.

1320 The Tughluq dynasty begins when Ghiyasuddin Tughluq replaces the Khalji rulers in Dehli.

1324 Mansa Musa makes a pilgrimage to Mecca.

1325 Muhammad Ibn Tughluq becomes the sultan of Delhi. The sultanate's territories reach their greatest extent under his reign.

1325 Ibn Battuta, a Moroccan Muslim, begins his celebrated travels through Egypt to Arabia and into various other parts of western Asia.

1325 Mali takes the city of Gao on the Niger River.

c. 1325 The eastern African gold and ivory trade is monopolized by the Arab trading town of Kilwa, built on an island off Tanzania.

1326 The Byzantine city of Bursa in western Anatolia is captured by the Ottomans, who make it their capital.

1326 Ottoman ruler Osman dies. His son Orhan inherits his empire.

1327 The sultan of Delhi, Tughluq, founds a new capital at Daulatabad in the Deccan. However, he cannot control the north and returns to Delhi.

1331 The Byzantine town of Nicaea in western Anatolia is seized and renamed Iznik by the Ottomans.

1331 Ibn Battuta records his visits to the wealthy city-states of Africa's eastern coast.

1333 Celebrated medieval Arab historian Ibn Khaldun is born in Tunisia.

1333 The Byzantines are left with only a toehold in Anatolia when the Ottoman forces, led by Orhan, take the town of Nicomedia, which they rename Izmit.

1333 Ibn Battuta visits India and later travels to China as an ambassador for Tughluq.

1333 Islamic culture flourishes in Granada under Caliph Yusuf I.

1334 The governor of Madurai in southern India declares his independence from the sultans of Delhi.

1335 The Mongol Ilkhan dynasty of Persia ends with the death of the last khan, Abu Said.

1337 Mansa Musa dies; his brother Mansa Suleiman eventually inherits the kingdom.

1345 The Bhamanid dynasty is founded by Bhaman Shah, a Muslim noble, who revolts against the Delhi Sultanate. The dynasty rules the Deccan for almost two centuries.

1346 Muslim forces pillage the Kathmandu Valley in Nepal, destroying Hindu temples.

1346 The Byzantine emperor arranges the marriage of his daughter, Theodora, to Sultan Orhan in return for military aid.

1347 The Marinids of Morocco take Tunisia from its Hafsid rulers.

1348 The Black Death spreads through Egypt.

c. 1350 Syria and other parts of the Mamluk Empire become centers of refined glassmaking.

1351 Muhammad Ibn Tughluq, sultan of Delhi, dies and is succeeded by Firuz Shah, who rules for 37 years and consolidates the sultanate.

1352 Ibn Battuta explores the Sahara and lives in Mali for a year.

1352 Christians in Egypt are persecuted by the Muslim rulers. Coptic Patriarch Marco is imprisoned.

1352 The Marinids take Algeria.

1354 The Ottomans take the Gallipoli Peninsula on the western side of the Dardanelles Strait, gaining their first territory in Europe.

1360 Murad succeeds his father, Orhan, as Ottoman sultan. He puts down an uprising in Ankara (present-day Turkey).

1360 Mansa Suleiman dies and the Mali Empire falls into decline.

1361 The Ottomans take Adrianople in Bulgaria and rename it Edirne. It becomes the main Ottoman base in Europe.

1361 Timur becomes the leader of the Barlas tribe of Chagatai Mongols in Transoxiana, central Asia.

1365 Muslims sack southern Egypt and murder the Christian king of Makurra (Nubia).

1368 Persian poet Hafez compiles his masterpiece *Diwan* (Collected works).

1369 Geographer and traveler Ibn Battuta dies.

1369 Timur becomes ruler of all the Chagatai Mongols.

c. 1370 The Sultanate of Madurai is conquered by the Hindu Vijayanagar Empire.

1372 *The Lives of Animals*, the best-known Arabic zoological work, is written by al-Damiri.

1375 Mamluk forces conquer the kingdom of Armenian Cilicia in present-day southern Turkey.

1375 Ibn Khaldun writes the *Muqaddimah*, a philosophy of history and theory of society.

1375 Gao breaks away from Mali and eventually becomes the capital of the Songhai Empire.

1379 Bairam Khawaja establishes the independent principality of the Kara Koyunlu ("Black Sheep") Turkmen. Its capital is Van in Armenia.

1381 Timur invades Persia.

1382 Barquq establishes himself as the first Egyptian Mamluk ruler of the Burji (Circassian) line, taking power from the Bahri (Turkic) rulers.

1382 Ibn Khaldun is made a professor and judge in Cairo.

1384 Timur establishes Sultaniyya in northwestern Persia as his military base for campaigns into the north and west.

1388 Firuz Shah dies, and the Delhi Sultanate falls into decline.

1389 The Serbs are defeated by the Ottomans at Kosovo; however, Sultan Murad I is killed on the battlefield.

1389 Bayezid I, son of Murad I, becomes the Ottoman sultan.

1390 The last territories of the Byzantines in Anatolia fall to the Ottomans.

Tuaregs are an Islamic nomadic people whose range covers northern and western Africa.

■ **Africa**   ■ **Americas**   ■ **East Asia**   ■ **Europe**   ■ **South and Central Asia**   ■ **Western Asia**

1393 Timur captures Baghdad.

1394 Under an independent Muslim dynasty, Jaunpur in northern India breaks free of the Delhi Sultanate.

1395 In southern Russia, Timur defeats the rival Mongol Empire of the Golden Horde. He razes its capital at Sarai on the Volga River.

1396 Bayezid I and his Ottoman forces defeat European crusaders at Nicopolis on the Danube River.

1398 Timur enters India and sacks Delhi, destroying the power of the Delhi Sultanate.

1399 Mamluk sultan Barquq of Egypt dies. His 10-year-old son al-Nasir Faraj inherits the throne.

❖ 1400 ❖

1400 Timur enters Syria and ravages Damascus.

1401 Timur sacks Baghdad.

1402 Timur enters Anatolia and defeats and captures Bayezid.

1402 Bayezid dies in captivity and his sons contest the succession, throwing the Ottoman Empire into disorder.

1405 Timur dies and his territories are split between his sons Miranshah and Shah Rokh.

1407 Shah Rokh becomes sole ruler of the Timurid Empire in Persia and central Asia on the death of his brother Miranshah; he makes Herat (in Afghanistan) his new capital.

1410 The Kara Koyunlu (Black Sheep Turkmen) take Baghdad and found a dynasty there.

1412 The last Tughluq sultan of Delhi, Nasiruddin Muhammad, dies.

1413 Mehmed I regains Ottoman dominance over Anatolia from the Timurid Empire.

1414 Founder of the Sayyid Dynasty, Khizr Khan, takes control of a much-reduced Delhi Sultanate.

1415 Muslims lose Ceuta, on the coast of Morocco, to the Portuguese, giving them territory on mainland Africa.

1415 Ethiopian forces attack Seylac, a port on the Red Sea. They kill its Muslim ruler.

c. 1415 Under Sultan Firuz Shah Bahmani, the Kingdom of Bahmani in the northern Deccan flourishes as a center of Islamic culture.

1417 Bahmani is defeated in a battle by Vijaynagar and is forced to abdicate two years later.

1422 Ottoman Turks besiege Constantinople. They leave when the Byzantine emperor agrees to pay tribute.

1423 The Ottomans capture Salonika, in northern Greece, during a war with Venice for mastery of the Adriatic Sea.

c. 1425 The capital of Bahmani moves from Gulbarga to Bidar (Karnataka) under the rule of Shihab-ud-Din Ahmad I.

1426 Cyprus is raided by Mamluks from Syria and Egypt.

c. 1430 Coffee from eastern Africa reaches Arabia.

1433 Tuareg nomads take control of the trading city Timbuktu in Mali.

1434 Portuguese navigator Gil Eanes opens the way for European explorers when he sails around Cape Bojador on the coast of Morocco.

1434 Mubarak Shah, the Sayyid sultan of Delhi, is murdered.

1437 A Portuguese expedition, led by Prince Henry the Navigator, to capture Tangiers in northern Africa from Muslim rule ends in disaster.

1438 The Golden Horde of the Mongols fragments into smaller khanates, including Crimea, Astrakhan, and Kazan.

1439 Patron of architecture and calligraphy Jahan Shah becomes leader of the Kara Koyunlu (Black Sheep Turkmen).

1441 Portuguese traders take the first slaves—many of whom are Muslims—from Africa to Europe.

1443 A Persian traveler visiting the city of Vijayanagar describes it as having "no equal in the world."

1443 János Hunyadi, a Hungarian soldier leading resistance to the Ottoman advance in Serbia and Transylvania, is defeated at the Battle of Zlatica.

1444 A crusade launched by the pope against the Ottoman Turks is defeated at Varna on the Black Sea.

1444 Sultan Murad II hands over the Ottoman throne to his son Mehmed II. However, he resumes power two years later to put down a rebellion.

1445 The Muslim state of Ifat is defeated in battle by Zara Yakob, emperor of Ethiopia.

1448 The Second Battle of Kosovo results in the Ottomans gaining the Danube River as their frontier in the Balkans.

c. 1450 Around this time, Damascus and Aleppo in Syria are centers for the textile trade between Asia and Europe.

c. 1450 Mali is subsumed by the growing Songhai Empire.

1451 Ottoman Sultan Murad II dies and is succeeded by his son Mehmed II.

1451 Afghan noble Bahlul Lodi founds the Lodi dynasty when the last Sayyid sultan surrenders Delhi.

1453 Constantinople falls to Mehmed II.

1453 Jahan Shah, leader of the Kara Koyunlu (Black Sheep Turkmen), extends his domains in Iraq and western Persia.

1453 With the capture of Constantinople by the Ottomans, the Byzantine Empire comes to an end.

1454 The name Istanbul begins to be widely used instead of Constantinople. Construction of the sultan's residence—the Topkapi Palace—begins.

1455 Construction of the Great Bazaar starts in Istanbul.

1456 "Vlad the Impaler" becomes prince of Wallachia, present-day southern Romania. He is believed to have impaled 20,000 prisoners during an attack against the Turks.

1460 Mehmed II overruns and conquers Morea in southern Greece, wiping out the last claimants to the Byzantine throne.

1463 Mahmud Gawan is made chief minister of the Bahmani Kingdom on India's Deccan Plateau. He soon begins successful campaigns against Vijayanagar and Orissa.

1467 The Ak Koyunlu (White Sheep Turkmen) of northern Iraq defeat the Kara Koyunlu (Black Sheep Turkmen); Jahan Shah dies, and the Ak Koyunlu win his territories.

1468 The longest-ruling Mamluk sultan of the Burrji dynasty, Qa'itbay, begins his 28-year reign. He orders restoration work on the shrines of Mecca and Medina.

1468 The Songhai of Gao become the leading power in western Africa after Emperor Sunni Ali seizes Timbuktu.

1473 The Ottomans extend their territory eastward in Anatolia after a victory against the White Sheep Turkmen.

1476 Vlad the Impaler dies in a battle near Bucharest.

1479 A 15-year war between the Ottomans and Venice ends with the Treaty of Constantinople.

1480 The Greek island of Rhodes is besieged and Otranto in Italy taken by an Ottoman fleet.

1480 Russian ruler Ivan the Great refuses to pay tribute to the rulers of the Khanate of the Golden Horde.

1481 Mehmet II dies and his son Bayezid II inherits the Ottoman throne. In Bayezid's 31-year reign, the Ottoman Empire expands further.

1492 Sultan of Delhi, Sikandar II Lodi, annexes the state of Bihar and extends Muslim rule westward.

1492 Many Muslims and Jews are forced into exile in northern Africa after Granada—the last Moorish state in Spain—falls to Christian leaders Ferdinand and Isabella.

1493 The Songhai Empire's Askiya dynasty is founded by Askiya Muhammad. During his reign, the empire absorbs much of the Manding Empire, and the Sankoré Mosque in Timbuktu becomes a renowned center of learning.

1497 Persia's Turkmen White Sheep Dynasty ends with the death of Rustam Shah.

1499 War breaks out anew between the Ottomans and Venice. The Ottomans gain new territories in the Balkans.

❖ 1500 ❖

1501 Shah Ismail founds the Safavid dynasty in the northeastern part of present-day Iran.

1502 The Mongol Golden Horde falls into decline and Russia expands its territories into the Caucasus.

1503 The Ottoman war against Venice and Hungary ends.

1504 Venice proposes the construction of a Suez Canal to the Ottomans.

1504 In Sudan, the Christian rulers of Sennar are defeated in battle by the Muslim Funj.

1504 The Mughal army under the leadership of Babur begins a series of conquests in Afghanistan. The Mughals will eventually rule most of the Indian subcontinent.

1505 The first slaves from Africa arrive in the Americas, at Santo Domingo (in present-day Dominican Republic).

1505 Kilwa on the coast of eastern Africa (in modern-day Tanzania) is sacked by the Portuguese.

1508 Lebna Denegel, a Christian, ascends to the throne of Ethiopia and struggles against spreading Islamic influence.

1509 Spain begins a campaign to capture northern African cities after taking Oran in Algeria.

■ **Africa** ■ **Americas** ■ **East Asia** ■ **Europe** ■ **South and Central Asia** ■ **Western Asia**

1509 An earthquake in Istanbul kills 10,000 people.

1509 The Hindu state of Vijayanagar defeats an attack by Sultan Mahmud of Bidar.

1509 An Egyptian-Gujarati fleet is defeated by the Portuguese at Diu (an Island off the northwestern coast of India), securing Portuguese control over the spice trade.

1510 The Uzbeks are driven out of the disputed region of Khurasan by Shah Ismail I of Persia. He makes the Shiite branch of Islam the official religion of Persia.

1511 Ottoman sultan Bayezid II is deposed by his son Selim I ("the Grim"), who orders the death of 40,000 Shiite Muslims. The Ottoman Empire will double in size during his nine-year reign.

1511 The Portuguese take Malacca on the Malay Peninsula, center of the spice trade.

1512 In western Africa, the Songhai Empire, ruled by Askia Mohammed, and the Hausa Confederation vie for supremacy in the region.

1513 The Portuguese reach the Moluccas (eastern Indonesia), the fabled "Spice Islands." They dominate the nutmeg and mace trade for almost a hundred years.

1514 In western Sumatra, Ali Mughayat Syah becomes the first sultan of Aceh.

1514 The Ottoman Empire expands southward and eastward after the Safavid shah Ismail's defeat by Selim's Ottoman army at the Battle of Chaldiran.

1514 The Taklamakan Desert region (in present-day China) falls under the Islamic rule of Khan Sayid of Kashgar.

1515 Hormuz, at the mouth of the Persian Gulf, is taken by the Portuguese.

1517 Mecca surrenders to Selim and comes under Ottoman rule.

1517 The last Mamluk sultan of Egypt, Tuman Bey, is hanged after Ottoman forces pillage Cairo.

1518 The states of Tunis and Algiers are founded on the coast of northern African—soon becoming infamous as bases for raids on sea traffic in the Mediterranean.

1518 The transatlantic slave trade gathers momentum as the Spanish export 4,000 African slaves to America.

1519 Babur leads the first Mughal invasion of India.

1520 Selim dies and his son Suleiman I, "the Magnificent," becomes the Ottoman sultan.

1521 Suleiman invades the Kingdom of Hungary.

1521 Ottoman forces take Belgrade (present-day Serbia).

1522 The Ottomans conquer the island of Rhodes.

1523 Greek-born Ibrahim Pasha, who was sold into slavery by pirates, is made Suleiman's grand vizier.

1524 Egypt's governor Ahmad Pasha al-Khair attempts to set himself up as an independent ruler, but his plans are thwarted by the Ottomans.

1524 The founder of Persia's Safavid dynasty, Shah Ismail, dies. His 10-year-old son succeeds as ruler.

1524 Babur takes Lahore (in present-day Pakistan).

1525 Babur's forces enter the Punjab.

1526 The sultan of Delhi is defeated by Babur at the Battle of Panipat. Babur's army occupies Delhi and Agra.

1526 The Ottomans defeat the Hungarians at the Battle of Mohacs.

1527 Babur defends his conquests of the previous year by defeating the Hindu Rajputs at Khanua.

1529 Babur takes control of the Delhi Sultanate as far east as its frontier with Bengal.

1529 The Ottomans help the buccaneer Khayr ad-Din, also known as Barbarossa, take Algiers.

1529 Suleiman's Ottoman forces fail to take Vienna.

1530 Babur dies and his son Humayun becomes Mughal emperor of India. However, Humayun has to share his territories with his brothers.

1531 Ethiopian king Lebna Denegel loses territory to Muslim leader Ahmad Gran.

1534 Barbarossa takes Tunis for the Ottomans.

1534 Baghdad surrenders to Suleiman I and becomes part of the Ottoman Empire.

1535 The Ottomans are driven out of Tunis by Genoese admiral Andrea Doria, working for Holy Roman Emperor Charles V.

1535 Muslim Ahmad Gran rules most of Ethiopia, with Christian resistance in the mountain areas.

1536 King Francis I of France and Ottoman Sultan Suleiman I form an alliance against the Hapsburg Empire.

1538 A Christian fleet is defeated by the Ottoman navy at Prevesa, off the western coast of Greece.

1538 The entire Red Sea coast of Arabia falls under Ottoman rule when a naval expedition conquers Aden.

1538 The Portuguese are expelled from Diu after a joint attack by the Ottoman navy and the Gujarati army.

1539 Humayun loses Bengal after a rebellion led by Sher Shah Sur, an Afghan chieftain.

1539 Suleiman makes Mimar Sinan chief of the Corps of Royal Architects. He remains the most famous of all Muslim architects.

1540 Uzbek raids on the eastern provinces of the Safavid Empire end with the death of ruler Ubayd Allah Kahn.

1540 The Ottoman navy, led by Barbarossa, defeats Charles V's fleet off the island of Crete.

1540 The Afghan Sher Shah Sur seizes Delhi after defeating Humayun.

1541 Barbarossa defeats the Christians again off Algiers.

1542 Lebna Denegel attacks Ahmad Gran with military aid from the Portuguese.

1542 A new Islamic state, Banten (in modern-day western Java), is founded by Sunan Gunung Jati. It soon dominates its neighboring Hindu kingdoms.

1543 Sher Shah Sur's realm extends to the Indian Ocean.

1543 Ahmad Gran dies during fighting, ending the Muslim threat to control Ethiopia.

1543 The Ottomans conquer Hungary.

1543 The Ottoman fleet and French allies sack Nice.

1544 Italian coastal towns are raided by Barbarossa's fleet.

1545 Sher Shah Sur captures Chitor, completing his conquest of Rajasthan (present-day northwestern India).

1546 The Gujarati port of Diu is besieged by Ottomans.

1547 Suleiman and Ferdinand of Austria sign a peace treaty.

1547 The Ottomans take the port of Basra (present-day Iraq). Former pirate Piri Reis commands the Ottoman navy in the Indian Ocean.

1548 Alqas Mirza, governor of Khurasan, fails to overthrow his brother, Persia's Shah Tahmasp, even with military aid from the Ottoman army.

1548 Piri Reis regains Aden, which had fallen under Portuguese rule.

1550 Moroccan forces cross the Sahara to overthrow the Songhai Empire, which is now in decline.

1550 The Saadi dynasty rules Morocco after the Marrakech warlord al-Shaykh captures Fez.

1551 The Ottomans take Tripoli (present-day Libya) from the Knights Hospitallers.

1551 Piri Reis expels the Portuguese from the port of Muscat (present-day Oman).

1552 The former Mongol Khanate of Khazan is conquered by the Russians. This conquest opens the way for later expansion across the Urals into Siberia.

1553 Suleiman invades Persia for a second time. His attack ends with the treaty known as the Peace of Amasya, signed in 1555.

1553 Suleiman has his son Mustafa executed after suspecting a conspiracy.

1555 An uprising by Mustafa's supporters is suppressed in Anatolia.

1555 Humayun occupies Lahore and reestablishes Mughal power in Delhi.

1555 Thirteen-year-old Akbar becomes Mughal ruler, under the supervision of a regent, on the death of his father Humayun.

1556 Mughal forces defeat a Hindu army at Panipat in northern India. The victory confirms Akbar's authority as leader of the Mughals.

1556 Ismail, son of Shah Tahmasp, becomes governor of Khurasan. Suspected of plotting a coup, he spends the next 19 years imprisoned.

1557 The Süleimaniye Mosque in Istanbul is inaugurated after six years of construction.

1557 An Ottoman fleet retakes the Red Sea ports previously captured by the Portuguese.

1557 Morocco's ruler al-Shaykh is assassinated by the Ottomans. However, it does not stop his Saadi successors from reviving the country's power.

1559 Suleiman's sons Bayezid and Selim contest the succession of the Ottoman throne—even though their father is still alive. Bayezid escapes to Persia, where he seeks protection from Shah Tahmasp.

1561 Shah Tahmasp hands over Bayezid to his father Suleiman to prevent further war with the Ottomans.

■ **Africa**   ■ **Americas**   ■ **East Asia**   ■ **Europe**   ■ **South and Central Asia**   ■ **Western Asia**

1561 Akbar takes the reins as Mughal emperor, dispensing with the services of his regent. During Akbar's reign, the Mughal Empire enjoys a golden age.

1564 The Gakkhar rulers of Punjab and the Gonds of eastern India are brought to heel by Akbar's army.

1565 In India, a Muslim alliance called the Deccani Sultanates is victorious over the Hindu Vijayanagar Empire at the Battle of Talikota.

1565 Christian missionaries flee the Molucca Islands after suffering relentless raids by Sultan Hairun of Ternate.

1565 Malta stands firm after a four-month siege by the Ottoman navy.

1566 Suleiman dies and is succeeded by his son Selim II, also known as "the Sot."

The Süleimaniye Mosque was completed in 1557. It was designed by Mimar Sinan, a Muslim convert from a Greek Orthodox family.

1567 A Yemeni Shiite group called the Zeydis rebel against Ottoman rule. They are suppressed but retain a presence in the mountains.

1568 Tsar Ivan IV of Russia approaches the Safavid shah to join him against the Ottomans; Pope Gregory XIII backs the alliance, which he views as a "crusade."

1568 The Rajput stronghold of Chittor in Rajasthan is besieged and destroyed by Akbar, with the death of about 30,000 Rajputs.

1569 Muslim Spaniards who converted to Catholicism (known as Moriscos) revolt when Philip II orders them to give up their language (Arabic) and culture.

1569 Akbar takes the last Rajput fortress, Rathambor.

1569 The Ottomans recapture Tunis on the coast of North Africa from its European rulers.

1570 The Ottomans declare war on Venice and invade the island of Cyprus.

1570 The Saharan Kingdom of Kanem Bornu emerges as a power under its Muslim king, Idris III Aloma.

1571 Crimean Tatar forces sack Moscow.

1571 The Ottoman navy is defeated by a Christian fleet, commanded by Don John of Austria, at the Battle of Lepanto off the coast of Greece.

1572 One-third of the population of Algiers dies during an epidemic.

1574 Christian forces attempt to retake Tunis but are driven back by the Ottomans.

1574 Selim II dies and his son Murad III inherits the Ottoman throne.

1574 The Mughal Empire gains access to the Indian Ocean after the conquest of Gujarat.

1576 Akbar pays for and organizes the first annual pilgrimage from India to the holy cities of Mecca and Medina.

1576 Mughal forces take Bengal from the Afghans. The Mughal Empire now extends across all of northern India.

1576 After the death of the Safavid shah Tahmasp I, his son Ismail II succeeds him after 19 years in prison. He is assassinated after less than a year on the throne.

1578 Murad III wages war against the Safavid Empire.

1578 King Sebastian I of Portugal is defeated and killed by the Moroccans at the Battle of Kasr al-Kabir.

1579 A property tax on non-Muslim subjects called *jiziya* is abolished by Akbar.

c. 1580 Akbar commissions a Persian translation of the Hindu religious epic the Mahabharata.

c. 1580 To strengthen his hold over the trade routes of the eastern Sahara, Idris III Aloma buys firearms from the Ottomans.

c. 1580 The *devshirme* system of recruiting Christian boys for the janissaries—the elite palace guard of the Ottoman sultan—goes into decline under Murad III.

1581 The Moroccans under Ahmed al-Mansur of the Sharifian dynasty occupy Tuat in the northern Sahara.

1582 Renowned for his love of display, Murad III holds a festival in Istanbul to celebrate his son's circumcision. The festivities last 55 days and include banquets and mock battles.

1582 To reconcile the different faiths of his subjects, Akbar sets out the doctrine *Din-I Ilahi* (Divine faith), which incorporates ideas from other Asian religions, including Jainism and Hinduism, as well as Islam.

1583 Ottoman forces capture Baku, a Safavid-ruled city on the western coast of the Caspian Sea.

An architectural masterpiece completed in 1618, the Sheikh Lotf Allah Mosque, in Isfahan, Iran, was built on the orders of Shah Abbas I, Safavid ruler of Persia.

1585 The Sultan of Aceh signs a trade agreement with Queen Elizabeth of England.

1585 Lahore in Punjab becomes the capital of the Mughal Empire.

1588 After Shah Mohammed's death, his son Abbas I inherits the throne. The greatest of the Safavid rulers, Abbas is famed for his patronage of the arts.

1589 The memoirs of Babur, the first Mughal emperor, are translated into Persian. Lavishly illustrated, they promote the authority of the Mughal Empire.

1590 The Ottomans and Safavids make peace and agree on the Caspian Sea as a border between their empires.

1591 A new city, called Hyderabad, is founded on the Musi River (present-day Andhra Pradesh) by the sultan of Golconda, a ruler of India's Deccan Plateau.

1593 After building Fort Jesus outside Mombasa, a Muslim trading port on the eastern coast of Africa, the Portuguese sack the city.

1595 On the death of Murad III, his son Mehmed III inherits the throne and orders the murder of 20 of his younger brothers (and many of his sisters) to prevent rival claims to the throne.

1595 Afghanistan falls under Mughal rule when Akbar's forces take Kandahar.

1597 Abbas makes Isfahan the Safavid capital of Persia. He commissions many new fine buildings.

■ Africa ■ Americas ■ East Asia ■ Europe ■ South and Central Asia ■ Western Asia

1597 Uzbek incursions in Khurasan in northeastern Persia are halted by Safavid forces.

1598 Akbar moves his capital to Agra after maintaining stability in the northwest of his empire.

❖ 1600 ❖

1601 Akbar's son Salim rebels against his father but is later forgiven.

1602 The English establish a trading station at Bantam in Java (Indonesia).

1602 Shah Abbas of the Safavids initiates a campaign against the Ottomans to regain territory in Iraq.

1603 Thirteen-year-old Ahmed I inherits his father Murad III's throne to become the sultan of the Ottoman Empire.

1604 The Hapsburgs are forced out of Transylvania by an alliance of Protestant and Ottoman forces.

1605 The Ottoman governor of Egypt is murdered by rebels.

1605 Salim succeeds his father Akbar as Mughal emperor and takes the title of Jahangir, meaning "conqueror of the world."

1605 The Dutch take the island of Amboina in Indonesia from the Portuguese. Amboina becomes the center of the spice trade to Europe.

1605 Arjun, the fifth Sikh guru, is executed on Jahangir's orders for supporting an uprising led by Jahangir's son Khusrau.

1606 Khusrau is blinded on the orders of Jahangir, and many of his followers are put to death.

1606 Austria and the Ottoman Empire make peace by signing the treaty of Zsitvatörök.

1609 Work begins on the Mosque of Ahmed I, commonly known as the Blue Mosque, in Istanbul.

1609 The Moriscos are expelled from Spain by King Philip III. This ethnic cleansing results in more than 300,000 deportations in the following five years.

1611 Jahangir marries Nur Jahan. The new empress becomes a powerful figure and effectively rules the Mughal Empire until Jahangir's death.

1612 The Moroccan army leaves western Sudan but maintains control of the Songhai Empire in eastern Africa.

1614 The Sultan of Mombasa's palace is attacked by the Portuguese. He visits Goa in India to complain to Portuguese authorities.

1614 Cossack pirates ravage the port of Sinope on Turkey's northern coast. Ottoman control of the Black Sea weakens.

1616 Warfare breaks out anew between the Ottomans and Persian Safavids.

1617 Ahmed I dies and his brother Mustafa I ascends the Ottoman throne.

1618 Mustafa, declared unfit to rule, is replaced by his brother Osman II.

1618 The Ottomans agree to leave Azerbaijan and Georgia, thereby renewing peace with the Safavids.

1618 Future ruler of the Mughal Empire, Aurangzeb (grandson of Jahangir), is born. Under his control the empire later reaches its greatest extent.

1619 Plague kills more than 300,000 Egyptians.

1622 Persians join forces with the English East India Company to capture Hormuz, which has been under Portuguese rule for more than a century.

1622 Osman II is assassinated by the janissaries after trying to suppress their power and influence.

1623 Osman's nephew Murad IV becomes Ottoman sultan and crushes the janissaries.

1623 Persian Shah Abbas I takes Mosul and Baghdad from the Ottomans and completes his conquest of Iraq.

1625 The Persians take Kandahar from the Mughals.

1627 Jahangir dies and is succeeded by his son Shah Jahan.

1628 From Batavia (present-day Jakarta) the Dutch launch repeated raids that spread their rule across Java.

1629 The governor of Kandahar defects from the Persian Empire to the Uzbek khanate, allowing the Uzbeks to take control of the city and surrounding region.

1629 Safi I inherits the throne of the Safavid Empire after the death of his grandfather Shah Abbas.

1630 The city of Hamadan in Persia is taken by the Ottoman sultan Murad IV.

1632 Shah Jahan orders construction of a tomb at Agra for his dead wife, Mumtaz Mahal. The tomb—the Taj Mahal—takes 22 years to build.

1632 Shah Jahan sets out to conquer the Deccan. At this time, the region is struck by a famine, which results in the death of about one million people.

1634 The Uzbeks are driven out of Kandahar by Shah Jahan's Mughal forces.

1637 The Netherlands is hit by "tulipmania." Tulips were introduced into Europe from the Ottoman Empire. One Dutchman is said to have swapped a house for three tulip bulbs. However, the prices of bulbs eventually crash by 95 percent.

1638 Ottoman forces recapture Baghdad from the Safavids after a month-long siege. Iraq now remains a province of the Ottoman Empire until 1918.

1639 With the signing of the Treaty of Qasr-i-Shirin, the Safavid ruler Shah Safi and Ottoman sultan Murad IV establish a fixed border between their empires.

1639 Construction begins on the walled city of Old Delhi. Shah Jahan makes it the capital of the Mughal Empire nine years later.

1640 Murad IV dies and is succeeded by his son Ibrahim the Mad, who rules disastrously.

1641 Half a century of female rule begins in the Indonesian sultanate of Aceh as Safiyat ud-Din Taj ul-Alam ascends the throne.

1642 Crimean Tatars and Ottomans join forces to drive the Cossacks from Azov, thwarting Russian plans for dominance of the Black Sea coast.

1642 Shah Safi of the Safavid dynasty dies. His son Shah Abbas II ascends the throne to begin a reign characterized by religious intolerance.

1646 The Mughal army sets out on a disastrous campaign in central Asia.

1646 Amangkurat I ascends the throne of Mataram (in Java). He orders the execution of many opponents and religious scholars.

1648 Shah Abbas II of Persia takes Kandahar from the Mughals.

1648 Sultan Ibrahim's janissaries have him assassinated.

1650 The Portuguese-controlled port of Muscat is captured by Sultan Bin Saif al-Yarubi of Oman.

1652 Zanzibar is taken from the Portuguese by Omani Arabs. A 70-year struggle ensues for control of the Swahili coast.

1656 After a period of near anarchy in the Ottoman Empire, Mehmed Köprülü is appointed as grand vizier and brings stability.

1658 A rebellion occurs in Anatolia, led by Abaza Hashan Pasha. Mehmed Köprülü later suppresses the revolt.

1658 Candia (present-day Heraklion), the capital of Crete, is besieged by the Ottomans.

1658 Shah Jahan is deposed and imprisoned by his son Aurangzeb. The new Mughal emperor enforces strict Sunni orthodoxy and represses other religions, such as Hinduism, Sikhism, and minority Islamic sects.

1659 The city of Bijapur in southwestern India is taken from the Mughals by Sivaji, a Hindu warlord.

1659 In Algiers, Ottoman janissaries rebel. They appoint their own governor.

1659 Ahmad el Abbas, the last Saadi sultan of Morocco, is murdered in Marrakech.

c. 1660 Muslim leader Nasir al-Din calls for a jihad in the kingdoms of northern Senegambia (between the Senegal and Gambia rivers) in response to growing Western influence.

1661 The Ottoman grand vizier Mehmed Köprülü dies, and his son, Ahmed, inherits the post, thus establishing a dynasty of grand viziers that will continue for more than a century.

1662 The English colony of Virginia authorizes slavery.

1662 Aurangzeb's Mughal forces conquer Assam in northeastern India; they are forced out four years later.

1664 The Mughals conquer Bengal in northeastern India.

1664 The Ottomans are defeated by European armies, led by the Austrian Hapsburgs, at the Battle of Saint Gotthard. However, the Ottomans hold on to their territories in the Peace of Vasvar thanks to the Köprülüs' diplomatic skills.

1664 Mulay Rashid becomes the ruler of the Alawid clan of southern Morocco.

1666 Mulay Rashid captures Fez from the Saadi Dynasty and as sultan of Morocco establishes his capital there.

1666 Mughal forces take the Portuguese-controlled port of Chittagong (in present-day Bangladesh).

1666 Shah Abbas II dies. He is succeeded by his son Shah Sulayman who continues to persecute non-Muslims in Persia.

■ **Africa** ■ **Americas** ■ **East Asia** ■ **Europe** ■ **South and Central Asia** ■ **Western Asia**

1666 The former emperor of the Mughals, Shah Jahan, dies imprisoned in Agra.

1668 The Ottomans take the port of Basra in southern Iraq from independent local chieftains.

1669 Aurangzeb takes another step to enforce Sunni Islam by banning Hindu worship in India.

1669 The Venetians lose Candia and all of Crete to Ottoman forces.

1672 Ottoman forces wage war against Poland, gaining the region of Podolia and parts of Polish Ukraine.

1672 Mulay Ismail succeeds his half brother Mulay Rashid as sultan of Morocco.

1673 Protestant French traveler Jean Chardin visits Isfahan on a great journey through Turkey and Persia. He published a full account, *The Travels of Sir John Chardin in Persia and the Orient*, in 1711.

1675 After his refusal to become a Muslim, the Sikh guru Tegh Bahadur is executed on the orders of Aurangzeb.

1675 The last of the Ten Gurus of Sikhism, Goband Singh, rebels against his Mughal rulers.

1676 Kara Mustafa succeeds his brother-in-law, Ahmed Köprülü, as grand vizier of the Ottoman Empire.

1677 Jean Chardin reaches India, where he experiences courtly life of the Mughal and Deccani sultans.

1677 After Cossack attacks in Ottoman territory, the Ottomans and Russians go to war.

1678 The Khanate of Kokand (present-day Uzbekistan) conquers the Khanate of Kashgar.

1679 Aurangzeb conquers the Rajput Kingdom of Marwar in western India.

1679 Aurangzeb reinstates the *jiziya* tax for non-Muslims.

1680 The Hindu ruler Sivaji dies having thwarted Aurangzeb and held on to his kingdom in the Deccan.

1681 Aurangzeb's son Akbar leads a revolt against his father. It fails and he is exiled.

1681 Kara Mustafa assembles a large Ottoman army to invade central Europe.

1682 Iyasu I, a Christian, becomes king of Ethiopia and opens the country to trade with both Europeans and Arabs.

1683 Vienna is rescued from an Ottoman siege by forces led by the Polish king John Sobieski.

1683 After defeat at the gates of Vienna, Kara Mustafa is executed in Belgrade and his head sent in a velvet bag to the Ottoman sultan Mehmed IV.

1684 The Holy League is established by Pope Innocent XI. The league comprises an alliance of Poland, Venice, and Hapsburg Austria with the aim to free Europe of the Ottomans.

1684 Morocco takes Tangiers on the coast of northern Africa after it is abandoned by the English.

1684 The French launch a concerted attack on pirate bases on the coast of northern African.

1684 The Dutch East India Company takes control of the Sultanate of Bantam on Java.

1685 On the orders of Aurangzeb, the English East India Company is expelled from its base at Surat, western India.

1686 The Muslim Sultanate of Bijapur in the northwestern Deccan falls to Aurangzeb.

1687 Aurangzeb takes Golconda, a sultanate in southern India famous for its diamonds.

1687 Ottoman sultan Mehmed IV is deposed and his younger brother, Suleiman II, ascends the throne.

1687 The Venetians besiege Ottoman-ruled Athens, Greece. During the fighting an ammunition dump inside the Parthenon catches fire, damaging the ancient Greek temple.

1688 The Holy League takes Belgrade from the Ottoman army.

1689 Suleiman II appoints Mustafa Köprülü as his grand vizier. Mustafa reforms the Ottoman army and administration.

1689 Captured by Mughal forces, the Hindu ruler Sambhaji—the son of Shivaji—is taken to Aurangzeb and executed.

1690 Sambhaji's brother and successor Rajaram is besieged in the great fortress of Senji in southern India by a Mughal army. The siege continues until 1698.

1690 The Austrian army is driven out of Serbia by Ottoman forces.

1691 Suleiman II dies and his brother Ahmed II inherits the Ottoman Sultanate.

1691 Ottoman grand vizier Mustafa Köprülü dies fighting the Austrian army at the Battle of Slankamen.

This wall painting from the Chehel Sotoun pavillion, Isfahan, depicts Shah Abbas II of the Safavid dynasty (in white) receiving and entertaining the king of Turkestan (top left).

1694 Shah Suleiman of the Safavid dynasty dies and is succeeded by his son Shah Hussein.

1695 Mustafa II succeeds his half uncle Ahmed II as the Ottoman sultan.

1696 Russian tsar Peter the Great takes the port of Azov from the Ottomans.

1697 The Ottomans are defeated by a Hapsburg force at the Battle of Zenta.

1698 Omani Arabs drive the Portuguese from Zanzibar.

1699 The Treaty of Karlowit ends the war between the Ottomans and the Holy League. The Ottoman Empire hands over most of Hungary to the Hapsburgs.

❖ 1700 ❖

1702 The last Muradid bey (Ottoman client ruler) of Tunis, Murad III, dies in a coup. An army officer, Husain ibn Ali, takes power in the ensuing confusion.

1703 Mustafa II abdicates and his brother Ahmed III becomes the Ottoman sultan.

1704 Hasan Pasha is made Ottoman governor of Baghdad; his family reigns there for more than 100 years.

1704 The First Javanese War of Succession breaks out. The claim of Pakubuwono I to the throne of Mataram is supported by the Dutch East India Company, although the Dutch demand concessions in return.

1705 The Husainid dynasty is founded in Tunis.

1707 Aurangzeb, the Mughal emperor, dies while campaigning in the Deccan. The Mughal Empire begins to rapidly decline.

1708 Led by Banda Bahadur, Sikhs rebel against Mughal rule in Punjab, northwestern India.

1708 Spain loses Oran to Algerian forces.

1708 French merchants and missionaries are given special privileges in Persia.

1709 Ghilzai Afghans, led by Mir Wais Hotaki, rebel against Safavid rule and occupy Kandahar.

1709 Swedish king Charles XII and the Cossack leader Mazepa seek asylum in Ottoman territory after defeat at the hands of Peter the Great.

1710 Banda Bahadur establishes an independent Sikh nation in Punjab.

1711 Russian troops are defeated by the Ottoman army at the Pruth River. The Ottomans regain their Black Sea territories.

1711 Discord within Lebanon's Druze community leads to the emigration of the defeated Yamani Druze to neighboring Syria. Their exodus results in Maronite Christians making up most of the Lebanese population.

1711 Civil war begins in Egypt between representatives of the Ottoman rulers and the local governors, known as the Mamluk beys.

1711 Ahmed Qaramanli is appointed Ottoman governor of Tripoli. He establishes a dynasty that increases the influence of the northern African city.

1712 The secession of Hyderabad as an independent state on the death of Mughal emperor Shah Alam (Bahadur Shah) initiates the breakup of the Mughal Empire.

1714 Ahmed III declares war on the Holy Roman Empire and the Venetian Republic.

1715 Sikh rebel Banda Bahadur is captured by the Mughals and executed. The rebellion he led is brutally suppressed.

1716 Former allies of the Safavids, the Abdali, capture the city of Herat in western Afghanistan.

■ Africa ■ Americas ■ East Asia ■ Europe ■ South and Central Asia ■ Western Asia

1716 The British East India Company obtains special trading privileges from the Mughal emperor Farrukhsiyar.

1717 Russian forces enter the Muslim Khiva khanate of Uzbekistan.

1718 War ends between the Ottoman and Holy Roman empires. In the Peace of Passarowitz, the Holy Roman Empire gains territory in the Balkans and Hungary.

1718 A time of cultural renewal throughout the Ottoman Empire, known as the Tulip Period, begins when Damad Ibrahim Pasha is made Ottoman grand vizier.

1719 Ghilzai Afghans—under the leadership of Mir Wais Hotaki's son Mir Mahmud—invade the Safavid Empire, attacking Irfan and besieging Isfahan.

1719 Farrukhsiyar is assassinated and Muhammad Shah becomes Mughal emperor.

1719 After the death of Pakubuwono I, the Second Javanese War of Succession begins.

1721 The Kingdom of Rohilkhand is founded in northern India by the Afghan Rohilla tribe.

1722 Afghan ruler Mir Mahmoud proclaims himself shah after defeating Safavid forces at the Battle of Gulnabad.

1722 To counter the Afghan threat, Russia and the Ottoman Empire both invade Persia. The Russian army occupies Persia's Caspian Sea coast.

1723 The Ottomans take over the Persian stronghold of Tiflis (present-day Tbilisi, Georgia).

1724 Mir Mahmoud, whose behavior has become increasingly insane, is executed and replaced by Shah Ashraf.

1724 Asaf Jah becomes the Mughal governor of Hyderabad.

1724 Kingdom of Oudh in northern India breaks free of Mughal rule.

1726 The Afghans lose the city of Isfahan back to the Safavids.

c. 1730 As the Mughal Empire declines, Bajirao I, Hindu ruler of Maharashtra in central India, expands his territories.

1730 The janissaries rebel in Istanbul. They depose Ahmed III and place Mahmud I on the Ottoman throne.

1730 After a defeat by Ottomans at Shiraz, Shah Ashraf is killed by his followers.

1730 The Ottomans suffer a heavy defeat at the hands of Persian general (and later shah) Nader Kuli at Nehavend in western Persia.

1730 Nader Kuli besieges Baghdad but is unsuccessful.

1731 Safavid shah Tahmasp II signs a peace treaty with the Ottomans after defeat at the Battle of Arijan. However, Nader Kuli denounces the treaty and deposes the shah.

1735 In an alliance with Russian forces, Nader Kuli captures Tbilisi from the Ottomans.

1736 The last Safavid shah, Abbas III, dies at the age of six. Nader Kuli ascends the throne, calling himself Nader Shah.

1738 Nader Shah campaigns eastward and takes Kandahar in Afghanistan.

1739 The Persians, led by Nader Shah, defeat Muhammad Shah's army at Karnal and overrun his capital, Delhi, accelerating the collapse of the Mughal Empire.

1739 Holy Roman Emperor Charles VI returns northern Serbia to the Ottomans after they advance on Belgrade.

1739 The Ottomans lose Azov to the Russians.

1740 Alvardi Khan becomes the ruler of Bengal. He maintains the pretence that he governs in the name of the Mughal emperor.

1743 The Ottomans and Safavids resume their hostilities.

1744 Much of Arabia falls under the control of Muhammad Ibn Saud and Muhammad Ibn Abd-al-Wahhab, founder of the Wahhabi sect.

1747 Persian ruler Nader Shah is assassinated by one of his Afghan bodyguards.

1747 After the death of Nader Shah, Ahmad Shah Durrani takes control of Afghanistan. This country will become the greatest Islamic state of the late 18th century.

c. 1750 Feudal lords, or *derebeys,* become semiautonomous rulers in Anatolia as centralized Ottoman power wanes.

1752 The Sultan Abu al-Qasim of Darfur, in Sudan, is killed fighting an invasion led by the sultan of Kordofan.

1752 Afghan leader Ahmad Shah Durrani captures Lahore.

1752 The ruler, or nizam, of Hyderabad loses territory to Hindu forces.

1754 Sultan Mahmud I dies and his younger brother Osman III succeeds to the Ottoman throne.

1755 Chinese forces enter Kashgaria (Chinese Turkestan) to suppress a rebellion by local Muslims.

1756 Siraj-ud-Dawlah, nawab of Bengal, takes Calcutta (Kolkata) from the British.

1757 British general Clive defeats Siraj-ud-Dawlah's army at the Battle of Plassey.

1759 The Islamic Khanate of Kokand recognizes the sovereignty of China's Qing (Manchu) dynasty.

1761 The Dutch replace the Indonesian sultan of Siak as a punitive measure.

1761 Prussia and the Ottoman Empire sign a treaty of friendship.

1761 Hyder Ali, a Muslim, captures the throne of Mysore in southwestern India.

1761 A joint Hindu and Sikh force is defeated by Ahmad Shah Durrani outside Delhi.

1762 The Hamadj dynasty become rulers of the Sultanate of Funj in northern Sudan.

1762 Mir Kasim, the Mughal nawab of Bengal, revolts against the British East India Company.

1763 The highly effective Ottoman grand vizier Raghib Pasha dies.

1764 Exiled Mir Kasim makes an alliance with Mughal forces, but they are routed by the British at Buxar.

1764 Mughal rule is nominally restored when Ahmad Shah Durrani's forces withdraw from Dehli.

1765 Muhammad Ibn Saud dies. His son Abd al-Aziz becomes emir and extends Saudi rule across the Arabian Peninsula.

1766 Muhammad Ibn Uthman Dey takes control of Algiers.

1767 In southern India, the First Mysore War breaks out between Hyder Ali and British forces.

1768 The Ottoman governor in Egypt is overthrown by Ali Bey al-Kabir.

1768 After Tunisia refuses to release ships taken by its corsairs, a French fleet attacks Tunisian ports.

1768 The Ottomans bring in France's Baron de Tott to modernize their army.

1768 The Ottomans declare war on Russia after becoming alarmed by Russia's invasion of Poland.

1768 Ottoman-held Bulgaria is invaded by the Russians.

1769 Mawlay Muhammad dislodges the Portuguese from Morocco.

1770 The Russians defeat an Ottoman fleet at the Battle of Chesme in the Aegean Sea.

1772 The Mamluk sultan of Egypt, Ali Bey, is defeated by the Ottomans. He is killed the following year.

1772 A Hindu army defeats Hyder Ali, ruler of Mysore.

1773 Kabul is made the capital of Afghanistan.

1774 A prisoner for 43 years, Abdülhamid I becomes Ottoman sultan when his brother Mustafa III dies.

1774 The Russo-Ottoman War ends with the signing of the Treaty of Kuchuk-Kainarji. The Russians gain territories.

1775 The ruler of Persia, Karim Khan Zand, takes Basra from the Ottomans.

1777 Christian slavery is abolished in Morocco.

1778 Taking advantage of the war between the English and French, Hyder Ali attacks the East India Company; he also resumes hostilities against the Hindus.

1779 Karim Khan Zand dies; succession is disputed by his sons.

c. 1780 Mahadji Sindhia, a Hindu, takes control of Delhi from the Mughal emperor.

1781 A Muslim rebellion in China's Gansu province is suppressed.

1782 Hyder Ali dies. His son Tipu Sultan, also known as the "Tiger of Mysore," succeeds him.

1783 The last Khan of Crimea, Shahin Girai, is deposed by the Russians, who found Sevastopol as their naval base on the Black Sea.

1786 The British acquire the island of Penang (Malaysia) from the sultan of Kedah as a trading base and colony.

1786 Ottoman sultan Abdülhamid I sends troops to Egypt to strengthen his control.

1787 The U.S. government pays Morocco $10,000 to stop Moroccan privateers from plundering American shipping.

1789 Tipu Sultan starts a new war by attacking British-protected Travancore, in southern India.

1792 British forces defeat Tipu Sultan in the Third Anglo-Mysore War. Tipu loses half of his territory, and his sons are taken hostage.

1792 After the Second Russo-Turkish War, the Ottomans regain some territory in the Treaty of Jassy.

1793 The janissaries oppose Ottoman sultan Selim III's attempts to reform the Ottoman army on European lines.

1794 After defeating and capturing Lotf Ali Khan—the last of the Zand dynasty—eunuch Agha Muhammad Qajar becomes ruler of Persia.

1794 Morocco closes its borders to foreigners.

1796 Agha Muhammad is crowned as the first Persian shah of the Qajar dynasty.

1797 Agha Muhammad is assassinated. His nephew Fath Ali Shah succeeds him as shah of Persia.

1798 Napoleon Bonaparte's French forces occupy Egypt, but the British defeat them at the Battle of the Nile.

1798 The Fourth Anglo-Mysore War breaks out between British forces and Tipu Sultan, who dies the following year when British forces storm his capital at Seringapatam.

❖ 1800 ❖

1800 Captain John Malcolm of the British East India Company seeks the support of the Persians against Russia.

1801 After their defeat, French troops leave Egypt.

1801 In an attempt to end piracy, U.S. ships attack Tripoli and Algiers in northern Africa.

1803 The Wahhabi sect occupies the Hejaz, a region in Arabia that includes the holy cities of Mecca and Medina.

1804 After Russia annexes the Kingdom of Georgia, Persia's ruler Fath Ali Shah declares war on Russia.

1804 Serbian national leader Kara George leads a revolt in Belgrade against the ruling Ottomans that spreads throughout Serbia.

1804 In the Hausa kingdoms of northern Nigeria, reformer Usman dan Fodio spearheads an Islamic revival and jihad.

1805 Janissaries seize Aleppo in Syria.

1805 An Albanian officer in the Ottoman army, Muhammad Ali, proclaims himself viceroy of Egypt. He introduces many reforms during his long reign.

1807 Ottoman sultan Selim III is deposed by janissaries, who are opposed to his reforms. He is replaced by his cousin Mustafa IV.

1808 Selim III is killed during a revolt to restore him to the throne; his cousin Mahmud II takes the Ottoman throne. Deposed Mustafa IV is later murdered.

1809 The British sign a treaty with the ruler of Afghanistan, Shoja Shah.

1811 Muhammad Ali, viceroy of Egypt, is sent by Ottoman sultan Mahmud II to recapture the Arabian Peninsula from the Saud dynasty and their Wahhabi supporters.

1811 The Dutch surrender Java in Indonesia to British forces. They regain the island in 1816.

1812 A sheikhdom is founded in Kuwait by Jabir al-Sabah.

1813 Russia and Persia end their war. In the Treaty of Gulistan, Persia loses territory in the Caucasus region.

1813 Kara George's Serbian forces lose Belgrade back to the Ottomans.

1814 The ruler of Oman, Said Ibn Sultan, strengthens his control over the Swahili coast of eastern Africa.

1815 More than 92,000 people die when Mount Tambora, a volcano in Indonesia, erupts. So much ash is thrown into the atmosphere by the explosion that the following year will be recorded in history as "the year without a summer."

1817 Usman dan Fodio founds the Sokoto Caliphate in the Hausa lands (present-day northern Nigeria and southern Niger).

1817 The Ottomans grant the Serbs limited self-government.

1818 Shehu Ahmad Lobbo founds an Islamic state in Masina (present-day Mali). He makes Hamdallahi its capital.

1819 After pirate attacks on British shipping in the Indian Ocean, British warships attack ports along the Persian Gulf.

1819 The British found a trading station, Singapore, at the southern tip of the Malay Peninsula.

1819 Sikh leader Ranjit Singh takes Kashmir from Muslim rule.

1820 Egyptian viceroy Muhammad Ali sends an army, led by Ishmail Pasha, to conquer Sudan.

1821 The Greeks begins a war against the Ottomans to gain independence.

1821 Persia and the Ottoman Empire resume hostilities. Neither side wins any lasting territories.

1822 An Ottoman army of about 30,000 troops enters Greece to try to end the Greek War of Independence.

1823 The city of Khartoum in Sudan is founded by Muhammad Ali.

1824 Britain imposes itself as the dominant colonial power in Malaya and Singapore after signing a treaty with the Dutch.

1825 An Islamic revolt begins against the Dutch on Java. Hostilities continue until 1830.

1826 The power of the janissaries in Istanbul ends when Sultan Mahmud II stamps out their last mutiny.

1826 Dost Mohammad becomes the ruler of Afghanistan.

1826 Sayyid Ahmad of Bareli calls for a jihad against the Sikhs in northern India.

1827 A joint British, French, and Russian fleet destroys the Ottoman navy at the Battle of Navarino.

1828 Mahmud II introduces Westernized dress. He also replaces the traditional turban with the fez.

1828 The Second Russo-Persian War ends with the Treaty of Turkmanchay.

1828 The Russians declare war on the Ottomans, who are already fighting the Greeks.

1829 The Ottoman Empire recognizes Greece's right to rule itself. However, full independence is not granted until 1832.

1829 Russia and the Ottomans make peace. In the Treaty of Adrianople, Russia gains territory on the coast of the Black Sea.

Stone Town, Zanzibar, was the capital of the Sultanate of Oman between 1840 and 1856. During this period, it was the center of a thriving commercial empire.

1830 French forces invade Algeria. The ruler, or dey, is deposed and coastal towns are occupied.

1831 The French Foreign Legion is established in Algeria.

1831 Muhammad Ali revolts; as a result, Egypt becomes autonomous within the Ottoman Empire. Ali's heirs will rule until 1952.

1832 Muhammad Ali takes control of Syria from the Ottomans.

1833 Austria, Prussia, and Russia agree to uphold the territorial integrity of the declining Ottoman Empire.

1833 Britain passes a law to abolish slavery in its empire.

1833 Russia and the Ottoman Empire sign the Treaty of Unkiar Skelessi. The treaty closes access to the Black Sea to all but Russian warships in the event of war.

1833 A peace treaty is signed between the Ottoman Empire and Muhammad Ali Pasha. It grants partial control of Syria to Muhammad Ali's son but does not confer independence on Egypt.

1834 The ruler of Oman, Said Ibn Sultan, moves his capital from Muscat, Oman, to Stone Town, Zanzibar.

1834 Ranjit Singh's Sikh forces take the city of Peshawar from the Afghans.

1835 Dost Mohammad proclaims himself emir of Afghanistan and establishes the Barakzai Dynasty.

1838 Thousands of enslaved Africans—many of whom are Muslims—are emancipated in Sierra Leone.

1838 The first of the Afghan wars begin when British forces invade Afghanistan to block Russia's southward expansion. Emir Dost Mohammad is taken prisoner.

1839 Shah Shuja, an unpopular puppet ruler, is installed by the British in Afghanistan.

1839 The Ottoman army invades Syria but is defeated by the Egyptians at the Battle of Nizip (in present-day Turkey).

1839 Mahmud II dies as the weakened Ottoman Empire is under threat of breaking up.

1839 The Ottoman Empire launches a program of reform known as the *tanzimat* (reorganization) under new sultan Abdul Mejid.

1840 Britain, Austria, Russia, and Prussia force Muhammad Ali to restore land to the Ottoman Empire.

1841 James Brooke is made raja of Sarawak in Borneo for helping the sultan of Brunei crush piracy.

1842 The British withdraw their troops after a revolt in Kabul. From an original army of more than 16,000, only 121 survive the retreat, marking the end of the First Afghan War.

1843 Charles Napier's army defeats the emirs of Sind and the Punjab at the Battle of Hyderabad after they refuse to cede sovereignty to the British East India Company.

1844 Ilija Garasanin leads southern Serbian nationalists against Ottoman rule in the Balkan region.

1848 Nasr al-Din begins a 48-year reign as shah of Persia. He will introduce some Western ideas to his realm.

1848 After 40 days as Egyptian viceroy, Muhammad Ali's son and successor, Ibrahim Pasha, dies.

1848 Algeria, now controlled by France, is split into three "departments," or administrative divisions.

1849 The Russian army occupies the Ottoman Danubian principalities of Walachia and Moldavia.

1850 A Persian Islamic mystic called the Bab is executed for heresy. His followers are persecuted and eventually expelled from Persia.

1852 The Bab's successor, Baha Ulla, founds the Baha'i faith.

1854 France establishes its dominance over Senegal in western Africa.

1854 Competition between France and Russia concerning authority over Christians in the Ottoman-controlled Holy Land leads to war between Russia and the Ottoman Empire. France and Britain join the Ottoman side in what becomes known as the Crimean War.

1855 Frenchman Ferdinand de Lesseps is commissioned to build the Suez Canal, which will link the Red and Mediterranean seas.

1856 A railroad is laid down between Cairo and the Mediterranean port of Alexandria in Egypt.

1856 Said Ibn Sultan, ruler of Zanzibar, dies.

1856 British and French forces take the Russian fortress town of Sevastopol in the Crimea after a 322-day siege.

1856 The Treaty of Paris ends the Crimean War. It declares the Black Sea a neutral zone, setting back Russian influence in the region.

1856 Persian forces come into conflict with the British when they occupy the city of Herat in northwestern Afghanistan.

1857 Afghanistan's independence is recognized by Shah Nasr al-Din of Persia.

1857 A mutiny by sepoys (Indians fighting for the British) erupts in India. The mutiny quickly escalates to a more general rebellion against British rule. The last Mughal emperor, Bahadur Shah Zafar, is named by the rebels as the emperor of India.

1858 The Indian rebellion is defeated by the British and their Indian allies. The British exile the Mughal emperor and execute his male heirs. For their perceived support of the rebellion, Muslim leaders are marginalized by the colonial administration in India.

1859 The city of Tetuán in Morocco is conquered by Spain.

1861 Abdul Aziz becomes sultan of the Ottoman Empire. His empire opens up to Western influences during his reign.

1863 Muslims rebel in China's Gansu, Qinghai, and Shanxi provinces.

1863 The new ruler of Egypt, Ismail, launches an ambitious program of modernization.

1863 Dost Mohammad, ruler of Afghanistan, dies, and civil war erupts.

1865 Tashkent in central Asia is taken by Russian forces. It becomes the capital of Russian Turkestan in 1867.

1866 Crete rebels against Ottoman rule. Abdul Aziz sends troops to suppress the uprising.

1867 Abdul Aziz becomes the first Ottoman sultan to travel to Europe when he visits the Great Exhibition in Paris.

1868 Shir Ali Khan reestablishes himself as ruler of Afghanistan two years after being deposed by his brothers.

1868 Russia conquers the Islamic khanates of Samarkand and Bukhara (in present-day Uzbekistan).

1869 The Ottoman army is modernized, following the Prussian army as a model.

1869 Midhat Pasha is appointed as Ottoman governor of Baghdad. Rapid modernization occurs during his three-year administration.

1869 The Suez Canal is opened.

1870 Abdallah, emir of Saudi Arabia, is deposed and succeeded by his brother, Saud Ibn Faysal.

1871 The Ottoman Empire expands into Arabia with the conquest of Hasa in the Gulf Coast region. Kuwait also yields to Ottoman overlordship.

1871 Chief minister of Persia, Mirza Husayn, launches a program of modernization but is forced out of office in 1873 by conservative factions.

1872 The Ottoman army conquers Arabia's Red Sea coast and parts of Yemen.

1873 Moulay al-Hassan becomes sultan of Morocco. His quest to modernize the state is at odds with conservative clerics.

1873 The League of the Three Emperors—William I of Germany, Francis Joseph of Austria, and Alexander II of Russia—is established against the Ottoman Empire.

1873 Russia annexes the Islamic khanate of Khiva (in present-day Uzbekistan).

1874 Disorder and confusion fall on the Ottoman Empire after a financial crisis leaves it bankrupt.

1875 Bosnians rebel against Ottoman rule.

1875 The British suppress an uprising in the Malay states.

1875 Abdallah Ibn Faysal reclaims the throne of Saudi Arabia from his usurping brother Saud.

1875 Britain becomes the majority owner of the Suez Canal after purchasing the Ottoman Empire's share.

1876 A group of dissatisfied Ottoman nobles depose Abdul Aziz and install his nephew Murad V as sultan. Murad is soon declared insane, however, and replaced by his brother Abdülhamid II.

1876 Abdülhamid II gives the Ottoman Empire its first written constitution as a deference to Western criticism.

1876 The finances of a bankrupt Egypt are put in the hands of an Anglo-French commission.

1876 The Ottomans suppress a Bulgarian uprising against their rule.

1876 Russia takes the Islamic Khanate of Kokand in eastern Uzbekistan. The khan of Kalat (in present-day Pakistan) cedes the city of Quetta to the British, who hope to use the city as a defense against further Russian expansion.

1877 Russia aids Serbs and Montenegrins, who are rebelling against Ottoman rule. Britain forms an alliance with Austria against Russian expansion in the Balkans.

1878 Under the terms of the Treaty of San Stefano, Sultan Abdülhamid II cedes most Ottoman possessions in Europe. At home, he takes dictatorial power.

1878 Britain starts the Second Afghan War after Shir Ali Khan makes overtures to Russia. Shir Ali stands down as ruler in favor of his son Yaqub Khan. The British conquer Afghanistan the following year.

1879 The French expand their empire in western Africa, moving eastward from Senegal into the Niger Valley.

1880 In return for protection from the British, the sheikh of Bahrain surrenders control over foreign policy. Other sheikhdoms of the Persian Gulf follow suit.

1880 The British depose Yaqub Khan as ruler of Afghanistan and replace him with his cousin Abd al-Rahman Khan.

1880 The Kurds—a mainly Islamic ethnic group from western Asia—rebel under Shaykh Ubaydallah. The revolt is put down by joint Ottoman and Persian forces.

1881 The Decree of Muharram is issued by Sultan Abdülhamid. The decree establishes a Public Debt Administration to repay foreign creditors.

1881 A French army takes possession of Tunisia. Although still part of the Ottoman Empire, the country has been largely independent.

■ **Africa**   ■ **Americas**   ■ **East Asia**   ■ **Europe**   ■ **South and Central Asia**   ■ **Western Asia**

British general Charles Gordon was killed during a siege of Khartoum, Sudan, by the Muslim Mahdi's forces in 1885.

1882 After the threat of a coup by his officers, the Ottoman governor of Egypt, Tawfik Pasha, invites the British to occupy the country.

1882 The "First Aliyah," a wave of Jewish settlement, starts in Ottoman Palestine. About 30,000 Jews from eastern Europe and Yemen arrive in the course of the next two decades.

1884 Muhammad Ahmad, self-styled Mahdi, or Muslim Messiah, and his followers besiege Britain's General Charles Gordon and his troops in Khartoum, Sudan.

1884 European colonial powers divide Africa up into spheres of influence at the Berlin Conference.

1885 The Mahdi takes Khartoum; General Gordon is killed.

1886 The Qajar Shah, Nasr al-Din, invites the Muslim visionary Jamal ad-Din al-Afghani to help with affairs of state, but he soon falls from favor.

1887 Armenian exiles in Geneva, Switzerland, found the Henchak, a revolutionary socialist group. The group's aim is to gain Armenia's independence from the Ottomans.

1888 The Young Turk movement—secret meetings of army officers and intellectuals—begins in Ottoman Turkey in response to Sultan Abdülhamid's despotic rule.

1889 Abdallah Ibn Faysal, emir of Saudi Arabia, dies. His successor is al-Rahman Ibn Faysal.

1890 Britain takes Zanzibar under its control.

1891 Jamal ad-Din al-Afghani is evicted from Persia after persistently criticizing the shah's government.

1891 Muhammad Ibn Rashid, ruler of Jabal Shammar (a region in present-day Saudi Arabia), defeats Saudi forces. The Saudi royal family flees.

1893 The British and Abd al-Rahman Khan, ruler of Afghanistan, draw up the Durand Line, marking the border between India and Afghanistan.

1895 A rebellion against British rule breaks out in Chitral (present-day northern Pakistan). It is eventually put down by British forces.

1895 The Ottomans begin massacres of Christian Armenians living in Turkey. Over the next few years, up to 200,000 Armenians are killed.

1896 The shah of Persia, Nasr al-Din, is murdered by a follower of Jamal ad-Din al-Afghani.

1896 Crete revolts against its Ottoman rulers. In 1898, European powers impose an international administration to end the hostilities.

1897 Jamal ad-Din al-Afghani dies in Istanbul.

1897 The entire leadership of the Young Turks is sent into internal exile by the Ottoman government.

1897 Austro-Hungarian journalist Theodor Herzl and his Zionist Congress propose Palestine as a homeland for Jewish people.

1898 German emperor William II makes a state visit to Istanbul, strengthening the growing friendship between his country and the Ottomans.

1898 British troops defeat the Muslim Mahdists of Sudan at Omdurman after two years of fighting.

1898 British troops push southward to confront French colonists at Fashoda (Kodok) in southern Sudan, sparking a diplomatic conflict known as the Fashoda Incident.

1899 Construction of the Istanbul-Baghdad Railroad begins, with German involvement upsetting rival European powers.

❖ 1900 ❖

1901 Zionist leader Theodor Herzl meets with Ottoman sultan Abdülhamid II in an attempt to be granted land in Palestine for a Jewish state.

1901 British citizen William Knox D'Arcy is granted a 60-year monopoly on oil-exploitation rights in Persia. He finds oil in 1908 and the following year establishes a company that later becomes British Petroleum (BP).

1902 Exiled Abdul Aziz al-Saud returns to capture Riyadh and creates a Saudi state.

1903 Rioting breaks out in the Persian cities of Isfahan and Yazd. Violence is directed against members of the Baha'i faith.

1903 The British conquer northern Nigeria and rule the region as a protectorate through the existing Sokoto Caliphate.

1904 Abdul Aziz al-Saud defeats an Ottoman force dispatched to Arabia.

1905 George Nathaniel Curzon, Britain's viceroy in India, divides Bengal into a mainly Hindu Western Bengal and a largely Muslim Eastern Bengal and Assam.

1906 Persian shah Muzaffar ud-Din is forced by unrest in his country to concede a constitution. A constituent assembly, or *majlis*, is established.

1906 European powers recognize France and Spain as rulers of Morocco after signing the Treaty of Algeciras.

1906 A group of leading Muslims, known as the Simla Deputation, calls on Lord Minto (Gilbert John Elliot), the newly appointed viceroy of India, to improve the rights of Muslims in the country.

1906 The All India Muslim League is established to fight for the rights of India's Muslim minority.

1908 The Young Turks start a revolution in Ottoman Turkey. They demand a constitutional government while keeping Abdülhamid II as head of state.

1908 Crete, taking advantage of the troubles in Ottoman Turkey, declares union with Greece.

1908 Bulgaria declares independence from its Ottoman rulers.

1909 Supporters of a Persian constitutional government depose Shah Muhammad Ali. They place his young son Ahmad on the Peacock Throne, with a regent.

1909 Ottoman sultan Abdülhamid II is deposed after an unsuccessful counterrevolutionary coup. He is replaced with his more malleable brother, Mehmed V.

1910 Charles Hardinge becomes viceroy in India. In 1911, he annuls the partition of Bengal to the approval of Hindus.

1911 Italian forces invade Tripoli.

1911 In protest against Italy's annexation of Tripoli—an Ottoman territory—the Ottoman Empire unsuccessfully wages war on Italy.

1911 The Agadir Incident in Morocco causes tension between France and Germany.

1912 France imposes a protectorate on southern Morocco; the northern part of the country becomes a Spanish protectorate.

1912 Bulgaria, Greece, Serbia, and Montenegro unite against the Ottomans in the First Balkan War (−1913). A new nation, Albania, is created.

1913 In the Second Balkan War, Serbia, Greece, Romania, and Ottoman Turkey join forces to defeat Bulgaria. The boundaries between the various countries are redrawn.

1913 Enver Pasha leads the Young Turks in a coup against Sultan Mehmed V's ministers, following Ottoman losses in the First Balkan War.

1914 The Ottomans ally with Germany in World War I.

1914 The British take control of Malay.

1915 After landing at Gallipoli in the Dardanelles, British and ANZAC (Australia and New Zealand Army Corps) forces are driven back by the Ottoman army.

1915 Deportations and massacres of Armenians living in Turkey result in a genocide of up to 1.5 million people.

1916 Arabs, led by Sharif Husein, revolt against Ottoman rule. Aqaba, Baghdad, and Damascus are captured with the aid of the British.

1916 Russian tsarist forces suppress a rebellion in Uzbekistan and kill thousands.

1917 Britain declares its support for the establishment of a Jewish national home in Palestine.

1918 The Ottoman Empire disintegrates after the end of World War I.

1918 Soviet forces conquer Turkestan, resulting in widespread bandit, or *basmachi*, resistance by tribes in central Asia.

■ **Africa**   ■ **Americas**   ■ **East Asia**   ■ **Europe**   ■ **South and Central Asia**   ■ **Western Asia**

1919 Egyptian nationalist leaders are exiled by the British authorities, causing an uprising that is suppressed by force.

1919 Upper Volta (present-day Burkina Faso) gains independence from French Sudan (Mali).

1920 In keeping with the terms of the Treaty of Sèvres, Greece attempts to divide Turkey, but nationalist leader Mustafa Kemal heads a successful resistance (–1922).

1920 Nations in central Asia become autonomous soviet socialist republics (ASSRs) of the Soviet Union.

1921 Spain, seeking to extend its territories around Tangiers, sparks a rebellion that spreads into French Morocco.

1922 Muhammad Abd el-Krim, leader of the rebellion against French and Spanish rule, founds the Rif Republic.

1922 Egypt becomes independent under King Fuad I. However, Britain retains its control over defense and foreign policy, the Suez Canal, and the administration of neighboring Sudan.

1922 The League of Nations mandates that Britain will rule Palestine and that France will govern Syria and Lebanon after the disintegration of the Ottoman Empire.

1923 The new republic of Turkey is internationally recognized in the Treaty of Lausanne. Its leader, Mustafa Kemal, makes Ankara the capital and secularizes the traditional Muslim society.

1924 Soviet central Asia is redefined again as small nations are subsumed into four socialist republics: Kazakhstan, Kirgizia, Turkmenistan, and Uzbekistan.

1924 Saudi forces take Mecca. The following year they conquer all of Arabia.

1925 Iran's ruling assembly, the *majlis*, deposes Ahmad Shah—ending the Qajar dynasty—and elects Reza Khan as first shah of the Pahlavi dynasty.

1925 Druze tribesmen rebel unsuccessfully against the French in Syria.

1925 Kemal assumes emergency powers after a revolt by Kurds in eastern Turkey.

1927 The Nationalist Party of Indonesia (NPI) is founded by Ahmed Sukarno to press for independence from the Netherlands.

1928 Mustafa Kemal replaces Arabic with Latin script for written Turkish.

1928 France establishes an assembly in Syria, but it is suspended after voting to end French rule.

1928 An Islamic revivalist organization, the Muslim Brotherhood, is founded in Egypt by Hasan al-Banna.

This mausoleum, overlooking Ankara, contains the remains of the father of modern Turkey, Mustafa Kemal Atatürk.

1929 Formerly part of Uzbekistan, Tajikistan becomes a separate Soviet republic.

1929 About 250 people are killed during hostilities between Jews and Arabs in Palestine.

1932 Britain retains a military presence in Iraq but gives it independence under King Faysal I.

1932 The Kingdom of the Hejaz is renamed the Kingdom of Saudi Arabia.

1932 Oil is discovered in Bahrain, an island in the Persian Gulf.

1934 Women are allowed to vote in Turkey.

1934 The two Italian colonies of Tripoli and Cyrenaica are united as Libya.

U.S. civil rights activist Malcolm X, a Muslim African American, was assassinated in 1965.

1935 Persia is renamed Iran.

1935 The Turkish national assembly gives Mustafa Kemal the title Atatürk ("Father of the Turks").

1936 Jewish immigration to Palestine is limited by British authorities following hostile clashes with Arabs.

1937 Afghanistan, Iran, Iraq, and Turkey sign a nonaggression pact.

1938 Oil is discovered in Saudi Arabia.

1938 Mustafa Kemal Atatürk dies.

1938 Gandhi and Muhammad Ali Jinnah, leader of the Muslim League, meet but fail to settle differences between the Congress Party and India's Muslims.

1940 The Muslim League demands that the regions of India in which Muslims are the majority should become independent states.

1940 British and Australian forces defeat an Italian attempt to invade Egypt from Libya.

1941 Germany's Afrika Korps regain land in northern Africa until checked by the Allies at El Alamein in 1942.

1941 British and Soviet forces unite to invade Iran, which is sympathetic to the Germans. They depose Reza Khan in favor of his son, Muhammad Reza, who becomes the second shah of the Pahlavi dynasty.

1943 Lebanon becomes independent of France.

1945 The Arab League is established with seven initial member states.

1945 Militant Jewish organizations attack British military targets in Palestine.

1946 Syria and Transjordan gain their independence, respectively, from France and Britain.

1946 Jewish militants bomb the King David Hotel in Jerusalem, killing 91 people.

1946 Hostilities between Hindus and Muslims pressure the British to form a separate Muslim state (Pakistan).

1947 After securing independence from Britain, India and Pakistan are partitioned into separate states. The Muslim-majority state of Pakistan is divided into two parts—West Pakistan and East Pakistan (later Bangladesh). About 14 million people are resettled, and at least half a million are killed en route.

■ **Africa**   ■ **Americas**   ■ **East Asia**   ■ **Europe**   ■ **South and Central Asia**   ■ **Western Asia**

1947 The United Nations agrees to a plan to split Palestine into a Jewish and an Arab state.

1948 War breaks out between India and Pakistan over the frontier state of Kashmir.

1948 The Jewish state of Israel is created.

1948 Israel gains territory after the Arab-Israeli War. More than 1 million Palestinians leave Israel, while about 250,000 Holocaust survivors arrive from Europe.

1949 Transjordan takes the West Bank and renames itself the Hashemite Kingdom of Jordan.

1949 The Netherlands recognizes Indonesia's independence.

1952 In Egypt, a group of Egyptian army officers led by Gamal Abdel Nasser overthrows the monarchy and founds a republic.

1953 In Iran, Mohammed Mossadegh's nationalist government is deposed after a CIA-backed coup. Reza Pahlavi is reinstated as shah.

1954 The National Liberation Front launches a war of independence against the French authorities in Algeria.

1955 Newly independent African and Asian states meet at Bandung, Indonesia, committing themselves to anticolonialism and peace between East and West.

1956 Gamal Abdel Nasser, Egypt's leader, nationalizes the Suez Canal. In the crisis that follows, Britain and France send troops to Egypt but are forced to withdraw them by international opinion.

1956 Israel invades the Sinai Peninsula.

1956 Pakistan becomes the first Islamic republic.

1958 General Ayub Khan imposes millitary rule in Pakistan.

1958 The Iraqi monarchy is deposed by a military coup and Iraq becomes a republic.

1958 Syria and Egypt unite to form the United Arab Republic. Syria secedes from the union in 1961.

1960 With the exception of Algeria, France's colonies in Africa gain independence.

1960 The colonies of British and Italian Somaliland unite to form the independent state of Somalia.

1961 Kuwait gains independence from Britain.

1962 After eight years of war, Algeria gains independence from France.

1963 The Federation of Malaysia is established, comprising Malaya, North Borneo, Sabah, and Sarawak.

1964 The Palestine Liberation Organization (PLO) is established.

1964 After criticizing the shah, the Islamic cleric Ayatollah Ruhollah Khomeini is exiled from Iran.

1965 Singapore declares its independence from Malaysia.

1965 Militant African American Malcolm X, a Muslim, is assassinated in New York City.

1965 India and Pakistan resume hostilities over Kashmir.

1967 In the Six-Day War, Israel defeats its Arab neighbors. Israeli forces occupy the West Bank, Gaza Strip, Sinai Peninsula, and Golan Heights.

1969 Libya's monarchy is deposed by Colonel Muammar al-Qaddafi, who declares himself the new ruler.

1970 After King Hussein expels members of the Palestine Liberation Organization from Jordan, civil war breaks out.

1971 East Pakistan rebels against West Pakistan—they are located 1,000 miles (1,600 km) apart—and gains independence as Bangladesh the next year.

1973 Egypt, Syria, Iraq, and Jordan unite to attack Israel during Yom Kippur, a day of religious observance. Israel manages to drive back the invaders after initial setbacks.

1973 Arab oil producers refuse to supply the Western nations that supported Israel in the Yom Kippur War. In the ensuing crisis, the price of crude oil increases fourfold.

1974 Turkish troops invade northern Cyprus (mainly inhabited by Turkish Cypriots) and partition the island to prevent its union (*enosis*) with Greece.

1974 The PLO is recognized as the representative body of the Palestinian people by the Arab League.

1974 In Tunisia, Habib Bourguiba is proclaimed president for life.

1975 Bangladesh's premier since independence, Mujibur Rahman, is deposed and assassinated in a military coup.

1975 Civil war breaks out between Christian and Muslim forces in Lebanon. Hostilities will continue for many years.

1975 East Timor declares independence from Portugal but is soon invaded by neighboring Indonesia.

1976 King Hassan II of Morocco invades the Western Sahara. His forces are resisted by guerrillas aided by Algeria.

1977 Somalia and Ethiopia go to war over a disputed region. Ethiopia prevails the following year.

1978 Israel intervenes in the Lebanese civil war. A UN peacekeeping force is stationed in southern Lebanon to prevent attacks against Israel.

1979 Israel agrees to withdraw from the Sinai Peninsula and promises autonomy to the Palestinian occupants of the West Bank after signing the Camp David Accords.

1979 Shah of Iran Reza Pahlavi is forced to step down. Ayatollah Khomeini returns from exile to set up an Islamic state.

1979 Radical Iranian students take over the U.S. embassy in Tehran. They take 66 staff hostage and demand the shah's extradition from the United States, where he is undergoing treatment for cancer.

1979 The Soviets invade Afghanistan. They become embroiled in an unsuccessful nine-year war.

1980 A military coup in Turkey suspends democracy.

1980 A border dispute between Iran and Iraq leads to a war that lasts for eight years and takes more than a million lives.

1981 Israeli warplanes destroy a reactor under construction at Osirak, thwarting Iraq's attempt to acquire nuclear power.

1981 President of Egypt Muhammad Anwar al-Sadat is assassinated by Islamic extremists opposed to the Camp David Accords, which Egypt signed with Israel.

1982 Israeli troops enter Lebanon, starting an occupation that lasts until 1985.

1982 Israeli-backed Christian Phalangists attack and kill hundreds of unarmed Palestinians in refugee camps in West Beirut.

1983 More than 300 peacekeeping troops in Beirut are killed by suicide bombers driving truck bombs into army compounds.

1984 A famine strikes Ethiopia and Sudan, resulting in about 100,000 deaths.

1985 The Italian cruise ship *Achille Lauro* is hijacked by Palestinian terrorists, who kill one passenger.

1986 In retaliation for Colonel Qaddafi's support for international terrorism, Libya's capital Tripoli is attacked by U.S. warplanes flying from British bases.

1987 A Palestinian uprising, or *intifada*, is launched against the Israeli occupation of the West Bank and Gaza.

1988 The eight-year conflict between Iran and Iraq ends.

1988 The Iraqi army uses chemical weapons to attack the Kurdish town of Halabja, killing about 4,000 civilians.

1988 A terrorist bomb on a U.S. airplane flying over the Scottish town of Lockerbie kills 270 people. A Libyan agent will eventually be convicted of the attack.

1988 Benazir Bhutto becomes Pakistan's prime minister. Her father, Zulfikar Ali Bhutto, was Pakistan's prime minister from 1971 until his execution in 1979.

1989 Soviet troops withdraw from Afghanistan.

1989 Iran's Ayatollah Khomeini issues a death sentence against British novelist Salman Rushdie, whose novel *The Satanic Verses* is considered to insult Islam.

1990 Iraq invades Kuwait.

1990 Accused of corruption, Benazir Bhutto is relieved of her post as prime minister of Pakistan.

1991 U.S.-led coalition forces Iraq to withdraw from Kuwait.

1992 More than 1,000 people die in rioting, after Hindu militants destroy a 16th-century mosque at Ayodhya, in India.

1992 Conflict between UN peacekeeping troops and warlord General Aideed erupts in Somalia. Fighting will continue until 1995.

1993 A bomb planted by Islamist terrorists makes a 100-foot (30-m) hole in the basement floors of the World Trade Center in New York.

1993 Palestinian leader Yasir Arafat and Israeli prime minister Yitzhak Rabin sign a peace agreement.

1994 Israel and Jordan sign a peace treaty, ending 46 years of hostility.

1994 Heavy casualties result when Russia invades the central Asian republic of Chechnya, where Muslim separatists are campaigning for independence.

1995 Yitzhak Rabin is assassinated by an Israeli nationalist opposed to dialogues with the Palestinians.

1995 Led by Yasir Arafat, the Palestine National Authority takes over the West Bank and Gaza.

1995 Civil war ends in Bosnia. It is divided between a Muslim-Croat federation and a Bosnian Serb republic.

Africa **Americas** **East Asia** **Europe** **South and Central Asia** **Western Asia**

1996 Afghanistan is taken over by the Taliban, hard-line Muslim fundamentalists.

1997 Iran elects reformist Mohammad Khatami as its new president.

1998 The Yugoslav province of Kosovo is attacked by Serbian forces, who conduct ethnic cleansing. The forces withdraw after NATO orders airstrikes against Serbia.

1998 Islamist terrorists affiliated with Al-Qaeda bomb U.S. embassies in Africa, killing more than 200 people.

1999 Abdullah II succeeds his father Hussein as king of Jordan.

1999 A military coup in Pakistan overthrows the government. General Pervez Musharraf becomes head of state.

❖ 2000 ❖

2000 Israel ends its occupation of southern Lebanon.

2000 Serbian president Slobodan Milosevic is ousted. He will later be indicted for war crimes.

2001 Islamist terrorists hijack airplanes and fly them into the World Trade Center in New York City and the Pentagon in Washington, D.C. A fourth plane crashes in Pennsylvania. About 2,750 people die in the attacks.

2001 U.S. forces lead an invasion of Afghanistan, whose government is believed to harbor terrorists. Pakistan is a major ally of the United States.

2002 About 200 die when Islamic terrorists bomb nightclubs in Bali, Indonesia.

2002 East Timor gains independence from Indonesia.

2003 The United States invades Iraq.

2003 Unrest breaks out in the Darfur region of Sudan. Government troops kill about 180,000 people and displace another two million.

2004 Yasir Arafat dies; Mahmoud Abbas becomes head of the Palestinian National Authority.

2005 Kurdish leader Jalal Talabani becomes president of Iraq. He begins a second term the following year, elected under Iraq's new constitution.

2005 Saudi Arabia holds its first municipal elections, although only men are allowed to vote.

2005 Syria withdraws its troops from Lebanon.

2005 Kuwaiti women are given the right to vote.

2005 Four explosions by Islamist extremist suicide bombers kill 56 people in London.

2005 Controversial drawings of Muhammad are printed in a Danish newspaper.

2005 An earthquake beneath the Indian Ocean triggers a tsunami that kills approximately 310,000 people in Indonesia, Thailand, Sri Lanka, India, and other countries ringing the ocean.

2006 Iran admits to producing a few grams of low-grade enriched uranium.

2006 In Iraq, Al-Qaeda leader Abu Musab al-Zarqawi is killed in a U.S. air raid.

2006 Israeli troops invade Lebanon. A cease-fire takes effect a month later.

2006 The Islamic State of Iraq is established.

2006 Saddam Hussein is sentenced to death by hanging.

2007 Suicide bombings kill 572 people in northern Iraq.

2007 Former Pakistani prime minister Benazir Bhutto is assassinated at an election rally in Rawalpindi.

2008 Thousands of Palestinians cross into Egypt after part of the border is blown up by militants.

2008 Iran opens its first space center and launches a rocket into space.

2008 Kosovo declares independence from Serbia.

2008 A series of terrorist attacks in Mumbai, India, by Pakistan-based Islamic militants kills 195 people.

2008 Israel initiates airstrikes followed by an invasion of Gaza, killing at least 1,300 people.

2009 Barack Obama—whose father grew up in a Muslim family in Kenya—is inaugurated as the 44th president of the United States.

2009 Iran launches its own satellite, *Omid*, into Earth orbit on an Iranian-built rocket.

2009 Mahmoud Ahmadinejad is reelected as the president of Iran. Thousands of opposition supporters protest the result in the streets.

2009 Tension mounts in northern China between ethnic Muslim Uighurs and Han Chinese.

2010 Millions of Iraqis participate in nationwide parliamentary elections.

Dictionary of Persons

Abbas, Mahmoud (1935–)
Politician
Mahmoud Abbas, also known as Abu Mazen, became chairman of the PLO (Palestine Liberation Organization) in 2004 and president of the Palestinian National Authority in 2005.

Born in the Arab-Israeli town of Zefat, Abbas and his family went into exile in Syria during the 1948 Arab-Israeli War. He studied at Damascus University before going on to law school in Egypt. In the late 1950s he was a cofounder of the Palestinian political party Fatah. Considered less extreme than PLO chairman Yasir Arafat, Abbas negotiated with Israel in the early 1990s and, when he became Palestinian prime minister in 2003, demanded an immediate end to the *intifada* (the Palestinian uprising). Abbas soon resigned, citing lack of support from the United States, Israel, and Arafat. When Arafat died in November 2004, Abbas became head of the PLO. In January 2005 he was elected president of the new Palestinian Authority until 2009.

Abbas the Great (1571–1629)
Safavid shah of Persia (1588–1629)
Abbas, third son of Shah Soltan Muhammad, came to the throne in 1588 and set about strengthening the weakened Safavid dynasty. Abbas created a permanent army that fought against invading Ottomans and Uzbeks and won back much of the territory previously lost by the Safavids, including Khorasan. With his enemies repelled, Abbas concentrated on strengthening the empire. He transferred his capital from Kazvin to Isfahan, which he turned into one of the most beautiful cities in the world. Abbas built mosques, theological colleges, public baths, and caravansaries (inns for traders and their caravans) amid wide streets and beautiful public gardens. Foreigners flocked to the city to trade and forge diplomatic ties. Textile production flourished, as did ceramics, bookbinding, illumination, and, particularly, painting. Tolerant of other religions, Abbas encouraged the presence of Christian convents and monasteries in Isfahan.

Abd Allah (c. 1923–)
King of Saudi Arabia (2005–)
Abd Allah became *de facto* king of Saudi Arabia in 1995 when a stroke incapacitated his half-brother King Fahd; he became king in his own right in 2005. Abd Allah had served in a number of high governmental roles,

including as commander of the National Guard and deputy prime minister, and became King Fahd's crown prince in 1982. On coming to power in 2005, Abd Allah faced problems with Islamic extremists who saw him and the Saud dynasty as pro-Western. When it became apparent that many of the extremists taking part in terrorist activities around the world were Saudi nationals—including some of the terrorists responsible for the 9/11 attacks in the United States—he cracked down on their activities, seizing bank accounts and assets thought to belong to extremist groups. In other areas, he showed himself to be a moderate, including appointing the country's first female deputy prime minister. He also tried to lessen Saudi Arabia's economic reliance on oil. Saudi relations with the United States became strained when the king refused to back the U.S.-led invasion of Iraq in 2003.

Abd al-Malik (646/647–705)
Umayyad caliph (685–705)
Abd al-Malik, fifth caliph of the Umayyad dynasty based in Damascus, Syria, reorganized the government, imposed Arabic as the administrative language, and introduced a special currency for the Muslim world.

Abd al-Malik was born in Mecca and raised in Medina (both in present-day Saudi Arabia), where he received religious instruction. He lived in Medina with his father until 683 when Medinese rebels, revolting against the central government in Damascus, drove them out of the city. His father enjoyed a brief period as caliph before Abd al-Malik succeeded on his death.

Abd al-Malik's early rule was marked by warfare among competing tribes before he finally captured Iraq, which he ruled as an enemy territory, and territory in North Africa, including the city of Carthage. While military victories strengthened Umayyad rule, Abd al-Malik's religious piety also gave him strong moral authority throughout the Islamic world. Among his notable contributions to Islam was construction of the Dome of the Rock in Jerusalem.

Abdelaziz, Mohamed (1947–)
Rebel leader
Mohamed Abdelaziz is secretary general of the Polisario Front political party and president of the self-proclaimed Sahrawi Arab Democratic Republic fighting for the independence of the Western Sahara from Morocco.

Born in Morocco to a Bedouin family, Abdelaziz was educated at Moroccan universities, where he became involved in the movement for a free Sahrawi State. He cofounded the Polisario Front, which started an armed struggle for independence in the Western Sahara in 1973. Since 1976, he has been the party's president. Now living in exile in western Algeria, he has tried unsuccessfully to enlist support from the United States and the European Union for his cause. He condemns terrorism and claims that the Polisario does not use violent tactics.

Abdel Raziq, Ali (1888–1966)
Scholar and jurist
Born in Egypt, Ali Abdel Raziq was an Islamic scholar and Sharia judge who is considered the father of Islamic secularism. His controversial book *Islam and the Foundations of Governance* (1925) opened a heated debate about whether Islam has a political component. Abdel Raziq argued that Islamic law does not specify which political party to follow, and that separating Islam from the state would protect Islam and Muslims from political abuse. Many Muslims disagreed. In 1947, Abdel Raziq published *Consensus in Islamic Law*. He also served in the Egyptian government as minister of endowments.

Abduh, Muhammad (1849–1905)
Scholar and jurist
Egyptian scholar, lawyer, and reformist Muhammad Abduh played a key role in the 19th-century drive to modernize the institutions and teachings of Islam. Educated at Al-Azhar University in Cairo, he later became a follower of the Persian radical writer and political activist Jamal-ad-Din al-Afghani (1838–1897). After al-Afghani was expelled from Egypt by the government, Abduh followed him to Paris and helped to publish the revolutionary newspaper *The Unbreakable Link*. During his exile he also spent time in Lebanon, where he helped to set up an Islamic educational system and taught in Beirut. Abduh returned to Egypt in 1888 and served as a judge before in 1899 becoming the country's leading mufti (authority on Islamic law). He made reforms in Islamic legal administration, notably in the law surrounding religious endowments, as well as in the curriculum and workings of the Al-Azhar University. He also wrote *Treatise on the Unity of God* and a commentary on the Koran.

Abdülhamid II (1842–1918)
Ottoman sultan (1876–1909)
Abdülhamid II was an autocratic ruler of the Ottoman Empire whose Islamic beliefs influenced him to turn the empire away from Western influence and toward Asia.

Abdülhamid II came to the throne in 1876 in place of his mentally ill older brother. He created the first Ottoman constitution later that year, largely to protect his empire from European influence. In 1877 he dismissed parliament; the following year, he suspended the constitution and ruled for 30 years as a dictator. At times he relied on European help but he preferred to turn to Muslim states. He built the Hejaz railroad with contributions from across the Muslim world, built 18 new schools and the University of Istanbul, reformed the judiciary, and improved infrastructure. He was overthrown in 1909 by a popular uprising.

Abdul-Jabbar, Kareem (1947–)
Basketball player
Born Ferdinand Lewis Alcindor in Harlem, New York, Kareem Abdul-Jabbar changed his name in 1971 to reflect the Muslim beliefs he had adopted at college. Helped by his enormous height—he was 6 feet 8 inches (2 m) tall by eighth grade and eventually reached 7 feet 2 inches (2.2 m)—he excelled at basketball in high school and helped the University of California at Los Angeles (UCLA) Bruins win three successive NCAA championship titles (1967–1969). As a professional, he played for the Milwaukee Bucks (1969–1975) and the Los Angeles Lakers (1975–1989). He retired in 1989, holding NBA records for most minutes on court, most career field goals, and most career points. His point average was 24.6 per game, and he was named NBA MVP six times.

Abdullah II (1962–)
Hashemite king of Jordan (1999–)
Abdullah II is known for his efforts to modernize Jordan and introduce a form of democracy. The son of King Hussein and his British-born wife, Princess Muna, Adbullah was educated in Great Britain and the United States before training as an officer at Britain's elite Royal Military Academy in Sandhurst. King Hussein had originally named Abdullah's uncle, Prince Hassan, as his heir but changed his mind shortly before his death. Since taking the throne, Abdullah has been known for his pro-Western stance and his stand against Islamist terrorism. He is eager to improve the position of Jordanian women and bolster the weak economy. In 1993, Abdullah married a Palestinian, Queen Rania, with whom he has four children.

Abdullah Ahmad Badawi (1939–)
Malaysian politician
Tun Abdullah bin Haji Ahmad Badawi was until April 2009 prime minister of Malaysia. The Malay people affectionately call him *Pak Lah*, or "Uncle Lah."

Abdullah was born into a well-respected religious family of Arab descent on his father's side and Chinese descent on his mother's. After graduating from university, he joined the Malay civil service and became a career politician. He became a member of parliament in 1978, deputy prime minister between 1999 and 2003, and prime minister from 2003 until April 2009. King Tuanku Mizan Zainal Abidin gave him the title "Tun" in recognition of his public service when he stepped down.

Abdullahi, Sidi Ould Cheikh (1938–)
Mauritanian politician
Sidi Ould Cheikh Abdullahi is a long-serving politician and former president of Mauritania. He was born in the south of the country when it was still controlled by the French. He completed his education in France before returning to Mauritania in 1968 to work in the government. During the 1970s and 1980s he held ministerial positions. From 1989 until 2003 Abdullahi lived in Niger, where he worked for the Kuwait Fund as an adviser. He won the 2007 presidential election in Mauritania after a long period of absence but was forcibly removed from office by a bloodless coup in August 2008. Since then, Abdullahi has tried unsuccessfully to regain the presidency.

Abid al-Jabiri, Muhammad (1936–)
Arab philosopher
Born in Morocco, Muhammad Abid al-Jabiri is one of the early 21st century's leading Arab philosophers. He has argued that Arab and Islamic philosophy developed alongside and in response to philosophies from other cultures, including ancient Greek ideas. He has criticized contemporary Arab society for failing to reconcile tradition and modern life, and has accused many Arab leaders of seeking to remake the present on the basis of an idealized vision of the distant past. An internationally celebrated author and an authority on the 15th-century Arab historian Ibn Khaldun, he is probably best known for his *Critique of Arab Reason*, published in four volumes between the 1980s and 2001.

Abu Abdallah Muhammad al-Fazari (d. 796 or 806)
Muslim astronomer and mathematician
Abu Abdallah Muhammad ibn Ibrahim al-Fazari was born in either Persia or the Arabian Peninsula. His father, known as Ibrahim al-Fazari, was also an important astronomer who served in the court of the Abbasid caliph Harun al-Rashid (763–809). Al-Fazari followed his father and translated many scientific texts into Arabic and Persian; the two may have collaborated in a translation of the astronomical text *Brahmasphuta-siddhanta* (628), by the Indian astronomer and mathematician Brahmagupta (c. 598–670). However, al-Fazari's most important contribution was the invention of the Islamic world's first astrolabe, a device that astronomers used to predict the position of stars and planets in the sky.

Abu al-Abbas Abdullah As-Saffah (722–754)
Abbasid caliph (750–754)
Abu al-Abbas Abdullah was the first Abbasid caliph; his nickname, As-Saffah, means "slaughterer" in Arabic and refers to his destruction of the rival Umayyad dynasty.

As-Saffah led a branch of the Banu Hashim, a Muslim sect that believed he was a descendant of the Prophet Muhammad who had come to lead them; many Muslims of the period saw the struggle as one between good, represented by As-Saffah, and evil, represented by the Umayyads. As-Saffah defeated the Umayyads in battle, then destroyed any hope of their returning to power; he invited them to a banquet where he murdered them all except Abd ar-Rahman, who escaped to al-Andalus (in southern Spain). As-Saffah set about restoring the caliphate, reforming the army, and encouraging education and commerce, but he died only four years after the civil war from smallpox.

Abu al-Faraj (897–967)
Persian scholar
Abu al-Faraj al-Isbahani collected and preserved ancient Arabic lyrics and poems. Born in Isfahan, Persia (present-day Iran) in 897, he was a direct descendant of the last Umayyad caliph of Syria, Marwan II. Abu al-Faraj was educated in Baghdad, Iraq, where he spent much of his life under the patronage of the Buyyid emirs. He later lived in different parts of the Islamic world including Aleppo, Syria, and Rayy, Iran. Abu al-Faraj is best known for *Kitab al-Aghani* (Book of songs), a collection of poems and songs from the earliest Arabian literature until the ninth century. The collection is an invaluable source of information about the life and customs of early Arabia and contains entries on songs, composers, poets and musicians. A Shiite, despite the opposition of his family, Abu al-Faraj also wrote *The Slaying of the Talbis*, a biography of Shiite martyrs beginning with Ali ibn Abi Talib.

Abu Ali al-Hasan ibn al-Haytham (965–1039)
Arab mathematician and physicist
Abu Ali al-Hasan ibn al Haytham, better known by the Latin version of his name, Alhazen, made an outstanding contribution to the study of optics. Alhazen documented his experiments with light—in particular, on refraction and reflection, and his work with lenses and mirrors—in *Kitab al-Manazir*. The work

included the first explanation of vision as the effect of light coming from an object into the eyes. *Kitab al-Manazir* appeared as a Latin translation in 1270 and influenced European scientists such as Roger Bacon (1220–1292) and Johannes Kepler (1571–1630).

A popular story records that Alhazen once presented to Caliph al-Hakim (985–c. 1021) a plan for controlling the annual flooding of the Nile River. It was only when he visited the site that the scholar realized that his plan would not work. Fearing the caliph's anger, Alhazen pretended to be mad until al-Hakim's death.

Alhazen traveled widely, reportedly visiting Syria, Baghdad, Egypt, and Spain. His writing influenced the development of science until the European Renaissance, some 500 years after his death.

Abu al-Qasim, Khalaf al-Zahrawi (936–1013)
Spanish-Arab physician

Known in the West as Albulcasis, Abu al-Qasim was born in the city of El Zahra in southwestern Spain and spent most of his life in Córdoba. He studied medicine there and became court physician to the Caliph of Córdoba, Hakam II (died 976).

Abu al-Qasim developed a range of surgical instruments, such as scalpels and the surgical needle, and introduced the use of dissolvable catgut for internal stitches. However, his most significant contribution to his field was the publication of a 30-volume encyclopedia entitled *Kitab al-Tasrif*. Completed in 1000, the volumes covered a wide range of medical subjects from dentistry to nutrition. The work also included details of Abu al-Qasim's innovations in surgery. Translated into Latin by Gerard of Cremona (c. 1114–1187), *Kitab al-Tasrif* influenced European physicians for more than 500 years after his death.

Abu Bakr (c. 573–634)
Companion of the Prophet

Abu Bakr was the Prophet Muhammad's closest friend and his successor. He came from the ruling merchant tribe of Quraysh at Mecca. Most Muslim scholars doubt claims that he was the first convert to Islam, but his importance to and influence on the Prophet are clear. Muhammad married Abu Bakr's daughter and chose Abu Bakr to be his companion on his journey to Medina (the *hijra*). Abu Bakr advised the Prophet and took over prayers when the Prophet was too sick to conduct them. After the Prophet's death in 632, he was appointed his successor to avoid any rebellions. During his rule from 632 to 634, he stamped out uprisings and expanded Muslim territory into present-day Syria and Iraq.

Abu Nuwas (c. 747/762–c. 814)
Abbasid poet

Abu Nuwas was an important poet from the early Abbasid period. Born in Alvaz, Persia, to an Arab father and Persian mother, he was allegedly sold to a merchant from Basra, Iraq, where he studied the Koran, grammar, and religious scripts at the mosque. Abu Nawas moved to Baghdad, where his witty poetry about sex, humor, wine, and drinking was initially poorly received; it combined traditional Arab forms with modern, urban themes. Later the poems became a favorite of the caliph Harun al-Rashid, and particularly of his son al-Amin, under whom Abu Nuwas wrote most of his poetry. Eventually, Nuwas's outrageous verse shocked even al-Amin, and the poet was imprisoned. According to some accounts he died in prison; others state that he was poisoned.

Abu Talib (549–619)
Companion of the Prophet

Abu Talib was the brother of the Prophet Muhammad's father, Abdullah ibn Abdul Muttalib. Following the death of Muhammad's parents, Abu Talib became the boy's guardian and oversaw Muhammad's upbringing from age eight. Abu Talib was a member of the very first group of Arabs to hear Muhammad preach the Islamic faith in about 613. As leader of the Banu Hashim clan to which Muhammad belonged, he protected the Prophet from the interference of other clan leaders. Abu Talib was married to Fatima bint Asad and was father of Ali ibn Abi Talib, who was the fourth caliph of the Islamic empire and is revered by Shiite Muslims as the first imam.

Adam
Cross-cultural figure

In the Islamic tradition (as in Judaism and Christianity), Adam is the first man in the account of the creation of the world. Muslims see Adam as a prophet of Islam, the first in a long line that included Noah, Abraham, Moses, and Jesus and culminated in the Prophet Muhammad. In the Koranic account, God created Adam in Paradise from clay, issuing the command "Be," then taught him the names of all things and all the angels. He also created the first woman, Eve (called Hawa in Arabic), and commanded the first couple not to eat the fruit of a forbidden tree. When God ordered his angels to bow down before Adam, all obeyed except Iblis, afterward known as Shaitan. God punished Shaitan by expelling him from Heaven. Shaitan then tempted Adam and Hawa with the promise of immortality and boundless knowledge if they would disobey God and eat the fruit of the tree. Afterward God sent Adam and Eve from

Paradise down to Earth. The Koran relates that Adam repented of his sin and that God forgave him. Adam thus became the first Muslim (a person who submits to God).

Adivar, Halide Edip (1882–1964)
Turkish writer

One of Turkey's leading women writers, Edip Adivar was a social activist who wrote about real events, including women's position in Turkish society.

Adivar was born in Istanbul to a privileged family and educated at home and at the American College for Girls. She became involved in Turkish nationalist and literary movements and in the Turkish Hearth clubs that used lectures as a way to encourage national progress. Adivar became a well-known figure in the struggle for independence, fighting in the war against Greece. Her best-known novel *Atesten Gömlek* (Shirt of fire, 1923) is the story of a woman working for the liberation of her country, based on real events.

After independence, Adivar traveled abroad for long periods. She returned to Turkey in 1939 and set up the English Department of Istanbul University, where she worked as a professor until 1950. She became involved in politics after 1950, when she was elected to Parliament as a deputy of the Democratic Party.

Adonis (1930–)
Syrian poet

A highly influential modernist poet and literary critic, Adonis—pen name of Ali Ahmad Said—was born to a rural Syrian family. He received no formal education until age 14, when the opportunity to recite a poem to the Syrian president led directly to his attending a French-speaking school. After graduating from university in Damascus in 1954, Adonis was imprisoned for his political views. He and his wife moved to Beirut, Lebanon, and later took Lebanese citizenship. In 1957, he cofounded the influential literary review *Shi'r* (Poetry). In the 1960s, Adonis invented a new form of Arabic poetry. He earned his doctorate and took up university posts in Beirut before moving to Paris, France, in 1980 to escape the Lebanese Civil War. Nominated for the Nobel Prize for Literature on several occasions, Adonis remains highly controversial. Writing in Arabic, he rebels against traditional rhythmic forms and sets his provocative and often political themes in free verse.

Afghani, Jamal-ad-Din al- (1838–1897)
Writer and activist

Jamal-ad-Din Al-Afghani was a political activist and writer who urged Muslims to unite against the Western imperial powers of the 19th century, such as Britain,

France, and Russia. He proposed that Muslims needed to cooperate and adopt modern technology to resist Western influence. Al-Afghani often claimed to be an Afghan and a Sunni Muslim but was in fact born in Iran and raised as a Shiite. He was an adviser to Afghan rulers from about 1858 to 1868, then moved to Cairo, Egypt. Later he traveled widely and lived in cities including Moscow, London, Munich, and Paris. In 1884 in Paris he published an Islamic newspaper called *The Unbreakable Link* with his pupil and fellow thinker Muhammad Abduh. Al-Afghani died and was buried in Istanbul, but in 1944 the government of Afghanistan moved his body to a specially built mausoleum in the Afghan capital, Kabul. Today he is honored there and in Iran as a major Islamic thinker. A square in Tehran, capital of Iran, is named after him.

Aga Khans
Shiite imams

The title Aga Khan (chief commander) was created in 1818 by the shah of Iran and bestowed on Hasan ali Shah (1800–1881), governor of the Iranian province of Kerman. The title is hereditary: to date there have been four Aga Khans. The first Aga Khan was the spiritual leader of the Nizari Ismaili sect of the Shiite Muslims; he later fled from Iran to India. His eldest son succeeded his father as the imam, but his imamate was short. He died in India in 1885.

The third Aga Khan (1877–1957), only son of the second Aga Khan, became imam on his father's death. He took a leading role among India's Muslim minority and advocated to improve the rights of Indian Muslims. He was involved in international politics following World War I, but during World War II he left the political scene and retired to Switzerland to breed thoroughbred horses. The fourth Aga Khan (1936–) is known for his business holdings and for the Aga Khan Foundation, which gives large sums of money to Muslim projects and causes.

Ahmadinejad, Mahmoud (1956–)
Iranian president

Mahmoud Ahmadinejad became president of Iran in 2005; after a controversial first term, he was reelected in a disputed election in 2009.

The son of a blacksmith, Ahmadinejad was raised in Tehran, where he studied civil engineering. During the Iranian Revolution (1978–1979), he organized demonstrations against the shah; Ahmadinejad denies reports that he was also involved in the siege at the American Embassy in Tehran. After the fall of the shah, Ahmadinejad joined the Revolutionary Guards and held a number of positions until he became governor

of the newly established province of Ardabil in 1993. When his term ended, he became a university lecturer but also cofounded a new political party, Developers of an Islamic Iran. The party won city council elections in Tehran in 2003 and Ahmadinejad became mayor. He ran for the presidency in 2005 and surprised many observers by easily defeating his more moderate opponent, former president Rafsanjani.

Ahmadinejad was a conservative president who promoted many of the stricter Islamic values. His foreign policy was seen by many as deliberately provocative; it was marked by anti-Israeli rhetoric, the development of a nuclear capability, and antagonism toward the West. Ahmadinejad's increasing unpopularity among the middle classes led many observers to think he would not be reelected in 2009. Ahmadinejad's suprise victory was alleged to be larger than was electorally possible and led to widespread demonstrations in Tehran and accusations of fraud. However, his victory was backed by the Council of Guardians led by Ayatollah Khameni.

Ahmad Shah Durrani (c. 1722–1773)
Afghan leader
The founder of the modern state of Afghanistan, Ahmad Shah Durrani built an empire that stretched from the Amu Darya River to the Indian Ocean and from Khorasan (modern Iran) to northern India.

Ahmad, from the Sadozi tribe, became commander of an Abdali cavalry group under Nader Shah of Persia. When Nader Shah was assassinated, tribal chiefs elected Ahmad as shah. He was crowned close to Kandahar, which he made his new capital, in 1747. He then embarked on a program of expansion, invading India nine times and marrying the daughter of an Indian ruler to reinforce his position. Ahmad centralized government in a new capital, Ahmad Shahi, and ensured control of his territory by appointing advisors from the chiefs of the leading Afghan tribes.

Ahmed ibn Hanbal (780–855)
Theologian and jurist
Ahmed ibn Hanbal was an influential theologian who founded the Hanbali tradition, one of the four schools of *fiqh* (religious law) in Sunni Islam (the others are the Hanafi, Maliki, and Shafi'i schools). Born in what is now Turkmenistan to a family of the Banu Shaibah tribe, who came originally from Arabia, he began to study the Hanafi tradition of religious law as a boy. He traveled throughout the Islamic empire, serving as a soldier before becoming a famous mufti (authority on Islamic law) and settling in Baghdad, the heart of the caliphate. Ibn Hanbal compiled a large collection of Hadith (narratives), oral traditions about the Prophet's life, and attracted many students who promulgated his teachings after his death. Today Hanbali is the dominant form of *fiqh* in the Arabian peninsula.

Aisha (d. 678)
Wife of the Prophet
The third wife of the Prophet Muhammad, Aisha is an important source of Hadith (narratives), oral traditions about the Prophet's life. She is a role model for Muslim wives and is honored as a learned scholar. According to tradition, Aisha was Muhammad's favorite wife, and he died with his head in her lap. She was the daughter of Abu Bakr, the first caliph or ruler of the Islamic state. After his death in 644, she is said to have inspired a revolt in which the third caliph, Uthman, was killed in 656. She was defeated by the fourth caliph, Ali, near Basra, Iraq, the same year; because she directed her troops from the back of a camel, this clash is called the Battle of the Camel. Ali spared Aisha's life and sent her back to Medina, Arabia, where she died aged 65.

Ajram, Nancy (1983–)
Lebanese musician
One of the biggest superstars in the Arab world, Nancy Ajram is the third best-selling female artist in Lebanon. Raised a Christian in Lebanon, she has a huge following

Lebanese singer Nancy Ajram is popular throughout the Middle East for her Arabic-language pop music.

in the Muslim world. By 2007, she had sold more than 30 million records. In 2008, she won the World Music Award for the best-selling Middle Eastern act, the youngest musician to win the award. She sings in Arabic.

Akbar (1542–1605)
Mughal emperor
The greatest of the Mughal emperors, Akbar significantly increased the dynasty's power and territory. He was an enlightened ruler who reorganized his government and introduced reforms to unite his vast empire; despite being illiterate, he was a patron of poets, scholars, and artists. Akbar's respect for and inclusion of people of different faiths, such as Hindus and Christians, was resented by conservative Muslims.

Akbar counted both Genghis Khan and Timur among his ancestors. His father, Humayun, had to flee Delhi, the Mughal capital, before regaining the throne in 1555 and making Akbar, then aged 13, governor of the Punjab region. When Humayun died a year later, Akbar was victorious in a power struggle for the throne. Initially, Akbar was guided by his advisor, but in 1560 he began ruling on his own. He expanded his territory through a series of military victories; he left defeated princes in place in exchange for paying tribute but heavily punished those who did not acknowledge his authority. As the empire grew to stretch from Gujarat in the west to Bengal in the east and Kashmir in the north, Akbar organized his government to include as many different religions and ethnic groups as possible. He restructured his army so that his officers reported directly to him, reducing opportunities for local rebellions. He also centralized his financial system so that each provincial governor collected local taxes and reported directly to him.

At court, Akbar encouraged poets, artists, calligraphers, musicians, and scholars, although he himself was unable to read. His capital, Fatehpur Sikri, is a monument to his enlightened rule, with its Hindu and Muslim architecture, the emperor's paintings, and the texts he had translated from Sanskrit into Persian.

Akef, Mohammed Mahdi (1928–)
Egyptian political leader
Mohammed Mahdi Akef has been the leader of the Egyptian-based Islamic political movement known as the Muslim Brotherhood since 2004.

Born in the north of Egypt, Akef worked as a teacher after finishing his education and then studied law. He became associated with the Muslim Brotherhood as early as 1940; his involvement with the outlawed group led to his being sentenced to death on charges that included smuggling, but his sentence was commuted to

U.S. boxer and Muslim convert Muhammad Ali. During his 20-year career Ali won an Olympic gold medal and was heavyweight champion of the world three times.

life imprisonment. Following his release in 1974, he moved to Riyadh, Saudi Arabia, to work for the World Assembly of Muslim Youth, where he organized youth camps and conferences for Muslims across the globe.

Back in Egypt, Akef was elected as a member of parliament in 1987. He was imprisoned again in 1996 for being the head of the Muslim Brotherhood but was released three years later. He has never been far from controversy, and in 2005 questioned the extent of the Nazi Holocaust against the Jews.

Alavi, Bozorg (1904–1997)
Iranian writer
One of the most famous and influential writers in 20th-century Iran, Alavi was both a novelist and a translator. Born in Tehran, Alavi was sent to Berlin, Germany, to study in 1922. He returned to Iran in

1927, where he taught and translated German. In 1937, he was jailed for communist activities and served four years of a seven-year term. In prison, he wrote *Fifty-Three People,* about the members of a socialist group and what happened to them in prison.

After World War II, Alavi became a founding member of the communist Tudeh party. His most famous novel, *Her Eyes* (Chashmhayash), about a love affair between an upper-class woman and her revolutionary lover, was published in Iran in 1952 but promptly banned. The following year, he went into exile in Berlin, after a coup deposed the socialist prime minister. Alavi remained in exile until the 1979 revolution that deposed the shah. His return to Iran was short-lived, however, as he did not like the country's new political direction. He returned to Berlin, where he lived until his death.

Ali, Monica (1967–)
British writer
Ali was born in Dhaka, Bengal (now Bangladesh), to an English mother and Bengali father. She moved to Britain at age three, when civil war broke out, spending her early life in Bolton, northwest England, and studying at Oxford University. Ali's first novel, *Brick Lane*, named for a street in East London that is home to an immigrant Bangladeshi community, was published in 2003 to critical and public acclaim and was shortlisted for the prestigious Man Booker Prize. The novel explores the British immigrant experience through a Bangladeshi family's daily life and the conflict between tradition and integration. A movie version was released in 2007. Both the movie and book provoked anger among the Bangladeshi community in East London, who rejected the portrayal of their lives. Ali has published two other novels: *Alentjo Blue* (2006) is set in Portugal while *In the Kitchen* (2009) again examines multiculturalism and what it means to be British. Ali lives in London.

Ali, Muhammad (1942–)
U.S. boxer
Muhammad Ali is a three-time world champion who is considered to be the greatest heavyweight boxer of all time. Born on January 17, 1942, in Louisville, Kentucky, Cassius Marcellus Clay took up boxing at age 12. He achieved considerable success as an amateur, winning two national Golden Gloves boxing titles and two Amateur Athletic Union titles. In 1960, Clay won gold in the Olympic Games in Rome, boxing as a light heavyweight. On October 29, 1960, Clay won his first professional fight; within three years, he had 19 wins to his name, 15 of which came from knockouts. In

February 1964 Clay defeated Sonny Liston in a huge upset to become world heavyweight champion for the first time. A few days after the fight, Clay stunned the sports world by announcing that he had converted to Islam and changed his name to Muhammad Ali, under the influence of his spiritual mentor, Elijah Muhammad of the Nation of Islam. Ali won a rematch against Liston and a succession of title defenses. In 1967, Ali cited his Islamic beliefs to refuse to be drafted into the U.S. Army to fight in the Vietnam War. As a result, he was stripped of his title and had his boxing license suspended. He did not fight again for another four years.

In his comeback in 1971, Ali fought one of his most famous bouts, dubbed the "Fight of the Century." Ali lost to Joe Frazier in the final round—his first professional defeat. Ali won a rematch with Frazier in January 1974. In October he knocked out challenger George Foreman in Kinshasa, Zaire, a fight billed as the "Rumble in the Jungle." Ali fought Frazier again in a fight promoted as the "Thrilla in Manila"; Frazier retired after 14 rounds.

Ali successfully defended his WBA title until February 1978, when he was beaten by 1976 Olympic champion Leon Spinks. In a rematch in September 1978, Ali regained his title for a record third time. Ali retired a year later. In an unsuccessful comeback in 1980–1981, Ali was a shadow of his younger self.

In 1984, three years into his official retirement, Muhammed Ali was diagnosed with Parkinson's disease. He continued to remain an active public figure, however, and worked for humanitarian causes. He also became a serious student of the Koran and distanced himself from the racially separatist views of Nation of Islam leader Louis Farrakhan.

Ali, Samina (1971–)
U.S. writer and activist
Samina Ali is an Indian-born American writer whose debut novel *Madras on Rainy Days* (2004) looks at the choices facing many Muslim women. Ali was born to Muslim parents in Hyderabad, India, but moved to the United States when she was six months old. Growing up, she spent half of the year in India and the other in the Minneapolis area. Aged 19, she underwent an arranged marriage to please her parents but later divorced her husband. Her largely autobiographical novel explores the conflict of being raised in the United States but expected to follow traditional Muslim values.

Ali is cofounder of the Muslim American feminist organization, the Daughters of Hajar, and a prominent activist for Muslim women in the United States. She

was an organizer of a peaceful walk by women into the front entrance of a mosque in Morgantown, West Virginia, contravening Muslim tradition, and was featured in *Time* magazine. A year later, the Muslim Organization of America changed its official policy to allow women to attend mosques with men. Ali continues to work to change the image of Muslim women in the United States. She lives in San Francisco.

Ali, Tariq (1943–)
Pakistani-British writer

Tariq Ali is a prolific political campaigner, broadcaster, commentator, historian, and novelist. He was born and raised in Lahore, Pakistan, but has lived in Great Britain since the 1960s. His parents were both politically active and, as a child, his atheist parents taught him the fundamentals of Islamic belief so that he could argue against Islam. Ali studied at Punjab University before moving to Oxford University, where he was elected president of the Oxford Union in 1965. Inspired by the Vietnam War of the 1960s, Ali has actively campaigned against Western imperialism. In 2003, he criticized President George W. Bush's invasion of Iraq. In 1985, he wrote a screenplay for the BBC about the final days of Pakistan's President Zulfiqar Ali Bhutto. It was screened in New York in 2007, days before Bhutto's daughter and former president of Pakistan, Benazir Bhutto, returned to Pakistan after eight years in exile. Since 1990, Ali has written fiction about Islam, as well as nonfiction. He lives in London.

Alibhai-Brown, Yasmin (1949–)
British writer

Yasmin Alibhai-Brown is a British journalist and author who writes about immigration, diversity, and multiculturalism. She was born in Uganda, East Africa, and follows the Ismaili branch of Islam. Following her graduation from Makerere University in Uganda in 1972, she moved to Oxford, England, to study for her master's degree. She stayed in Great Britain to teach immigrants and refugees. In her mid-30s, she moved into journalism, writing for most of the major British daily newspapers. She also worked as an advisor on racial issues for the Labour government but severed her links with Labour following the 2001 invasion of Iraq. In 2001, she was made an MBE (Member of the British Empire) in recognition of her services to journalism. She returned the honor two years later, arguing that it reinforced a colonial attitude. She continues to explore issues of race and multiculturalism in Great Britain in her column in *The Independent* newspaper. She lives in London.

Ali ibn Abi Talib (600–661)
Caliph (656–661)

The cousin and son-in-law of the Prophet Muhammad, Ali was caliph or ruler of the Islamic empire from 656 to 661. Sunni Muslims identify him as the fourth caliph, the last of the so-called *rashidun* (rightly guided caliphs). Shiite Muslims honor him as the first imam, a religious and political leader with complete authority and knowledge. Shiites view Ali and his descendants as Muhammad's rightful successors. They call Ali "Prince of the Faithful" and "Saint of God."

Ali's father, Abu Talib, was Muhammad's uncle and guardian, who raised and protected the Prophet. By tradition Ali was born in the Kaaba sanctuary in Mecca, the holiest place for Muslims. He accepted Islam at age 10, becoming the second person to do so after Muhammad's wife Khadija. In 622 Ali joined Muhammad in the *hijra* (migration) from Mecca to Medina. In 623 he married Muhammad's daughter Fatima. Ali was Muhammad's messenger and his defender in battle. He was also one of several scribes who wrote down Muhammad's teachings in the Koran. After Muhammad's death, his successors as caliphs or leaders of the Islamic state were Abu Bakr (reigned 632–634), Umar (reigned 634–644), and Uthman (reigned 644–656). Ali became caliph in 656 following the murder of Uthman, having fought off a rival claimant, Muawiyah, governor of Syria, and defeating rebels known as the Kharajites, who objected to Ali's interpretation of the Koran. Ali was stabbed to death by Kharajites as he prayed in the mosque at al-Kufah (now Kufa in present-day Iraq) in 661.

Ali is revered by Muslims for being brave, wise, honest, always loyal to Muhammad, and generous when forgiving enemies. Most Sufi religious orders trace their line of descent directly to Muhammad by way of Ali. Sufis declare that Ali inherited from Muhammad the religious power called *walayah,* which people need to make the spiritual journey to God.

Ali ibn Sahl Rabban al-Tabari (c. 838–c. 870)
Persian physician and psychologist

Ali ibn Sahl pioneered pediatrics but is most famous as the tutor of the Persian physician al-Razi (Rhazes). Born to a Jewish family in Merv on the Silk Road in Central Asia, Ali ibn Sahl converted to Islam under the Abbasids and became court physician to the caliph. He was a prolific author whose most important work was the encyclopedia *Firdous al-Hikmah*, which outlined his system of medicine in seven parts. The book included studies of child development and psychology, drawing on ancient Indian medicine

and Islamic philosophy. Unlike his student al-Razi, Ali ibn Sahl remained relatively unknown in Europe, most likely because the encyclopedia was never translated into Latin.

Arafat, Yasir (c. 1929–2004)
Palestinian politician

Yasir Arafat is best known internationally as the leader of the PLO (the Palestinian Liberation Organization). He was also the president of the Palestinian Authority and the leader of Fatah (the largest Palestinian political group). He was one of the recipients of the 1994 Nobel Peace Prize for the peace agreement between Israel and the Palestinians.

Arafat was born to a wealthy Palestinian family, although where and when remains unknown. He trained as an engineer. Politically motivated, he joined the Muslim Brotherhood and the Union of Palestinian Students, of which he was president. Moving to Kuwait, where he started his own engineering firm, he cofounded Fatah, a faction of the PLO. He became head of the PLO's political division and set about trying to solve the Israeli-Palestinian problem through dialogue rather than violence.

As head of the PLO in the late 1980s and 1990s, Arafat worked toward a peace settlement by acknowledging Israel's right to exist. Israeli-Palestinian relations suffered numerous setbacks during the period, however. In 2000, Arafat rejected Israel's offer to create an independent Palestinian state as it did not give the Palestinians control over East Jerusalem. This led to more violence, and relations again became highly strained. Negotiations came to a temporary end when Arafat fell sick and died in November 2004.

Ashari, al- (874–936)
Arab theologian

Abu al-Hassan Ali al-Ashari was an Islamic theologian who founded the Ashari school of philosophy and theology. Born in Basra, Iraq, he studied with al-Jubbai (d. 915), a renowned teacher of Mutazilite theology and philosophy. Until 912, al-Ashari was himself a Mutazilite but he later became a committed opponent of Mutazilite views. He argued that the Mutazilites relied too much on reason: al-Ashari and his followers believed that humans were not capable of understanding God's nature and character, and that people could not use reason to work out their own moral positions. From 915 to his death al-Ashari lived and worked in Baghdad, where he gathered disciples who subsequently developed and spread his religious philosophy. According to tradition, al-Ashari wrote more than 100 books, but only four or five have survived. Among his books are

Theological Positions of the Muslims, *The Luminous Volume*, and *A Statement of the Principles of Islam*.

Aslam, Nadeem (1966–)
Pakistani-British writer

Nadeem Aslam is a critically acclaimed novelist whose work examines the position of Muslims in modern society, although he considers himself a "nonbeliever."

Aslam was born in Pakistan but moved to Great Britain at age 14 when his communist father escaped the regime of President Zia-ul-Haq. The Aslam family moved to Huddersfield in northern England. Aslam studied at Manchester University but left before graduation to be a writer. His first novel, *Season of the Rainbirds*, was published in 1993. Set in rural Pakistan, it was short-listed for a number of prizes and won the Betty Trask Award for a first novel. His second novel took 11 years to complete. *Maps for Lost Lovers* was set in an immigrant Pakistani community in a northern English town; it won the 2005 Encore Award. His 2009 novel is set in Afghanistan; *The Wasted Vigil* takes its name from a painting by a Pakistani artist.

Assad, Bashar al- (1965–)
Syrian president (2000–)

The president of Syria, Bashar al-Assad inherited the position on his father's death in 2000. Bashar was not the original heir. His older brother, Basil, was killed in an auto accident, and Bashar became the heir apparent.

Bashar studied medicine at Damascus University, graduating as a general practioner in 1988. Further studies took him to London, but in 1994 he was summoned to return to Syria on his brother's death. He trained at a military academy and became a colonel in the Presidential Guard. After the death of his father, he was elected president for a seven-year term. His presidency enacted some minor economic reforms, but he continued his father's policy of strong rule that did not tolerate dissent. In 2007, he was elected to serve a second term.

Assad, Hafiz al- (1930–2000)
Syrian president (1971–2000)

Hafiz al-Assad's authoritarian and oppressive rule brought relative stability to Syria after years of unstable military rulers and reasserted its importance in West Asian international affairs.

Al-Assad was born into a poor family that belonged to the Alawites, a minority Islamic sect. While a student, he joined the Ba'ath party. In 1952, he enrolled in military school and trained as an air force pilot. When the Ba'ath party took power in 1963, he became

commander of the air force. He was part of the coup that overthrew the civilian government, and he became minister of defense. He became involved in a power struggle that finally resulted in his becoming president in 1971.

As president, al-Assad built up the Syrian military with money from the Soviets and embarked on a public building program paid for by Arab donors. He dealt harshly with political dissidents, including the Muslim Brotherhood, and his efforts to turn Syria into the leader of the Arab world made him many enemies within the Middle East, including Iraqi leader Sadam Hussein.

Atatürk, Kemal (1881–1938)
Turkish statesman

One of the key figures of the 20th century, Atatürk is revered as the father of modern Turkey. He steered Turkey's recovery from the remnants of the Ottoman Empire. As its first president, he embarked on a radical program of modernization that created a new country.

Mustafa Kemal was born in Salonika (now Thessalonica, Greece) when it was a busy port in the Ottoman Empire. He was educated in a modern, secular school, so that he could work in a government position, but decided to enter a military secondary school, graduating as a captain in 1905. As a student, he and his friends were already planning ways of ousting the unpopular Ottoman sultan. Their plot was discovered, nearly ending his career, but he proved his loyalty in a number of battles during the two Balkan wars. During World War I (1914–1918) he became a national hero for repelling the Allied forces from the Gallipoli Peninsula.

In 1919, Kemal became the leader of the Turkish national liberation struggle. Sent to Anatolia by the Ottoman sultan, he abandoned his commission and told the Turks of Anatolia that he was there to liberate them. Although he had resigned his commission, he had the backing of a general who commanded 18,000 men. Kemal set up a new government and capital city in Ankara, attracting exiles from the sultan's government in Istanbul. Kemal set out to push the Greeks from Anatolia and to control the Armenian state in the Turkish War of Independence (1919–1922). Following the Battle of the Sakarya, the Grand National Assembly voted to get rid of the sultanate, and the sultan fled. The Ottoman Empire was at an end.

In 1923, Atatürk became the first president of the new republic of Turkey and set about bringing his country into the 20th century with far-reaching reforms. Between 1926 and 1930, he abolished Islamic religious rule and made the country a secular state. He introduced education for women and compulsory

elementary education for all. He also gave women more rights, including the vote. One of his most significant reforms was to replace the Arabic script with the Latin alphabet, confirming his desire to make Turkey look toward Europe rather than Asia. When a new law in 1934 required Turks to take surnames, the government awarded him the name Kemal Atatürk, "Kemal, father of the Turks."

Atatürk was president for 15 years before he died from cancer. His death was met with an outpouring of grief from his people; he is still revered in Turkey, where there are statues of him everywhere, and his words are chiseled on important buildings. A mausoleum in Ankara holds his remains.

Ayyub
Cross-cultural figure

Ayyub is the Muslim name for the biblical figure of Job, who lost his wealth, family, friends, and health but maintained his faith in God. In the Koran, Ayyub is

Kemal Atatürk seized control of Turkey from European powers in 1923. His radical secularist reforms transformed the country from an Islamic monarchy to a secular democracy.

celebrated as a Prophet of Islam and praised for his patience and fortitude in suffering. In the narrative told by Muslims, Ayyub lost all his cattle when his farm was raided by thieves, lost all his sons and other relatives when the roof of his house fell in, and was afflicted with terrible sores that crawled with worms. These sufferings were brought on him by Shaitan (the angel Iblis, the Islamic counterpart of Satan). Finally even Ayyub's faithful wife Rahima prayed for his death. Through all this Ayyub prayed to God and called him merciful, and at last God restored his prophet: he commanded Ayyub to stamp on the ground, and a holy stream burst forth. Ayyub bathed in the stream and was healed, then his family and wealth were restored to him and even increased. Because he suffered from infected skin, Ayyub is often seen as a patron of leprosy and other skin diseases.

Baba, Gul (d. 1541)
Turkish saint

Gul Baba was a Turkish dervish whose tomb in Buda, Hungary, became a site of pilgrimage. (A dervish is a Sufi holy man known for energetic dancing and singing). Little is known about Baba; even the origins of his name are a mystery. Gul means "rose" and Baba means "father," so he was known as "father of the roses." One account says he was named Gul after his tomb was covered in roses. It is known that he arrived in Hungary in 1541 with the sultan Suleiman I. Baba died during the Turkish siege of Buda. According to legend, Suleiman carried Baba's coffin, and the third pasha (1543–1548) had a tomb built on his grave.

Babur (Zahir-ud-Din Muhammad; 1483–1530)
Mughal emperor

Babur was the founder of the Mughal dynasty and emperor between 1526 and 1530. A descendant of the most powerful men in the region's history, Genghis Khan and Timur, Babur was a skilled military commander, an accomplished poet, and a notable diarist.

Babur was born into a tribe of Mongol descent but was greatly influenced by Turkic culture. His father was one of a number of local rulers who sought to extend power over the earlier Timurid Empire; Babur inherited his father's campaigns, but his early reign was marked by a failure to capture Samarkand and unsuccessful raids into India. On his fifth raid, in November 1525, Babur met the Sultan of Delhi in battle. Despite having far fewer men and no elephants, he outmaneuvered the sultan and captured the city. Further battles expanded the empire south through India as far as Agra and east to Lucknow, where Babur

defeated the ruling Afghans. Barbur had created a vast empire but it was not controlled nor pacified; that task fell to his son, Humayan.

Badran, Rasem (1945–)
Arab architect

The award-winning architect Rasem Badran was born in Jerusalem in 1945 and educated in neighboring Ramallah. His father, a famous Islamic craftsman, was an important early influence on the young man. Following architectural studies at the Technical University of Darmstadt, Germany, Badran graduated in 1970 and worked in Germany before settling in Jordan in 1973. As well as living in Jordan, Badran has lived in Damascus, Syria, and Tripoli, Libya.

Badran is best known for his 1992 design of the Great Mosque of Riyadh, Saudi Arabia, and the redevelopment of the old city center of Riyadh. Badran's architecture reflects his cultural heritage. He designed the Great Mosque with no domes because domes are usually associated with tombs and are thus not compatible with the Wahhabi philosophy of the Saudis. Badran received the Aga Khan Award for architecture for his design in 1995. Badran continues to practice in Jordan, and his ideas have gained great importance in the developing world.

Bakri, Abu Ubayd Abd Allah al- (1014–1094)
Spanish-Arab geographer and historian

Al-Bakri was born in the province of Huelva in southwestern Spain; he spent his entire life in Spain, living in the city of Córdoba.

Al-Bakri wrote informative accounts of countries in the Arabian Peninsula and North Africa, based on the accounts of merchants and travelers who had been there and on the works of other scholars. Al-Bakri contributed to an ambitious encyclopedia of the world, which set out to give objective accounts of countries and their people and customs, as well as facts about the climate and geography of each area and lists of major cities and their landmarks.

Banna, Hasan al- (1906–1949)
Egyptian political thinker

A teacher and reformer, al-Banna founded and led the highly influential religious and political organization the Muslim Brotherhood. After becoming a Sufi at age 12, he studied from age 16 in Cairo, where he was troubled to see that young people were moving away from Islam under the influence of Western secular ideas. He founded the Muslim Brotherhood in response to this insight in 1928. The organization, which argued that an Islamic society should return to the Koran and Hadith (traditions

about the Prophet Muhammad's words and deeds), spread throughout Egypt and into Sudan, Palestine, Lebanon, and Syria in the 1930s. After about 1938 the organization became overtly political, calling on Muslim countries to reject modernization and all Western influences. In 1948, after the Muslim Brotherhood sent volunteers to fight on the side of Palestine in the Arab-Israeli War, there were rumors in Egypt that its members were planning a coup: Egyptian prime minister Mahmoud an-Nukrashi Pasha forcibly disbanded the organization and jailed several of its members. In retaliation, a member of the Muslim Brotherhood assassinated the prime minister. Al-Banna was himself assassinated, perhaps by the government's secret service, on February 12, 1949.

Battani al-Harrani as Sabt, Abu Abd Allah Muhammad ibn Jabir ibn Sinan al- (c. 858–929)
Arab astronomer and mathematician

Also known by his Latin names Albategni or Albatemius, al-Battani made important advances in astronomy and mathematics. Born in Harran in southeastern Turkey, al-Battani worked and lived in ar-Raqqah and Damascus in Syria. Al-Battani used trigonometry to calculate improved values for the length of the year (at 365 days, 5 hours, 46 minutes, and 24 seconds), the precession of the equinoxes, and the inclination of Earth on its axis. Al-Battani also published a set of astronomical tables that would, through a Latin translation by the 12th-century Italian scholar Plato of Tivoli, influence European astronomers for centuries to come.

Ben Ali, Zine al-Abidine (1936–)
Tunisian president (1987–)

After an education that included military school in France and engineering school in the United States, Ben Ali headed the Tunisian military security between 1964 and 1974 before entering the government. He held various senior positions, including state secretary for national security in 1984 and minister of the interior in 1986. During this time, he earned a reputation as a hard-liner, particularly for his campaign against the violent extremists of the Islamic Tendency Movement. President Bourguiba, who had ruled Tunisia since its independence from France in 1956, appointed Ben Ali prime minister in October 1987. The following month, Ben Ali deposed him in a peaceful coup. As president, Ben Ali has been criticized for his record on human rights. Leading a somewhat secular government, he has suppressed religious extremists. He has been reelected overwhelmingly at each presidential election since he took office.

Ben Bella, Ahmed (c. 1918–)
Algerian president (1963–)

The first president of the North African state of Algeria, Ahmed Ben Bella was the main leader of the War of Independence against Algeria's French rulers.

Ben Bella was educated in the colonial education system and soon became aware of the inequalities between the French rulers and the local Algerians. He was obliged to serve in the French military but then joined an underground independence movement. His activities led to his imprisonment and he fled to Egypt. In November 1954, he formed the National Liberation Front (FLN) to fight the French. After a long and bloody campaign, the French withdrew from Algeria in 1962. Confusion followed their withdrawal until Ben Bella was elected unopposed to the presidency in 1963.

The new president faced an enormous task to restore order. Despite numerous achievements, his policies were often poorly planned or executed. In 1965, he was deposed in a coup and placed under arrest until 1980. He went into exile, only returning to Algeria in 1990. Ben Bella reentered Algerian politics with a new party, the Movement for Democracy in Algeria, but the party was banned in 1997.

Bhikha, Zain (1974–)
South African musician

Zain Bhikha was born in Pretoria, South Africa. He sang from an early age but only began a singing career after he won a radio competition in 1994. His Islamic faith is of supreme importance to him, and his music is about his beliefs. Bhikha's first album, *A Way of Life*, was an English-language compilation of a cappella Islamic songs that looked at different aspects of the faith. More albums followed, including *1415 The Beginning*, released in 2009; it contained a single, "Freedom will Come," in support of the Palestinian people. Bhikha collaborates with musicians such as Yusuf Islam and often works with children. Most of his songs are adapted from poems and traditional Arab songs and encourage Muslims to be proud of their faith. Bhikha and his family now live in Dubai.

Bhutto, Benazir (1953–2007)
Pakistani prime minister (1988–1990, 1993–1996)

Benazir Bhutto was the first woman to lead a Muslim country, serving as prime minister of Pakistan on two occasions. Bhutto was the daughter of Zulfikar Ali Bhutto, the Pakistani president and prime minister. Educated at Harvard and Oxford universities, she became the head of her father's party, the Pakistan People's Party (PPP), following his execution by the military dictator Muhammad Zia-ul-Haq in 1979. During the

Pakistani politician Benazir Bhutto, pictured greeting the public on her return to Pakistan in October 2007. Bhutto was the first woman to lead a Muslim state.

1980s, she was frequently placed under house arrest, but following Zia-ul-Haq's death in 1988 she entered politics. The PPP won elections and she became prime minister of a coalition government in December 1988.

Bhutto's first term in office achieved little against Pakistan's entrenched problems of poverty and corruption. She lost the next election but returned to power in 1993. In 1996, the president fired her on charges of corruption, mismanagement of the economy, and a decline in law and order. Bhutto and her husband were dogged by charges of corruption throughout the 1990s and into the new century. He served a prison term for corruption, and Bhutto went into self-imposed exile in London and Dubai. While in exile, she continued to press for the charges against her and her husband to be dropped.

In 2007, rumors started that Bhutto planned to return to Pakistan. When President Musharraf finally gave her the amnesty against corruption she wanted, she returned to Karachi in October 2007. She was assassinated two months later by Islamic extremists associated with the Taliban and Al-Qaeda as she campaigned for the forthcoming elections. Her husband, Asif Ali Zardari, was subsequently elected president of Pakistan.

Bhutto, Zulfikar Ali (1928–1979)
Pakistani president (1971–1973)

Bhutto was a popular president (1971–1973) and prime minister (1971–1977) of Pakistan until he was overthrown in a military coup.

Bhutto came from a prominent family that had converted to Islam. He studied at the University of California at Berkeley and at Oxford University before returning to Pakistan to set up his law practice. While working in Karachi, he joined the government and served in various senior roles, including as foreign minister (1963–1966). Bhutto resigned from the government over his opposition to peace with India following the 1965 war over Kashmir and formed his own party, the Pakistan People's Party (PPP).

Following the war between East and West Pakistan that led to the creation of the new state of Bangladesh, Pakistan's ruler, General Agha Muhammad Yahya Khan, made Bhutto president. Bhutto created a new constitution in 1973 that made the presidency a ceremonial role and became prime minister. He started a process of Islamization in Pakistan but sensed that he was losing public support. Bhutto ordered new elections for 1977 but was overthrown by the army chief of staff, General Muhammad Zia-ul-Haq. Soon after, Zia sentenced Bhutto to death and he was hanged in 1979.

Bin Laden, Osama (1957–)
Islamist leader

The terrorist attacks on New York's World Trade Center and the Pentagon on September 11, 2001, brought to world attention Osama bin Laden, who had been waging a war against the West and non-Muslims for more than a decade.

Bin Laden was born in Riyadh, Saudi Arabia, into an extremely wealthy Saudi family. He joined the Afghan resistance to fight the Soviet Union's invasion of Afghanistan in 1979 and remained in Afghanistan until the Soviet withdrawal in 1989. When he returned to Saudi Arabia, he was treated as a hero. He became disillusioned with the pro-Western stance of the Saudi government during the Persian Gulf War of 1990–1991, and by 1993 he had formed a militant Islamic group, Al-Qaeda (Arabic for "the base"), to fight against the West and non-Muslims. Backed by bin Laden's wealth, Al-Qaeda organized and funded attacks worldwide, including killing tourists in Egypt in 1997 and bombing the U.S. embassies in Nairobi, Kenya, and Dar es Salaam, Tanzania, in east Africa. Bin Laden also masterminded the 1993 bombing of the World Trade Center and the 2000 suicide bombing of the U.S. warship USS *Cole* in the port of Aden, Yemen.

The Saudi government revoked bin Laden's passport, but he fled to the Sudan before moving to Afghanistan, where he was protected by the ruling Taliban militia. Since the U.S.-led invasion of Afghanistan in 2001, bin Laden is thought to be in hiding in Pakistan. His stated aim is to create a war between the United States and the Muslim world and to reestablish a single Islamic state.

Bint Wahb, Amina (d. 577)
Mother of the Prophet

The mother of the Prophet Muhammad, Amina bint Wahb was a member of the Banu Hashim group of the Quraysh tribe of Mecca. Muhammad's father, Abdullah ibn Abdul Muttalib, died before Muhammad was born. Amina sent the young Muhammad to live among the Bedouin tribes of the desert in the care of a poor woman named Halima. There Muhammad learned the purest form of Arabic. Amina died in 577, when Muhammad was aged six, leaving the young boy in the care of his grandfather Abd al-Muttalib.

Biruni, Abu ar-Rayhan Muhammad ibn Ahmad al- (973–1048)
Arab scholar

Known also as Alberuni, al-Biruni was born in what is now Khiva in Uzbekistan. After studying math and astronomy under Abu Nasr Mansur (960–1036), he was invited to travel with Sultan Mahmud of Ghazni (971–1030) on a campaign to India. Over the next 20 years, al-Biruni visited India many times and became the first Muslim scholar to write extensively about the Indians and their religion. His most famous work, *Ta'rikh al-Hind*, is an account of his travels in India.

Al-Biruni's scientific studies covered subjects as varied as geometry, geography, math, and medicine. His major works included an encyclopedia of astronomy, *al-Qanun al-Masudi*, as well as a medical text, *Kitab as-Saydalah*. Al-Biruni's interests also included social sciences such as history, psychology, and law, and he was fluent in several languages, including Arabic, Persian, Turkish, Hebrew, and Sanskrit.

Along with his contemporary Avicenna, al-Biruni is considered to be one of the greatest Islamic scholars. He died in Afghanistan in 1048, having written more than 146 books. Al-Biruni has been honored on postage stamps issued in Afghanistan and the former Soviet Union; the Al-Biruni Crater on the Moon is named for him.

Bourguiba, Habib (1903–2000)
Tunisian president (1957–1987)

Considered the father of Tunisia, Bourguiba was the first president of the North African country, having led the movement for independence from France.

Habib Bourguiba was born in a fishing village to a former army lieutenant. He returned to Tunisia in 1927 after finishing his education in France and became involved in the struggle for independence. He formed a political party, the New Destour, to press for change. Bourguiba's activities led to prison on a number of occasions, but when Tunisian nationalists began to use violence in 1954, the authorities asked Bourguiba to start negotiating the end of French rule. The negotiations were complete by 1957, and Bourguiba was elected president of the independent country.

The new republic was an Islamic state, but Bourguiba's government was secular. He radically improved the position of women and made education a priority. His foreign policy was practical; he attracted Western support to help Tunisia modernize. After 30 years in power, Bourguiba was removed from office in a bloodless coup; he spent the rest of his life under house arrest.

Bouteflika, Abdelaziz (1937–)
Algerian president (1999–)

Bouteflika's election as president of Algeria marked a spectacular comeback for a man who had spent almost 20 years out of Algerian politics.

Bouteflika played a significant role in the struggle against France, and on independence he became foreign

minister in the government of Houari Boumedienne. His Westernized lifestyle earned him criticism as a "dandy diplomat," and after Boumedienne's death in 1978, Bouteflika fell from favor and went into self-imposed exile. He returned to Algeria in 1987 and became involved in the unrest that would mark the next decade. In 1999, backed by the army, he ran for the presidency and won on a platform to grant thousands of Islamists amnesty. Bouteflika's actions won approval in the West, where he was largely credited with saving Algeria from a full-scale civil war. He ran again in 2004 and was reelected amid allegations of vote rigging. In 2008, he announced a change to the constitution to allow him to run for a third term. In April 2009, he announced he had won the presidential election to serve for another five years.

Bukhari, Muhammad al- (810–870)
Islamic theologian

Muhammad ibn Ismail al-Bukhari was an Islamic scholar who compiled the *Sahih Bukhari* collection of Hadith (traditions about the words and deeds of the Prophet Muhammad), which is viewed by Sunni Muslims as the most authentic of all books of Hadith and the second most important sacred book in Islam after the Koran. Al-Bukhari was born in Bukhara (in present-day Uzbekistan) and his ancestors were Persian-speaking Tajiks. He studied Hadith from the age of 11 and began writing in his teenage years; before age 16 he made the hajj pilgimage to Mecca. Afterward he traveled widely for 16 years, studying under great teachers and collecting Hadith. Then he returned to Bukhara, where he wrote the *Sahih Bukhari*. According to tradition, he collected 600,000 narratives about the deeds and words of the Prophet, of which he included 7,275 in his book. After 864 he lived for a period in the city of Nishapur, now in Iran. In Nishapur he taught Muslim ibn al-Hajjaj, who became his disciple and himself wrote a well-known collection of Hadith, the *Sahih Muslim*.

Chappelle, Dave (1973–)
U.S. comedian and actor

Dave Chappelle is an American stand-up comedian, movie actor, scriptwriter, producer, and television star, known particularly for the hit television show *Chappelle's Show* (2003–2004) and for the documentary movie *Dave Chappelle's Block Party* (2006). He is noted also for his conversion to Islam in 1998. He was born David Khari Webber Chappelle in Washington, D.C., the son of university academics. His mother was a minister of Unitarian Universalism, a liberal religion with roots in Christianity. He studied theater arts at Duke Ellington School of the Arts in Washington, D.C., then moved to New York City to establish himself as a stand-up comedian in the early 1990s. He began to get roles in Hollywood movies, including *Robin Hood: Men in Tights* (1993), *The Nutty Professor* (1996), *Con Air* (1997), and *You've Got Mail* (1998), before making his mark with *Chappelle's Show* on cable TV channel Comedy Central. Chappelle does not normally make public statements about his Muslim faith. He lives on a farm in Ohio with his wife and two sons, Sulayman and Ibrahim.

Chughtai, Ismat (1911–1991)
Indian writer

Chughtai was an Indian-born writer who was widely considered to be one of the best writers of Urdu fiction. She was a trailblazing, outspoken, and often controversial feminist.

Chughtai was born in Badayu, Uttar Pradesh, and grew up in Jodhpur, Rajasthan, the ninth of ten children. When she earned her bachelor of education after her bachelor of arts degree, she was the first Indian Muslim woman to hold both degrees. In 1936, she joined the Progressive Writers' Association and started to write secretly. Her first short story was published in a prestigious literary magazine. The British, who still controlled India, prosecuted her for obscenity for her 1941 short story, "Linaaf" (The quilt), about lesbianism, but she was acquitted. Chughtai continued to write short stories, novels, and political essays, as well as film scripts with her husband, winning many awards. Her subject matter dealt with the position of women and often was autobiographical. She died in Bombay (now Mumbai).

Dada, Nayyar Ali (1945–)
Pakistani architect

Nayyar Ali Dada remains the only Pakistani architect to have received the Aga Khan Award for Architecture, in 1998. Born in Delhi, India, Dada moved with his family to the newly created Pakistan in the 1950s. He studied at Punjab University before training as an architect at the National College of Arts (NCA) in Lahore. When he graduated in 1964, he became a lecturer at NCA and was made a fellow of the college in 1976.

Dada is best known for bringing modern architecture to Pakistan. He designed the Open Air Theater in Lahore (1993) in the shape of a drum and decorated it with blue tiles, traditionally associated with mausoleums. His Al Hamra Arts Complex, also in Lahore, brought him worldwide attention. It used handmade red bricks to echo the two most historically important buildings in Lahore, the Fort and the Badshahi Mosque. As well

as designing buildings in Lahore and Islamabad in Pakistan, Dada has worked on projects in Sri Lanka and the Maldives.

Dalokay, Vedat (1927–1991)
Turkish architect

Turkish architect Vedat Dalokay is best known for his work outside his home country. He was born in Elazig, Turkey, in 1927. He graduated from the faculty of Architecture of the Istanbul Technical University in 1949 and then undertook further studies at the Sorbonne University in Paris, France.

Dalokay won an architectural competition to design the Kocatepe Mosque in Ankara but, controversially, his design was never built. Instead, it became the winning design for the Faysal Mosque in Islamabad, Pakistan (largely funded by King Faysal of Saudi Arabia). Completed in 1986, the Faysal Mosque was designed in the shape of a Bedouin desert tent. It occupies a central role as Pakistan's national mosque. Uniquely, the mosque contains none of the traditional domes and arches of other mosques. Dalokay also designed the Islamic Development Bank in Riyadh, Saudi Arabia, in 1981. He was killed in a traffic accident in 1991.

Daneshvar, Simin (1921–)
Persian writer and academic

Simin Daneshvar is a Persian academic, translator, and well-known novelist and writer in her native Iran. Born in Shiraz, she moved to Tehran in 1942. In 1948, she became the first Iranian woman to be published when her collection of short stories appeared. After completing a doctorate in 1949, she traveled to the United States on a Fulbright Scholarship and studied creative writing at Stanford University. She returned to Iran, where she held an associate professorship at the University of Tehran until 1979.

In 1969 Daneshvar became the first Iranian woman to be published with the release of her novel *Savushan* (Mourners of Siyavosh). Set in Shiraz, it remains Iran's best-selling novel. Daneshvar writes about the lives of Iranian women and the social problems of Iran during the 1960s and 1970s. Daneshvar was married to a famous Iranian writer, Jalal Al Ahmad, who died shortly before *Savushan* was published. In 1981, she wrote a moving monograph about her late husband. *A Persian Requiem* (1992) looks at modern Iran. She lives in Tehran.

Darwish, Mahmoud (1941–2008)
Palestinian poet

Author and politician Mahmoud Darwish is credited with helping the Palestinian people create a sense of identity. His poems are taught in schools throughout the Arab-speaking world, and there is an ongoing debate about whether to teach them in Israeli schools.

Darwish was born in Birwa, a village in western Galilee, in 1941. When he was six, Israeli troops attacked the village and the family fled. They returned to find their house destroyed and their land occupied. Darwish perceives his childhood, as an Arab Israeli, to be spent as a second-class citizen. He wrote poetry from an early age and published his first books from 1964. Darwish continued to write poetry after he was sent to prison for belonging to the Communist Party. He left Israel in 1971 and, when he was banned from returning, lived in numerous countries. All his poetry was written in Arabic, and he published more than 30 volumes of poetry and eight books of prose. He won many awards and was considered Palestine's national poet.

Daud Khan, Mohammed (1909–1978)
Afghan politician

Mohammed Daud Khan was an Afghan prince who overthrew the monarchy in 1973 and made Afghanistan a republic. He served as prime minister from 1953 to 1963 and as president from 1973 until his assassination in 1978.

After a military career, Daud Khan became prime minister in 1953. His term was notable for his pro-Soviet stance and his attempts to modernize Afghan society, particularly the position of women and of Pashtun peoples in both Afghanistan and neighboring Pakistan. The relationship between the two countries deteriorated and led to Daud Khan's resignation. In 1964 members of the royal family were banned from holding political office.

In July 1973 Daud Khan led a coup that overthrew his cousin, King Zahir Shah. He declared Afghanistan a republic with himself as president. Once in power, Daud Khan used brutal measures against his opponents. He also sought to reduce Soviet influence in Afghanistan and tried unsuccessfully to engage with the West and the United States. In April 1978 Daud Khan was killed with most of his family in a coup that brought the communists to power.

Dawud
Cross-cultural figure

Dawud is the historical and biblical figure known by Jews and Christians as King David. In Jewish and Christian tradition, David (reigned c. 1000–c. 962 BCE) established a united kingdom in Israel, with its capital at Jerusalem, and is revered as an ideal ruler and ancestor of Jesus. In the Muslim view, Dawud was a prophet of Islam and messenger of God who received

the revelation of a holy book, the Zabur (the Book of Psalms), one of three sacred books—along with the Tawrat (or Torah) and the Injil (New Testament)—that God revealed before the Koran. The biblical narrative in which as a young boy David killed the Philistine warrior Goliath is celebrated in the Koran, and Muslims also honor Dawud as a great king, but they do not accept biblical accounts in which David committed adultery with Bathsheba and sent her husband, Uriah, to his death in battle. According to Hadith (traditions of the Prophet's words and deeds), Muhammad reported that Dawud's fasting and praying were the most perfect of any man's in the eyes of God. Muslims also say that Dawud had the most beautiful voice of any man ever born, and that when he sang and recited the Zabur the fish would leave the sea to listen.

Dhur Rummah, Ghaylan ibn Uqbah (c. 696–c. 735)
Bedouin poet

Considered the last of the Bedouin poets before the arrival of Islam, Ghaylan ibn Uqbah was also known as Dhur Rummah; his full name was Abu al-Harith Ghaylan ibn Uqbah. His poetry described the difficult nomadic life led by the Bedouins in the desert. The poems were recounted by a narrator as the men sat around a campfire. In pre-Islamic society, poets occupied many roles. Dhur Rummah was a historian, fortuneteller, and propagandist. As Islam emerged as a faith, its clerics were suspicious about the power of the poet and his poetry. After Dhur Rummah, poets were employed by the ruling sultans. Leading a comfortable life at court, they wrote verses about love.

Diab, Amr (1960/1961–)
Egyptian musician

The Egyptian superstar Amr Diab is the best-selling Arab recording artist of all time and has won the World Music Award on three separate occasions in 1999, 2002, and 2007.

Diab was born in Port Said, Egypt, to an upper-middle class family, and he made his first singing appearance on the radio at the age of six. He graduated in music from the Cairo Academy of Art in 1986. His first album, *Ya Tareeq*, was an instant hit and has been followed by 16 best-selling albums. Diab has created a new kind of music that blends Western music with West Asian music and Egyptian rhythms known as *jeel* music. His appeal goes far beyond Egypt: he is a best-selling artist across the Arab world and is popular as far away as South Africa and South America. Diab has also acted in several movies and was the first Egyptian singer to appear in music videos. His album, *Wayah*, released in 2009, had more than 1.5 million downloads within only a few months.

Din Attar, Farid al- (c. 1142–c. 1220)
Persian poet and mystic

Al-Din Attar was one of the greatest Muslim mystical writers and thinkers; he wrote more than 45,000 couplets and a large volume of prose.

Al-Din Attar was born in Nishapur, northeastern Iran, in about 1142, but the exact dates of his birth and death are not known, and there are few details about his life. It is known that as a young man he traveled widely around Egypt, Syria, Arabia, India, and Central Asia. "Attar" means "perfumer," and he may have practiced as a pharmacist, writing poetry between dispensing to his patients.

Al-Din Attar's best-known and greatest work is *Manteq al-teyr* (The conference of the birds), an allegorical poem describing the journey of 30 birds. Other important works include the *Book of God* and the *Book of Affliction*, both mystical allegories. His most famous prose work, *Tadhkirat al-Awilya* (Biographies of the saints), is an important source of information on early Sufis. His poetry inspired many others. There is a statue honoring him in Nishapur.

Djebar, Assia (1936–)
Algerian writer

Assia Djebar is one of Algeria's most important women writers, known for her feminist stance. She was born Fatima Zohra Imalayen in a small coastal town. Writing in French, the language of the colonial power, she published her first novel in 1957. *La Soif* (translated as *The Mischief*) was published under a pen name because she was afraid of her father's reaction. Like *La Soif*, Djebar's second novel dealt with colonial bourgeois life and the obstacles faced by Algerian women. During the Algerian War (1954–1962) Djebar lived abroad before returning to teach history at the University of Algiers. She also started to make films. In 1995, she moved to the United States and became a professor at New York University. In 2003, Djebar wrote a book that examined the relationships between the French and Arabic languages. In 2005, she was elected to the highly respected Académie Française. She has been nominated for the Nobel Prize for Literature on a number of occasions.

Ebadi, Shirin (1947–)
Iranian reformer

Shirin Ebadi is a prominent Iranian lawyer who was awarded the Nobel Peace Prize in 2003 for her work promoting human rights, especially those of women,

children, and refugees. Ebadi studied law in Tehran and became a judge, but after the Iranian Revolution of 1979, the new religious government declared that women could not serve as judges. Ebadi protested and eventually requested retirement, becoming a law lecturer at Tehran University. In 2001 she cofounded the Defenders of Human Rights Center (DHRC) in Tehran: through the DHRC she defended Iranian intellectuals, journalists, and dissident writers against the authorities. In August 2006 the government declared the DHRC illegal and in December 2008 shut down the center's offices in Tehran. In her 2006 book *Iran Awakening,* Ebadi argued that authentic Islam allows for equality and democracy and that people misinterpret the religion when they use it to justify confining women to lowly positions. In June 2009, following the victory of President Mahmoud Ahmadinejad in a disputed election, Ebadi declared that a new election should be held under the oversight of international observers.

Elijah Muhammad (1897–1975)
U.S. political leader
Elijah Muhammad, born Elijah Poole, was leader of the black nationalist American religious movement Nation of Islam (NoI) from 1934 to 1975.

The son of a Baptist pastor named Willie Poole, Elijah was born in Georgia and in his twenties moved to Detroit, Michigan, where he worked in an auto plant. He converted to Islam and became a follower of preacher Wallace D. Fard, who founded the movement that became the NoI. After becoming head of NoI in 1934, Elijah Muhammad told members to avoid being drafted into the military in World War II and was jailed in 1942–1946. After the war he built membership in NoI and developed a program calling for a separate nation for black Americans following a religion derived in part from Islam. This religion declared that black Americans were God's chosen people.

Ellison, Keith (1963–)
U.S. politician
Keith Ellison became the first Muslim to be elected to the U. S. Congress when he was elected as a Democratic representative for Minneapolis, Minnesota.

Ellison was raised a Roman Catholic in Detroit, Michigan, but converted to Islam as a student at Wayne State University, Detroit. He then attended the University of Minnesota Law School and wrote a number of articles that supported Louis Farrakhan, the leader of the Nation of Islam. When Ellison ran for public office in 2006, his articles caused controversy, but he was elected nevertheless.

Fahd I (1923–2005)
King of Saudi Arabia (1982–2005)
Although Fahd was officially king of Saudi Arabia from 1982 to 2005, he had actually ruled on behalf of his brother, Khalid, between 1975 and 1982, as Khalid had little interest in governance. Fahd's own reign was effectively ended when he suffered a serious stroke in 1995, although he remained nominal head of state until his death in 2005.

Faud's father, Ibn Saud, founded Saudi Arabia. Educated at court as was the custom, Fahd became minister of education in 1953. Realizing the gaps in his own education, he returned to study to improve his knowledge. Fahd held different positions in the government of his half brother, King Faysal. Following Faysal's assassination, Fahd became crown prince but was, in reality, ruling the country. He became a familiar figure in the West, traveling to the United States in 1977, where he met President Jimmy Carter. As king, Fahd sought to reduce the power of the Soviet Union in western Asia. When Iraq invaded Kuwait in 1990, he allowed Western forces to be based in Saudi Arabia, provoking shock among Arab nations. He was a figurehead for the last 10 years of his reign, after his stroke left him severely weakened.

Faisal, Toujan al- (1948–)
Jordanian politician
A human rights activist and former TV journalist, Toujan al-Faisal was Jordan's first female member

U.S. Muslim convert Keith Ellison, who in 2006 became the first Muslim to be elected to the U. S. Congress.

of parliament. Her work as an activist for women's rights has brought her into direct conflict with Jordan's religious leaders and government. Before she was elected to parliament, she was charged with apostasy (turning away from Islam), but the case was dismissed. Al-Faisal served as a member of parliament between 1993 and 1997 but was allegedly prevented from running for reelection.

In 2002, al-Faisal wrote an open letter to King Abdullah II, accusing the Jordanian prime minister of corruption. Her accusations led to her being imprisoned, despite an international outcry. She was granted a royal pardon after she went on a hunger strike, but her conviction was not overturned, preventing her from running in any future elections.

Faiz, Faiz Ahmed (1911–1984)
Pakistani poet

Faiz Ahmed Faiz was one of Pakistan's most famous Urdu poets. A lifelong Marxist, he was the first Asian poet to win the Lenin Peace Prize, the Soviet Union's equivalent of the Nobel Prize.

Faiz was born into a well-off literary family in Sialkot, Punjab, India. Following partition in 1947, he decided to live in the newly created Pakistan and settled in Lahore, where his education involved learning the basics of Islamic belief. In 1936, Faiz founded a branch of the Progressive Writers' Movement; he taught at university and briefly joined the British Army. In 1947, he became the first editor-in-chief of the *Pakistan Times*, the leading daily newspaper of the time. His communist beliefs led him into conflict with the new Pakistani government, and he was jailed for his alleged involvement in a failed coup. While in prison for four years he wrote two of his greatest volumes of poetry, *Dast-e-Saba* and *Zindan Nama* (1953, 1956). His poetry followed the favorite form of Urdu poetry, the *ghazal*, and reflected his belief in Sufism and its saints.

Farabi, Abu Nasr al- (c. 878–c. 950)
Philosopher

Known also as Alpharabius or Avennasar, al-Farabi (Muhammad ibn Muhammad ibn Tarkhan ibn Uzalagh al-Farabi) was one of the greatest Muslim scientists and thinkers, making important contributions to astronomy, music, philosophy, physics, and psychology.

The first record of al-Farabi comes from Baghdad, where he moved in 901 and remained for 40 years, until he was invited to Aleppo under the patronage of the Syrian ruler Sayf ad-Dawlah. Al-Farabi commented on the works of early philosophers such as Greek scholars Plato and Aristotle, as well as establishing his own Islamic philosophy, "Farabism." Al-Farabi was known as "the Second Teacher," after Aristotle. His work paved the way for future Islamic philosophers such as Avicenna.

Farah, Nuruddin (1945–)
Somali writer

One of Africa's greatest writers, Somali-born Nuruddin Farah concentrates on women's liberation in postcolonial Somalia and how people combine multiple cultural identities into a single identity. Writing in English, which is not his first language, his work attracts an international audience.

Farah was born in 1945 in Italian Somaliland (now Somalia), the son of well-known Somali poet, Aleeli Faduma. Farah was educated in Ethiopia and Mogadishu and studied at university in India, where he wrote his first novel. *From a Crooked Rib* (1970) described one woman's struggle to escape from an arranged marriage. After the publication of his second novel, *A Naked Needle* (1976), which examined post-revolutionary life in Somalia, the Somali government issued a warrant for his arrest. Farah began 22 years of self-imposed exile, living in Europe, Africa, the United States, and India. He returned to Somalia for the first time in 1996. His 2007 novel, *Knots*, was about an exile's return to Mogadishu. He lives in Cape Town, South Africa.

Farouk I of Egypt (1920–1965)
King of Egypt (1936–1952)

Farouk I, Egypt's second king after independence from Great Britain, was originally a popular ruler, but his eccentric behavior and extravagance turned his subjects against him.

Farouk's rule was marked by the continuing rivalry between his family and the popular Wafd Party. During World War II, the British forced Farouk to take the Wafd leader, Mustafa al-Nahhas Pasha, as prime minister. As a result, Farouk could no longer maintain the Egyptian neutrality he had planned, as al-Nahhas initiated the Arab League, a group of Arab states that could act together. When Egypt was defeated in war by the newly created Israel in 1948, army officers blamed Farouk for the defeat and his inability to get rid of the British. They forced him to stand down in favor of his young son. Shortly after, Egypt became a republic.

Farrakhan, Louis (1933–)
U.S. religious leader

Louis Farrakhan is the leader of the black American political-religious movement the Nation of Islam.

Born Louis Eugene Walcott, he was raised as a Christian in Boston, Massachusetts, and after training to be a teacher, became a nightclub calypso singer. In

1955 he joined the Nation of Islam (NoI), a movement founded by Wallace D. Fard in the 1930s. As developed by its leader Elijah Muhammad, the movement drew on elements of Islam and called for a separate nation for black Americans. NoI members rejected their surnames because they were those of white slave owners. Like many others, Walcott at first took the surname X and became known as Louis X before Elijah Muhammad gave him the name Abdul Haleem Farrakhan.

In the 1960s Farrakhan became one of the leading figures in the NoI. After Elijah Muhammad died in 1975, the NoI split: one group, led by Elijah's Muhammad's son Wallace Muhammad (later called Warith Deen Mohammed), aligned itself with orthodox Sunni Islam and changed its name. Louis Farrakhan led a second group that kept the name Nation of Islam and carried on the radical black nationalist teachings of Elijah Muhammad.

Fathy, Hassan (1900–1989)
Egyptian architect

The most famous Egyptian architect of modern times, Fathy was distinguished by the housing he designed for poor people. In a long career, he built in many countries, designing both private houses and public buildings.

Hassan Fathy was born in Alexandria, Egypt, and graduated from the University of Cairo in 1926. In 1937, he built the first mud-brick structures that would become a key part of his work, which was influenced by ancient architectural techniques and design. For example, he used dense brick walls and traditional courtyards to create passive cooling for low-income housing. Fathy was a pioneer who aimed to create affordable indigenous architecture and searched for alternative energy sources. His contribution to architecture was recognized when he served as a consultant to the United Nations Refugee World Assistance in 1950. In 1980, Fathy was awarded the Aga Khan Award for Architecture.

Fatima (c. 616–633)
Daughter of the Prophet

Daughter of the Prophet Muhammad and wife of Ali ibn Abi Talib, Fatima is seen as a role model for Muslim women. Shiites particularly honor her because they see her sons Hasan and Husayn as the inheritors, through their father Ali, of the authority of Muhammad. Shiites declare that, like her father, Fatima was infallible: everything she believed and said was true. They say that she did not sin, was always compassionate, and shared what she had with others. In 632 she nursed the Prophet during his final illness. After Muhammad's death, Fatima supported the claim of Ali to succeed him and argued with Abu Bakr, the first leader of the Islamic Caliphate. She died in 633, the year after the Prophet's death.

Faysal (1906–1975)
King of Saudi Arabia (1964–1975)

King Faysal ruled Saudi Arabia between 1964 and his assassination in 1975. An influential figure in western Asia, he wanted to reduce Soviet involvement in the region. He was also an outspoken critic of Israel.

The son of Saudi Arabia's founder, Ibn Saud, Faysal held high ministerial positions before becoming crown prince in 1953. He became king in 1964 after King Saud was deposed by a coalition of religious leaders, the Council of Ministers, and senior members of the ruling family. The king initiated economic and educational reforms. He continued to rule despite being in poor health. He was shot dead by his mentally ill nephew, who wanted revenge for the death of his brother during a demonstration 10 years earlier.

Faysal I (1885–1933)
King of Iraq (1921–1933)

The first king of Iraq, Faysal I was an important leader who worked to advance Arab nationalism. The son of the emir and grand sharif of Mecca, Husayn ibn Ali, Faysal played a key role in organizing Arab leaders to fight against their Ottoman rulers during World War I. Led by his father, they revolted against the Ottomans in 1916. With Arab soldiers occupying Damascus, Faysal was declared king of Syria; he hoped for British support to create an Arab state, but at the Paris Peace Conference the French demanded to be involved in the government of Lebanon and Syria. They invaded Syria and forced Faysal into exile. The British installed Faysal as king of Iraq in 1921, although he had no previous connection with the country. He was a popular ruler, however, and negotiated with the British for full Iraqi independence and membership in the League of Nations by 1932.

Faysal II (1935–1958)
King of Iraq (1939–1958)

Faysal II, grandson of Faysal I, was the last king of Iraq. He came to the throne at age four after his father was killed in an auto accident. In April 1941, the prime minister seized power, and Faysal left Iraq with his mother. When she died in 1950, his uncle became his guardian. In 1953, when he reached 18, Faysal became king. His cousin, Hussein ibn Talal, became king of Jordan later the same year. The two new rulers were

rivals for the leadership of the Hashemite clan. Faysal became head of the Arab Federation that united Iraq and Jordan. Faysal attempted to modernize Iraq with building projects, but he grew increasingly unpopular. In 1958, General Abd al-Karim Qasim overthrew the monarchy; Faysal was killed in the fighting.

Fiasco, Lupe (1982–)
U.S. musician
Lupe Fiasco is the stage name of Wasalu Muhammad Jaco, a hip-hop recording artist. He was born in Chicago, Illinois, and came to attention with his critically acclaimed debut album, *Lupe Fiasco's Food and Liquor* (2006).

Fiasco was raised a Muslim in an African American family on the West Side of Chicago. His father played African drums in his spare time. Fiasco began to rap after he heard Nas's 1996 album, *It Was Written*. After joining a number of bands, Fiasco went solo and was signed by Atlantic Records in 2004. The rapper and pop mogul Jay-Z helped produce his debut album, which was nominated for three Grammies. A second album, *Lupe Fiasco's The Cool*, appeared in 2007, followed by *Lasers* in 2009.

Firdawsi, Hakim Abu al-Qasim Mansur (c. 935–c. 1020/1026)
Persian poet
Firdawsi, pen name of Abu al-Qasim Mansur, was one of the most important poets to come from the ancient Khorasan region (now partly in Iran). Writing in classical Persian, he wrote the famous epic *Shah-nameh* (The book of kings).

Firdawsi was born to a well-to-do family of landowners in Tus, Khorasan. He spent almost his whole life in Khorasan, except for a period in Baghdad, Iraq. He traveled to and lived in all the cities of Khorasan to learn about pre-Arab life. By age 30, Firdawsi had learned much about ancient Iranian history through his study of ancient chronicles and oral histories. By age 40 he was ready to start writing; he started *Shah-nameh* in 975, finishing it in 1010. In more than 50,000 rhyming couplets, it chronicles the legends and histories of the Iranian kings from prehistoric times to the Arab conquest in the seventh century.

Fuad I (1868–1936)
King of Egypt (1922–1939)
Fuad I was Egypt's first king after independence from Great Britain.

Brought up and educated overseas, Fuad held a number of administrative posts in Egypt before being chosen by the country's British governors to be the

The Persian poet Firdawsi is an Iranian cultural icon. This is a building on Firdawsi Street, Tehran, that is decorated with bas-reliefs depicting characters from the poet's Shah-nameh.

sultan of Egypt. In 1919, the British decided to start discussions about Egyptian independence. They were uncertain, however, about whether to talk to Fuad, as sultan, or to the Wafd Party, which had emerged as the leader of the nationalist movement. When no agreement was reached, the talks collapsed. The British granted independence anyway, provided they could still have a say in Egyptian affairs. Fuad took the title of king in 1922.

His reign was overshadowed by the popularity of the Wafd Party, although he tried to choose ministers who were not associated with it. The 1931 elections resulted in a parliament without any Wafd members, and Egypt enjoyed a period of calm until 1935. Fuad died before the completion of negotiations with Great Britain about Egypt's future.

Ghalib, Mirza (1797–1869)
Indian poet
Also known as Mirza Asadullah Baig Khan, Mirza Ghalib was a classical poet who wrote in both Urdu and Persian. He adopted the pen name Ghalib, which means "dominant." He became famous posthumously, and he remains the most widely read and influential Urdu poet.

Ghalib was born in Agra in British-controlled India; he was supported by state patronage and by his friends in order to concentrate on his poetry. He wrote about historical events as he witnessed the decline in power of the Mughal Empire and the rise of the British. Although he wrote in Persian, he is most famous for

his *ghazals*, traditional love poems he wrote in Urdu. As well as writing about love, Ghalib wrote about philosophy and daily life, thereby expanding the subject matter of *ghazals*. An accomplished and prolific correspondent, Ghalib introduced a new style of informal letter writing, using popular Urdu. He also wrote religious verse but remained skeptical about interpreting too literally the Islamic scriptures. He died in Delhi, India.

Ghazali, al- (1058–1111)
Persian mystic
Al-Ghazali, sometimes known as Algazel, was a Persian philosopher, theologian, and mystic whose work played a key role in making Sufi mysticism acceptable to orthodox Sunni Muslims.

Born in Tus (now in Iran), he enrolled in a madrassa at age 12 to study *fiqh* (religious law) and rose to become one of the most important scholars of his day. He taught and lectured in Baghdad; then, at the height of his achievements, he withdrew from public life in 1095 to live as a mystic. His book *The Revival of Religious Sciences* described how Islamic religious practices can be brought to expression in mystical Sufi devotions. It inspired many later poets. *The Incoherence of the Philosophers* attacked ancient Greek philosophers as unbelievers and criticized earlier Muslim philosophers such as Avicenna, who were inspired by ancient Greek philosophy. Another philosophical work, *The Aims of the Philosophers*, was among the first Arabic texts translated into Latin for European readers in the 12th century.

Guerrouj, Hicham el- (1974–)
Moroccan athlete
Hicham el-Guerrouj was a middle-distance runner who, at his retirement in 2006, held the world records for 1,500 meters, the mile, and the outdoor 2,000 meters. He won gold medals for the 1,500 meters in four successive World Championships (1997, 1999, 2001, and 2003) and achieved double gold in the 2004 Olympic Games, winning the 1,500 meters and 5,000 meters races. His success earned him the title "King of the Mile." In recognition of his Olympic success, el-Guerrouj was awarded the prestigious Cordon de Commandeur by King Mohammed VI of Morocco in 2004. Following the 2004 Olympics, el-Guerrouj decided to retire from competition, and he became a member of the International Olympic Committee (IOC) Athletes' Commission.

Hadid, Zaha (1950–)
British architect
Born in Baghdad, Iraq, but a long-time resident of Britain, Zaha Hadid occupies a unique position in modern architecture. In 2004, she became the first woman to win the prestigious Pritzker Architecture Prize.

Zaha Hadid was born in 1950 and educated in Baghdad. She studied mathematcs at the American University of Beirut, Lebanon, before moving to London in 1972 to study at the Architectural Association School of Architecture. She started her own architectural practice in 1980. Her groundbreaking designs have won many international competitions, including in 1994 the unbuilt Cardiff Bay Opera House in Wales and the Aquatic Center for the 2012 London Olympics, which is under construction. Hadid's work has a sculptural quality, and collections of her concept drawings and design sketches have been exhibited at art galleries around the world. Hadid has also been a visiting architecture professor at many of the world's leading universities.

The interior of the Bridge Pavilion in Saragossa, Spain, designed by British-Iraqi architect Zaha Hadid.

Hafez, Mohammad Shams od-Din
(c. 1325–c. 1390)
Persian poet

Known simply as Hafez, this Persian lyric poet is revered throughout Iran. Most Iranians know his poetry by heart, and many Iranian homes keep a copy of his collected works, *Divan*, alongside the Koran.

Hafez was born and died in Shiraz. His tomb, in the beautiful Musalla Gardens, is a popular site of pilgrimage for Iranians. The details of Hafez's life are largely unknown, but academics think he must have been well educated because of the quality of his writing. Hafez wrote hundreds of *ghazal*s and took as his themes love, a celebration of drinking, and exposing the hypocrisy of those in power. Many of his verses have been set to music or used in Persian calligraphy. Since the 1940s there has been a concerted effort to compile a definitive scholarly edition of his work. This is difficult because the precise number of poems he wrote is unknown.

Hagar
Cross-cultural figure

The second wife of the patriarch Ibraham (Abraham), originally the handmaiden of his first wife Sarah, Hagar gave birth to Ibraham's first son, Ismail (Ishmael), ancestor of the Arab peoples. According to one tradition, the birth of Ismail caused difficulty with the childless Sarah, and Ibraham took Hagar and Ismail away to start a new life. The angel Jibril (known as Gabriel in the Judeo-Christian tradition) guided them to the place where the Kaaba shrine would be built in what would become the holy city of Mecca. After Ibrahim left his wife and child there, they ran out of water, and Hagar made seven trips in desperate search of water up two nearby hills, al-Safa and al-Marwah, until finally Jibril caused a miraculous spring to burst from the ground. The spring, called the Zamzam Well, plays an important role in pilgrims' devotions today.

Hakim, al- (985–c. 1021)
Fatimid caliph (996–1021)

Al-Hakim was the sixth caliph or ruler of the Egyptian Shiite Fatimid dynasty. Followers of the Druze religion believe he was the reincarnation of God.

Al-Hakim became ruler in 996, supported by the army. Once in power, his rule was highly eccentric. He persecuted Christians, Jews, and Sunni Muslims. He had dogs killed because he did not like their barking, and he banned various shellfish and vegetables; he also sacked the city of al-Fustat (near present-day Cairo). However, al-Hakim could also be a tolerant ruler, promoting the arts and education, building mosques, and distributing food during times of famine. In 1017

the caliph started to promote the teachings of a sect of Islam that claimed he was an incarnation of God; those teachings gave rise to the Druze religion. Al-Hakim disappeared in 1021 while out walking; his remains were never found.

Hallaj, Mansur al- (c. 858–922)
Persian mystic

Mansur al-Hallaj was a Persian mystic and Sufi teacher, who was accused of claiming to be God, imprisoned, and eventually executed. Born in the province of Fars, al-Hallaj learned the Koran by heart as a young boy. On his first pilgrimage to Mecca, he stayed for a year, then traveled widely, gathering followers and making two more journeys to Mecca. Later he settled in Baghdad, capital of the Abbasid caliphate (now the capital of Iraq). After al-Hallaj said in a trance "I am the Truth," opponents alleged that he was claiming to be God because in Islamic tradition "the Truth" is one of the 99 names of God. Al-Hallaj also said "There is nothing in my turban but God." Supporters argue that al-Hallaj was teaching that God lives deep in the human heart and can be directly experienced by people who learn to reduce self-will.

Hamad bin Khalifa al-Thani (1952–)
Emir of Qatar (1995–)

Sheikh Hamad bin Khalifa al-Thani is the emir of the Gulf state of Qatar, the smallest of the Middle Eastern counties. He was trained at the prestigious Sandhurst Royal Military Academy in Britain and commanded the Qatari armed forces while his father was on the throne. Hamad was made crown prince and minister for defense in 1977; from 1992, he was responsible for administering the country's day-to-day affairs, including the development of Qatar's massive oil and natural gas resources. Hamad mounted a bloodless coup against his father on June 26, 1995, and has ruled Qatar since then.

Hariri, Rafiq (1944–2005)
Lebanese businessman and politician

Rafiq Hariri was a successful Lebanese businessman who became prime minister before he was assassinated.

Hariri was born into a poor Sunni family in Sidon, Lebanon. After university he moved to Saudi Arabia, where he set up a construction company with interests across western Asia. He expanded his businesses to include banking, insurance, and telecommunications and became very rich. With some of his wealth, he set up a charitable foundation to fund the education of thousands of Lebanese students around the world.

Hariri returned to Lebanon and became a politician. In 1992, he was appointed the country's prime minister

under a constitution that required a Sunni head of government. His government successfully rebuilt the country after years of Israeli occupation and civil war. He negotiated a peace agreement with Israel, ending terrorism both at home and abroad. Hariri resigned in 1998 but was reelected in 2000; he resigned again in October 2004 over continuing Syrian interference in Lebanon. On February, 14, 2005, Hariri was assassinated by a bomb in Beirut. Protests over his death led to massive political change in Lebanon, including the withdrawal of Syrian troops.

Hariri of Basra, al- (1054–1122)
Arab scholar
Born in Basra, Iraq, Abu Muhammad al-Qasim ibn Ali al-Hariri was an Arabian scholar and Seljuk government official best known for his elegant style and wit. His stories, *Maqamat al-Hariri* (The assemblies of al-Hariri), are regarded as some of the most important literary works in the Arab-speaking world after the Koran.

Maqamat al-Hariri is made up of stories, written in rhyming prose, that mix parts of the Koran with well-known proverbs and phrases and classical poems. As well as imparting a moral, the stories taught the listener rules of grammar, rhetoric, and poetry. They allowed al-Hariri to criticize the social order of the day in a refined, stylized way. The stories all shared the same narrator, a traveler who encountered the subjects of the tales.

Harun
Cross-cultural figure
Harun is the Arabic name for Aaron, brother of Moses (Musa), who led the Israelites out of captivity in Egypt. Like Musa, he is viewed in Islam as a Prophet. Harun had a gift for prophecy and public speaking and helped Musa in his work. When the Israelites were in the wilderness after leaving Egypt, Musa left his people in the care of Harun while he communed with God on a mountaintop; when he returned, he found that the people had abandoned monotheism and were worshipping a golden calf. He initially blamed his brother, but Harun explained that he had been forced to accept the change. Then Musa prayed to God for forgiveness for himself and Harun. According to Islamic tradition, Harun lived to the age of 122.

Harun ar-Rashid (763/766–809)
Abbasid caliph (786–809)
Harun ar-Rashid was the fifth and most famous Abbasid caliph who ruled when Islam was at its peak. His famous court was immortalized in the stories of *The Thousand and One Nights*.

Harun was born in Rayy, in modern-day Iran, the son of the third caliph. From 780 to 782, he led an expedition against the Byzantine Empire that reached the Bosporus, opposite Constantinople, where he made a peace treaty, which favored the Muslims. His success was rewarded with the title of ar-Rashid, which means "the one following the right path." Following the deaths of his father and elder brother, Harun became caliph in 786 and ruled an empire that reached from the western Mediterranean as far east as India until his death in 809. During his reign, the caliphate prospered as trade and commerce increased. Science, culture, religion, and the arts were encouraged, and there were many storytellers at court. Harun's rule and his legendary court inspired many stories. The most famous were written in *The Thousand and One Nights*.

Hasan ibn Ali (624–680)
Shiite saint
Hasan ibn Ali was the grandson of the Prophet Muhammad and the older brother of Husayn ibn Ali. He is a member of the Ahlul Bayt (the household of Muhammad), the group of the five holiest people of the Shiite faith.

When his father Ali became caliph, Hasan fought in several battles to help secure his father's position. After Ali's murder in 661, many of his followers pledged their loyalty to Hasan as the next caliph, although his father had died without naming an heir. Muawiyah, governor of Syria, wanted the caliphate for himself and raised an army to fight Hasan. Hasan, outnumbered and fearing more bloodshed, renounced the caliphate. Hasan retired to Medina, angering many of his supporters. His wife poisoned him on the orders of Muawiyah.

Hassan II (1929–1999)
King of Morocco (1961–1999)
The deeply religious Hassan II, 16th sovereign of the Alawite dynasty, was considered by some Muslims to be a direct descendant of the Prophet Muhammad.

He ruled Morocco as a religious state, taking his authority from his proclaimed role as Commander of the Faithful. Seen as having held Morocco together in a difficult period, Hassan was, at the time of his death, the Arab world's longest reigning monarch, despite attempts on his life, repeated military coups, and popular unrest. In order to divert attention from the kingdom's social problems, Hassan sought to unite the country behind his campaign to expand Morocco's border south into the mineral-rich Western Sahara. He also played an important

behind-the-scenes role in the Middle East peace process and is credited with being a key influence in the signing of the 1979 peace treaty between Israel and Egypt. Throughout his reign he maintained friendly relations with the West, but his often heavy-handed approach to domestic human rights attracted strong international criticism.

Hawa
Cross-cultural figure

Hawa is the first woman in the Islamic account of the creation of the world, the counterpart of Eve in the Jewish and Christian traditions. As in the biblical account, in the Islamic narrative Adam and Hawa defy God's ban on eating the fruit of a particular tree after being tempted to do so by the fallen angel Shaitan (Satan), they and are expelled from Paradise. Hawa's role is different from that of Eve in one important way: in the biblical account, Eve is tempted by the serpent, sins by eating the forbidden fruit, and then tempts Adam to do so; in Islamic tradition, Adam and Hawa are tempted together by Shaitan and both sin at the same time. In one Islamic tradition, Adam and Hawa were expelled from Paradise separately: Adam to Ceylon (Sri Lanka) and Hawa to Arabia. They were apart for around two centuries before they met near Mount Arafat, when Hawa bore 20 pairs of twins to Adam. Another tradition says that they came separately to the hills near Mecca, Adam to al-Safa and Hawa to al-Marwah, and after Adam spent 40 days in tearful repentance God sent down the Kaaba shrine and taught Adam the duty of making the hajj pilgrimage.

Hikmat, Nazim (1902–1963)
Turkish writer

Nazim Hikmat is one of Turkey's best-known writers, whose poetry, novels, and plays have been translated into more than 50 languages. His radical political views frequently brought him into conflict with the Turkish government, however, and he spent most of his adult life in prison or living in exile in the Soviet Union.

Hikmat was born in Salonika, Greece, and grew up in Anatolia, later fighting in the Turkish War of Independence against the Greeks. He published his first poetry at seventeen. He studied at Moscow University in 1922 and, influenced by the 1917 Russian Revolution, became a Marxist in 1924. On his return to Turkey he continued his outspoken activism for communist causes, resulting in frequent imprisonment that culminated, in 1938, in a 28-year sentence for inciting unrest. In prison, he wrote prolifically, creating a style that combined Soviet modernism and free-verse with the lyricism of Turkish poetry.

His best-known work, *Human Landscapes* (1941–1945), was written during his time in prison, but was not published until years later. In the 1950s well-known intellectuals and activists around the world lobbied for his release. He left Turkey permanently in 1951 and was stripped of his citizenship as a result. Following his death in Moscow in 1963, his work, previously censored, started to appear again in Turkey. His Turkish citizenship was returned posthumously in 2009.

Hoxha, Enver (1908–1985)
Prime minister of Albania (1944–1955)

Enver Hoxha was the prime minister of Albania and was responsible for turning Albania into a communist state and making it the most isolated and tightly controlled country in Europe.

Born in Albania and educated at university in France, Hoxha returned home to be a teacher. After the Italian invasion of Albania in 1939, he left teaching and became an active Communist. In 1941, Hoxha founded the Albanian Communist Party. He became the party's first leader and commander of its military arm, the Army of National Liberation. He was prime minister of Albania from its liberation from German and Italian control in 1944 until 1954. As first secretary of the Party of Labor's Central Committee, he retained effective control of the government until his death in 1985.

Hoxha turned Albania from a semi-feudal remnant of the Ottoman Empire into an industrialized economy. To achieve this, he confiscated private property and turned farms into large-scale collectives that made the country largely self-sufficient in food. However, his rule was also notable for its brutality. He imprisoned, executed, or exiled thousands of his political opponents. He shut down places of worship. He was determined to keep Albania free from the influence of other countries, effectively closing the country to the outside world.

Husayn ibn Ali (629–680)
Shiite saint

Husayn ibn Ali was the grandson of the Prophet Muhammad and the younger brother of Hasan ibn Ali, the second Shiite imam. He is revered by Shiite Muslims as one of the twelve imams believed to have been the rightful successors to Muhammad.

Husayn opposed what he considered to be the unjust rule of the Umayyad caliph Muawiyah's son and successor, Yazid. In 680 Husayn decided to overthrow Yazid and seize power for himself. However, Husayn and his followers were encircled near the banks of the Euphrates River, in the city of Karbala, Iraq. Although

outnumbered by the forces sent to arrest him, Husayn refused to surrender. He was beheaded and his men were killed. His head was sent to Yazid in Damascus, Syria, where it was put on display in the Umayyad Mosque.

The anniversary of his death, known as Ashura, is a day of mourning for Shiite Muslims and is still observed on the tenth day of the month of Muharram.

Hussein, Saddam (1937–2006)
President of Iraq (1979–2003)

Saddam Hussein was an Arab ruler who became internationally notorious as the leader of a totalitarian state who engaged in costly wars with his neighbors and used ruthless methods to silence internal opposition.

Hussein was born in Iraq to a poor Sunni family. As a young man, he joined the Ba'ath Party, which advocated nonreligious Arab socialism. In 1959, after a failed assassination attempt on the Iraqi prime minister, he escaped abroad. He did not return to Iraq until the Ba'ath Party took power in Iraq in 1963. After the party was overthrown later the same year, Saddam spend several years in prison. He returned to politics when the Ba'ath Party retook power in 1968.

As vice president and the effective leader of Iraq, Saddam created a security service that kept a tight control over the country. In the early 1970s, he nationalized the Western-owned Iraq Petroleum Company. In 1979, he became president of Iraq. His secret police crushed any opposition, particularly

King Hussein of Jordan standing with Palestinian leader, Yasir Arafat, during Arab-Israeli peace talks. Hussein was an important figure in the peace talks of the 1990s.

among the Shiite and Kurdish populations, and he fostered a cult of personality among the Iraqi people.

In September 1980, Saddam launched a war against neighboring Iran, which soon settled into a bloody stalemate. During the war Hussein authorized the use of chemical weapons, such as nerve gas, which were used indiscriminately against Iranian soldiers, civilians, and Iraqi dissidents. The war cost hundreds of thousands of lives on both sides and dragged on until 1988. In August 1990, Iraq invaded the neighboring oil-rich country of Kuwait. A U.S.-led coalition forced Saddam's army out of Kuwait in the Gulf War, which ended in February of 1991 with Saddam still in power but weakened by UN sanctions and military losses.

In March 2003, Iraq was invaded by the United States and its allies. Saddam went into hiding but was captured by U.S. forces in December 2003. He was put on trial, and in November 2006 he was convicted and sentenced to death by hanging. Saddam was executed in Baghdad on December 30, 2006.

Hussein bin Talal (1935–1999)
King of Jordan (1953–1999)

King Hussein took control of Jordan in the aftermath of the assassination of his grandfather, King Abdullah, by forces hostile to a possible peace with Israel. Hussein's

reign was defined by generally pro-Western reformist policies that maintained the stability of the country in the face of regional conflicts.

King Hussein was educated at the Sandhurst Royal Military College in England before succeeding his father, King Talal, who was declared unfit to rule. Because he was only 16, Hussein was not enthroned until 1953. From the early years of his reign, Hussein's policies were primarily motivated by the desire to maintain stability and development in his country, an attitude that brought him into conflict with his allies in the West and in the Arab world when his internal concerns took precedence over regional ones.

Jordan was forced to join the Arab side in the Six-Day War of June 1967 against Israel, but it was costly to Jordan, which lost the West Bank and East Jerusalem. The war caused 250,000 additional Palestinian refugees to flood into Jordan.

By September 1970, the Palestine Liberation Organization was causing problems within Jordan; in a campaign known as "Black September," Hussein drove them out. In the following years he maintained good relations with Israel, the West, and the Arab nations.

Following the Israeli-Palestinian peace accords of 1993, King Hussein signed a peace treaty that formally ended more than 40 years of hostile relations between Jordan and Israel. Even though he was seriously ill, he helped further peace negotiations between Israelis and Palestinians in October 1998. He died of cancer in 1999.

Ibn Abd-al-Wahhab, Muhammad (1703–1792)
Arab scholar

Muhammad Ibn Abd-al-Wahhab was an Arab theologian whose teachings were the basis of the conservative Islamic movement known as Wahhabism. The movement he started rose to prominence after it was adopted by Ibn Saud, the founder of the Saudi royal family.

Al-Wahhab urged Muslims to return to the purity of Islam as it was thought to have been practiced in the first three generations after the death of the Prophet Muhammad. Followers were encouraged to base their lives on a strict interpretation of the Koran and Hadith. He attacked the *bida*, or innovations, of some Muslims, such as visiting the tombs of former religious leaders or praying to God through a Shiite imam or Sufi saint.

Born in Uyaynah, Arabia (now Saudi Arabia), he was educated in Medina, then taught in Basra and Baghdad. On his return to Uyaynah in 1740, his teachings caused controversy, and in 1744 he was forced to leave. In the town of ad-Diryah he made an alliance with local ruler Ibn Saud, making Saud and his descendants leaders of the movement, in return for the promise that Ibn Saud would spread Abd-al-Wahhab's teachings. After many years of fighting, the Saud family founded the Kingdom of Saudi Arabia in 1932, establishing it as a Wahhabi state. Saudi Arabia is still governed in line with the teachings of Abd-al-Wahhab. Followers of Abd-al-Wahhab's teachings do not call themselves Wahhabi, but Muwahiddun (unitarians) or Salafis (predeccessors).

Ibn al-Arabi (1165–1240)
Sufi teacher and mystic

One of the most profound mystics in the history of Islam, Ibn al-Arabi was an Arab Sufi philosopher and poet who lived and worked both in Al Andalus (Muslim Spain) and Syria. Born in Arabia (modern Saudi Arabia), he lived from age eight to 35 in Al Andalus, then made the hajj pilgrimage to Mecca, where he lived for three years before settling in Damascus, Syria. He wrote a 37-volume work, *The Meccan Illuminations*, a study of Islamic knowledge and traditions interpreted from the standpoint of mystic insight, which he said was based on a vision he had at the Kaaba in Mecca. He also wrote a shorter book, *The Bezels of Wisdom*, a spiritual study he said was dictated to him by the Prophet Muhammad himself in Damascus in 1229, together with a large number of poems, collected in the five-volume *Diwan*. He taught that divine unity lies behind the world's varied forms, and that humans could go beyond the individual self to become aware of unity. His work is highly regarded in the Islamic tradition both from a literary and theological perspective.

Ibn al-Bawwab (d. 1022 or 1031)
Arab calligrapher

Abu al-Hasan ali ibn Hilal ibn al-Bawwab was an Arabic calligrapher in the age of the Abbasid caliphs (750–1258), known for developing the cursive Muhaqqaq and Rayhani calligraphic scripts and for refining the Nashki and Tawqi scripts.

Born in Iraq, he was of humble origins—his name means "son of the doorkeeper"—and he began his career as a house painter before becoming an illuminator of books. He was very well educated, however, and studied under noted calligraphers and scholars. He worked in Baghdad, where he served as imam in a mosque, and in Shiraz, where he established his own style of calligraphy that survived until the 13th century. He collected many manuscripts of the earlier calligrapher Ibn Muqlah (886–940), who had created the first cursive calligraphic script, the Nashki. A number of Korans written in Ibn al-Bawwab's elegant hand can be found in museums around Europe and the Muslim world.

Ibn al-Farid (1182–1235)
Arab Sufi poet

Ibn al-Farid was a poet whose work includes some of the most highly regarded and widely read examples of Arab mystical poetry. He was born and died in Cairo, Egypt, and lived for a period in Mecca. His father was an important Syrian-born official, and al-Farid studied law for some time before abandoning his legal studies to study Sufism. In Mecca, he met the famous Sufi al-Suhrawardi of Baghdad.

Al-Farid is best known for two important poems, "Nazm-as-suluk" (The wine ode) and "Khamriyah" (The poem of the way). His poems are odes, known as *qasidah*; using the convention of love poetry, he describes a lover's longing to be with his loved one. Like many Sufi poets, al-Farid used the language of love and romance as a metaphor for religious devotion. Al-Farid is considered to be a saint by many Sufis, and his tomb in Cairo is still a site of pilgrimage.

Ibn al-Hajjaj, Muslim (821–875)
Muslim scholar

Muslim ibn al-Hajjaj was author of the *Sahih Muslim*, a very important collection of Hadith (narratives), oral traditions about the Prophet's life. Sunni Muslims regard the *Sahih Muslim* as the second most authentic collection of Hadith after the *Sahih Bukhari* of al-Bukhari (810–870). Al-Hajjaj was born in Nishapur, in what is now Iran, a descendant of the Arab tribe of Qushair. He traveled to Arabia, Egypt, Iraq, and Syria, studying with great teachers in many places, then returned to Nishapur. There he became a friend of al-Bukhari. The *Sahih Muslim* and *Sahih Bukhari* have around 1,900 Hadiths in common.

Ibn Anas, Malik (711–795)
Arab scholar

Malik ibn Anas was one of the best-known teachers and scholars of *fiqh* (religious law) in Sunni Islam. He founded the Maliki school or tradition of religious law (the others are the Hanafi, Hanbali, and Shafi'i schools). As a young man Malik memorized the Koran and studied with the great teachers of his day, including Abu Hanifa (699–765), founder of the Hanafi school of *fiqh*. Over a period of 40 years, Ibn Anas compiled the Muwatta, a statement of Muslim law and correct customs; the Muwatta contains the earliest surviving collection of Hadith, traditions about the Prophet Muhammad's words and deeds. This book and its Hadith collection are a widely used resource for those studying or implementing Sharia law. Malik ibn Anas died, age 89, in Medina, where he had lived his whole life.

Ibn Battuta (1304–1369)
Explorer and writer

Ibn Battuta was an Islamic explorer and traveler who wrote an account of his journeys to the furthest reaches of the Muslim world, *Rihlah* (Travels), which provides a detailed picture of the Muslim world as it was in the 14th century.

He was born and died in Morocco, but he spent thirty years traveling through the Muslim world. He probably traveled around 75,000 miles, which was more than his contemporary, the European explorer Marco Polo. Ibn Battuta was born into a family of Islamic legal scholars and studied Muslim law, giving him a vocation that he often relied on in his travels. At the age of 21, in 1325, he set off to perform the hajj. It took him 16 months to reach Mecca, and he did not return to Morocco for 24 years. He visited as many of the Islamic holy sites as he could. On his return, the sultan of Morocco, Abu Inan Faris, ordered him to dictate an account of his travels, to a scribe, Ibn Juzayy. Ibn Battuta kept no notes during his travels so the account was compiled from memory, supplemented with extracts from other travel journals copied by Ibn Juzayy. The book was not rediscovered until the 1800s, when it was translated from Arabic and published around the world.

Ibn Firnas, Abbas Qasim (810–887)
Spanish-Arab inventor

Abbas Qasim ibn Firnas was born in Córdoba in the Muslim province of al-Andalus in Spain. Best known for his pioneering experiments with flying machines, Ibn Firnas made many other contributions to science and technology, as well as being an accomplished musician and poet. Ibn Firnas came up with a process of manufacturing colorless glass and made magnifying lenses for reading, which he called "reading stones." His method of cutting rock crystal provided a way for Spanish mines to cut quartz, rather than exporting the stone to Egypt to be cut. He designed a water clock called "al-Maqata" and also made a machine that demonstrated the motion of the planets and stars in space. Ibn Firnas experimented with a flying machine with wings that flapped like those of a bird, but he was badly injured in a test flight.

Ibn Jubayr (1145–1217)
Traveler and writer

Ibn Jubayr was a Spanish Muslim who wrote a book about his pilgrimage to Mecca. His book, *Rihlah*, translated as "The Travels of Ibn Jubayr", gives valuable insight into the culture, politics, and peoples of the Muslim world in the 12th century.

He was born in the city of Balansiya in al-Andalus (present-day Valencia, Spain). After he completed his education, his father secured a position for Ibn Jubayr as the secretary to the Almohad governor of Granada.

It is not known what prompted Ibn Jubayr to suddenly abandon his career in order to travel to Mecca. According to one account, he decided to perform the hajj to atone for a sin he was obliged to commit for the governor of Granada. He set off in 1183 and returned to Granada two years later. He describes his journey across the Mediterranean on Genoese ships, his travels on land through Egypt and then back through Iraq, Syria, and Sicily. He made two further journeys to the East in 1189–1191 and 1217 but did not record those trips.

Ibn Rushd, Abu al-Walid Muhammad ibn Ahmad ibn Muhammad (1126–1198)
Islamic philosopher and physician

Abu al-Walid Muhammad ibn Ahmad ibn Muhammad ibn Rushd, better known by his Latin name Averroës, was an influential Islamic philosopher and physician. He trained in medicine under the great physician Ibn Zuhr (1091–1161) and eventually became physician at the Almohad court. Later, Ibn Rushd served as a judge in the courts of Seville and Córdoba in southern Spain, but he fell out of favor and was banished; he was reinstated shortly before his death in 1198.

Ibn Rushd was a prolific author whose work covered many areas of science, including astronomy, mathematics, medicine, religion, and law. His most famous medical text, *Kulliyat*, discussed a range of medical problems and treatments, including the condition now known as Parkinson's disease. However, Ibn Rushd is best known for his works of philosophy. He wrote a series of commentaries on the works of Greek philosophers Aristotle (384–322 BCE) and Plato (c. 428–348 BCE). His most important philosophical ideas were published in his masterpiece, *Tahafut al-Tahafut* (The incoherence of the incoherence), in which he combined ancient Greek ideas with his own ideas about Islam in an attempt to create a harmony between religion and philosophy. His work became well-known in the West through the numerous translations that appeared shortly after his death.

Ibn Saud (c. 1880–1953)
First king of Saudi Arabia (1932–1953)

Abdul Aziz al-Saud, commonly known as Ibn Saud, was the founder of the modern state of Saudi Arabia and was largely responsible for the nation's current political and economic status. He came from the Saud tribe, which has ruled over significant areas of the Arabian Peninsula since the 1740s.

Ibn Saud was born in Riyadh around 1880, when his family ruled much of Arabia. When he was still a child, his family was usurped by their rivals, the Rashids. The Sauds were exiled to Kuwait. When he was 21, Ibn Saud decided to reclaim his family's territories. After two years of raids, he and his followers had temporarily conquered half of central Arabia.

Ibn Saud was an extremely devout Muslim who followed the Koran literally. Before World War I he decided to restore his dynasty's support for Wahhabism, which was a puritanical form of Islam. Ibn Saud's aim was to use religious fundamentalism to further his territorial gains. With the support of the British, he expanded his territory, including the Hejaz region along the Red Sea and Mecca.

The vastly increased Saudi territory remained poor until May 1938 when oil was discovered. At the end of World War II commercial oil extraction began. Ibn Saud saw his income increase over three years from a total of $200,000 for the year 1950 to $2,500,000 a week in 1953. Saud's ailing health overtook him before he could make any major decision on what to do with Saudi Arabia's newfound wealth; he died in November 1953 after naming his oldest son, Saud, as his successor.

Ibn Sina, Abu Ali al-Husayn ibn Abd Allah (980–1037)
Persian scientist, physician, and philosopher

Ibn Sina, also known by the Latin name Avicenna, was a Persian scholar who made important advances in many different fields of intellectual enquiry.

He was born in a village near Bukhara in present-day Uzbekistan, where he studied before traveling widely. He learned many classical Arab texts and mastered astronomy, Greek, mathematics, and all the available texts on medicine. At age 18 he became a court physician, then became vizier at the Buyyid court in Hamadan, and from 1024 was physician to several sultans. In addition to his medical work, he wrote a number of commentaries and translations that introduced the works of Aristotle to the Islamic world. Avicenna wrote more than 100 works himself on science, philosophy, and religion. His medical textbook *Canon of Medicine*, written in 1000, remained a standard work for centuries in both Europe and the Muslim world, earning him the nickname Galen of Islam—a reference to the ancient Greek medical authority.

Ibn Taymiyah (1263–1328)
Turkish scholar

Taqi ad-Din Ahmad ibn Taymiyyah was a celebrated Turkish theologian who was strongly committed to *tawhid* (the unity of God) and to jihad (struggle in

God's work). He is celebrated by modern Sunni Muslim Salafi traditionalists (also known as Wahhabis). Ibn Taymiyyah worked in Damascus, Syria, in the period of the Mongol invasions of the region. He was from a family of well-established theologians and was taught by the finest scholars of the day, studying Arabic literature, mathematics, calligraphy, and philosophy, as well as learning Hadith, theology, and the Hanbali tradition of religious law. He was uncompromising in his beliefs and outspoken in criticism of opponents, so he often came into conflict with the authorities. He was jailed on several occasions for advocating jihad against rulers he perceived to be unjust or impious.

Ibn Tumart (c. 1080–c. 1130)
Berber scholar

Abu Abd Allah Muhammad ibn Tumart was a Berber religious teacher who inspired the rise of the Almohad rulers of North Africa and Spain. He was a member of the Masmuda, one of the Berber tribes of the Atlas Mountains (in present-day Morocco). A very religious youth, he traveled first to Córdoba in Spain and then to Mecca, where he established himself as a religious teacher. After he returned to Morocco, ibn Tumart declared himself the Mahdi, the Islamic redeemer who according to prophecy will purify the world in the last days of history. He inspired a Berber soldier named Abd al-Mumin, who led a revolt against the Almoravids and established the Almohad dynasty of rulers. Ibn Tumart died in a monastery he had established at Tinmal before Abd al-Mumin rose to power.

Ibn Zuhr, Abu Marwun Abd al-Malik (c. 1090–1162)
Spanish-Arab physician

Known by his Latin name Avenzoar, Ibn Zuhr was one of the greatest physicians of his time. During his lifetime he made important advances in the field of surgery as well as outlining new methods of medical research.

Born in Seville in southern Spain, he studied at the university in Córdoba before falling out with the Almoravid rulers of the region and fleeing to Morocco. He returned to his homeland when the Almohad dynasty conquered Seville in 1147 and devoted himself to the study and teaching of medicine; his students included Ibn Rushd, or Averroës (1126–1198).

Ibn Zuhr wrote extensively about many areas of medicine; his most famous text, *al-Taisir*, discussed experimental methods in surgery, such as tracheotomy—the procedure to open an airway in the throat directly through the windpipe. The book also discussed radical ideas such as use of animal experimentation as a precursor to human surgery. Ibn Zuhr became famous throughout Europe thanks to the Latin and Hebrew translations of his work. His books remained popular until well into the 18th century.

Ibrahim
Cross-cultural figure

Ibrahim is the patriarch of the Islamic, Jewish, and Christian religions, known as Abraham in the Judeo-Christian tradition. Muslims regard Ibrahim as a *hanif* (founder or pioneer of monotheism) and a prophet; he is called a "friend of God." His son Ismail is said to be the father (ancestor) of the Arabs, while his other son Ishaq (called Isaac by Jews and Christians) is reputedly an ancestor of the Jews. In the Islamic narrative Ibrahim, his second wife Hagar, and son Ismail were guided by the angel Jibril (Gabriel) to the place where the holy city of Mecca would later rise; Ibrahim left them there, trusting them to God's care, in order to return to his first wife, Sarah. Ibrahim returned to visit Ismail and built under God's guidance the sacred Kaaba (the cube-shaped shrine in Mecca); a footprint in stone outside the Kaaba is said to be that of Ibrahim. Later God called on Ibrahim to sacrifice his son Ismail, and Ibrahim was willing to obey, but at the last moment Ismail was spared by God, who provided a ram for sacrifice in his place. (In the Jewish and Christian traditions, God commanded Abraham to sacrifice Isaac, not Ismail.)

Ilyas
Cross-cultural figure

Ilyas is the Arabic name for the prophet known as Elijah in the Judeo-Christian tradition. Ilyas is celebrated by Muslims as a prophet of Islam and mentioned in the Koran alongside Isa (Jesus) and Yahya (John the Baptist) as being in the ranks of the righteous. In the Islamic narrative (as in the biblical account), Ilyas was called to warn people against neglecting God and worshipping the Middle Eastern fertility deity Baal. He was ignored, and he prophesied drought and famine as God's judgment. For three years the people suffered until at last Ilyas prayed to God to be merciful. God sent rain, and the people abandoned Baal and returned to monotheism. Ilyas disappeared into a whirlwind sent by God.

Iman (1955–)
Somali model

Somali Muslim model, businesswoman, and occasional actress, Iman was born Iman Mohamed Abdulmajid in the Somalian capital Mogadishu, the daughter of a former Somali ambassador to Saudi Arabia. She was educated in Egypt and Kenya, studying political science at the University of Nairobi, before settling in the United States after becoming a model in 1976. She

appeared as an actress in TV shows and in movies. She married American basketball player Spencer Haywood in 1977 and, after that marriage ended in divorce in 1987, wed British rock star David Bowie in 1992. She was the first black model to win advertising contracts from major names including Calvin Klein and Yves Saint Laurent. She launched IMAN Cosmetics and Skincare in 1994, IMAN Make Up in 2000, and IMAN Global Chic in 2007. She is a spokeswoman for the charity Keep a Child Alive, which works to provide drugs for African children and families affected by AIDS.

Iqbal, Muhammad (1877–1938)
Indian Muslim poet and politician

Iqbal was an Indian-born Muslim poet, philosopher, and politician who was an important figure in the Pakistani indepence movement. Each year, Pakistanis celebrate Iqbal Day on the anniversary of his birth on November 9.

Iqbal was born in Sialkot, India, now in Pakistan. He trained as a lawyer in Europe and set up his own law practice on his return to India. He was already writing poetry in Arabic, Urdu, and Persian when he lived in London. Back home, he started to write scholarly articles on a number of subjects, including politics. However, his reputation was made by his poetry. He was made a Knight of the British Empire for his Persian poetry collection *Asrar-e Khudi* (The secrets of the self).

Iqbal wrote in a classical style that was intended to be read out loud. His poetry was very popular, and millions of illiterate people learned his poems by heart. Iqbal's themes concentrated on the early glories of Islam and his dissatisfaction with what he perceived as the contemporary need for unity and reform. He died in 1938 after many years of ill health and did not live to see Pakistan become an independent state in 1947.

Isa
Cross-cultural figure

Isa is the Arabic name for Jesus. Seen by Christians as the Son of God, Isa is regarded by Muslims as a righteous man sent by God as a prophet, a source of blessings to all, and a profound teacher who had the power to perform miracles. Like all the prophets before Muhammad, Isa is considered to be a Muslim in that he taught that people should submit to God's will. His teachings were revealed to him in the form of the *Injil* (New Testament). He performed miracles including curing a leper, raising the dead, putting the breath of life in clay birds, and speaking while still in his infancy. According to Islam, Isa was not crucified and did not rise from the dead (as in the Christian tradition) but was raised alive into heaven by God. In Islamic tradition Isa will return at a time near the end of the world, when the Mahdi, or prophesied Islamic redeemer, is fighting against the Dajjal (false Messiah); it is believed that Isa will support the Mahdi in his battle. According to this tradition, Isa will rule after the death of the Mahdi, at a time of universal peace in which Islam will be accepted by all.

Ishaq
Cross-cultural figure

Ishaq was the second son of the Prophet Ibrahim (Abraham) and is known as Isaac in the Judeo-Christian tradition. He was the younger brother of Ismail, forefather of the Arabs. Muslims view Ishaq as a prophet of Islam, a righteous and generous man who was God's chosen servant. Ishaq's birth was miraculous, for he was born when his father was age 100 and Ibrahim's wife Sarah was age 90 and had long before given up hope of having a child; an angel visited the couple to announce that it was God's will that the child be born. (Ismail had been born earlier to Ibrahim and his second wife Hagar, who was originally Sarah's servant.) Ishaq married Rebecca and had twin sons, al-Eis and Yaqub (Esau and Jacob in the Jewish and Christian traditions). He lived to age 180 and was buried at Hebron (now a city in the West Bank) alongside Ibrahim and Sarah.

Islam, Yusuf (1948–)
British musician

One of the most prominent Western converts to Islam, Yusuf Islam, since his conversion in 1977, has worked to promote a better understanding of Islam and Muslims in the West.

Born Steven Demetre Georgiou and brought up in Central London, Islam had a highly successful musical career as a singer-songwriter under the name Cat Stevens. His 1975 *Greatest Hits* album sold more than four million copies in the United States.

At the height of his fame, he converted to Islam in 1977. His conversion was the end of a long spiritual quest to find meaning in his life, and he described it as a gradual move. Following his conversion he abandoned his musical career and spent a number of years away from the public eye, during which time he worked with the Muslim community in London and concentrated on studying the Koran. In the 1980s he began to work as an advocate of several Muslim charities. During the 1980s and 1990s he performed occasionally at charity concerts before returning to music in 2005. A long-time opponent of Islamic extremism, Islam has fought all allegations that he or his charitable foundations are in any way linked to terrorist groups.

Ismail
Cross-cultural figure

Ismail was the first-born son of the prophet Ibrahim (Abraham), by his second wife Hagar, and is regarded by Muslims as the father of all Arab peoples. Under God's instructions, Ibrahim took Hagar and Ismail to the Hejaz region of Arabia while Ismail was still a tiny baby and left them there. In a place near the spot where the sacred Kaaba stands today, God created a miraculous spring to provide water for the mother and child. When Ismail was a boy of age eight or nine, God told Ibrahim that He required his son's life as a sacrifice; Ibrahim tied Ismail's arms and legs, placed him on the ground and prepared to cut his throat, but at that moment the angel Jibril (Gabriel) appeared and declared that God had instructed Ibrahim to kill Ismail as a test, and that he was pleased with the Prophet's obedience and was willing to spare the child. Then a ram appeared and Ibrahim slaughtered it in Ismail's place before the angel announced that Ibrahim would have a second son, Ishaq (called Isaac in the Judeo-Christian narrative). (In the Jewish and Christian version, Abraham was instructed to sacrifice Isaac rather than Ismail.) In one tradition, Ismail later helped Ibrahim construct the sacred Kaaba at the settlement that became the holy city of Mecca. Ismail had many sons and was a direct ancestor of the Prophet Muhammad.

Jafar ibn Muhammad al-Sadiq (702–765)
Shiite saint

Regarded by the Twelver and Ismaili Shiite Muslims to be the sixth imam, their spiritual leader and successor to the Prophet Muhammad, Jafar is the last imam recognized by both Ismaili and Twelver sects. The dispute over who should succeed him led to the split of the Ismailis from the Twelver Shia branch of Islam.

Jafar was the son of Muhammad al-Baqir, the fifth imam, and great-grandson of the fourth caliph, Ali, who is considered to have been the first imam and founder of Shia Islam. He developed the belief that the imam was never wrong and was all-wise and that loyalty was owed to him as the sign of being a good Muslim. Jafar had many talents. He was an astronomer, alchemist, imam, scholar, Islamic theologian, writer, philosopher, physician, physicist, and scientist.

Jahiz, Abu Uthman Amr ibn Bahr ibn Mahbub al- (c. 776–868 or 869)
Muslim theologian and scientist

The son of slaves from Ethiopia, al-Jahiz was born to a poor family in Basra in what is now Iraq, where he attended lectures at the main mosque and read widely—everything from Arabic translations of Greek philosopher Aristotle (384–322 BCE) to detailed studies of the Koran. In about 816, al-Jahiz moved from Basra to Baghdad to study at the newly founded "House of Wisdom,"—a vast library built under the patronage of the Abbasid Caliphate. Al-Jahiz's vast body of writing covered a range of material, from poetry and psychology to dicussions of philosophy. He is perhaps best known for *Kitab al-Hayawan* (Book of animals). The seven-volume encyclopedia discussed ideas such as food chains and the effects of the environment on the characteristics of animals. Some of his ideas bear many similarities to later theories of natural selection formulated by British naturalist Charles Darwin (1809–1882).

Jiang, Haji Noor Deen Mi Guang (1963–)
Chinese Muslim calligrapher

Haji Noor Deen Mi Guang Jiang is a Chinese Muslim master of Arabic calligraphy, whose work combines Chinese and Arabic traditions in calligraphy. He was born in Shandong province, eastern China. He undertakes research into Islamic culture at the Henan Academy of Sciences and lectures in Arabic calligraphy at the Islamic College in Zhengzhou, Henan province. He has given many lectures and workshops in the United States and in western Europe, notably at Harvard University, University of California-Berkeley, MIT (Massachusetts Institute of Technology), and the University of Cambridge, England. In 1997, he was awarded the Egyptian Certificate of Arabic Calligraphy and was admitted to the Association of Egyptian Calligraphy—the first Chinese Muslim to achieve this feat. He has exhibited his work in many prestigious galleries and museums, including the "Word into Art" exhibit at the British Museum, London, in 2006.

Jinnah, Muhammad Ali (1876–1948)
Pakistani politician, governor-general of Pakistan (1948–1949)

In Pakistan, Mohammed Ali Jinnah is officially known as the Father of the Nation. He was the founder of Pakistan, serving as leader of the Muslim League and the first governor-general of the newly created Pakistan.

He trained as a lawyer in England and while studying in London he studied the British political system. He also took an active interest in Indian students living in London. On his return to Bombay (now Mumbai), still British-controlled, he set up a law practice. He joined the Muslim League and worked closely with the Indian National Congress to support Hindu-Muslim unity and achieve home rule.

However, his differences with Mohandas Gandhi and the Indian National Congress led him to work for the splitting of India after the end of British rule and the

creation of a separate Muslim state. After the British granted independence to India in 1947, Pakistan was carved out of India and created as an independent country the same year, amid bloodshed. Jinnah became its first head of state. He died in 1948.

Kabbani, Hisham (1945–)
Sufi scholar

Shaykh Muhammad Hisham Al-Kabbani is a Sufi and world-renowned Muslim scholar, author, and lecturer.

He was born in Lebanon but moved to the United States in 1991 on the orders of Sufi scholar and religious leader, Nazim al-Qubrusi. He opened a number of centers specializing in spreading Sufism (the mystical branch of Islam). He is chairman of the Islamic Supreme Council of America and the Sufi Muslim Council.

Kabbani received his Islamic Law Degree in Syria, a bachelor's degree in Chemistry from the American University of Beirut, and he studied medicine in Belgium.

As chairman of the Islamic Supreme Council of America (ISCA), a nonprofit religious organization based in Washington, D.C., aimed at increasing religious tolerance and understanding, he has for many years publicly condemned all acts of terrorism and the use of Islam to promote terrorist agendas.

Afghan president Hamid Karzai (left) meeting with Pakistani president Asif Ali Zardari soon after Zardari's inauguration in 2009. On the wall behind the two men are portraits of Ali Jinnah, founder of Pakistan, and assassinated Pakistani politician Benazir Bhutto, Zardari's former wife.

In this role of spreading the message of Islam and peace, Kabbani has met with many heads of state like President George W. Bush and President Bill Clinton.

Kahf, Mohja (1967–)
U.S. poet

Mohja Kahf is a Muslim American poet and journalist whose work focuses on the topics of cultural identity and the challanges that come with being a Muslim in the United States today.

Kahf was born in Damascus, Syria, to Egyptian parents and moved to the United States in 1971 before she turned four. Her father went into exile because he was a member of the banned Muslim Brotherhood. Kahf was raised in a devout Muslim household, but many of her views on Islam have angered devout Muslims. Kahf's debut collection of poetry, *Emails from Scheherazad* (2003), was a finalist for the Paterson Poetry Prize. She published her first novel, *The Girl in the Tangerine Scarf*, in 2006. It is set in 1970s Indiana, where she grew up, and examines the lives of a group of young Muslim women. She has also written a scholarly examination of Muslim women (*Western Representations of the Muslim Woman*, 1999).

She is associate professor of comparative literature at the University of Arkansas and a member of the Muslim Women's League of the United States.

Karamanli, Ahmed (1686–1745)
Ruler of Tripoli (1711–1745)

Ahmed Karamanli founded the dynasty of the same name (1711–1835), which ruled the region of Tripoli or Tripolitania (present-day Libya). He ruled from 1711 to 1745, having expelled the ruling Ottoman governor. His title was the first Karamanli pasha of Tripolitania.

By the start of the 18th century, the Ottomans were starting to lose control of North Africa. Karamanli seized his opportunity, murdered the Ottoman governor, and took control of the region. He persuaded the Ottomans to accept him as governor, then gave himself the title of pasha and made his position hereditary. In doing so, he largely liberated Tripoli, which was able to function as an independent kingdom and only had to pay a small tribute to the Ottomans.

Karamanli was an extremely able ruler who improved the fortunes of Tripoli, particularly its economy. He forced all foreign ships passing close to his waters to pay a protection fee to him.

Karzai, Hamid (1957–)
President of Afghanistan (2004–)

Hamid Karzai is the first president of the Islamic Republic of Afghanistan to take office since the overthrow of the Taliban.

Karzai comes from the Popalzai tribe of the Pashtun people in the Kandahar region of Afghanistan. His father was the hereditary chief of the Popalzai, and after his father's murder he became the next chief.

He was studying in Simla, India, when the Soviet Union invaded Afghanistan in the early 1980s. He worked for the mujahideen resistance during the Soviet invasion, providing financial and military support and working as a CIA contact when the United States funded the mujahideen. After the Soviets' withdrawal, the Taliban took control of the country.

Originally a supporter of the Taliban, by the late 1990s Karzai had begun to organize opposition against them. He became a prominent figure in Afghan politics after the removal of the Taliban regime in late 2001. In December 2001, he became the chairman of the transitional administration; then served as interim president from 2002 until he won the 2004 presidential election. He emerged victor in the disputed presidential election of 2009 and has survived several assassination attempts.

Khadija (555–619)
Wife of the Prophet
The first wife of the Prophet Muhammad, Khadija supported the Prophet when he received his revelations and developed the new faith of Islam. She is generally believed to have been the first person to accept Islam. Khadija inherited wealth from her father and was herself a very successful merchant. She hired Muhammad to be her agent. When Muhammad and Khadija married, she was about 40 years old and he was about 25. She had twice been married, but both her husbands had died. Khadijah bore Muhammad at least six children. According to tradition she was very kind and always helped the poor. It was normal for husbands to have several wives, but while Khadija was alive Muhammad did not marry any other woman. Muhammad was deeply distressed when she died in 619, in the same year that his guardian and uncle Abu Talib died. Because the Prophet lost two people he loved so deeply, 619 is traditionally called "the Year of Sorrow" by Muslims.

Khalid of Saudi Arabia (1913–1982)
King of Saudi Arabia (1975–1982)
Khalid ibn Abdul Aziz al-Saud was king of Saudi Arabia between 1975 and 1982. Khalid was chosen as crown prince after his half brother Faysal succeeded their oldest half brother, Saud, as king. He became king after the assassination of Faysal by his mentally ill nephew.

Unlike many of his brothers, he did not study abroad. Instead, he took an interest in the Bedouin and desert projects, making him very popular among the

Ayatollah Ali Khameni, the religious and political ruler of Iran. He was president of Iran for eight years before assuming the position of grand ayatollah.

Bedouin people. During his reign the Saudi government funded major projects to upgrade the country's infrastructure, health care, and military. Because of poor health, however, his public role was limited even before he became king. He left most of his duties to his half brother Prince Fahd, who became king after Khalid's death.

Khalifa bin Zayed al-Nahyan (1948–)
President of the United Arab Emirates (2004–)
Sheikh Khalifa is the current president of the United Arab Emirates (UAE) and also emir of Abu Dhabi since November 2004, inheriting both positions from his late father.

After the establishment of the UAE in 1971, Sheikh Khalifa became deputy prime minister of the federal state under his father, who was president. In May 1976 he became deputy commander of the UAE armed forces. The region's vast oil reserves make him one of the world's wealthiest men. He is head of the Supreme Petroleum Council, which regulates the oil and natural gas industry in the UAE.

Sheikh Khalifa is known for his interest in sports, particularly in horse and camel racing. He is generally regarded as a pro-Western modernizer.

Khameni, Ali (1939–)
Ayatollah of Iran (1989–)

Ali Khameni is an Iranian Shiite Muslim cleric who served as president of Iran between 1981 and 1989 and as its supreme leader, or ayatollah, since 1989.

He was born in Mashhad, Iran, to a family of Islamic clerics. As a young man he studied under Ayatollah Ruhollah Khomeini, later the leader of the 1979 Iranian Revolution. Khameni became a member of Khomeini's movement against the shah, Reza Pahlavi, and was an important figure in Iran while Khomeini was still in exile.

Khameni was a strong supporter of the Islamic Republican Party (IRP) and believed in religious rule. He was elected state president in 1981 and reelected in 1985. On Khomeini's death in 1989, he resigned and became the country's supreme spiritual leader and was given the highest religious title of ayatollah.

Khameini enjoyed a good working relationship with President Hashemi Rafsanjani in the early 1990s, but his relations were strained with the reformist president Mohammad Khatami, who served from 1997 to 2005. In the 2005 presidential elections, the hard-line Mahmoud Ahmadinejad received vital support from Khameini, and again in the disputed presidential election of June 2009, Khameini backed Ahmadinejad's contested victory.

Khan, Ahmad Raza (1856–1921)
Sunni scholar

Ahmad Raza Khan was the Indian founder of the Sufi-influenced Sunni Muslim Barelvi movement. Born in what is now Bangladesh, Ahmad Raza Khan became an internationally renowned mufti (authority on Islamic law) and wrote an encyclopedic 12-volume book of fatwas (legal opinion on Islamic law) called the *Fatawa Ridawiyya*. He also made a translation of the Koran into Urdu, published in 1912. He founded the Barelvi movement in 1904 when he was troubled by what he saw as an intellectual and moral decline among Indian Muslims; he intended the movement to promote conservative Islam, mainly in the Hanafi school of religious law. Today the Barelvi movement has more then 200 million followers, principally in Bangladesh, India, Pakistan, South Africa, and the United Kingdom.

Khan, Imran (1952–)
Pakistani athlete and politician

Imran Khan is a retired Pakistani cricket player who played between 1971 and 1992 and served intermittently as captain between 1982 and 1992. Khan is considered to have been one of the best all-around players in international cricket. In 1982, Khan took over as captain of Pakistan's national team from Javed Miandad. In 48 international fixtures as captain, Khan only lost eight matches. The highlight of Khan's cricket career came in 1992 when he guided his team to victory in the World Cup. Following his retirement from cricket in 1992, Imran Khan pursued a career in politics. In 1996 he founded his own party, Pakistan Tehreek-e-Insaf, and was elected as a member of parliament in 2002. Many people have criticized Khan's political career, however, claiming he is cashing in on his celebrity status.

Khan, Sayyed Ahmed (1817–1898)
Indian politician

Sayyed Ahmed Khan was an Indian educator and politician who worked to modernize Islamic education in India.

He was born into a family of Mughal nobility and was educated at home as was the custom. He was well versed in the Koran and studied Arabic and Persian. Following the death of his father in 1838, the family found itself without money, and Ahmed Khan had to find work. He joined the British East India Company before working in the legal profession and worked his way up to become a judge.

Loyal to the British rulers of India, he believed that Muslims in India were threatened by the inflexibility of Islamic orthodoxy and their reluctance to work with the British rulers of India. He wanted Muslims to become more moderate and less rigid. To accomplish this, he founded the Aligarh College in 1875. He spent the rest of his life working with his Aligarh education movement, which sought to modernize education for Muslims.

Khan, Shahrukh (1965–)
Indian actor

An internationally known Indian actor in Bollywood movies, as well as a television host and movie producer, Shahrukh Khan was born into a Muslim family in New Delhi, India, in 1965. After completing his university education, he decided to defer his postgraduate study and pursue a career in acting.

His first movie was *Deewana* (1992), and later hits include *Dilwale Dulhaniya le Jayenge* (The lover will take the bride, 1995), the New York-set *Kabhi Alvida Naa Kehna* (Never say good bye, 2006) and *Kabhi Khushi Kabhie Gham* (Sometimes happy, sometimes sad, 2001), the last becoming one of the highest grossing Indian movies of all time. In addition to his on-screen success, Khan runs several production companies.

Khan married Hindu actress Gauri Chibber in 1991. The couple have two children who are encouraged to

follow both Hinduism and Islam. Khan stated that the key thing was for his children to "know the value of God." He holds the Padma Shri, a civilian award given by the Indian government, and received the Ordre des Arts et des Lettres (Order of Arts and Literature) from the French government. He is popularly known as "King Khan."

Khatami, Mohammad (1943–)
President of Iran (1997–2005)

Mohammad Khatami was the moderate, reformist president of Iran between 1997 and 2005.

Khatami was the son of a well-known religious teacher and studied at a madrassa in Qom before becoming a teacher. Unusually for a religious cleric and a direct descendant of the Prophet Muhammad (signified by the black turban he wears), he also studied at the secular universities of Tehran and Isfahan.

During the 1960s and 1970s he was known for his opposition to the shah, and during the 1980s he held various positions in the new Islamic revolutionary government under Ayatollah Khomeini.

In 1997 he was the most moderate of the four presidential candidates and was elected with a massive majority. He was reelected in 2001, again with a large majority. His terms as president were notable for the tensions between him and more conservative elements within Iran. He favored closer relations with the United States, which other religious leaders opposed. He was barred by the constitution from running for a third term. In 2009 he supported the presidential campaign of the reformist Mir-Hossein Mousavi.

Khidr, al-
Sufi saint

Al-Khidr is a wise man who is the subject of a narrative in the Koran and of various Hadith and is viewed as a saint by Sufis. His name is a contraction of the Arabic al-Kahadir (Green one). In the Koran, Musa (Moses) and his servant encounter a man of God (later identified as al-Khidr) who performs a series of troubling actions. The man of God damages a boat, kills a young man, and then, after he has been turned away from a village, repairs a wall there. He explains to Musa why these acts are in fact merciful. Sufis associate al-Khidr with the founding of several orders. Many Sufis believe that al-Khidr remains alive. In some traditions al-Khidr is green because he dove into the well of life; in others he is linked with plants.

Khomeini, Ruhollah Musavi (1902–1989)
Ayatollah of Iran (1979–1989)

Ruhollah Musavi Khomeini, better known as Ayatollah Khomeini, led the Iranian Revolution of 1979 that deposed the shah of Iran. He then turned Iran into an Islamic Republic and ruled the country as its charismatic leader until his death in 1989.

A descendant of the Prophet Muhammad, he was the son and grandson of mullahs and became a Shiite religious scholar. During the 1950s, Khomeini rose to the rank of ayatollah, and by the early 1960s he had received the title of grand ayatollah, making him one of Iran's supreme religious leaders.

His opposition to what he perceived as the decadence of the shah's rule and the influence of the West led to his being exiled from Iran for the next 15 years, first to Iraq and then to France. He was uncomprising in his call for Islamic purity and the creation of an Islamic state. He continued to campaign against the shah while in exile. As the Iranian people grew increasingly disillusioned with the shah, Khomeini's popularity grew.

Civil unrest in late 1978 forced the shah to flee from Iran on January 16, 1979. Khomeini arrived in Tehran on February 1, 1979, and was acclaimed as the religious leader of Iran's revolution. He appointed a government and killed many of the shah's supporters. In December of that year Khomeini was named Iran's political and religious supreme leader for life.

Iran became an Islamic state with religious leaders running the country and Khomeini having the final say. Any opposition was put down; Iranian women were required to wear the veil; Western music and alcohol were banned; and Islamic law brought in. Khomeini rejected the Shah's pro-Western position, and Iran became unfriendly to many non-Islamic states. In 1979 the United States embassy staff in Tehran were held hostage for over a year with his approval.

During the Iran-Iraq war (1980–1988) Khomeini refused the peace treaty offered by the Iraqis in 1982, instead ordering a counterinvasion of Iraq in an attempt to depose Saddam Hussein and make Iraq part of the Islamic Republic. This invasion soon settled into a stalemate that lasted for six years and cost millions of military and civilian lives.

Although Iran's economy suffered greatly and many people fled to exile, he remained supreme political and religious leader until his death in 1989. His funeral was one of the largest ever held, and his gold-domed tomb in Tehran remains a place of pilgrimage for many Shiite Muslims.

Khusro, Amir (1253–1325)
Indian poet

A classical Persian poet, Amir Khusro Dehlari was the royal poet for more than seven rulers of the Delhi

Sultanate. Famous throughout the Indian subcontinent, he was also an accomplished musician.

He was born Ab'ul Hassan Yamin al-Din in Patiyali, Uttar Pradesh, India, to a Turkish father and Indian mother. He adopted the pen name Amir Khusro. His grandfather worked at the royal court, so Khusro was exposed to court life from an early age. Khusro was a disciple of the Sufi saint Hazrat Nizamudding Auliya, and he is regarded as the father of the *qawwali*, the devotional music of the Indian Sufis.

Khusro wrote his poetry mainly in Persian, but he also wrote in Hindavi (a combination of Bhojpuri and Persian), the forerunner of the Hindi and Urdu languages. He also introduced Persian and Arabian elements to Hindustani classical music, and he is also credited with the invention of the tabla, the traditional Indian drum. Some people even credit him with inventing the sitar, India's popular lute. Many of his poems are still sung today.

Khwaja (1141–1230)
Sufi teacher
Khwaja, also known as Muin-ad-din Chishti, was a Persian Sufi teacher-saint who founded the Chishtiyah Sufi order in India and Pakistan. Born in Sijistan (now Sistan in eastern Iran), he was orphaned at age 15. After a devout youth, he set out on pilgrimages to Islamic religious centers in Samarkand and Bukhara (now both in Uzbekistan), then to Mecca and Medina. By tradition the Prophet Muhammad visited Khwaja in a dream and encouraged him to travel to India. He settled at Ajmer, northern India, and established the Chishtiyah order. Members were expected to renounce all worldly wealth and possessions, to accept no gifts from rulers, to be generous and tolerant, and to be pacifists. They aimed for unity with God and practiced this by reciting the names of God. Khwaja and his followers claim descent from the Prophet Muhammad through the Shiite imam Jafar al-Sadiq (702–765).

Khwarizmi, Abu Abdallah Muhammad ibn Musa al- (c. 780–c. 850)
Arab mathematician
Al-Khwarizmi is widely considered one of the greatest Muslim scientists. His work influenced scientists in Europe and the Islamic world for centuries. There are few accurate accounts of al-Khwarizmi's life, although it is known that he traveled to Baghdad soon after the Muslim conquest of Persia to study at the new "House of Wisdom," built by the Abbasid caliph Abu Jafar Abdullah al-Mamum (786–833).

Al-Khwarizmi's most important contribution was in mathematics. In around 830 he wrote *Al-Kitab al-mukhtasar fi hisab al-jabr wa-al-muqabala* (The compendious book on calculation by completion and balancing), which laid the foundations for modern algebra. Al-Khwarizmi also introduced the Arabic number system and decimal notation, both developed from Indian mathematics.

Al-Khwarizmi was also an astronomer, publishing a set of astronomical tables and calculations around 820. He also improved on the design of the sundial, which was used at mosques to determine the time for prayer. He also invented the first quadrants, using them for astronomical calculations and to determine the time. In two other books, al-Khwarizmi wrote about the design and construction of astrolabes. He also translated and revised the *Geography* written by the 2nd-century CE scholar Ptolemy.

Kindi, Yaqub ibn Ishaq as-Sabah al- (died c. 870)
Arab philosopher
Popularly known as the "philosopher of the Arabs," al-Kindi lived in Baghdad and studied at the House of Wisdom established by the Abbasid caliph Abu Jafar Abdullah al-Mamum (786–833). Like many of his contemporaries, including al-Khwarizmi (c. 780–c. 850), al-Kindi was skilled in astronomy, mathematics, and geography, as well as medicine and music. Al-Kindi was one of the first Arab philosophers to study the works of the ancient Greek philosophers, including Aristotle (384–322 BCE) and Plato (c. 428–348 BCE). He also attempted to unite the ideas of Aristotle and Plato with his own philosophy. Al-Kindi was a prolific author, publishing more than 270 treatises by the time of his death around 870.

Lahauri, Ustad Ahmad (1580–1649)
Indian architect
Little is known about much of the life of Ustad Ahmad Lahauri, the man who is thought to have been the chief architect of the Taj Mahal in Agra, India. Also known as Ahmad Mimar (Ahmad the Architect), Lahauri was the principal architect to the Mughal emperor Shah Jahan (ruled 1628–1658). When Shah Jahan's wife, Mumtaz, died giving birth to their 14th child, the emperor decided to build the most beautiful mausoleum to honor her memory.

The Taj Mahal sits on the banks of the Yumana River in Agra. Working alongside the emperor, Lahauri designed the mausoleum in white marble. A large dome, under which lie the sarcophagi of Mumtaz and Shah Jahan, sits in the center of the mausoleum. It is believed that Lahauri designed other buildings for Shah Jahan, including the magnificent Red Fort in Delhi.

Leo Africanus (c. 1485–c. 1554)
Spanish-Arab scholar

Known by the Latin name Leo Africanus, the Arab writer Hasan al-Fasi is best known for his book *Descrittione dell'Africa* (Description of Africa), about the geography of the continent. Leo Africanus was born in Granada, Spain, around 1494, but his family moved to Morocco when Muslim Granada fell to Spanish forces. After studying at the university in Fez, he traveled around North Africa and Arabia. In 1518, Leo Africanus—then a diplomat representing Sultan Muhammad II of Fez—was captured by Spanish pirates and was taken to Rome, where he was released and presented to Pope Leo X. In 1520, Leo Africanus converted to Christianity.

First published in 1526, *Descrittione dell'Africa* was so popular that it was reprinted five times and translated into many other languages. Most facts about the life of Leo Africanus are written in his book, and so little is known about him after its publication. One idea is that he left Rome shortly after the city was sacked in 1527

by the mutinous soldiers of Holy Roman Emperor Charles V (1500–1558). Eventually, he converted back to Islam and is thought to have died in Tunis, capital of Tunisia, in 1554.

Lut
Cross-cultural figure

Lut is the Islamic name for the figure known in the Jewish-Christian tradition as Lot, a preacher who tirelessly attempted to divert the sinful people of Sodom and Gomorrah from their wrongdoing. Honored by Muslims as one of the righteous and as a Prophet of Islam, he was a nephew of Ibrahim (Abraham) and a resident of the ancient city of Ur (modern Tell al-Mukayyar in Iraq). He was called by God to preach to the sinful and inhospitable people of Sodom and Gomorrah, but the people ignored his warnings, and God decided to destroy the cities. Before doing so He sent angels to warn Lut; they told him and his family to flee, and warned them not to look back. Lut and his family left the cities, which were destroyed by fire and flying rocks, but as they fled, Lut's wife looked back and was turned to a pillar of stone.

Mahfouz, Naguib (1911–2006)
Egyptian writer

Naguib Mahfouz was the first Arab writer to win the Nobel Prize for Literature (1988). He is best known for his Cairo Trilogy of novels (1956–1957) and for his allegorical novel *The Children of Gebelawi* (1959).

Mahfouz was born in Cairo into a devout Muslim family and had a strict Islamic upbringing. He started to write when he was 17. His first novel was published in 1939, and by 1952 he had published another ten novels while working as a civil servant. His work was informed by political events, including the Egyptian Revolution of 1919.

During the 1950s, he worked on the Cairo Trilogy, which secured his reputation internationally. The three novels follow a family in the parts of Cairo where he grew up from World War I to the 1950s. Retiring from the civil service in 1972, he worked full-time on his writing. In 1978, many Arab countries banned his work after he supported President Anwar Sadat's Camp David peace treaty. In 1994, at the age of 82, he was almost assassinated by Islamic fundamentalists. The damage to his hand limited his writing to a few minutes a day. He died, aged 94, in 2006 and was given a full state funeral.

Egyptian writer Naguib Mahfouz, the first Arab writer to be awarded the Nobel Prize for Literature. He published more than 30 novels in a career that lasted over 70 years.

Mahmud of Ghazni (971–1030)
Sultan of Ghazna (998–1030)

Under Mahmud the small kingdom of Ghazna in what is now Afghanistan and northeastern Iran spread its power deep throughout most of Iran and deep into India, where Mahmud first introduced Islam.

The son of a Turkish slave who had risen to become sultan, he possessed great ambition, matched by administrative ability. When he came to the throne himself, he made the kingdom wealthy through raids on his neighbors, particularly on the Punjab and northeastern India, where Mahmud led some 17 expeditions from 1001 to 1026. After a decisive victory in 1008 near Peshawar, Mahmud gained access to the heart of South Asia.

With the treasure he seized from the wealthy temples, he transformed his capital at Ghazna into a cultural center, with new gardens, mosques, and palaces, that drew renowned scholars and artists from throughout Central Asia and the Muslim world, including the Persian poet Firdawsi and the scholar al-Biruni.

Mahmud allowed his Indian subjects to remain Hindu and used Hindu troops in campaigns against Muslim states in Central Asia, which grew increasingly rebellious in the last years of Mahmud's rule. His chief legacy remains bringing the Muslim world and South Asia closer, easing trade and the exchange of ideas between them, and bringing Islam into the heart of India.

Malcolm X (1925–1965)
U.S. Muslim convert and political activist

Malcolm X was a key figure in the rise of the African American political and religious movement the Nation of Islam (NoI) in the 1950s and early 1960s.

Born Malcolm Little in Omaha, Nebraska, he was raised a Christian as the son of a Baptist minister who had once been a supporter of the black nationalist Marcus Garvey (1887–1940). After Malcolm's father was killed in a road accident and his mother was committed to an insane asylum, he drifted into a life of crime. He committed burglaries in Boston and in Harlem in New York City. In 1946 he was caught and sent to prison. While incarcerated he became interested in Islam and later joined the Nation of Islam. Like other NoI members he dropped his surname on the grounds that it had been given to his ancestors by a slave owner, and he took the name Malcolm X.

After leaving jail, he became minister of the NoI temple in Boston, then of the temple in Harlem, and was an articulate and charismatic public speaker for the movement, giving speeches at Oxford University, England, and Harvard University. However, in 1963–1964 he disagreed with NoI leader Elijah Muhammad and left the movement. He made the

hajj pilgrimage to Mecca, converted to Sunni Islam, and changed his name to el-Hajj Malik el-Shabazz. He argued that racial problems in the United States could be solved by Sunni Islam. He was assassinated while giving a speech in Harlem on February 21, 1965. Three NoI members were later convicted of his murder.

Maliki, Nouri al- (1950–)
Iraqi politician, prime minister (2006–)

Shiite activist and politician Nouri al-Maliki rose from relative obscurity in 2006 to become Iraq's first elected prime minister.

Al-Maliki grew up in the town of Hilla, close to the Shiite holy city of Karbala. After the Ba'ath party seized power in 1968, al-Maliki joined the Shiite opposition group Dawa, which organized protests and militant action against the Ba'ath party regime. He was driven into exile soon after Saddam Hussein became president in 1979.

Following the U.S.-led invasion of Iraq in 2003, al-Maliki returned to Iraqi politics. He was an advisor to the interim prime minister, Ibrahim Jafaari, and helped draft the Iraqi constitution. In 2005 he was chosen as Dawa's candidate for prime minister, primarily because he was a relatively uncontroversial figure. Al-Maliki proved popular with Iraqi voters, and his party was able to form a governing coalition with him as prime minister. Since assuming power in May 2006, al-Maliki has worked to reduce the influence of sectarian rivalries on politics and has overseen the handover of power by coalition forces.

Mansur, al- (709/714–775)
Abbasid caliph (754–775)

Although al-Mansur was the second Abbasid caliph—after his brother Abu al-Abbas as-Saffah—he is often credited with truly establishing the dynasty.

The Abbasids had moved to the city of Kufa in Iraq in the 8th century, with the intention of establishing enough political and military power to overthrow the Umayyad Caliphate. After the Umayyads were deposed by forces allied with the Abbasids, as-Saffah became caliph. During the brief reign of his brother, al-Mansur led campaigns against Umayyad resistance and set about killing former allies who might represent a challenge to the dynasty.

On becoming caliph on as-Saffah's death, al-Mansur used rebel support to put down threats from within the army and then continued his policy of eliminating rivals by murdering the leaders who had helped him to power. Al-Mansur also suppressed religious revolts by non-Muslim sects and Shiite Muslims, who were dismayed that overthrowing the Umayyads had not brought a descendant of the Prophet's nephew, Ali, to the throne.

Al-Mansur arranged for his own son to be his successor, establishing the dynasty. In 762 he moved the political center of the Muslim world from Damascus—where the Umayyads were based—to the purpose-built capital city of Baghdad. He died on his way to Mecca to perform the hajj in 775.

Manto, Sadaat Hassan (1912–1955)
Pakistani writer

Best known for his many short stories, the Pakistani writer Hassan Manto also worked as a journalist, critic, and scriptwriter. He was one of the most controversial Urdu short story writers of his generation, whose outspoken views and uncompromising language often bought him into conflict with the authorities.

He was born in the Punjab, India, in 1912 and had a difficult childhood, failing school tests and abusing alcohol and drugs. He enjoyed English, however, and read widely. A turning point came when he was 21 and he met a well-known Urdu writer, Abdul Bari Alig. Alig became a mentor to Manto, introducing him to many European novelists and to politics.

Manto became a published author soon after and by the age of 24 had published four stories as well as translations. In 1937 he moved to Bombay, where he became a celebrity after many more of his short stories appeared while he was still in his twenties. Like millions of other Muslims, he was forced to move from Bombay to Lahore in 1948 following the partition of India and Pakistan. In Lahore he started to drink heavily, and his last years were spent in ill health and poverty. He died of cirrhosis of the liver at the age of 42.

Marwaziyya, Karima al- (d. 1070)
Sunni scholar

Karima al-Marwaziyya was a Sunni Muslim teacher based in Mecca, who is celebrated as one of Islam's finest female scholars. She was seen in her time as the preeminent authority on the *Sahih Bukhari* collection of Hadith. Her father was from a village near the city of Merv (now called Mary in Turkmenistan) but had settled in Mecca. From this base she traveled widely with him, visiting Jerusalem, Isfahan, and other places in Iran, studying with great teachers as she traveled. In Mecca she lived and taught near the Holy Sanctuary. One of her pupils was the highly regarded Sunni scholar al-Khatib al-Baghdadi (1002–1071). According to tradition, Karima al-Marwaziyya lived to the age of 100.

Maryam
Cross-cultural figure

Maryam is the Arabic name for Mary, mother of Jesus. In Islam, Jesus is called Isa and is honored as a Prophet, while Maryam is said to be the most righteous woman in history and an honored servant of God. In Islam, as in Christianity, Isa (Jesus) is said to have been the result of a miraculous birth: Maryam (Mary) received by God's decree the gift of a holy son while still a virgin. Nevertheless, Muslims see Isa as a human being and not the son of God; in Islam, one of God's essential qualities is unity (*tawhid*) and so God can not be said to have a son. Muslims say that the birth of Isa without a human father is like that of Adam, the first man, who was made by God from clay but was not divine. In the Christian tradition, Jesus was born in a manger at an inn and was visited by three Wise Men from the East; in Islam, Maryam is said to have given birth alone beneath a dead palm tree. When she was alone, weak and desperate beneath the tree, God instructed her to shake the trunk, and despite the fact that the tree was dead, dates fell to nourish her.

Mawardi, al- (972–1058)
Sunni scholar

Al-Mawardi, also known as Alboacen, was an Arab expert in Islamic law who, in his masterpiece *The Ordinances of Government*, made a key statement of Sunni Muslim theory on the authority of the caliph, the duties of officers, and the administration of government. A follower of the Shafi'i school of *fiqh* (religious law), he was a judge in Iraq and served as an ambassador of the Abbasid caliphs to other Muslim rulers. He lived at a time when the emirs of the Shiite Buyyid dynasty were in effective control of the caliphate and had forced the caliph to take a subsidiary role. Al-Mawardi was often an intermediary between the two sides. He was commissioned by the caliph to write *The Ordinances of Government* at a time when the Buyyids' power was weakening.

Mawdudi, Sayyid Abu'l-A'la (1903–1979)
Pakistani philosopher and writer

Sayyid Abu'l-A'la Mawdudi was a Pakistani Muslim philosopher, theologian, and writer, and founder of the Islamic revivalist party Jamaat-e-Islami. Born in Aurangabad, at that time part of the princely state of Hyderabad (now the Indian state of Maharashtra), he was descended from Khwaja (also known as Muin-ad-din Chishti), founder of the Chishtiyah Sufi order.

Mawdudi was a newspaper editor before he founded the Jamaat-e-Islami (JI) in 1941. JI was a political movement that promoted Islamic values. Following the partition of India in 1947, the JI split into various pro-Islamic groups; Mawdudi was president of JI in Pakistan from 1947 to 1972. He worked to make

Pakistan an Islamic state governed by Sharia law and, over a period of 30 years, translated the Koran into Urdu. Mawdudi was several times imprisoned for writing pamphlets and was sentenced to death in 1953. His sentence was subsequently commuted to life imprisonment and later annulled. In the 1970s he developed serious health problems and traveled to the United States for treatment. He died in Buffalo, New York, aged 76.

Mehmed II (1432–1481)
Ottoman sultan (1444–1446; 1451–1481)

Mehmed II's achievements earned him the title Mehmed Fatih, Turkish for "Mehmed the conqueror"; he was an outstanding military commander who expanded the Ottoman heartland into southeastern Europe.

The son of Murad II and a slave girl, Mehmed first came to the throne at age 12, when his father abdicated. However, a military crusade against the empire led by Hungary, the Byzantine Empire, and Venice, coupled with palace intrigue against the young prince, led to Murad's recall from retirement to repel the invaders and eventually his reaccession to the throne. On Murad's death in 1451, Mehmed II came to the throne in Edirne for a second time. There he severely repressed the janissaries—a military force gathered from the Christian countries in the Ottoman Empire—whom he perceived as opposed to him.

Mehmed spent many years planning the capture of the Byzantine capital, Constantinople. After making peace treaties to keep Venice and Hungary neutral, rebuilding fortifications, enlarging his navy, and commissioning the largest artillery guns anywhere in the world at the time, Mehmed commanded the assault on the city in 1453. After Mehmed captured the city—now known as Istanbul—he guaranteed the rights of foreign traders and resettled loyal Christians and Muslims from throughout the empire there. He converted the church of Hagia Sophia into a mosque, but also reestablished the patriarchate of the Orthodox Greek church in the city.

Mehmed's attempts to make Istanbul the heart of an international trading empire were so successful that by 1478 it was the largest city in Europe. Seeing himself as both the heir of the Eastern Roman Empire and the champion of Islam, Mehmed sought to extend the empire further, securing dominance of the Balkans and Anatolia. He launched numerous raids, including on the Italian peninsula, which he may have been planning to invade at the time of his death in 1481. After his death, critics of Mehmed's reforms placed on the throne his son Bayezid, whom the emperor had previously disowned.

Mir, Mir Taqi (1723–1810)
Indian poet

Muhammad Taqi—known by his pen name, Mir Taqi Mir—was one of the leading Urdu poets of the 18th century. He specialized in the *ghazal* and was a pioneer who helped shape the modern Urdu language.

Mir Taqi Mir was born in Agra, India, in 1723 when the Mughals ruled. After his father's death, when he was eleven, he left Agra for Delhi, where he finished his education and became a courtier-poet. When Delhi came under sustained attack, starting in 1748, he left the city for Lucknow, in the north, and remained there for the rest of his life. He mourned the destruction of Delhi and died in Lucknow in 1810 having lost his entire family.

He was extremely prolific, writing more than 13,585 couplets. His *ghazal*s concentrated on themes of love and compassion. He helped give form to the new Urdu language, mixing everyday expressions with Persian imagery.

Mirza, Iraj (1874–1926)
Iranian poet

Mirza was a famous Iranian poet who used everyday language in his poetry, which was known for its satire and witticisms. His poetry was often politically motivated as he criticized the social conditions of Iran.

Mirza was a direct descendant of the second shah of the Qajar dynasty; his father, Gholam Hossein Mirza, was the official court poet and poet laureate. Mirza was well educated and considered to be one of Iran's finest calligraphers. At the age of 19, he inherited his father's position of court poet but left the Royal Court to join the court of the government of East Azerbaijan. In 1905, he moved to Tehran and worked as a civil servant.

One of his best-known poems is "The Story of Zohreh and Manouchehr," based on the Greek myth of Venus and Adonis. Many of his poems were pederastic (homosexual relations between adults and adolescents). His colloquial style and use of everyday Persian became known as Iraj after him.

Mirza, Shazia (1975–)
British comedian

British Asian stand-up comedian Shazia Mirza has achieved international success, appearing on the U.S. NBC television show *Last Comic Standing* in 2008, at the World Performing Arts Festival in Pakistan (also 2008) and on British television and radio shows. Raised a Muslim in Birmingham, England, she studied biochemistry at Manchester University and began a career as a physics teacher in London before launching

her career as a comedian. She began her stand-up career appearing in *hijab* and included jokes touching on Islamic fundamentalists and terrorists. She is also a columnist for the British current-affairs magazine *The New Statesman* and won the Columnist of the Year award in 2008. In 2009 she was named one of the 20 most successful Muslim women in the United Kingdom in the first Muslim Women's Power List.

Mohammed, Warith Deen (1933–2008)
U.S. Muslim leader

Warith Deen Mohammed was born Wallace D. Muhammad, the seventh son of Elijah Muhammad, leader of the African American religious group the Nation of Islam (NoI). Even before he was born, his rise to become leader of the movement was prophesized by Wallace D. Fard, founder of NoI.

Warith Deen Mohammed became minister of the NoI temple in Philadelphia in 1958, but his adherence to conventional Sunni Islam often brought him into conflict with the leadership of the NoI. He was expelled from the NoI more than once, but each time he was allowed to rejoin.

On the death of his father in 1975, Mohammed became leader of the movement. As leader he rejected the more unorthodox teachings of the NoI, including belief in the divinity of Wallace D. Fard and the racial superiority of African Americans. He gradually brought the teachings of NoI into line with mainstream Sunni Islam. Starting in the late 1970s, Mohammed started disbanding the organization as a distinct religious denomination and merging it with mainstream Sunni Muslim congregations in the United States. The organization that presently calls itself the Nation of Islam is a splinter group led by Louis Farrakhan that reestablished the Nation of Islam along the lines envisaged by Elijah Muhammad.

In later years Mohammed continued to work with the Muslim community in the United States, attempting to strengthen ties between mosques that were formerly part of the NoI and mosques established by immigrant Muslim communities.

Mohammed Reza Shah Pahlavi (1919–1980)
Shah of Iran (1941–1979)

Mohammed Reza ruled as shah of Iran for 38 years. His reign brought a period of prolonged economic prosperity but also oppressive treatment of his political opponents. He was overthrown by the revolution that established the Islamic Republic of Iran in 1979.

Mohammed Reza Pahlavi was born on October 26, 1919, in Tehran. He went to school in Switzerland but returned to Iran to enroll at the military academy in Tehran, graduating in 1938. In 1941, in the middle of World War II (1939–1945), British and Soviet forces invaded Iran. They forced Reza Shah Pahlavi, his father, from power and put Mohammed Reza Pahlavi in his place, as he was expected to be more cooperative.

In 1951, Iran nationalized the country's profitable oil industry under the direction of Mohammed Mossadegh (1882–1967), who became prime minister a month later. Britain had invested a lot of money in Iran's oil industry, and they decided to depose Mossadegh, with the support of the shah and the United States. The plot initially failed, and Mohammed Reza Pahlavi fled into exile. When Mohammed Reza Shah Pahlavi returned to Iran shortly after, the plot reignited. Despite strong opposition, Mossadegh was eventually defeated. Mohammed Reza Shah Pahlavi returned to power.

In his later years, Mohammed Reza Shah Pahlavi embarked on a program of modernization in Iran, named the White Revolution. He improved education and extended suffrage (the power to vote) to women. He also maintained good relations with foreign powers, especially the United States. It was this special relationship with the United States that ultimately led to the Iranian Revolution of 1979. Mohammed Reza Shah Pahlavi fled Iran on January 16, 1979, and traveled the world. Following surgery in the United States, Mohammed Reza Shah Pahlavi eventually returned to Egypt but died shortly after he arrived.

Mos Def (1973–)
U.S. rapper

Mos Def is the stage name of Dante Terrell Smith, a U.S. rapper and actor who has been nominated for both an Emmy and a Golden Globe award.

Mos Def was born in Brooklyn, New York, and converted to Islam along with his brothers. Their father first introduced them to Islam when Mos Def was thirteen, but he did not convert until he was nineteen, after he met other Muslim-convert rappers.

He worked in a number of bands before launching his solo career. To date he has made four solo albums, the most recent, *The Ecstatic*, in 2009. Today, he is as well known for his TV and movie roles. He is also involved in several social and political causes, motivated by the devastation caused by Hurricane Katrina in New Orleans in 2005.

Moshiri, Farhad (1963–)
Iranian artist

Farhad Moshiri is an internationally renowned Iranian artist. Born in Shiraz, he studied fine art and film making at CalArts (the California Institute of the Arts)

in Valencia, California, graduating in 1984; he returned to Iran to settle in Tehran in 1991. A series of paintings representing ancient Iranian earthenware jars with Persian calligraphy first brought him wide attention, and later works developed the use of Islamic calligraphy and *abdjad* (an ancient Arabic code). He is known also for his combination of traditional Iranian styles and forms with the products of global popular consumer culture in works such as his installation *Golden Love Super Deluxe* (2002). He is a frequent collaborator with fellow-Iranian artist Shirin Aliabadi. Their *Sofreh* (Tablecloth) series examined ways in which watching television soap operas has affected traditional Iranian dining. He has been exhibiting his work since 1987 and has held or contributed to shows in Barcelona, Berlin, Dubai, Geneva, Los Angeles, New York City, and London, as well as Tehran.

Muawiyah (c. 602–680)
Umayyad caliph (661–680)

Both a controversial and widely admired figure in Muslim history, Muawiyah rose from a non-Muslim tribal background to become the first caliph of the Umayyads; his caliphate greatly influenced the development of early Islam, although some historians argue that the increased secularization of his caliphate means that he would be better termed a *malik*—or king—rather than than caliph.

He converted to Islam after the Prophet Muhammad subdued Mecca, serving as a scribe. After the Prophet's death, Muawiyah was sent to Syria by the caliph Umar, where he built up a tribal army that defeated the forces of the Byzantine Empire on land and at sea and sent expeditions into Anatolia (present-day Turkey).

When Muhammad's cousin, Ali ibn Abi Talib, became the fourth caliph on the assassination of Uthman in 656, Muawiyah rejected Ali's caliphate on the grounds that he had not punished Uthman's murderer. Muawiyah cast doubt on the legitimacy of Ali's succession, encouraging some of the caliph's supporters—the Kharijites—to rebel in Iraq, allowing Muawiyah to seize control of Egypt.

When Ali was assassinated in 661, Muawiyah was the most powerful candidate to become the fifth caliph; he bought off the claim of Ali's son Hasan. Muawiyah's caliphate was based in Syria, where Damascus became the new center of the Islamic world, and was supported by his tribal army, whose loyalty he ensured by adopting traditional Arabic political institutions: the *shura*, or tribal council, and the tribal delegations that visited the caliph. However, as the caliphate grew, Muawiyad also adopted government structures that were better suited to the growing territory; these he inherited from the Byzantine Empire. Muawiyah introduced ministries to look after the chancellery and the postal service, to improve communications; many of the senior bureaucrats were Christians who had previously served the Byzantine Empire. He also introduced the practice of hereditary rule by passing the caliphate to his son Yazid, thus again adopting a secular tradition in place of the less stable practice of electing previous caliphs.

Today, some Sunni Muslims still criticize what they say was a deviation from the caliphate as established by the Prophet; Shiites meanwhile condemn his usurpation of the caliphate from Ali. However, Muawiyah's administrative and military reorganization of the Arabs allowed Islam to continue to expand.

Mubarak, Hosni (1928–)
Egyptian president

Muhammad Hosni Said Mubarak is the current president of Egypt, a role that he has occupied since 1981. His presidency has been marked by improved relations with the West and Israel.

Mubarak was born in the Nile Delta and studied at Egypt's military and air academies, including training from the Soviet Union, before president Anwar el-Sadat made him chief of the air force in 1972. In 1975 he was named Sadat's vice president, a position in which Mubarak took a leading role in negotiations in the Middle East, including those that led to the Egypt-Israel peace accords in 1979.

Mubarak became president after the assassination of Sadat in 1981 and reaffirmed peaceful relations with Israel. Egypt received significant aid from the United States during the 1980s. Elected for a second term in 1987, Mubarak continued to mediate peace between Israel and the Palestine Liberation Organization and was a prominent supporter of the U.S.-led coalition that drove Sadam Hussein out of Kuwait. His third term, which began in 1993, was marked by increasing challenges from Islamist terrorists and calls for Egypt's first free elections since 1950. Mubarak was elected again in 1999 and, in 2005, triumphed easily in multiparty elections that were condemned by observers as being flawed and unfair.

Muhammad, Sayyid Ali (1819–1850)
Shiite mystic

Sayyid Ali Muhammad, or the Bab. was a Persian Shiite mystic who founded the Babi religion and became one of the three key figures in the Baha'i faith. In 1844 Muhammad declared himself to be the Bab (Gateway) to the hidden imam (the 12th Shiite imam, who is said to have been in hiding since the 9th century), then gathered a group of 18 disciples whom he dispatched as missionaries in the provinces of Persia. His actions

provoked the opposition of the religious authorities and he was arrested and jailed. He later declared that he was not the gateway to the hidden imam but the hidden imam himself, and then later still announced that he was an embodiment of the divine.

In 1848, while the Bab was in prison, his followers declared that they were breaking from Islam and forming their own faith, Babism. Muhammad was executed by the Iranian government on July 9, 1850. Subsequently, Muhammad's brother Mirza Yahya and an associate, Mirza Hoseyn, took control of the movement, and in 1867 Mirza Hoseyn declared himself the Mahdi or promised Islamic redeemer. Mirza Hoseyn later called himself Baha Ullah and founded the Baha'i faith.

Muhammad VI (1963–)
King of Morocco (1999–)
Born Muhamamd ibn al-Hassan, the crown prince studied law in Morocco and later in France. Although he acquired a reputation as a wealthy socialite in his youth, in the 1990s the prince returned to his home country to assume control of many aspects of government that his father, Hassan II, was too frail to manage. During this time he took command of the armed forces and represented Morocco abroad. He took the throne on his father's death in 1999 and was expected to continue his policies of moderation and cooperation with the West.

Muhammad Ahmad al-Mahdi (1844–1885)
Religious leader
A religious leader and Sufi teacher, Muhammad Ahmad declared himself the Mahdi—an Islamic redeemer who is prophesied to perfect society at the end of the world. Ahmad launched a jihad in 1881 in a bid to drive Egyptians and British forces from Sudan. In 1885 he captured the capital Khartoum and established an independent Islamic state in Sudan. Ahmad died in 1885, but the Islamic state he created lasted until 1899, when the territory was recaptured by the British. Ahmad's father was a boatbuilder; his great-grandfather was a religious scholar. His family claimed descent from the Prophet Muhammad. Ahmad built a mosque in western Sudan and was a well-known religious teacher before he became a military leader.

Muhammad Ali (1769–1849)
Pasha and viceroy of Egypt
Born in Kavala, Greece—then part of the Ottoman Empire—Muhammad Ali, also known as Mehmed Ali, founded the dynasty that ruled Egypt until 1953. After working as a local administrator in Kavala, Muhammad Ali was made commander of a small Ottoman army

sent to recapture Egypt after the withdrawal of the French emperor Napoleon Bonaparte, who had occupied the country for three years.

Through skilled political maneuvering, Muhammad Ali managed to have himself appointed as the Ottoman sultan's viceroy in Egypt, with the rank of pasha. The French occupation had disrupted traditional Egyptian society, offering Muhammad Ali the opportunity to continue to undermine the power of the traditional aristocracy—the Mamluks—to introduce controls on commercial activity, and to repress opposition among the lower classes. Modern historians criticize the pasha for being more interested in reinforcing his own dynasty than in advancing Egyptian society.

His sweeping modernizations included bringing agriculture under state control, introducing new cash crops, reforming the government, and introducing Western-style education. However, his attempts to introduce industrialization failed, and Muhammad Ali found himself engaged in expensive wars to increase his own power against the sultan; he won military victories over the Ottomans, but instead found his power limited by an alliance of European powers that supported the sultan while also granting Muhammad Ali and his successors the right to rule Egypt.

Muizz, al- (c. 930–975)
Fatimid caliph (953–975)
On the death of his father, the caliph al-Mansur, in 953, al-Muizz inherited a caliphate that extended over much of what is now Morocco, Tunisia, and Algeria. Al-Muizz conquered the island of Sicily and sent his general Jawhar to reinforce Fatimid authority in places where it had become weak. Al-Muizz is best known, however, for bringing Egypt under the control of the Fatimid caliphate. Jawhar's initial invasion failed but—after a delay said to have resulted when al-Muizz's mother was treated kindly by the Egyptian ruler during a pilgrimage to Mecca—a second invasion succeeded in 969. A few years later, al-Muizz moved the capital of the caliphate to Cairo, a new city founded by Jawhar near the old city of Al-Fustat, which under al-Muizz and his son al-Aziz became a cultural center of the Islamic world. Meanwhile, Fatimid power extended east as far as Syria.

Mukhtar, al- (622–687)
Shiite leader
Al-Mukhtar ibn Abi Ubayd al Thaqafi was a Shiite leader who attempted to bring down the Sunni Muslim Umayyad Caliphate in 686–687. He proclaimed the imminent return of the Mahdi, a prophesied savior who would create a perfect and equal society in the

last days of the world. Among his supporters were non-Arab converts to Islam (*mawali*), who complained that they were not treated as equals by Arabs.

Al-Mukhtar preached that all Muslims should be equal. His army was defeated and he was killed in battle near al-Kufah (now Kufa in present-day Iraq) in 687.

Mullah Omar (c. 1959–)
Taliban leader
Muhammad Omar was born in poverty in Afghan's Kandahar province. He joined the Islamic mujahideen to fight the Soviet occupation after 1979 and against the pro-Soviet Afghan regime after the Soviet withdrawal. Having lost an eye in battle, he became a village mullah and a madrassa teacher in rural southern Afghanistan.

As mujahideen groups struggled for control after the Soviet withdrawal, Mullah Omar gathered a group of armed followers whom he called the Taliban—the Students—and soon began to gain local power in Kandahar and Herat, offering a popular campaign against the corruption of previous rule. Dubbed "Commander of the Faithful" by his followers, Omar captured Kabul in September 1996 and imposed Sharia law on Afghanistan. He remained head of the Supreme Council and head of state until the U.S.-led invasion of 2001 in reprisal for the Taliban's harboring of Al-Qaeda terrorist bases. Mullah Omar fled but is believed to be directing the Taliban campaign against U.S. and NATO forces in Afghanistan.

Musa
Cross-cultural figure
Musa is the Arabic for Moses, the patriarch who led the Israelites out of slavery in Egypt in the 13th century BCE and in the Judeo-Christian tradition received the Ten Commandments from God. In Islam, Musa is honored as a Prophet. Many details in the narrative of Musa given in the Koran align with those in the Judeo-Christian version. Musa was born in Egypt the son of Israelite parents, abandoned in a reed basket on a river, then raised at the court of the ruling pharaoh. He fled Egypt after killing an Egyptian who had been mistreating an Israelite and lived in Madyan (the northern part of the Hejaz region of Arabia), where he married Safoorah (Zipporah in biblical tradition). He had an encounter at a burning bush with God, who commanded him to free the Israelites from Egypt, then returned to Egypt, attempted without success to convert the pharaoh to monotheism and eventually led the Israelites to freedom. He communed on a mountaintop with God and returned with tablets bearing precepts for leading a righteous life. When he did, he found that his people had abandoned the worship of the one God and were bowing down before a golden calf. He destroyed the calf and made the people repent. He tried to lead the Israelites into the land of Palestine, but they were not willing to fight the local tribes and were punished by God. According to Islamic tradition, Musa lived to the age of 120.

Musharraf, Pervez (1943–)
President of Pakistan (2001–2008)
General Pervez Musharraf is the former president of Pakistan, who rose to power following a military coup in 1999. As one of Pakistan's longest-serving rulers, General Musharraf presided during a period of instability—both in Pakistan and around the world—before resigning in 2008.

Pervez Musharraf was born in Delhi, India, on August 11, 1943. Following the partition of the Indian subcontinent in 1947, Musharraf's family moved to Pakistan. Musharraf went to school in Karachi and then Lahore, before entering the Pakistan Military Academy. Musharraf had a distinguished military career. He fought in the Indo-Pakistani wars of 1965 and 1971 and later in the Kargil War in 1999, when India and Pakistan again entered into combat over the disputed Kashmir territory.

By this time, General Musharraf had risen through the ranks to become chief of Army Staff. Following calls for the army to take control of Pakistan, General Musharraf removed Prime Minister Nawaz Sharif (1949–) from office in a bloodless coup in October 1999. With approval from Pakistan's Supreme Court, General Musharraf became "Chief Executive." General Musharraf eventually took over as president on June 20, 2001, following the resignation of President Muhammad Rafiq Tarar (1929–).

Just three months into his presidency, world politics plunged into turmoil following the 9/11 terrorist attacks in New York and Washington, D.C. General Musharraf pledged support for the United States in its "war against terror"—a position that contributed to the domestic problems that plagued his presidency. General Musharraf clashed with Islamic militants who supported the Taliban and Al-Qaeda, and he became increasingly isolated. In 2007, General Musharraf struck a deal to remain president if he resigned as head of the army. A year later, the coalition government forced General Musharraf's resignation.

Mustansir, al- (1029–1094)
Fatimid caliph (1036–1094)
Born in Cairo, Egypt, on July 5, 1029, Abu Tamim Maad al-Mustansir Billah, commonly known as al-Mustansir, succeeded his father as caliph in Egypt at the age of six.

He went on to rule for the next 60 years—the longest serving caliph in the Islamic world.

During the early part of his reign, his mother advised him in state affairs. An able vizier named Ali bin Ahmad Jarjarai (died 1045) succeeded his mother. With the notable exception of Abu Muhammad Hasan bin Abdur Rehman Yazuri (died 1058), who served between 1050 and 1058, a succession of incompetent viziers followed, who plundered the royal treasury. The state of the caliphate deteriorated further as a result of Berber raids, which destroyed irrigation systems and caused major food shortages.

In 1067 a revolt by the Turkish mercenaries hired to protect the caliph destabilized the caliphate. The Turks sold what remained of the royal treasury, including works of art and gemstones. Turkish general Nasir ad-Dawla took control of Cairo where he found al-Mustansir hiding in his palace, served by three slaves and surviving on two loaves of bread a day. For the next few years al-Mustansir was allowed to live but was treated with contempt by the Turks. In 1074, Nasir ad-Dawlah was assassinated by his own followers. His death left Egypt in turmoil. Al-Mustansir continued to rule until his own death in 1094.

Nabhani, Taqiuddin al- (1909–1977)
Islamic scholar and politician

Sheikh Muhammad Taqiuddin ibn Ibrahim al-Nabhani was an Islamic scholar, theologian, and founder of the Islamic political party Hizb ut-Tahrir.

Taqiuddin al-Nabhani was born in Ijzim, Haifa, in 1909—a descendant of the ancient Arab tribe of Bani Nabhan from northern Palestine. His father was a lecturer in Sharia law. His mother was also a respected scientist and scholar, whose own father, Sheikh Yusuf an-Nabhani (1849–1932), was a famous poet and judge. Like his parents, al-Nabhani decided to follow an academic career. He studied Sharia law at the Al-Azhar University and the Dar-ul-Ulum college of Cairo. He graduated in 1932 and returned to Palestine to work first as a teacher and then as a jurist, rising to the rank of Sharia judge in the court of appeal.

The occupation of Palestine by the newly formed state of Israel in 1948, as well as his failed coup in Jordan, played an important part in the formation of Taqiuddin al-Nabhani's political ideology, resulting in his political party called Hizb ut-Tahrir. The party formed early in 1953 and was immediately banned in Jordan. Al-Nabhani was banned from returning to the country and settled in Beirut, Lebanon. He continued to meet with opposition, and eventually he retired from public life, fearing assassination. He died on December 20, 1977, aged 68.

Naderpour, Nader (1929–2000)
Iranian poet

Nader Naderpour was an Iranian writer who died in exile in Los Angeles. He was nominated for the Nobel Prize for Literature.

Born in Tehran, he came from a literary and artistic family. Following the Allied occupation of Iran in 1943, he became politically active. He moved to Paris in 1950 to study at the Sorbonne and while there started to write freelance articles. His first volume of poetry, *Chashmha va Dastha* (Eyes and hands), appeared in 1954, and more volumes followed. He lived between Iran and Europe for the next decade. In 1968, he was one of the founding members of the first Association of Writers in Iran but severed his links with them in 1977.

Following the Iranian Revolution of 1979, he went into self-imposed exile, first in Paris and later in California, where he lived until his death in 2000. He taught for more than 14 years at the University of California at Los Angeles. His knowledge of Iran's recent history was unmatched, and his classes were a meeting place for exiled Iranians. His poetry is banned in Iran.

Nasir-i-Khusraw (1004–c.1077)
Persian poet

One of the greatest of all Persian writers, Khusraw wrote devotional poetry that reflected his great faith. His most famous work is *Safarnama* (The book of travels), an account of his travels through the Muslim world.

He was born in modern-day Tajikistan (then Greater Khorasan, an eastern province of Iran) and died in present-day Afghanistan. He was extremely well educated, as the language of his poetry reveals, and worked at court in a high administration position. Then, in 1046, inspired by a dream, he gave up his job and undertook a pilgrimage to Mecca and Medina.

He journeyed for seven years and covered more than 10,000 miles. His account of the places he visited and the people he met in Safarnama provide us with an invaluable insight into the Muslim world in the 11th century. He became an Ismaili follower having studied the different Islamic schools to better understand the Islamic faith. He became a missionary for the Ismaili faith before retiring to the Pamir Mountains, where he lived as a hermit from around 1060 until his death.

Nasser, Gamal Abdel (1918–1970)
President of Egypt (1956–1970)

Gamal Abdel Nasser is considered to be one of the most important figures in modern Arab history. Nasser was the second president of Egypt, ruling between 1956 and his death in 1970. He is best known for his

nationalist policies and provided the inspiration for revolutions in neighboring Arab states, including Libya, Iraq, and Yemen.

Gamal Abdel Nasser was born to a wealthy family in Alexandria on January 15, 1918. His mother died when he was eight years old, and Nasser moved to Cairo to live with his uncle. After attending various schools in Cairo, Nasser applied to the Abassia Military Academy and graduated as a lieutenant in the infantry. He worked with Italian forces during World War II (1939–1945), aiming to expel British forces from Egypt. After serving in the Arab-Israeli War in 1948, Nasser worked as an instructor at the Royal Military Academy in Cairo.

Nasser realized his political ambitions in 1953. Following a coup, Nasser helped General Muhammad Naguib (1901–1984) take control of Egypt. Following a three-year transition period, Nasser forced Naguib from power and officially took over as president of Egypt in 1956. Nasser soon became unpopular in the West, striking deals with the former Soviet Union and communist China to secure funding for the Aswan High Dam, as well as supporting uprisings in Algeria and other Arab states. His most unpopular act was the nationalization of the Suez Canal, which prompted an invasion by British, French, and Israeli forces. In 1957, the invasion ended when the United Nations intervened. However, Nasser's stand against the West made him extremely popular in the Arab world.

Following defeat in the Six-Day War with Israel in 1967, Nasser offered his resignation. This was rejected by Egyptians, who took to the streets to support him. His popularity continued until his death on September 28, 1970.

Nawawi, al- (1234–1278)
Muslim scholar
Al-Nawawi, often known as Imam Nawawi, was a Syrian Sunni Muslim authority on *fiqh* (religious law) and Hadith (traditions concerning the words and deeds of the Prophet Muhammad). Al-Nawaki takes his name from his birthplace Nawa, in Syria. He studied in Damascus from age 18, then in 1253 made the hajj pilgrimage to Mecca and established his home there. According to tradition, al-Nawawi was virtuous, ascetic, and profoundly knowledgeable. He is considered the highest authority in the Shafi'i school of religious law (the other three schools are Hanafi, Maliki, and Hanbali), collected and exhaustively researched the sources of 40 Hadith, and wrote a very popular commentary on the *Sahih Muslim* book of Hadith. He was a Sunni Muslim, but Shiites also honor him, and several of his works have been translated into Persian.

N'Dour, Youssou (1959–)
Senegalese musician
The Senegalese singer and composer Youssou N'Dour is one of the best-known African musicians in the world. His music, known as *mbalax*, blends different influences, including Sufi-inspired Muslim religious chants along with traditional Senegalese sounds.

He was raised by devout Muslim parents in Dakar, Senegal, and started to perform in neighborhood religious ceremonies when he was twelve. His international career was launched by Senegalese taxi drivers in France and Italy, who played his music in their cabs. As his popularity grew, Youssou N'Dour performed with many Western singers. One of his most popular songs, "7 Seconds," with Neneh Cherry, sold more than 2 million copies worldwide and won many music awards.

In 2005, he released *Egypt*, an album intended to promote the more tolerant face of Islam; although praised by critics in the West, the album was denounced by Senegalese religious leaders as blasphemous. In 2009, his movie *I Bring What I Love* was given a limited theatrical release in the United States. It is a behind-the-scenes look at the making of his controversial album.

Nedim (c. 1681–1730)
Ottoman poet
Ahmet Nedim Efendi, better known by his pen name of Nedim, was one of the most celebrated Ottoman poets whose work shows the European influence on the Ottoman Empire in the period known as the Tulip period. Nedim's poetry reflects and depicts the decadence of the Ottoman Empire in that period.

He was born the son of a judge and learned both Arabic and Persian before becoming a scholar of Islamic law. He wanted to be a poet, however, and wrote several poems for the grand vizier, Ibrahim Pasha, who became his patron. Nedim's fame came during the reign of Ahmed III, called the Tulip period (1718–1730) because of the popularity of the tulip flower in Turkey at the time.

As well as writing classical poetry to celebrate holidays, weddings, and other special occasions, he specialized in writing about the city of Istanbul and clothing. He wrote in Turkish, moving away from Persian and Arabic. His songs are still sung today. Nedim was killed during the revolts that brought the Tulip period to an end.

Nuh
Cross–cultural figure
Honored by Muslims as a righteous man, pious and sincere, and a Prophet of Islam, Nuh is the Islamic

name for Noah, who was told by God to build an ark to survive the great flood that would sweep sinful men from the Earth. In Nuh's time, people had turned from God and worshipped many false deities. On God's command, Nuh told people to turn away from their evil ways and return to monotheism, but the people made fun of him and ignored his message. Nuh called on God to wipe out the sinners, but to spare his relatives and close associates, and then God instructed Nuh to build an ark, opened the gates of heaven and unleashed a great flood with waves as tall as mountains. Nuh took representatives of all animal species on the ark. After the flood subsided, the animals and people climbed down from the ark and repopulated the land. They were faithful to God for many generations.

Olajuwon, Hakeem Abdul (1963–)
Nigerian-American basketball player

Hakeem Abdul Olajuwon is a retired basketball player who is considered to be one of the greatest centers ever to play the game.

Olajuwon was born in Lagos, Nigeria, on January 21, 1963, and only started playing basketball when he was 15. He moved to the United States to play for the

University of Houston after being spotted by a scout. Following a successful college career, Olajuwon was drafted by the Houston Rockets in 1984 and remained there until 2001, when he was traded to the Toronto Raptors. The next year, he announced his retirement from the sport. Olajuwon won numerous awards throughout his professional career, including two consecutive NBA titles with the Rockets (1994, 1995), Most Valuable Player (1994) and Defensive Player of the Year (1993, 1994). In 1996, he played in the famous "Dream Team 3" that won Olympic gold at the Atlanta games. In 1996, Olajuwon was named one of the 50 Greatest Players in NBA History and was elected to the Naismith Memorial Basketball Hall of Fame in 2008.

Although Olajuwon came from a Muslim community in Nigeria, he did not become a practicing Muslim until 1991. For the rest of his professional career, Olujawon made sure that his career did not interfere with the correct observance of his faith. During the month of Ramadan, for example, he continued to play while observing his fast.

Omar Khayyam (c. 1048–c. 1131)
Persian poet, philosopher, astronomer, and mathematician

Omar Khayyam was a Persian polymath, accomplished in fields as diverse as philosophy, astronomy, and math. Best known in modern Iran for his scientific achievements, he is known in the English-speaking world for his poetry, principally the *Rubaiyat of Omar Khayyam.*

He was born in Nishapur, Khorasan, now in Iran, but spent many years in Isfahan, at the invitation of the sultan, where he worked on reforming the astronomical calendar. His calendar proved to be more accurate than the Gregorian calendar used in the West. He undertook a pilgrimage to Mecca and returned to Nishapur, where he taught and worked as the court astrologer.

Khayyam wrote around 1,000 four-line verses, known as quatrains. Each quatrain is a complete poem; after Edward Fitzgerald (1809–1883) translated them from Persian to English, they became very popular in Europe. Fitzgerald combined a number of quatrains to make a longer elegy. The translated poems reveal a thoughtful man who posed many questions about life, its transitory nature, and his relationship with God. Many of the quatrains have become popular quotes.

Senegalese Muslim musician Youssou N'Dour combines traditional African and Islamic musical forms with modern Western styles and arrangements.

O'Neal, Shaquille (1972–)
American basketball player

Shaquille O'Neal is an American basketball player who has won four NBA Championships—three consecutive NBA titles with the Los Angeles Lakers (2000, 2001, 2002) and one with the Miami Heat (2006).

Shaquille O'Neal was born on March 6, 1972, in Newark, New Jersey. His parents split up when O'Neal was an infant. His stepfather, a Muslim convert, introduced him to Islam. Shaquille excelled at basketball at high school and college, helped by his enormous size. As a professional, he has played for the Orlando Magic (1992–1996), Los Angeles Lakers (1996–2004), Miami Heat (2004–2008), and Phoenix Suns (2008–2009). In 2009 Shaquille played for the Cleveland Cavaliers. Shaquille has won numerous awards throughout his career, including Rookie of the Year (1992–1993) and Most Valuable Player (2000). Off the court, Shaquille O'Neal is a popular celebrity and has forged a successful career as a rap artist and an actor.

Pamuk, Orhan (1952–)
Turkish writer

Orhan Pamuk is Turkey's greatest living writer and the first Turkish citizen to receive the Nobel Prize for Literature (2006). His novels examine the city of his birth, Istanbul, and the tensions between East and West.

Pamuk was born to an affluent family. He originally wanted to be a painter and studied architecture at university before switching to journalism. He started to write fiction at the age of 22 but did not publish his first novel until he was thirty. Since then, his work has been translated into 55 languages and sold more than 7 million copies. His first novel, translated as *Cevdet Bey and His Sons* (1982), told the history of an Istanbul family during and after the establishment of the Turkish Republic. His novel *Museum of Innocence*, was published in Turkey in 2008.

Currently writer in residence at Bard College, New York, Pamuk also taught at Columbia University for a number of years. There was international outrage in 2005 when the Turkish government charged him with insulting the Turkish Republic for his assertion that the Armenian massacre had taken place. The government was forced to back down under international pressure.

Parveen, Abida (1954–)
Pakistani musician

Often referred to as the "Queen of Sufi Music," Parveen is a Pakistani folk and devotional singer known for her interpretations of traditional *kafi* and *ghazal* music.

She was born in Sindh Province in Pakistan. A classically trained singer, her father was her original teacher, and she later studied under Ustad Salamat Ali Khan. Her professional career began in 1973; since then she has been prolific in her output. She sings in a number of languages including Urdu, Sindhi, Seraiki, Punjabi, and Persian.

Famous throughout South Asia, she is seen as the female equivalent of the famous singer Nusrat. She considers her singing to be a chance to praise God and get closer to God, and her music is informed by her deep commitment to Sufism. In 1982 she was awarded the President of Pakistan Pride of Performance award. She tours regularly in the United States and Europe as well as South Asia.

Qabbani, Nizar (1923–1998)
Syrian poet

Nizar Qabbani was a Syrian poet, diplomat, and publisher, whose personal life inspired his desire to change conservative Arab society through his writings. His poetry is popular throughout the Arab world with its themes of love, feminism, religion, and Arab nationalism.

Qabbani was born into a middle-class family in Damascus and studied law. At college he wrote his first collection of poetry, *The Brunette Told Me* (1944), which shocked Damascene society. Well-connected, he asked the minister of education to write the foreword of the volume to help get around society's disapproval.

Qabbani worked for the foreign ministry and spent much of his career overseas, where he continued to write poetry. Over fifty years he wrote 35 volumes of poems.

His sister's suicide, to avoid an arranged marriage when she was 15, motivated much of his writing. The death of his son, aged 17, led to his famous poem, "To the Legendary Damascene." He lived in London for the last 15 years of his life but was buried in Damascus as he requested.

Qaboos bin al-Said (1940–)
Sultan of Oman (1970–)

In 1970, Qaboos bin al-Said took over as sultan of Oman and has remained in power ever since. At the time, Oman was an isolated Arab state, with strict laws and poor living conditions for its people. When he came to power, Sultan Qaboos promised reforms that would improve the quality of life for the people of Oman.

Qaboos bin al-Said was born in Salalah, Dhofar, on November 18, 1940. After studying in Salalah, he trained as an officer cadet at Sandhurst Military Academy in England. He then entered service for the British Army. Following military service, Qaboos bin al-Said traveled the world, returning to Oman in 1964. For the next six years, Qaboos bin al-Said studied Islam and learned about the history of his country and its people.

Qaboos bin al-Said became sultan of Oman in 1970, following a coup that deposed his father, Said bin Taymur. Immediately, Qaboos bin al-Said called for all Omani citizens to return to Oman and help rebuild their country. Oman joined the League of Arab Nations and the United Nations in 1972 and has since entered diplomatic relations with many countries. The long period of modernization is continuing and has seen the introduction of new schools and universities, housing and health programs, improvements to women's rights, and reform of the military.

Unlike most other Arab leaders, Qaboos bin al-Said has not named an heir to the Omani throne. He has no children, and the line of succession is unclear.

Qaddafi, Muammar al- (1942–)
Libyan head of state (1969–)

Also known as Colonel Qaddafi (or Gadhafi), Muammar al-Qaddafi has been the leader of the North African state of Libya since 1969. His policies as leader have left his country internationally isolated, although he is currently seeking to build bridges with Western states.

He was born in 1942 to a Bedouin family. After university he attended military academy. As a military officer, he took control of the country in a coup, deposing the pro-Western king, Idris I. Promoting himself from the rank of captain to colonel, he formed the Libyan Arab Republic and abolished the monarchy. He called his new regime's political ideology "Islamic socialism." Under its umbrella, he took control of foreign-owned oil companies, outlawed alcohol and gambling, and imposed rule following Islamic law.

Over the years, Qaddafi helped revolutionary and terrorist groups. In 1988, a Pan American airplane was blown up over Lockerbie, Scotland. Libya's involvement in the bombing led to further sanctions and isolation. After Qaddafi turned in the alleged bomber in the late 1990s, United Nations sanctions against Libya were lifted in 2003. The United States has since dropped most of its sanctions, and Libya and Colonel Qaddafi are no longer completely isolated. His cause has been helped by his charitable foundation, the Qaddafi International Charity and Development Foundation (GICDF), headed by his son, which has intervened in difficult situations involving hostage crises.

Qaradawi, Yusuf al- (1926–)
Sunni Islamic scholar

Yusuf al-Qaradawi is a high-profile Egyptian Sunni Muslim preacher and writer, widely viewed by Muslims as a moderate but seen by many Western media outlets as a promoter of terrorism. He is known particularly for having founded a Web site, IslamOnline, and hosting a TV program *Islamic Law and Life* on the Qatar-based Arabic satellite network Al Jazeera.

Born in a village in the Nile Delta, al-Qaradawi was extremely devout in his youth and reputedly had memorized the Koran by age 9. He became a follower of Hasan al-Banna (1906–1949) and a member of his Muslim Brotherhood organization. Al-Qaradawi studied at the Al-Azhar University in Cairo, graduating in 1953, and has lived in Qatar since 1963. He has never been shy of controversy, and he has made public statements in support of Palestinian attacks on Israel and of Palestinian suicide bombings, which he has called "martyrdom in God's name." In 2009 he was at the center of an uproar after making verbal attacks on the Jewish holy books of the Torah and on the Jewish people. A Sunni Muslim, he has also made public verbal attacks on Shiites. However, he has issued several condemnations of terrorism.

Qasim, Muhammad bin (695–715)
Umayyad military leader

Muhammad bin Qasim died at the age of twenty, but by the time of his death he had conquered Sindh (modern-day Pakistan).

When he was a child, his father died, leaving his mother to raise him. She ensured that bin Qasim was educated in different subjects, including religious instruction. He was taught military tactics and swordsmanship by his uncle, Hajjaj bin Yousaf.

When he was sixteen, he served under General Qutayba bin Muslim and showed his military skills. Only a year later, when he was seventeen, his uncle gave him the command of the army that was to invade Sindh. As well as being a brilliant soldier, bin Qasim was a skilled administrator. His tolerant rule made him popular among the people he conquered.

After these early successes, however, he was the victim of changing circumstances. When a new ruler was installed who hated his uncle, he found himself imprisoned, and he died in prison at the age of twenty.

Qazvini, Arif (1882–1934)
Iranian poet

Often referred to as Iran's national poet, Arif Qazvini was the first Persian songwriter to compose political anti-dictatorship songs. He was a poet, lyricist, and musician who composed many poems about Iran as well as writing many lyrics for songs. Many of Persia's popular singers have sung his songs.

Qazvini's singing talent became apparent at an early age. From 13 he studied Persian vocal music with Haji Sadeq Kharrazi. He sang at religious ceremonies, led by

his father Molla Hadi Vakil. Qazvini moved to Tehran, where he performed at the court of the shah.

During the Iranian Constitutional Revolution of 1906, he wrote political and pro-revolutionary songs. Early in World War I, he moved to Istanbul, where he continued his political activities. Later in life, he moved to Hamadan, where he lived in poverty before dying at the age of 52.

Qutb, Sayyid (1906–1966)
Egyptian Muslim radical

Sayyid Qutb was an Egyptian intellectual whose radical writings on the political role of Islam were reputedly a major influence on Ayman al-Zawahiri (born 1951) and other prominent figures in the international Islamic jihadist group Al-Qaeda.

Born in the village of Musha, Qutb studied in Cairo, then worked as a teacher, novelist, and critic. Between 1948 and 1950 he traveled to Washington, D.C., and Colorado to study the education system in the United States. He was strongly critical of the American way of life. On returning to Egypt he joined the Muslim Brotherhood founded by Hasan al-Banna, but he was jailed by the government in 1954. In 1966 he was accused of plotting the assassination of the Egyptian president and was executed with six other members of the Muslim Brotherhood.

His books have been very influential in the Arab world. In works such as *Milestones* (1964), he took a strongly anti-Western position, argued that all existing governments (even those in Muslim countries) were subject to *jahiliyyah* (not being enlightened by God), and called on Muslims to launch a revolution that would attack *jahiliyyah* using "physical power and jihad." After his death, his theories were promoted by his brother, Muhammad Qutb, an Islamic studies professor.

Rabia al-Adawiyya (717–801)
Sufi saint

Rabia al-Adawiyya was a poet and the first female Sufi saint. She is revered throughout the Islamic world. Rabia did not leave any written works, and what little is known about her today comes from other sources. Much of what we know about Rabia comes from her biographer, the medieval poet, Farid ud-Din Attar.

Rabia was born in Basra, Iraq. It is thought that she was the fourth daughter of a poor family. Following her parents' deaths, she was taken into slavery. According to legend, she was freed when her master saw her praying. She then dedicated her life to prayer, despite receiving many offers of marriage. She never studied under a spiritual master; instead she prayed directly to God to teach her.

She was one of the first Sufis to teach others that love alone was enough to guide a person on the mystic path and that they could pray directly to God without going on a holy pilgrimage to Mecca.

Rafsanjani, Ali Akbar Hashemi (1934–)
Iranian president (1989–1997)

Ali Akbar Hashemi Rafsanjani is a former president of Iran who continues to be an influential politician in his country. As chairman of the Assembly of Experts, Rafsanjani is responsible for the election of the supreme leader of Iran. He is also chairman of the Expediency Council, which resolves conflicts between different bodies in the Iranian administration.

Ali Akbar Hashemi Rafsanjani was born on February 15, 1934, to a family of farmers from Rafsanjan in central Iran. He studied theology in Qom and became an active critic of Mohammed Reza Pahlavi (1919–1980) during the 1960s and 1970s. He rose to power following the Iranian Revolution of 1979, when Ayatollah Ruhollah Khomeini (1902–1989) became the new president of Iran. Rafsanjani was appointed speaker of the parliament and eventually took over as commander of the armed forces during the Iran-Iraq War (1980–1988).

Rafsanjani took over as president of Iran following Ayatollah Khomeini's death in 1989. During his two terms in office, Ayatollah Rafsanjani built new relationships with Western governments and reestablished Iran as a regional power. He stepped down from power in 1997 and took up political office in the Iranian administration. He ran for presidency again in 2005 but was defeated by the conservative candidate, Mahmoud Ahmadinejad (1956–).

Rahman, A. R. (1966–)
Indian composer

Allah Rakha Rahman is a successful and prolific Indian composer who has sold more than 100 million records of his movie scores and soundtracks. He is one of the world's best selling recording artists of all time.

Rahman was born in Chennai, India, into an influential Tamil family. His father was a Chennai-based composer who died while Rahman was young. His mother's family was Muslim. His musical training began at an early age. As a child, Rahman played keyboard and arranged music for bands. He played lots of different instruments because his family rented out musical instruments. In 1992, he began his own recording studio in his house. It was then India's most advanced recording studio. Asked by a movie director, Mani Ratnam, to compose

a soundtrack for a Tamil movie, *Roja*, his score won him the prestigious Best Music Director at the Indian National Film Awards.

Rahman has gone on to win many more awards for his scores, including two 2009 Academy Awards for Best Original Music and Best Original Song for *Slumdog Millionaire*. In 2009, *Time* magazine listed him in the 100 Most Influential People List.

Ramadan, Tariq (1962–)
Swiss Muslim academic

Tariq Ramadan is an academic who writes about the position of Muslims in Western societies. He argues that Muslim leaders in Europe should foster the development of a new "European" Islam, adapted to the social and economic conditions of the Western world. He maintains, however, that Muslims should continue to respect the Koran and Sharia law.

He was born in Geneva, Switzerland, where his father was living in exile. His grandfather and father were both prominent figures in the Muslim Brotherhood. Ramadan completed his academic studies with a doctorate in Islamic Studies. He has taught at universities across Europe, including the University of Oxford, England, and subsequently at the University of Rotterdam, Netherlands. In addition to teaching, he lectures across Europe and is involved with a number of influential European think tanks.

In 2004 Ramadan was forced to turn down a teaching post at the University of Notre Dame, Indiana, after the U.S. government barred him from entering the United States. It was alleged that Ramadan had made donations to charities knowing that they were passing money on to the terrorist organization Hamas—a claim that Ramadan denies. In July 2009 a U.S. court ruled that barring Ramadan from the country infringed the rights of the organizations that had invited him. It remains to be seen whether he will subsequently be allowed to speak in the United States.

Razi, Abu Bakr Muhammad ibn Zakariya al- (c. 865–c. 923)
Persian physician and philosopher

Known in the West as Rhazes, al-Razi was one of the greatest Muslim physicians and a prolific author. Born in Rayy, near modern-day Tehran, Iran, al-Razi was a musician before he concentrated on medicine. Al-Razi became chief physician of the hospitals at Rayy and Baghdad. It was in these hospitals that he gained the experience that led him to reject many of the incorrect assumptions of his time. He made advances in the understanding of the mechanisms of fever and infection, allergic reactions, and pediatrics. His most

important contribution, however, was in his book *Al-Judari wa al-Hasbah,* which was the earliest medical text to distinguish between smallpox and measles.

Al-Razi also made important contributions to chemistry, including his discovery of sulfuric acid and the use of techniques such as distillation. Al-Razi challenged the established ideas of Greek philosophers such as Aristotle (384–322 BCE) and Galen (129– c. 199 CE). His ideas were later criticized in turn by Persian scholars Avicenna (980–1037) and al-Biruni (973–1048). Al-Razi wrote more than 180 books; many were translated into Latin and later influenced scientists in Europe. In recognition of his life and work, Iranians celebrate "Razi Day" every year on August 27.

Reza Abbasi (1565–1635)
Persian artist

Aqa Reza Reza-e Abbasi, usually known as Reza Abbasi, was a Persian miniaturist painter and calligrapher, celebrated as one of the greatest of all Iranian artists and founder of the Isfahan school of art (1597–1722).

Born in Mashhad, Iran, he was trained in the artistic studio of his father, Ali Asghar of Kashan, and began to work in the royal workshop of Shah Abbas I while still a young man. By age 31 he was regarded as being without equal among Persian artists, but later he effectively abandoned his calling and left the protection of the royal workshops for a period, spending time in wider society among wrestlers and athletes, before returning to royal employment in 1610 for the remainder of his life.

He developed a mannered, impressionistic style in miniature painting, often representing scenes of court life in stylized poses, rather than illustrating subjects from books as had been traditional for two centuries or more in Persian art. One of his masterpieces, *Two Lovers*, is held in the Metropolitan Museum of Art in New York City.

Reza Shah Pahlavi (1878–1944)
Shah of Iran (1925–1941)

Reza Shah Pahlavi ruled as the shah of Iran from 1925 until he was forced to abdicate by Britain and the Soviet Union in 1941. During his reign he began the process of modernizing Iran.

Reza Shah Pahlavi was born in the village of Alasht in Mazandaran on December 15, 1878. As a young man, he served in the Iranian army and the Persian Cossack Brigade, eventually rising through the ranks to become brigadier general.

In 1921, Reza Shah Pahlavi staged a coup, which forced Ahmad Shah Qajar (1898–1930), the last shah of the Qajar dynasty, from power. Reza Shah Pahlavi

became prime minister of Iran in 1923 and took full control as the the the first shah of the Pahlavi dynasty on December 15, 1925.

During his reign, Reza Shah Pahlavi commenced major road construction and promoted education by sponsoring Iranian students in European universities, as well as establishing the University of Tehran. He also promoted the role of women in society, encouraging them to take jobs and abandon traditional Muslim dress such as the chador and *hijab*.

Reza Shah Pahlavi's domestic reforms also started to alienate Iran in international circles. His reforms of the oil industry brought him into conflict with the British government, and he also fell out of favor with the Soviet Union. When World War II broke out in 1939, Nazi Germany was one of Iran's closest economic allies. British forces decided to occupy Iran and open up a supply route to the Soviet Union. The invasion in August 1941 came as a surprise, and Reza Shah Pahlavi fled in exile to South Africa, where he died in 1944 of heart failure. Under the direction of British and Soviet forces, Mohammed Reza Shah Pahlavi (*see under* Mohammed) replaced his father as the second shah of the Pahlavi Dynasty.

Rudaki (859–c. 941)
Persian poet

Rudaki was the pen name of Abu Abdollah Jafar ibn Mohammad. In his time he was renowned as a fine singer and instrumentalist, but today Rudaki is better known as the father of a new style of Persian poetry. He wrote in the Arabic alphabet and is thought to have composed as many as 100,000 couplets, although fewer than 1,000 survive today.

Rudaki was born in Khorasan, Persia, now in Tajikistan. Historians think he was completely blind, but his description of colors in his poetry suggests that this may not be true. He served as court poet to the Samanid dynasty until he fell from favor in 937. His poetry is notable for its simple style. His poems changed in tone over his lifetime from happy to sad as he ended his life in poverty and out of favor.

His contribution to Islamic literature was guaranteed when he translated a collection of Indian fables, the *Kalilah wa Dimnah*, from Arabic into the new Persian language.

Rumi (1207–1273)
Sufi poet and mystic

Jalal ad-Din ar-Rumi, better known as Rumi, was the greatest and probably most influential Sufi mystic and poet writing in Persian. His poetry has been widely translated and is popular around the world. To celebrate

A minature painting by Persian artist Reza Abbasi. Under the Safavid rulers of Persia, the traditional prohibition of representational artwork was lifted and painters were given royal patronage.

the 800th anniversary of his birth, UNESCO designated 2007 the year of Rumi.

Rumi was born in Balkh, present-day Afghanistan, but his family left Balkh because of the ongoing Mongol invasions. They traveled extensively before settling in Konya, Turkey, where Rumi spent much of his life. His father was also a mystic and teacher, and Rumi was exposed to Sufism at a young age. The most important moment in his life came when he met Shams al-Din, a wandering holy man. Rumi abandoned his pupils and family and spent his time with Shams. Their exact relationship is still debated, but it produced some of the greatest *ghazal*s about love ever written in Persian.

Rumi rarely wrote down his poetry. He dictated it while spinning around in a trance. His two best-known

works are two epic poems, *Diwani Shamsi Tabrizi* and *Mathnawi* (seen as an explanation of the Koran), which he composed concurrently.

Rushdie, Salman (1947–)
Indian author

A highly accomplished author, Salman Rushdie is best known for two of his novels, the award-winning *Midnight's Children* (1981) and *The Satanic Verses* (1988), which resulted in a fatwa (religious instruction) being issued that called for his execution.

Rushdie was born in Bombay, India, and was educated in India and England. After graduating from Cambridge University, he lived briefly with his family, which had moved to Pakistan in 1964. Apart from a period he spent working in advertising, Rushdie has always worked as a writer. Following the success of *Midnight's Children*, Rushdie found himself at the center of an international storm when the Iranian leader Ayatollah Khomeini issued a death sentence against Rushdie for *The Satanic Verses*. The Iranian leader considered the novel blasphemous because of its depiction of the Prophet Muhammad. Forced into hiding, Rushdie continued to write. The fatwa remained in effect for the next decade.

Knighted by the queen of England in 2007, Rushdie published his novel *The Enchantress of Florence* in 2008. Rushdie lives in London.

Saadawi, Nawal el- (1931–)
Egyptian author

Egyptian-born el-Saadawi trained as a psychiatrist, but she is better known for her novels and feminist activism. For more than 40 years, she has campaigned for the rights of women across the Arab world.

El-Saadawi was born into a large family in a small village. Although her parents were poor, she studied medicine, graduating from the University of Cairo in 1955. Her work as a doctor allowed her a unique perspective on the suffering of Egyptian women, particularly the issue of female circumcision. She was circumcised herself at the age of six. Although the practice is now banned in Egypt, it is still practiced by some communities in the Muslim world.

She became politically active as a result of what she witnessed, clashing with the Egyptian government on many occasions, and losing jobs as a result. She started to write while a student, and her first novel was published in 1957. In 1972, she published her first nonfiction work, *Women and Sex*, which led to her dismissal from the Ministry of Health.

Since the mid-1990s she has worked in the United States and Europe and is based in Atlanta, Georgia. Her novel *Zeina* was published in 2009.

Sadat, Muhammad Anwar al- (1918–1981)
President of Egypt (1970–1981)

Muhammad Anwar al-Sadat ruled as the third president of Egypt. He took over from Gamal Abdel Nasser in 1970 and served for ten years before his assassination by Islamic extremist Khalid Ahmed Showky al-Islambouli (1955–1982).

Al-Sadat was born in Mit Abu al-Kom, north of Cairo, in 1918. He graduated from the newly formed Royal Military Academy in Cairo and was posted to Sudan. There he met Gamel Abdel Nasser (1918–1970), and the two men started to plot a revolution to rid Egypt of British control. Their dream became a reality in 1953 when King Farouk I (1920–1965) was overthrown. Three years later, Nasser became president of Egypt. After holding various positions in the Egyptian government, al-Sadat eventually became vice president from 1964–1966, and again from 1969–1970.

When President Nasser died in 1970, al-Sadat became the third president of Egypt. Many thought his presidency would be short-lived, but al-Sadat confounded his critics by serving for the next ten years. He presided over the Egyptian-Israeli peace treaty, which was signed in Washington, D.C., in 1979. In recognition of his contribution to peace in the Middle East, al-Sadat was awarded the 1978 Nobel Peace Prize, along with Israeli prime minister Menachem Begin (1913–1992).

The final years of President al-Sadat's reign were marked by allegations of corruption and political unrest. Following months of turmoil in Egypt, President al-Sadat was assassinated by Islamic extremists. He was succeeded by Vice President Hosni Mubarak (1928–), who continues to rule as president of the Arab Republic of Egypt.

Sadi (1213–1291)
Persian poet

Known simply as Sadi, Musharrif al-Din ibn Muslih al-Din was an important Persian poet of the medieval period. His best-known works are *Bustan* (The orchard, 1257) and *Gulistan* (The rose garden, 1258).

Sadi was born in Shiraz, Iran, and left to study in Baghdad, Iraq. Forced to leave Persia after the Mongol invasion, Sadi traveled widely in the Islamic world. Between 1271 and the end of his life, he traveled thousands of miles to Anatolia, Syria, Egypt, Iraq, Pakistan, India, and central Asia. He lived among the poor and traveled to remote places where he preached and practiced his sermons. When he finally returned to Shiraz as an old man he had become well-known.

He wrote odes about human life and political events, such as the devastating Mongol invasion. His

greatest works were written in verse (*Bustan*) and prose (*Gulistan*). *Bustan* concentrates on Muslim virtues, while *Gulistan* recounted personal anecdotes and stories. Both works are considered pillars of Iranian literature.

Sadr, Muqtada al- (1973–)
Iraqi Shiite jurist

Muqtada al-Sadr has been an influential figure in Iraqi politics since the fall of Saddam Hussein (1937–2006) and his regime in 2003.

Following the occupation of Iraq by the Coalition Provisional Authority (CPA), al-Sadr organized an armed rebellion, dubbed the Mahdi Army. The Mahdi Army was set up to protect Shiite Muslims in the holy city of Najaf, but al-Sadr's forces soon spread to Iraqis living in Sadr City, Baghdad, and Basra in southern Iraq. Al-Sadr set up a weekly newspaper, *al-Hawzah*, to appeal to Shiite Muslims. As a result, coalition forces banned the paper in 2004, accusing al-Sadr of inciting violence.

Following a standoff, culminating in the siege of Fallujah in March and April of 2004, negotiators eventually agreed to a cease-fire in June 2004. Al-Sadr agreed to disband his Mahdi Army and called for hostilities in other parts of Iraq to stop. Iraqi officials and coalition forces agreed to include al-Sadr in the political process as long as the violence stopped.

Unfortunately, al-Sadr did not keep his promises, and fighting resumed on August 5, 2004. In the days that followed, the Mahdi Army suffered severe losses when they came under attack by U.S. Marines and Iraqi security forces. Conflict continued through 2006, when al-Sadr's Mahdi Army seized control of Amarah in southern Iraq. Hundreds of al-Sadr's followers battled local police and rival Shiite Muslims to take control of the area.

In 2007, al-Sadr announced a truce for six months following sectarian fighting in Karbala. Many observers feel that al-Sadr's movement has run its course. They believe that many Iraqis loyal to al-Sadr have split from his leadership and follow different beliefs. However, al-Sadr still enjoys enormous popularity in Iraq. According to some sources, he is studying to become an ayatollah with a view to improving his religious standing among respected older Iraqi clerics.

Said, Shakir Hassan al- (1925–2004)
Iraqi artist

Shakir Hassan al-Said was a notable Iraqi artist and a very influential teacher and writer. Born in Samawa, Iraq, he studied social sciences at the Higher Institute of Teachers in the Iraqi capital, Baghdad, graduating in 1948, then took courses in art at the Baghdad Institute of Fine Arts, graduating in 1954, before studying art history with artist Jewad Selim, with whom he founded the Baghdad Modern Art Group in 1951. The group looked for inspiration in Iraqi and Islamic tradition while also attempting to take account of modern styles. After winning a scholarship, he was a student at art schools in Paris from 1955 to 1959, then went back to Baghdad.

Under the influence of Sufi Islam, Said wrote the *Contemplative Art Manifesto* in 1966, arguing that artists were called to engage in contemplation of God's work rather than in the creation of their own, and that in this form, art was an act of worship. He taught painting in Saudi Arabia from 1968 to 1969, then was a teacher of art history at the Institute of Fine Arts, Baghdad, from 1970 to 1980. In 1971 he set up the One Dimension group, examining and working through the characteristics of the Arabic script in art. He continued to work and exhibit in many countries, including Tunisia, Jordan, India, and Brazil, up to his death.

Said ibn Husayn (r. 903–934)
Founder of the Fatimid dynasty

Known as Said ibn Husayn, Abdul Allah al-Mahdi Billah was the first Fatimid imam; he established his rule from a newly built capital in al-Mahdiyyah (Madhia) in Ifriqiya (modern-day Tunisia). During his short reign, Said ibn Husayn extended his influence over most of North Africa.

Said ibn Husayn founded the Fatimid dynasty in 903 based on a claim through descent to the Prophet Muhammad (c. 570–632) by his daughter, Fatimah (c. 605–632). He named the dynasty "Fatimid" in her honor. Muslim historians are divided about the legitimacy of his claims.

Said ibn Husayn began his conquest of North Africa by traveling through the region disguised as a merchant. Aghlabid ruler Ziyadat-Allah (died 916) captured Said ibn Husayn and locked him in a dungeon at Sijilmasah. In 909, Said ibn Husayn was rescued by his chief, Abu Abdullah al-Husayn ibn Ahmad ibn Zakariyya al-Shii (died 911). Said ibn Husayn then expelled the Aghlabids—the last of the Sunni Muslim rulers—from North Africa. Having changed his name to Ubayd Abdul Allah al-Mahdi, he established himself ruler at the former Aghlabid palace at Raqqadah in Tunisia. Over the next ten years, he extended his power from Morocco in the west as far east as Egypt. In 920, he built his new capital, named al-Mahdiyyah in his honor, on the coast of what is now Tunisia. Following Ubayd Abdul Allah al-Mahdi's death in 934, his son, Muhammad al-Qaim Bi-Amrillah (893–946), succeeded him.

Sakkal, Mamoun (1952–)
Syrian designer

Mamoun Sakkal is a Syrian calligrapher, designer, and architect. Born in Aleppo, the son of a teacher of Arabic, he emigrated from Syria and settled in the United States in 1978. He founded Sakkal Design, a graphic design and communications company, in Bothell, Washington, and from the 1990s onward the company has specialized in Arabic typography and calligraphy. Sakkal studied at the Plastic Arts Institute in Aleppo under master calligrapher Ibrahim Rifai, and he later earned degrees in architecture at the University of Aleppo and the University of Washington. He began his artistic life as a painter before becoming interested in calligraphy. He has worked as an architect, interior designer, and illustrator and has lectured on Islamic art and architecture at the University of Washington in Seattle and elsewhere. In 1993 he won the First Award in *Kufi* (a style of Arabic calligraphy) at the Third International Calligraphy Competition in Istanbul, Turkey.

Salah ad-Din Yusuf ibn Ayyub (c. 1138–1193)
Kurdish military leader

Known in the West by the latinized name Saladin, Salah ad-Din Yusuf ibn Ayyub was a Kurdish Muslim who ruled as sultan of Egypt and Syria between 1174 and 1193. He famously commanded the army that drove the Christian crusaders from most of the Holy Land.

Saladin was born in Tikrit, Iraq, around 1137, to a family of Kurds. Little is known about his early life, but he eventually settled in Damascus, where he studied the Koran. Eventually, he joined the military and fought against the crusaders. Following a series of military expeditions, Saladin settled in Egypt and eventually became vizier to Caliph al-Adid (died 1171). Three years after al-Adid's death, Saladin became sultan of Egypt, establishing the Ayyubid dynasty. Saladin expanded his empire across North Africa, Palestine, and Syria.

One of Saladin's greatest victories was in 1187, when he defeated the king of Jerusalem at the Battle of Hattin. Saladin marched victorious into Jerusalem. The victory stunned the Christian crusaders, and Pope Gregory VIII (c. 1100–1187) immediately ordered another campaign, the Third Crusade, to recapture Jerusalem from the Muslims. The campaign was led by Richard I of England (1157–1199).

By the time Richard arrived in the lands around Jerusalem he was very ill, and his soldiers were weakened by skirmishes and a lack of supplies. Richard appealed to Saladin for help. Saladin showed compassion and gave Richard's soldiers fresh water and sent his physician to treat Richard's fever. This galvanized Saladin's reputation among Christians as a generous and chivalrous opponent. In 1192, they signed a peace treaty. Saladin died of a fever a year later, shortly after Richard returned to England

Saleh, Ali Abdullah (1942–)
President of Yemen (1978–)

Ali Abdullah Saleh is president of Yemen—an office he has held since the unification of the country in 1990. From 1978 to 1990 Saleh held the position of president of North Yemen.

Saleh was born on March 21, 1942, in Bayt al-Ahmar. After leaving school, he enrolled as an officer cadet and quickly rose up the ranks, following many military commendations. In 1974, he was involved in a coup that put Ibrahim al-Hamdi (1943–1977) in power. Four years later, Saleh was promoted to deputy commander in chief of the Army. Following the assassination of Ahmad Hussein Ghasmi (1938–1978) in 1978, Saleh was promoted to chief of staff. A month later, he was elected president of the Yemen Arab Republic (North Yemen).

In 1990, following years of negotiations, North and South Yemen united. Saleh took control of the newly formed Republic of Yemen. In 1999, he was reelected in Yemen's first democratic elections, taking more than 90 percent of the votes. In 2002, Saleh announced his intention to resign from public office. He changed his mind, however, and was sworn in for another seven-year term following reelection in 2006.

Salih, Al-Tayyib (1929–2009)
Sudanese author

The Sudanese writer Al-Tayyib Salih was highly regarded as a short story writer across the Arab world. However, it was his 1966 novel *Mawsim al-hijra ila al-shamal* (Season of migration to the north) that established him as an important Arab writer.

Salih was born into a small rural community in a northern province of Sudan and left home to study at the University of Khartoum. He then moved to London, where he studied at the University of London. He lived in London for the rest of his life, working as a broadcaster for the BBC Arabic Service for many years.

Mawsim al-hijra ila al-shamal studies a clash of cultures between rural Africa and the cosmopolitan city life. In 1967, he published a collection of short stories, *Urs al-Zayn* (The wedding of Zein, and other stories), which was well received. In the late 1990s, the Sudanese government attacked his 1966 novel, claiming it violated Islamic teachings. He died in London in 2009.

Satrapi, Marjane (1969–)
Iranian author

Marjane Satrapi is an Iranian-born graphic novelist, illustrator, and movie director, best known for the graphic novel *Persepolis* and its subsequent film adaptation.

Born in Rasht, Iran, the daughter of an engineer father and a dress-designer mother, Satrapi is a great-granddaughter of Nasser al-Din Shah, shah of Persia (r. 1848–1896). She attended the French Lycée in Tehran, then was sent by her parents to Vienna, Austria, in 1983, at the age of 14, to escape the effects of the 1979 Iranian Revolution and the Iran-Iraq war. She returned to Iran to study visual communication at the Tehran Islamic Azad University School of Fine Arts. She married an artist but divorced at age 24 and moved to Strasbourg, France.

She achieved fame through the publication of her graphic novels *Persepolis* (2000) and its sequel *Persepolis 2* (2001), which showed her Iranian childhood and youth in Europe. The books have been translated into 24 languages and were made into an animated movie, also called *Persepolis* (2007), written and directed by Satrapi with French comic artist and filmmaker Vincent Paronnaud. The movie, with a French-language soundtrack, shared the Special Jury Prize at the 2007 Cannes Film Festival. An English-language version was nominated for the Academy Award for Best Animated Feature in 2008. She has written several other books, including *Chicken with Plums* (2006).

Seven8Six
U.S. pop group

Seven8Six is a Muslim boy band from Detroit, Michigan. Their influences are wide-ranging and include the Tamla Motown sound that comes from Detroit. Singing in harmony, the five members of the band sing to spread the Islamic message. Their name is a numeric shorthand for the Islamic saying, "In the name of Allah, the Beneficent, the Merciful."

The band formed in 2001. Their first performance was in 2002 at the Islamic Society of North America convention in Washington, D.C. Most of their live performances are at Muslim events. Both their albums, *786* (2003) and *The Straight Path* (2005), were international best sellers.

Shafi'i, ash- (767–820)
Islamic scholar

Ash-Shafi'i was an Arabic legal expert and teacher, regarded as the founder of the Shafi'i school of *fiqh,* or Islamic religious law. (Shafi'i is one of four schools

Iranian-born author Marjane Satrapi achieved fame through the publication of her autobiographical graphic novel Persepolis, *which was written and first published in her adopted home country, France.*

of *fiqh*—the others are the Hanafi, Maliki, and Hanbali schools.)

According to tradition, ash-Shafi'i was a member of the Banu Muttalib branch of the Quraysh clan. He was born in Ghazzah (now Gaza City in the Gaza Strip) but was raised mostly in Mecca before going to Medina to study with jurist and scholar Malik ibn Anas. After completing his studies in Medina he traveled to Yemen, where he was accused of sedition and was briefly jailed by Abbasid caliph Harun ar-Rashid (r. 786–809). After his release he traveled to Baghdad to study with the Hanafi legal expert al-Shaybani (709–805).

His celebrated book *al-Risala* established four sources for legal decisions: the Koran, the Sunna (the example of the Prophet Muhammad's words and deeds), the consensus of Islamic scholars, and finally the result of personal reasoning—usually involving drawing an analogy between the issue in question and an issue covered in the Koran. In the 12th century, Ayyubid ruler Saladin built a shrine and madrassa on the site of ash-Shafi'i's tomb, which became a major pilgrimage site.

Shah Jahan (1592–1666)
Mughal emperor (1628–1658)

Shah Jahan I was the fifth Mughal emperor of the Indian subcontinent. Shah Jahan is widely considered to be one of the greatest Mughal emperors—his reign has been called the "Golden Age" of Mughals.

Shah Jahan was born Prince Khurram Shihab-ud-din Muhammad on January 5, 1592. He was the third and favorite son of the emperor Jahangir (1569–1627), and his father soon selected him to be his successor. Serving under his father, Shah Jahan was a distinguished military commander.

Shah Jahan, the fifth Mughal emperor of the Indian subcontinent. During his reign Shah Jahan commisioned many beautiful monuments and mosques. He is best known today as the emperor who ordered the construction of the Taj Mahal.

Following the death of Jahangir in 1627, Shah Jahan succeeded the Mughal throne and immediately set about expanding his empire. The name Shah Jahan derives from the Persian, meaning "king of the world." His legacy is the splendid architecture he commissioned, which includes the stunning Taj Mahal—a tomb for his beloved wife, Mumtaz Mahal (1593–1631)—at Agra. In 1657, Shah Jahan fell ill, and his son, Aurangzeb (1618–1707), led a rebellion to assume power. Shah Jahan recovered from his illness, but Aurangzeb kept his father under house arrest in Agra Fort until his death in 1666.

Sharif, Nawaz (1949–)
Pakistani politician

Nawaz Sharif is a Pakistani politician who has twice been elected prime minister of his country. In 1999, he

was removed from office by General Pervez Musharraf (1943–). Following a period of exile, Sharif returned to Pakistan in 2007 and is forging another career in politics.

Sharif was born on December 25, 1947. After school, he attended the Punjab University and graduated with a degree in law. He started his political career as a member of the Punjab Provincial Council, eventually rising to become chief minister of Punjab.

Sharif successfully ran for prime minister in 1990 and held office for three years. He was reelected in 1997. During his second term, Pakistan carried out nuclear tests, which led to further hostilities with India. In 1999, General Pervez Musharraf led a successful coup and removed Sharif from office. He was exiled to Saudia Arabia and charged with corruption in his absence.

In 2007, after a lengthy legal battle, Sharif returned to Pakistan to challenge General Pervez Musharraf's leadership and resume his political career. In the 2008 elections, his party, The Pakistan Muslim League-Nawaz (PML-N), won three seats in the national parliament. Sharif is fighting a legal case to overturn a decision preventing him from holding public office—a result of his earlier corruption conviction.

Sharif, Omar (1932–)
Egyptian actor

Omar Sharif is an internationally celebrated actor, star of major Hollywood movies, including *Lawrence of Arabia* (1962) and *Doctor Zhivago* (1965).

He was born Michael Demitri Shalhoub in Alexandria, Egypt, to Roman Catholic Christian parents, but he converted to Islam in 1955 and married Egyptian Muslim actress Faten Hamama (1932–). The pair played as romantic lead characters in several Egyptian-language movies. Sharif's first acting role in English was as Sharif Ali in *Lawrence of Arabia*, directed by David Lean; he won a Golden Globe Award for Best Supporting Actor for the role. After a major success in the title role in *Doctor Zhivago*, again directed by David Lean, Sharif caused controversy in the Muslim world by playing opposite Barbra Streisand, a public supporter of Israel in conflict with Palestine and Arab states, in *Funny Girl* (1968) directed by William Wyler.

Due to conflicts with the government of President Nasser, he was for many years based in Europe, but he returned to live mainly in Cairo, Egypt, and has continued to appear in movies and television shows. He won widespread praise for his performance as Turkish Muslim shop-owner Ibrahim Demirci in the French-language movie *Monsieur Ibrahim el les Fleurs du Coran* (Mr. Ibrahim and the flowers of the Koran, 2003), set in Paris and Turkey, directed by François Dupeyron.

Shaykh, Hanan al- (1945–)
Lebanese author

Hanan al-Shaykh is a Lebanese writer whose works are known for their highly critical attitude to the traditional role of women in Arab societies. Her work has been banned in the more conservative parts of the Arab world because of her subject matter.

Al-Shaykh was born in Beirut, Lebanon, into a strict Shiite family and had a traditional education as a Muslim girl. Her father and brother exerted a strong control on her early life. Her writing, she claims, was a means of dealing with the anger she felt toward them. Writing in Arabic, a number of her novels have been translated into English. She published her debut novel in 1970. *Intihar rajul mayyit* (Suicide of a dead man) told the story of a middle-aged man obsessed with a young girl.

In 1976, she left Beirut when the civil war broke out, living in different countries before she settled in London. Her novel *The Story of Zahra* (1980), which she originally published at her own expense, brought her to public attention with its depictions of abortion, divorce, and illegitimacy. Her most recent novel, *Only in London*, was published in 2000 and explores people caught between the West and East.

Shihab ad-Din Ahmad ibn Majid (born c. 1421)
Arab navigator

Shihab ad-Din Ahmad ibn Majid was born in what is now the United Arab Emirates to a family of seafarers and spent most of his life on board ships, where he earned the nickname Shihan al-Dein, "Sea's Lion." He wrote more than 40 books. The most important, an encyclopedia of navigation written around 1490, described the history and basic ideas of navigation, and included accounts of star positions, monsoons and other seasonal winds, and details of the location of ports from East Africa to Indonesia. Portuguese explorer Vasco da Gama (c. 1460–1524) used a map from Ahmad ibn Majid's books to navigate around the Cape of Good Hope and sail across the Indian Ocean, establishing the first maritime trade route between Europe and India.

Sinan, Mimar (1489–1588)
Ottoman architect and engineer

Mimar Sinan ("Sinan the architect") was the chief architect and civil engineer to the rulers of the Ottoman Empire between 1539 and 1588. During the years he held this position, he was responsible for almost every major construction project in the Ottoman Empire, often personally supervising the construction of his designs. More than 450 structures have been credited to him, ranging from bridges and hospitals

to monumental palaces and mosques. Although it is doubtful he was fully involved in all of these, it is likely that either he or one of his students was involved in some capacity.

Sinan was born in 1489 to Greek Christian parents in Anatolia. He was conscripted into the Ottoman army in 1512 as a soldier and converted to Islam. He rose from the rank of cavalry officer to construction officer, distinguishing himself both as a soldier and engineer. When his commanding officer became grand vizier in 1539, he appointed Sinan his chief architect. In this position Sinan's everyday responsibilities were mostly those of a civil engineer—designing the bridges and roads that allowed the Ottoman Empire to function—but it is for his religious buildings and monuments that he is remembered today.

The vast central domes of Sinan's designs such as the Selimiye mosque and Suleimaniye mosque were a considerable engineering achievement at the time, and their beauty was renowned throughout Europe and the Muslim world. Sinan continued to teach and design buildings until his death in 1588 at the age of 99. He is buried in a small mausoleum of his own design on a street next to the Suleimaniye mosque in Istanbul.

Suharto (1921–2008)
President of Indonesia (1967–1998)

Suharto was the second president of Indonesia since it achieved independence in 1945. Suharto's presidency was a period of ecnomic growth and relative stability, marred by the violent oppression of political opponents.

Suharto was born on June 8, 1921, in the small village of Kemusu Argamulja in Central Java—then under Dutch colonial control. Suharto's parents divorced soon after his birth, and he spent his childhood with a series of foster parents.

In 1940, Suharto enlisted for the Royal Netherlands East Indies Army. A year later, he was accepted for training at the military school in Gombong in Central Java. Suharto enjoyed a distinguished military career, serving under the Japanese during World War II (1939–1945) and later with the Indonesian Army, rising through the ranks to commander of the army under President Sukarno (1901–1970).

In 1965, President Sukarno blamed an unsuccessful coup on the Indonesian Communist Party (ICP). The military waged a violent anticommunist campaign against them. Suharto and his army are thought to be responsible more than 500,000 deaths. President Sukarno's position eventually weakened, and Suharto took control. In 1967, he became the second president of Indonesia.

During Suharto's reign, Indonesia entered into a period of political stability and economic growth, with improved standards of education, health, and living. However, Suharto started to lose support following the Asian financial crisis in 1997–1998, especially given allegations of corruption. He resigned in 1998 and spent his last years alone in Jakarta. He died in January 27, 2008.

Sukarno (1901–1970)
President of Indonesia (1945–1967)

Sukarno was the first president of Indonesia, ruling from the country's formation to his deposition by Suharto.

The Selimiye mosque in Edirne, Turkey, designed by Mimar Sinan. During his 50-year tenure as chief architect to the Ottoman sultans, Mimar Sinan designed many monumental mosque complexes and public buildings.

Sukarno was born on June 6, 1901, the son of a Javanese aristocrat and his Balinese wife. Sukarno was educated at a Dutch-language school in Surabaya, and there he met Tjokroaminoto (1882–1934), who fostered Sukarno's interest in nationalism. In 1927, he helped found a pro-independence party, called Partai Nasional Indonesia. Two years later, Sukarno was arrested by the Dutch authorities for his nationalist stance, but he managed to defend himself and was released.

In 1945, following Japanese surrender at the end of World War II (1939–1945), Sukarno and his colleague, Mohammad Hatta (1902–1980), declared independence. On August 17, 1945, they formed the Republic of Indonesia. Sukarno assumed the role of president of the new republic and started to write a constitution and form a parliament. In the following years, Sukarno set out his vision, called "guided democracy," based on traditional Indonesian principles. In 1959, however, Sukarno dissolved the parliament and assumed the role of a dictator. In 1963, he proclaimed himself president for life. In that same year, the new Federation of Malaysia took its seat on the Security Council. In protest, Sukarno withdrew Indonesia from the United Nations.

In 1965, an attempted coup led to a violent anti-communist campaign in Indonesia. Under the command of one of Sukarno's generals, Suharto (1921–2008), the military killed at least half a million people. Eventually, Suharto wrested power from Sukarno and became Indonesia's second president. Suharto placed Sukarno under house arrest, and he stayed there until his death in 1970.

Sulayman
Cross-cultural figure

Sulayman is the historical and biblical figure known as King Solomon in the Judeo-Christian tradition. The son of King David (who is called Dawud by Muslims), Sulayman inherited his father's wisdom as well as his kingdom, and like Dawud is honored as a prophet of Islam.

In the Judeo-Christian narrative, Solomon (ruled in the 10th century BCE) is viewed as the greatest king of Israel, who consolidated the kingdom founded by his father, developed a powerful army, built a wealthy empire, constructed a great Temple in his capital Jerusalem, and was famous for his wisdom. In the Islamic tradition, God taught Solomon the language of the birds and animals, and he had tigers, lions, birds, and jinns (genies) in his army as well as men. Solomon also had power over the winds, and (as in the Judeo-Christian narrative) was known for his wisdom. He made contact with Bilqis, the Queen of Sheba (an

ancient kingdom either in the Horn of Africa or southern Arabia), whose people were sun-worshippers, and when she visited his kingdom she converted to Islam. In one tradition, he died while praying standing up supported by a staff, and neither his people nor the jinns realized he was dead until a worm sent by God to gnaw at the staff made both it and the king collapse.

Suleiman the Magnificent (1494–1566)
Sultan of the Ottoman Empire (1520–1566).

Suleiman was born on November 6, 1494. At the age of seven, Suleiman was sent to the Topkapi Palace in Istanbul for his education. Suleiman replaced his father as tenth Ottoman Sultan when Selim I (c. 1465–1520) died. Suleiman's reign was the longest of all the Ottoman sultans. He led several successful military campaigns and eventually presided over a huge empire, stretching over much of Europe, North Africa, and the Middle East. His navy dominated the seas, from the Mediterranean Sea to the Persian Gulf.

Suleiman's reign is noted for widespread reforms of education, taxation, and the law. Suleiman also ushered in the "Golden Age" of Ottoman culture. Suleiman himself was an accomplished poet, and Ottoman arts and architecture flourished under his patronage. Suleiman died in 1566 after 46 years in power. After a power struggle between the sons of his numerous wives and concubines, he was eventually succeeded by Selim II, his son by a Russian concubine.

Tabari, al- (839–923)
Persian scholar

Abu Jafar Muhammad ibn Jarir al-Tabari was a Sunni Muslim Persian historian and writer on the Koran, who consolidated the learning of many previous authors, and in his celebrated books the *Commentary on the Koran* and the *History of the Prophets and Kings* created the basis for a scientific study of history and of the Koran.

Although he was born in what is now Iran, and so spoke Persian, he wrote only in Arabic. According to tradition he had memorized the Koran by age 9 and left home at age 12, then traveled widely, studying with various authorities, before settling as a teacher and writer in Baghdad. His *History of the Prophets and Kings* was a success in his lifetime, and shortly afterward Samanid ruler Mansur ibn Nuh (r. 943–954) commissioned its translation into Persian around 963.

Taghmaoui, Said (1973–)
French actor

Said Taghmaoui is a French movie actor and screenwriter, born in the suburbs of Paris to a Muslim family of Moroccan Berber heritage. After dropping

out of school with the aim of becoming a boxer, he came to public attention when he co-wrote and starred in the French movie *La Haine* (Hatred, 1995) directed by Mathieu Kassovitz, about life in the suburban ghettoes of Paris in the wake of a riot. Taghmaoui speaks five languages and has become an internationally known actor, having performed in *Hideous Kinky* (1998), *Three Kings* (1999), and *The Kite Runner* and *Vantage Point* (both 2008).

Tagore, Sharmila (1946–)
Indian actress
Sharmila Tagore is an Indian movie actress, now known as Begum Ayesha Sultana after she converted to Islam and married Mansoor Ali Khan Pataudi, the nawab of Pataudi and a former Indian cricket player, in 1969. She was born in Bengal, the great-granddaughter of the renowned Bengali poet Rabindranath Tagore. She made her movie debut at age 14 in 1959 in *Apur Sansar*

Indian actress Sharmila Tagore at an awards ceremony. In addition to acting, Tagore works with UNICEF to raise awareness of HIV/AIDS among young people in India.

(The world of Apu), directed by Satyajit Ray; after appearing in several other Bengali films, she became a top Bollywood actress, following her success in the movie *Kashmir Ki Kali* (1964). In these years, before her marriage, she became known as a sex symbol, and she caused a sensation when she appeared wearing only a bikini in *Sawan Ki Ghata* (1966) and as a cabaret dancer in *An Evening in Paris* (1967). In the 1970s she played more staid roles as a wife and mother in several very successful movies opposite the male star Rajesh Khanna. Two of her three children, Saif Ali Khan and Soha Ali Khan, are Bollywood stars in their own right.

Talabani, Jalal (1933–)
President of Iraq (2005–)
Jalal Talabani became the president of Iraq when he was elected to the position by the Iraqi parliament in 2005. As president, he presided over the U.S. military's gradual handover of Iraq to Iraqi forces.

Born into a Kurdish Sunni Muslim family in northern Iraq, Talabani campaigned for Kurdish causes for more than 50 years. In the 1950s, he studied law and worked as a journalist. In the 1960s and 1970s, Talabani led Kurdish separatist fighting against the Iraqi authorities and also represented the Kurdish people in meetings in Europe and the Middle East. In 1975, he founded the Patriotic Union of Kurdistan. His campaign for Kurdish independence in Iraq led to the establishment of a Kurdish parliament in 1992. Talabani fostered close ties with Turkey and backed the U.S. coalition in the 2003 invasion of Iraq. Following the overthrow of Saddam Hussein, Talabani was a member of the Interim Iraq Governing Council. He was elected president of Iraq in 2005 by the Iraqi National Assembly and was reelected under the country's new constitution in 2007. Talabani is the first non-Arab president of an Arab state.

Timur (1336–1405)
Central Asian military leader
More commonly known in the West as Tamerlane, Timur was an Islamic Turkic conqueror born near Kesh (in present-day Uzbekistan). By 1370 he became ruler of Transoxiana, a region roughly comprising present-day Uzbekistan, Tajikistan, and southwestern Kazakhstan. A period of expansion followed, in which Timur led his army of nomadic Turks and Mongols to conquer Persia and other territories, including Mesopotamia, Georgia, and Armenia. In 1398 he invaded northern India and razed Delhi.

Renowned for his ruthlessness, Timur would place towers of severed heads from the massacred populations of cities outside their gates and raze to the ground any

city that opposed him. He later launched crushing campaigns against the Mamluk sultan of Egypt and the sultan of the Ottoman Empire. In 1404, Timur returned to the capital of his empire, Samarkand, in Transoxiana, which had thrived as the cultural and commercial center of Central Asia during his rule. The following year, Timur died in Chimkent (in present-day Kazakhstan) after setting out on an expedition to China.

Tughril Beg (c. 990–1063)
Seljuk military leader

Also known as Togrul, Tughril Beg was the founder of the Seljuk dynasty, which controlled Persia, Iraq, Syria, and Anatolia in the 11th to 14th centuries. Tughril Beg was the grandson of Seljuk, an Oghuz chief who converted to Sunni Islam. In 1037, Tughril conquered Khurasan, in eastern Persia, and took all of the Persian plateau by 1040, after defeating the Ghaznavid army at Dandanqan. Tughril Beg established Rayy (near present-day Tehran, in Iran) as his capital, from where he planned attacks on Iraq and Anatolia. In 1055, the Seljuks captured Baghdad and deposed its Shiite Buyyid ruler and restored the Sunni Abbassid caliph al-Qaim. Tughril crushed various plots to overthrow him, in one instance personally strangling his foster brother and rebel leader Ibrahim Yinal. In his final years, he waged small wars in northwestern Persia. He was succeeded by his nephew Suleiman.

Ulugh Beg (1394–1449)
Tatar prince and astronomer

Born Mirza Mohammad Taregh bin Shahrokh, Ulugh Beg took his nickname—which means "great ruler"—in 1447 when he became ruler of Turkestan. Born in Soltaniyeh in Persia, he was the grandson of the great conqueror Timur (1336–1405). Having traveled widely as a child, Ulugh Beg became governor of Samarkand and made the city a center of Muslim culture and learning. He built a large madrassa (college) in the city and invited some of the most important Muslim astronomers and mathematicians to attend.

Ulugh Beg was himself a talented astronomer and published a catalog of stars, making his observations from an observatory he founded in 1428. His catalog was an outstanding achievement and was a popular resource among European astronomers for many centuries after his death.

Umar ibn al-Khattab (c. 586–644)
Second Rashidun caliph (634–644)

A member of the Koreish tribe, Umar was born in Mecca around 586. Umar was at first opposed to his contemporary Muhammad's teachings but became a follower around 615. By the time Muhammad and his followers emigrated to Medina in 622, Umar was one of the Prophet's chief advisors. This relationship was cemented in 625 when Muhammad took Umar's daughter Hafsa as his wife.

On Muhammad's death in 632, Umar's close ally Abu Bakr became the first caliph, or ruler, and on Abu Bakr's death in 634, Umar succeeded him. During Umar's reign, the caliphate expanded into a world power as his Arab armies conquered Mesopotamia and Syria and began making inroads into Persia and Egypt. Umar is credited with laying down the principles for administering an empire that were followed by other caliphs for centuries to come. He was a respected but stern ruler and an expert jurist. Umar was assassinated by a Persian slave in 644.

Uthman ibn Affan (d. 656)
Third Rashidun caliph

Uthman was a member of the influential Umayyad clan of Mecca and a contemporary of the Prophet Muhammad. A wealthy merchant, Uthman was the first member of the Meccan elite to embrace the teachings of Muhammad, about five years after the Prophet began preaching in Mecca (most Umayyads at that time viewed Muhammad with suspicion). Muhammad valued his companion and allowed Uthman to marry one of his daughters.

When Umar, the second caliph, died in 644, Uthman was chosen to replace him. He consolidated the administration of the growing caliphate and oversaw the compilation of an official version of the Koran. Not as forceful a leader as his predecessor Umar, Uthman was often dominated by members of his clan, on whom he bestowed booty from conquests and governorships of regions of the caliphate. This made him unpopular with the army. Uthman was killed in 657 by rebels who beseiged his home in Medina. His death marked the beginning of religious and political divisions in Islam. He was succeeded by Ali as caliph.

Wadud, Amina (1952–)
American academic

Amina Wadud is an American Islamic feminist scholar and professor of Islamic studies. Born in 1952 in Bethesda, Maryland, she was the daughter of a Methodist minister father and a mother of Arabian and African descent. While studying at the University of Pennsylvania, she became a Muslim in 1972, and later she pursued academic work in Near Eastern studies, especially Arabic and Islamic subjects. She took courses at Cairo University and Al-Azhar University (also in

Cairo). Her books include *Quran and Woman: Rereading the Sacred Text from a Woman's Perspective* (1999) and *Inside the Gender Jihad: Women's Reform in Islam* (2006). The term *gender jihad* means the struggle for equality between the sexes in Islam. There was widespread comment and some controversy after she led Friday prayers for a congregation of both men and women in New York City on March 18, 2005—generally Muslims hold that women cannot lead Friday prayers or should do so only if the congregation is of women and not men.

Yahya
Cross-cultural figure

Known as John the Baptist in the Christian tradition, Yahya is identified as a prophet in Islam. In the Christian narrative, John was a preacher who called on people to be baptized in the River Jordan before God's prophesied final judgment; he is celebrated as a forerunner of Jesus, whom he baptized in the Jordan. John was beheaded by Herod Antipas, tetrach (ruler) of Galilee, to please Herod's stepdaughter Salome and her mother, Herod's new wife Herodias.

The Koran describes Yahya as devout, pure-minded, chaste, obedient to his mother and father, a prophet sent to confirm the word of God. By tradition his head lies within a shrine in the Umayyad Mosque in Damascus, Syria, since the mosque, built in 706–715, was raised on the site of a Byzantine Christian church named for John the Baptist. The tradition holds that Umayyad caliph al-Walid I (ruled 705–715) found Yahya's head during excavations and placed it in the shrine.

Yaqub
Cross-cultural figure

Honored by Muslims as a Prophet of Islam, Yaqub is known as Jacob in the Judeo-Christian tradition. With Al Eis (Esau), he was one of the twin sons of Ishaq (Isaac), son of Ibrahim (Abraham). Yaqub, also known as Israil (Israel), had 12 sons, including Yusuf (Joseph): ten of his sons were forefathers of tribes of Israel, while the other two tribes were founded by sons of Yusuf. As in the Judeo-Christian narrative, Yaqub quarreled with his twin brother and was forced to flee into the service of his uncle Laban; he married Laban's daughters, first Leah, then Rachel, after working seven years to earn the right to wed each woman. On his travels he had a dream of a ladder ascending to heaven and angels going back and forth on it, at the place where Jerusalem would be built. On his deathbed, according to the Koran, he called all his sons to him and asked them what God they would worship after he had gone, and they promised to worship the one God, the God of his fathers.

Yazid I (c. 645–683)
Umayyad caliph (680–683)

Yazid ibn Muawiyah was the second Umayyad caliph and son of Muawiyah, founder of the Umayyad dynasty. Before becoming caliph, Muawiyah sent Yazid to lay siege to Constantinople, an assault that lasted from 674 to 678. In 680, Yazid succeeded his father. In the same year, Yazid repressed a rebellion by Husayn, grandson of the Prophet Muhammad, at the Battle of Karbala. The death of Husayn caused a major and permanent rift in Islam between the majority Sunnis and the Shiites, who revere the descendants of Muhammad.

During his reign, Yazid built on the foundations laid down by his father. In various sources he is depicted as an indulgent ruler. In others, however, he is presented as an astute leader, consolidating his empire, especially its military and administrative structure, reforming the financial system and improving agriculture and the irrigation of Damascus, the Umayyad capital. Yazid was succeeded by his son, Muawiyah II, in 683.

Youshij, Nima (1896–1960)
Iranian poet

Nima Youshij was the pen name of Ali Esfandiyari. He was at the forefront of a movement to change and modernize Persian poetry and is widely considered to be the father of modern Persian poetry.

Youshij was ethnically a Tabarian and grew up in Yush, present-day Iran, where his father farmed. His early years were spent looking after animals and listening to stories around the campfire. Until he was 12 he received no formal schooling. Then he attended a French-speaking Roman Catholic school in Tehran. He remained a Muslim but was heavily influenced by his exposure to a different culture. He started to write poetry while still at school.

He introduced many innovations to Persian poetry, including varying the length of the line according to the thought it expressed and using everyday language. He also used symbols to express his ideas. His experimental poetry was considered unsuitable by the authorities, and it was not until the late 1930s that it started to be published. Youshij died of pneumonia and was buried in his native Yush as he requested.

Yunus
Cross-cultural figure

Yunus is the Arabic name for Jonah, a prophet of the Judeo-Christian tradition who was called by God

to convert the people of Nineveh in Assyria (close to modern-day Mosul in Iraq), but fled and in a great storm at sea was swallowed by a whale. In Islam he is viewed as a prophet and in the Koran is called "Lord of the Fish." The Islamic tradition follows the Judeo-Christian narrative, in which Jonah (Yunus) was commanded by God to warn the people of Nineveh that their wicked ways would bring God's judgment on them, but he ran from his responsibility and boarded a ship; when a great storm arose, the sailors—believing the storm to be God's judgment on an individual—drew lots as to who should be cast overboard, and Yunus was thrown into the waters and swallowed by a great fish. In the belly of the fish, Yunus prayed to God for forgiveness and was released by the fish onto land. He then returned to Nineveh and preached as God commanded, and the king and people repented.

Yusuf
Cross-cultural figure

The biblical figure of Joseph, the son of the patriarch Jacob who was given "a coat of many colors" and was sold into slavery but rose to high rank in Egypt, is called Yusuf and celebrated as a prophet in Islam. Muslims regard Yusuf as the perfect example of manly beauty, and he was reputedly identified by the Prophet Muhammad as the most honorable man in history. In the Islamic narrative, which largely follows that of the Judeo-Christian tradition, Yusuf was the favorite son of his father; becoming the victim of his eleven brothers' jealousy, he was cast into a well, taken by passing traders and carried to Egypt, where he was purchased by a rich man to serve his wife Zulaikhah. After Zulaikhah tried unsuccessfully to seduce him, he was thrown in prison, where God gave him the gift of interpreting dreams, and afterward he rose to become an advisor to the pharaoh, then finally was reconciled with his brothers and father. On his death Yusuf was buried in Egypt, but later the prophet Musa (Moses) carried the coffin with him when he led the Israelites out of Egypt, and Yusuf was buried in Palestine. The story of Yusuf and Zulaikha was a subject of a poem by the great Persian poet Firdawsi (935–1020).

Yusuf, Sami (1980–)
British musician

In 2006, *Time* magazine called Sami Yusuf "Islam's biggest rock star," and he is probably the most famous British Muslim in the world. He is a singer-songwriter who enjoys massive popularity across the Islamic world.

Yusuf was born in Tehran, Iran, but moved to Great Britain when he was three. He learned to play several instruments and trained classically at the Royal Academy of Music in London. He blends his Iranian and Middle Eastern heritage with his Western upbringing. He released his first album in 2003, *Al-Mu'allim*, which was extremely popular, as was his follow-up album, *My Ummah* (2005).

He sings about Islam and being a Muslim, but increasingly his songs are concerned with social and humanitarian issues. He sings in many different languages, which has increased his popularity. He sings in English, Arabic, Urdu, Turkish, and Persian. His charity work is a very important part of his life, and he has raised millions of dollars for different Islamic causes.

Zahir, Ahmad (1946–1979)
Afghan musician

Ahmad Zahir was a singer-songwriter and composer who dominated Afghan popular culture from the 1960s to the 1970s. Ahmad Zahir's music continues to be popular in Afghanistan and among Afghan exile communities around the world.

Zahir came from a powerful political family; his father was a prime minister and part of the royal court. Zahir's family was strongly opposed to his chosen musical career and often attempted to dissuade or prevent him from performing.

Zahir composed Persian songs based on the traditional rhythms of Persian poetry. During the 1970s, he released more than 22 albums. As his career progressed and the political situation in Afghanistan became more precarious, he began to introduce overtly political themes into his music.

On his thirty-third birthday, June 14, 1979, he was assassinated on the orders of a communist general concerned by the influence of his patriotic music on the Afghan people. His daughter was born the same day, but he did not live to see her.

Zahir Shah, Muhammad (1914–2007)
Shah of Afghanistan (1933–1973)

Muhammad Zahir Shah was the ruler of Afghanistan. He reigned from 1933 until 1973, when he was ousted in a coup. He was exiled and lived in Italy but returned to his homeland in 2002, earning the title "Father of the Nation."

Zahir Shah was born on October 15, 1914. He was the son of Muhammad Nadir Shah (1883–1933), who became shah of Afghanistan in 1929, following the execution of Habibullah Ghazi (c. 1890–1929).

Zahir Shah went to school in Kabul and continued his studies at the University of Montpellier in France. He returned to Afghanistan to help his father rule the country. In 1933, Nadir Shah was assassinated and Zahir Shah took control of Afghanistan. For the next

thirty years, he ruled with his uncles. In 1963, Nadir Shah ruled on his own and for the next decade took steps to modernize his country, building a university in Kabul and instituting democratic reforms.

In 1973, following a trip to Italy for eye surgery, Prime Minister Muhammad Daoud Khan (1909–1978) staged a coup. Nadir Shah remained in exile in Italy for the next 29 years. He returned to Afghanistan in 2002 after the fall of the Taliban, with the full support of the new administration. Nadir Shah remained in his homeland until his death in 2007.

Zawahiri, Ayman Muhammad Rabaie al- (1951–)
Islamic extremist

A leader of the Islamist terrorist organization Al-Qaeda, al-Zawahiri was born into a family of doctors and scholars in Cario, Egypt. In 1978, al-Zawahiri qualified as a surgeon. He was involved in the formation of the Egyptian Islamic Jihad, a group that aimed to overthrow the Egyptian government and create an Islamic state. After the assassination of Egyptian president Anwar al-Sadat in 1981, al-Zawahiri was arrested—along with hundreds of others—and imprisoned for three years for dealing in weapons. By 1991, al-Zawahiri was living in Peshawar, Pakistan, and had become the leader of the Egyptian Islamic Jihad. In Pakistan, he met Osama bin Laden and became involved in Al-Qaeda. During the 1990s, al-Zawahiri traveled widely using fake passports. He is known to have visited Afghanistan, the United States, Sudan, Russia, and Southeast Asia.

Viewed as Al-Qaeda's operational and strategic commander, he is under indictment in the United States for bombings and under death sentence in Egypt

French–Algerian soccer player Zinedine Zidane (right), playing for the French national team. In 1998 Zidane scored two goals against Brazil in the World Cup final, securing victory for France.

for antigovernment attacks. He is believed to be hiding in tribal Pakistan and has released various video and audio messages since 9/11.

Zayed bin Sultan al Nahyan (1918–2004)
Emir of Abu Dhabi (1966–2004)

Zayed was the youngest son of Sheikh Sultan bin Zayed bin Khalifa Al Nahyan, who ruled Abu Dhabi between 1922 and 1926. Zayed was governor of Abu Dhabi's Eastern Province from 1946 to 1966, when he deposed his brother in a bloodless coup and became emir. In 1971 he became president of the United Arab Emirates (U.A.E.)—a federation of seven emirates—in the formation of which he played a major role.

Zayed is credited with modernizing the U.A.E. He helped distribute the revenues from the country's oil reserves to raise the standard of living at home and abroad. A popular and relatively liberal leader, he was continually reelected as president. During his rule, gender equality advanced, U.A.E. became a major financial center, relations with the West improved, religious tolerance resulted in an influx of workers, private media were permitted, and irrigation projects were established to "turn the desert green." Zayed died in Abu Dhabi at the age of 86.

Zia-ul-Haq, Muhammad (1924–1988)
President of Pakistan (1978–1988)

Born in Jalandar in India, Muhammad Zia-ul-Haq was educated in Simla and Delhi. He served in the British Indian army during World War II, and after Pakistan was created in 1947 joined its army as a major. He trained in the United States from 1962 to 1964.

Between 1967 and 1970, Zia was stationed in Jordan and helped King Hussein retain power in the Black September operations. In 1976, Pakistani prime minister Zulfikar Ali Bhutto made Zia chief of Army Staff. However, public unrest and dissatisfaction with Bhutto's government led Zia to assume power as chief martial law adminstrator in 1977. Zia had Bhutto hanged on charges of attempted murder in 1979.

In 1978, after the resignation of President Fazal Ilahi Chaudhry, Zia became president of Pakistan. He assumed more and more power, declared martial law, dissolved parliament, and increased press censorship. A Sunni Muslim, Zia enforced many Islamic laws. In 1984, a controversial referendum was held, resulting in Zia's reelection as president. During the Soviet invasion of Afghanistan—which borders on Pakistan—Zia aided the mujahideen. He died in an airplane crash in 1988.

Zidane, Zinedine (1972–)
French soccer player

Zinedine Zidane is a retired midfield soccer player who played in the professional leagues of France, Italy, and Spain, as well as for the French national team. Zidane was born in Marseilles, France, on June 23, 1972. His parents, both Muslims, are of Algerian descent.

Zidane's soccer career began at AS Canne, where he played as a youth and won his first professional contract in 1988. Later he played for Bordeaux (1992–1996) and Juventus (1996–2001), and finally moved to Real Madrid in 2001, winning the UEFA Champions League the following year. Zidane first played for the French national team in 1994 against the Czech Republic, scoring twice to draw level and save the match. The highlight of Zidane's international career was the 1998 FIFA World Cup win, scoring twice in the final against Brazil. Two years later, France won the UEFA Euro 2000. Following an early exit from the UEFA Euro 2004, Zidane retired from international soccer. However, he came out of retirement in 2006, earning his 100th cap for France in a 1-0 win over Mexico. Later that year, France battled to the final of the 2006 FIFA World Cup. Zidane scored early in the game against Italy, but France eventually lost out on penalties.

Since retiring, Zidane has taken up an advisory position at Real Madrid. He does a lot of charitable work and has continued as United Nations Goodwill Ambassador, a role he has performed since 2001.

Zog I (1895–1961)
King of the Albanians (1928–1939)

Zog I was born Ahmet Muhtar Bey Zogolli in Albania into a Sunni Muslim family of landowners. He was educated in Constantinople (present-day Istanbul) and fought for Austria-Hungary during World War I (1914–1918). After the war, he became involved in Albanian politics, rising rapidly to become prime minister in 1922. A revolt forced Zog to flee Albania in 1924 but he returned—with the backing of Yugoslav and White Russian troops—and became president in 1925. A major reformist, Zog set about ridding the nation of serfdom. In 1928, Zog was crowned king of the Albanians. In 1929, he abolished Islamic law and adopted a civil code similar to the Swiss code.

Although Zog brought stability to Albania, financial dependence on Mussolini's Italy eventually led to an Italian invasion in 1939. Zog, his wife Geraldine, and infant son, Leka, fled Albania. They settled at first in England, then in Egypt, and finally in France, where Zog died in 1961.

DICTIONARY OF PLACES

Note: Place-names beginning with "al-" are alphabetizd by the following part of the name.

Abbasid Caliphate

The Abbasid Caliphate existed from 750 to 1258, although the caliphate had largely disintegrated by the mid-10th century. The capital city of the Abbasid Caliphate was Baghdad. The Abbasid era was marked by a consolidation of Islam and Islamic culture within the borders of the Muslim world rather than by military expansion. The period known as the "Islamic golden age" occurred during the reign of the Abbasids. The generous patronage of many Abbasid rulers helped create an era in which Muslim scholars were at the forefront of almost every form of intellectual or scientific inquiry, from medicine to philosophy. The Abbasid Caliphate ended in 1258, when the Mongol army of Hulagu Khan destroyed the city of Baghdad, massacred the population, and drove the few surviving members of the Abbasid dynasty into exile. The Abbasids settled in Cairo, where the Mamluk sultans of Egypt allowed them to claim authority on spiritual matters and remain nominal leaders of the Muslim world.

Al-Abbas Mosque, Karbala, Iraq
Shiite shrine

The tomb of Abbas, grandson of the prophet Muhammad and half brother to the second Shiite imam, lies at the center of this mosque in Karbala. The mosque also contains the tombs of Ali al-Akbar and Ali al-Asghar, the sons of Husayn, and all the Shiite dead from the battle of Karbala (680). The Al-Abbas mosque is linked to the shrine of Husayn ibn Ali, which it resembles in its design, by a broad, tree-lined avenue in the center of the town. The shrine was damaged during the reprisals directed at the Shiite population by Saddam Hussein's regime following the 1991 rebellion. Since the 2003 invasion of Iraq by a U.S.-led coalition, there have been many Sunni terrorist attacks on the shrine, killing more than 200 pilgrims in total, but failing to do any significant damage to the shrine itself.

Acre, Israel

The port of Acre, located on the coast of what is now northern Israel, was a strategically important location for the early Muslim empires and the site of fierce battles between Muslim armies and the Christian crusaders. The city was first brought under Muslim rule in 638 by the caliph Umar and remained part of the caliphate until it was captured by Christian forces in 1104. Over the next 200 years the city changed hands many times between the crusaders and the Arab armies; in 1187 Saladin captured the city, only to lose it four years later to Richard I of England. The city was beseiged by Napoleon's army in the early 19th century and was badly damaged when it was captured by Egyptian forces 40 years later. The modern city of Acre is a popular tourist destination.

Agra, India

The city of Agra is located around 140 miles (about 225 km) southeast of the Indian capital, Delhi, on the banks of the Jumna River. Between 1504 and 1638, Agra was the capital of the Mughal Empire, which spread across what is now northern India, Afghanistan, and Pakistan. The Mughal rulers of Agra commissioned many monuments and mosques, including the tomb of Akbar the Great and the famous Taj Mahal, which was commissioned by Shah Jahan (reigned 1628–1658) as a tomb for his wife. After the Mughals moved their capital to Delhi, the political and cultural importance of Agra waned. Today, Agra is an important industrial city with a predominantly Hindu population.

Akbar's Tomb, Sikandra, India

This mausoleum complex was constructed in the early 17th century to house the remains of the Mughal emperor Akbar (1542–1605). Set within a grand ornamental garden, the mausoleum is a large red sandstone structure, with four minaretlike towers and a colonnaded veranda on the upper floors. The external walls of the mausoleum are decorated with geometric mosaics, calligraphic inscriptions, and floral patterns, created by inlaying white marble into the red sandstone. Many of the architects and builders who worked on Akbar's tomb are known to have been involved in the design and decoration of the Taj Mahal 20 years later, and there are many similarities between the two structures.

Alhambra, Granada, Spain
Fortress

The name Alhambra comes from the Arabic name Qal'at al-Hamra—"red fortress"—a reference to the red clay hill on which it is built. The palace was built in several stages by the Moorish Nasrid rulers of Granada beginning in 1232. The original palace consisted of low square buildings arranged around central courtyards, and subsequent additions followed the style, usually adding new sections to the palace, rather than replacing existing ones. The most distinctive feature of the courtyards in the Alhambra is the prominent use of water in fountains, channels, and reflecting pools, both as decoration and as a means of keeping the surrounding

rooms cool. After the rulers of Christian Spain captured the city of Granada, the Alhambra was retained for use as a royal palace. Today it is one of Spain's most important tourist sites.

Apak Khoja Mausoleum Complex, Kashgar, China

The Apak Khoja mausoleum complex is located in the town of Kashgar on the eastern end of the Silk Road in northwest China. The complex is named after its patron, the local ruler and religious teacher Apak Khoja, whose imposing mausoleum lies at its center.

Most of the complex was built in the 17th century, beginning with a madrassa, cemetery, and small mosque. Later another, larger mosque was added to the site and the mausoleum was constructed. The architecture of the complex is a mixture of Chinese and Central Asian forms, which reflect the ethnic and cultural background of the local population. The two mosques were constructed using many structural and decorative elements unique to Chinese design, while the mausoleum itself is built in a style that closely

The Courtyard of the Lions, in the Alhambra Fortress. The courtyard is named for the stylized carvings of lions that surround the fountain.

resembles the funerary and religious structures of Bukhara, Uzbekistan.

Aqsab Mosque, Damascus, Syria

The Aqsab Mosque was constructed in 1234 by the Ayyubid king al-Ashraf on a site previously occupied by a Byzantine Christian church. The mosque was expanded and renovated under Mamluk rule in the 14th and 15th century as the Muslim population of the surrounding area grew. The mosque today consists of a prayer hall and other rooms arranged around a central courtyard, with a tall square minaret on one corner. The interior is decorated with brightly colored tiles and painted walls. The mosque contains a tomb believed to hold the remains of one of the companions of Muhammad, Aqsab al-Sadat.

Al-Aqsa Mosque, Jerusalem, Israel

The Al-Aqsa mosque is located on Temple Mount in Jerusalem, an area considered sacred by Christians, Jews, and Muslims. The Koran describes Muhammad's night ride to the Temple Mount on a flying horse guided by Allah to visit the Masjid al-Aqsa ("the farthest mosque"). The first mosque was built on the site in the late seventh century and expanded a few years later. Over the centuries the mosque has been destroyed several times by earthquakes and was used as a church and barracks by the Christian Knights Templar during the crusader occupation of Jerusalem, before being converted back into a mosque when Saladin retook the city in 1187. In 1969 the mosque was severely damaged by a fire started by a mentally ill evangelical Christian tourist, which destroyed an ornate wooden *minbar* installed by Saladin in 1188. An exact reconstruction was installed in the mosque in 2007.

Al-Askari Mosque, Samarra, Iraq
Shiite shrine

This mosque is one of the most important holy sites in Shia Islamic tradition. Built in 944, the mosque contains the remains of the tenth and eleventh Shiite imams as well as members of their families. Adjacent to the Al-Askari mosque is a smaller mosque called the Maqam Ghaybat, which marks the place where the twelfth imam, Muhammad al-Mahdi, is believed to have vanished from Earth in 874. The Al-Askari mosque is one of the places, along with Mecca and the Jamkaran Mosque in Iran, where it is believed that the Imam Mahdi will reappear with the prophet Isa (Jesus) on the Day of Judgment. Like other Shiite shrines in Iraq, the Al-Askari mosque is decorated with gold tiles on the dome and two minarets and decorative tiles on the walls. In 2006 Sunni terrorists associated with

Al-Qaeda in Iraq broke into the building, tied up the guards, and detonated several powerful bombs, destroying the golden dome and reducing many other parts of the building to rubble. Rebuilding efforts suffered a major setback in 2007 when another attack caused the mosque's two minarets to collapse. The rebuilding continued, however, and the reconstructed mosque was reopened to pilgrims in April 2009.

Attarin Madrassa, Fez, Morocco

The Attarin Madrassa was constructed in the early 14th century. It is located near the mosque and university of Al-Karaouine, part of the concentration of madrassas, libraries, and mosques that made Fez an important center of religious scholarship and intellectual inquiry. As is true of many madrassas, there is a stark contrast between the plain living quarters provided for the students and the richly ornamented public spaces and courtyards. The decorative style of the Attarin Madrassa is similar to that of the palaces and mosques of Muslim Spain.

Al-Azem Palace, Damascus, Syria

The al-Azem palace, constructed for the Ottoman governor of Syria in 1750, demonstrates the influence of Islamic social and religious convention in the construction of residential buildings. The palace was designed as two distinct and strictly separated areas: the harem and the *salamlik*. The harem is a private space reserved for the governor's family and household; it includes the kitchens, bedrooms, and bathhouse. The *salamlik*, on the other hand, is a public space intended to be used to entertain guests and conduct official business. The palace was damaged by French artillery during the Syrian revolution of 1925 but was fully restored in the 1980s.

Al-Azhar University, Cairo

Founded in 988, Al-Azhar University is one of the oldest institutions of higher education in the world. Throughout its history the university has been a major center of Sunni Islamic scholarship and holds one of the most comprehensive and important collections of early Islamic texts in the Muslim world. The University is attached to the Al-Azhar Mosque, which was completed in 972. When the university was founded, it had departments that conferred degrees in Arabic linguistics, Islamic astronomy, Islamic law, Islamic philosophy, and logic. In the 20th century the courses taught at the university were incorporated into a broader secular curriculum taught at other institutions in Cairo. In addition to teaching students, the scholars at Al-Azhar University are an important source of ethical and social guidance for many Muslims, responding to queries about the application of Islamic law. In recent years the scholars of Al-Azhar have provided judgments on topics as diverse as female genital mutilation, divorce law, and terrorism.

Babri Mosque, Ayodhya, India

The construction of the Babri Mosque was ordered by Babur, the first Mughal emperor of India, soon after his conquest of the region. The mosque had three domes, a well for drinking water, and a painted interior noted for its remarkable acoustics. Controversial investigations suggested that the mosque was built on the site of an earlier Hindu or Jain temple, but many Muslims rejected this theory, arguing that the investigations reflect an anti-Muslim prejudice among the Indian establishment rather than objective archaeological research. With the growth of Hindu nationalism in the 20th century, the mosque, which served the minority Muslim population, became the site of conflict. Some Hindus believed that the mosque should be destroyed or turned into a Hindu temple, and attempts were made throughout the late 20th century to achieve this. In 1992, despite an Indian Supreme Court ruling that the mosque should be preserved as a Muslim religious building, a mob of Hindu militants demolished the mosque, sparking protests and civil unrest in cities across India, Bangladesh, and Pakistan.

Badshahi Mosque, Lahore, Pakistan

The Badshahi Mosque, also known as the Emperor's Mosque, is one of the last great examples of Mughal era architecture. Built in 1673, the mosque is constructed from red sandstone inlaid with white marble; it has four minarets, one at each corner of the structure, which surrounds the central courtyard. The prayer hall has three white marble domes and is decorated on the inside with carved floral patterns. The mosque can hold 50,000 worshippers and was the largest mosque in Pakistan until the construction of the Faysal Mosque in 1986.

Baghdad, Iraq

The capital of Iraq stands at the confluence of the Euphrates and Tigris rivers in the center of modern Iraq. Baghdad was established in 762 by the Abbasid caliph al-Mansur on the site of an earlier settlement. The city was, from its founding, the capital of the Abbasid Caliphate, and royal patronage allowed the city to grow quickly, soon eclipsing the cities of the pre-Islamic Persian Empire. The Abbasids encouraged its development as a center of learning and commerce,

establishing caravansaries for traveling merchants and libraries for scholars. The most important of these libraries, known as the Bait al-Hikma ("House of Wisdom"), was responsible for translating books from many different languages into Arabic. This gave scholars in the city access to the philosophical, literary, and scientific works of the Persian, Roman, Indian, and Greek cultures. Disputes between powerful factions within the Abbasid dynasty slowed the growth of the city, and the capital was relocated to Samarra during the ninth century. In 1258 the Mongol army of Hulagu Khan attacked Baghdad, massacring the population, burning whole sections of the city, and destroying the infrastructure. After a turbulent period, during which the shattered city was fought over by competing Mongol rulers, Baghdad became part of the Ottoman Empire. Under Ottoman rule, Baghdad became large and prosperous again, although it did not recover its previous cultural and political importance. With the collapse of the Ottoman Empire in 1918, Baghdad became the capital of Iraq, first as a British colony and later as an independent state. As the capital, Baghdad was at the heart of the political conflicts that marked the 20th century in Iraq. The wars of the 20th and 21st centuries damaged many areas of the city, although there are plans for extensive reconstruction. Today the city is home to around 6.5 million people, making it one of the largest cities in the Muslim world.

Bagh-e Babur (Babur's Garden), Kabul, Afghanistan

Built in the 1530s in what are now the outskirts of Kabul, these ornate gardens contain the tomb of Babur (1483–1541), the first Mughal emperor. The gardens were laid out around a watercourse, with exotic plants surrounding a series of marble-lined pools, channels, and waterfalls. Around a century after Babur's death, his descendant, Shah Jahan (1592–1666), expanded the gardens and added a simple white marble mosque. Subsequent generations, however, allowed the gardens to fall into disrepair. The walls and structures of the gardens were damaged by an earthquake in 1842 and were rebuilt in a European style by the king of Afghanistan. Later, during communist rule, the gardens were turned into a playground, and a municipal swimming pool was constructed on the site. Finally, the gardens were almost completely destroyed during fighting between rival militant groups in 1992. Since the collapse of the Taliban regime in 2001, the gardens have been completely restored with funds and expertise from international Muslim charities and UNESCO. The site is now popular with locals and tourists, receiving many thousands of visitors every year.

Al-Bakiriyya Mosque, Sana'a, Yemen

The Al-Bakiriyya Mosque was constructed in 1597 by the Ottoman colonial governor of Yemen, Hasan Pasha. Like Ottoman mosques in Turkey and Syria, the design of the mosque consists of a large central dome supported by a number of smaller half-domes and arches. The domes cover a large internal prayer hall, which is decorated with calligraphic inscriptions and painted geometric patterns. The mosque fell into disrepair after the Ottomans were driven out of Yemen in 1626 but was fully restored when the Ottomans recaptured the city in the 1870s.

Blue Mosque, Yerevan, Armenia

This 18th-century mosque serves the small but long established Muslim community of Armenia's capital city. The mosque is decorated with the turquoise and blue tiles common to many Central Asian mosques. During the Soviet occupation of Armenia (1922–1991), many of Yerevan's mosques were demolished, and the Blue Mosque was turned into a museum. In the 1990s the mosque was extensively rebuilt and renovated with donations from the Iranian government, but local authorities in the majority Christian city have been reluctant to recognize it as a place of worship.

Bukhara, Uzbekistan

Bukhara was an important city on the ancient Silk Road—a network of trade routes that carried goods, people, and ideas between China, India, western Asia, central Asia, and Europe. The city first became part of the Islamic empire in 709 and thrived on revenues from trade. Between the 8th and 13th centuries, the patronage of Bukhara's wealthy rulers encouraged the development of the city as an important cultural and intellectual center. Bukhara's madrassas were home to some of the most important scholars in Islamic history, including Muhammad al-Bukhari, the most trusted collector of Hadith among Sunni Muslims. Poets, painters, and musicians found an appreciative audience in Bukhara and produced works that praised the city and its rulers. Most importantly, the diverse intellectual life of Bukhara and the great libraries kept by its rulers enabled those who studied there to explore many different avenues of intellectual inquiry. This is exemplified by the city's most famous resident, the philosopher, physician, astronomer, scientist, mathematician, and theologian Ibn Sina (also known by the latinized name Avicenna), whose reputation brought many scholars to study in the city. This golden age came to an end in 1226 when the city was razed by Genghis Khan's Mongol army. Bukhara's mosques, madrassas, and libraries were

destroyed, and the city never recovered its status as a cultural and intellectual center.

Cairo, Egypt

The area occupied by modern Cairo has been the site of several significant settlements. The ancient Egyptian city of Heliopolis, founded about 5,000 years ago, was located in an area now occupied by Cairo's northern suburbs. The first Muslim settlement in the area was the town of al-Fustat, which now forms part of Cairo's historic old town. It was the royal enclave of al-Qahira, founded by the Fatimid dynasty in 969, that gave the city its name. The Fatimid Empire, which extended from Morocco to Mecca, was ruled from Cairo until the dynasty's end in 1171. Under the Fatimids, Cairo became a center of Islamic scholarship and education and was home to one of the first universities in the world, the Al-Azhar University. The influx of refugees fleeing Mongol incursions in Persia expanded both Cairo and Fustat in medieval times, and the two settlements soon merged into one city. Between 1261 and 1517, Cairo was the center of the Mamluk Empire that controlled Egypt and the Levant. The Mamluk sultans were enthusiastic builders, and many examples survive of the monuments and mosques they commissioned. In the 18th and 19th century the Ottoman rulers of Cairo, influenced by French planning, remodeled large parts of the chaotic city with broad avenues that led to the west and north. Modern Cairo is the largest city in the Arab world, home to around 7 million people.

Chahar Bagh Madrassa, Isfahan, Iran

In 1704 the mother of Shah Hussein I of Persia made a charitable donation of a large amount of land and property in Isfahan to fund the construction of a new madrassa (theological school) in the city. A large set of residential buildings for the students surround an irrigated garden, which is connected to classroom buildings and a lavishly decorated mosque. The complex is often called the Shah Hussein Madrassa, as the complex is not only one of the most impressive remnants of his rule but also the location where he was imprisoned and subsequently executed after the city was taken over by an Afghan army.

Córdoba, Spain

Córdoba, on the banks of the Guadalquivir River in southern Spain, was the capital of the Roman province of Hispania Ulterior until the mid-sixth century. The city was conquered by a North African Muslim army in 711 and constituted the farthest outpost of the Umayyad Empire. In 929 the local rulers, who were descendants of the now-deposed Umayyad dynasty, declared independence from the Abbasid Caliphate, establishing Córdoba as their capital. As the heart of the Caliphate of Córdoba, the city became the prosperous center of Muslim Spain. The city was dominated by the Great Mosque of Córdoba, now a Catholic cathedral, which was once part of a complex of palace buildings and public institutions. Córdoba was captured by the Christian king Ferdinand II in 1236, and in the following decades most of the city's Muslim population were either forced to convert to Christianity or migrated to North Africa.

Damascus, Syria

Archaeological investigations reveal that the site of Damascus has been continuously inhabited for at least 10,000 years. Although it was an important city to the ancient Babylonians, Persians, and Romans, it was not until the rise of Islam and the early caliphs that the city became a place of cultural, political, and economic significance. Damascus was the capital of the Umayyad calipate from 661 to 750, serving as the political and cultural hub of the growing Islamic empire. This period was one of peace and prosperity, with the different religious groups in the city—including Christians, Jews, and a rapidly growing number of Muslims—coexisting relatively harmoniously. The city's great Umayyad Mosque was also built during this time. After the capital of the Islamic empire moved to Baghdad in 750, Damascus went into decline, but centuries of stability and peace under the rule of the Ottoman Empire allowed the city to recover. Ottoman rulers built grand public buildings, including many khans (guesthouses) for merchants who came to the city from Central Asia and the Mediterranean. After a brief period as a French colonial administrative capital, Damascus became the capital city of the newly independent state of Syria in 1946. Many mosques and historic buildings that fell into disrepair in the colonial and immediate postcolonial period are now restored or are being restored to their original function.

Darb-e Imam Shrine, Isfahan, Iran
Shiite shrine

The Darb-e Imam shrine, a mausoleum complex constructed next to an ancient cemetery, is the resting place of two descendants of the Imam Ali, venerated by Shiite Muslims. The first structures on the site were constructed in the 15th century, with additional decorative elements such as domes and tilework added in the early 17th century. The shrine is most notable for the complex geometric tilework that adorns the outside. The tiles are arranged in a huge nonrepeating pattern that follows a geometric form not discovered by Western mathematicians until the late 20th century.

Delhi, India

Delhi, in northern India, is believed to have been home to a small Muslim community of merchants from Arabia from as early as the eighth century. It was not until the 13th century, however, that Delhi came under Muslim rule. Even then, northern India remained outside the great caliphates of the Umayyads, Abbasids, and Ottomans, so its architecture and culture show little direct Arabic influence. Instead, Delhi reflects the combination of local Indian and Persian influences. The city was the capital of a number of short-lived kingdoms in the first few hundred years of Muslim rule but became part of the Mughal Empire in 1526. The Mughal emperors, especially Shah Jahan (reigned 1628–1658), built many impressive monuments and mosques in the city. In the early 20th century the British colonial governors of India commissioned the construction of a new, planned section of the town—known as New Delhi—to house the institutions of the national government. Today Delhi is one of the largest cities in the world, with around 1.6 million Muslim residents.

Dome of the Rock, Jerusalem, Israel
Shrine

The Dome of the Rock was constructed in 691 with funds supplied by Umayyad caliph Abd al-Malik. In a city that already housed many grand Christian cathedrals, the monument was designed to impress the population with its size and beauty. The structure is octagonal, with a wooden dome and stone foundation. The external walls and dome are decorated with brightly colored tiles and gold leaf, making the building stand out against the plain stone around it. Inside the shrine is a large stone on which it is said that the prophet Abraham was prepared to sacrifice his son Isaac. It is also believed that it was from this site that Muhammad ascended to heaven in 632.

Al-Fateh Mosque, Manama, Bahrain

Constructed in the 1990s, the Al-Fateh Mosque is one of the largest mosques in the world. Capable of accommodating more than 7,000 worshippers, the mosque is also notable for its unconventional construction techniques. The large traditional dome that covers the main prayer hall, for example, is made entirely of fiberglass.

Fatih Mosque, Istanbul, Turkey

This Ottoman mosque was built in the mid-15th century on the site of a Byzantine Christian church. When it was constructed, it formed the center of a large complex of public buildings, including madrassas, libraries, a hospital, public baths, and a kitchen that fed the local poor. The mosque was rebuilt in 1771, after the original was destroyed by an earthquake, to a design that incorporated many architectural and ornamental features found in the mosques designed by renowned Ottoman architect Mimar Sinan (1489–1588). Although some structural elements of the first building remain, little is known about the original design. Written references to the older building compare it to Istanbul's great Byzantine church, the Hagia Sophia, describing a vast dome covering a richly decorated prayer hall.

Fatima al-Masumeh Shrine, Qom, Iran
Shiite shrine

This Shiite shrine surrounds the tomb of Fatima al-Masumeh, daughter of the seventh imam descended from Muhammad, and sister of the eighth. Other female descendants of Muhammad are also buried here, including the daughters of the ninth imam, Muhammad al-Taqi. The shrine and the religious schools, libraries, and institutions that surround it were built as pilgrims flocked to the city to visit the tomb of Fatima. The shrine was badly damaged in the 13th century by Genghis Khan's Mongol army. The shrine and the surrounding buildings have been rebuilt and remodeled many times, and the current complex dates mostly from the 19th century. The city that grew up around the shrine, Qom, is the most important center of scholarship in Shia Islam.

The Dome of the Rock on Temple Mount, Jerusalem, constructed in 691 by the Umayyad caliph Abd al-Malik.

Fatimid Caliphate

The Fatimid Caliphate was founded in 909 in North Africa by the Fatimid dynasty, who were descendants of Muhammad. The Fatimid dynasty claimed the title of caliph in competition with the contemporary Abbasid dynasty, whose empire was by 969 restricted to Baghdad and the surrounding region. The Fatimid Caliphate is the only Islamic empire to have been ruled by a Shiite Muslim dynasty, who drew support from the many Shiite who were displaced by the policies of the Sunni Abbasids. The crusader invasion in the 11th century placed considerable pressure on the Fatimids, and many parts of the caliphate declared independence at around the same time. The Fatimid Caliphate was finally ended when the last Fatimid caliph was overthrown by one of his generals in 1171.

Fez, Morocco

Fez was founded in the ninth century at the intersection of various trade routes on the banks of the Fez River. The city has been ruled by many different dynasties, its relative isolation in the far west of North Africa placing it beyond the reach of most of the major caliphates. From 929 to 1031 the city was ruled by the Umayyad Caliphate of Córdoba, who were followed by numerous Berber dynasties. Fez became an important city during the 12th century, when it was made the capital of the North African Marinid Empire. The Marinid rulers of Fez built many madrassas and libraries in the area around the University of Al-Karaouine, helping strengthen Fez's position as an important center of scientific, religious, and cultural scholarship.

Great Mosque, Kufa, Iraq
Shiite mosque

The Great Mosque of Kufa is one of the earliest surviving mosques in the Muslim world. The current building dates from 670, with some later additions. Archaeological investigation, however, has revealed that some of the towers and minarets on the perimeter of the structure are built on top of much older foundations. Architecturally, the mosque bears many similarities to the palaces of pre-Islamic Persian kings and originally formed part of a compound that also included the palace of the town's governor. Buried within the mosque are family members of the first Shiite imams and prominent early supporters.

Great Mosque, Samarra, Iraq
Shiite mosque

The Great Mosque of Samarra was for a long time the largest mosque in the world. Built in 851, the mosque is a relatively unadorned building constructed from local sandstone. The structure has fallen into partial ruin over the centuries, and today little of the interior remains. The mosque is most notable for its minaret, the Malwiya, a 170-foot (52-m) tall tower with a spiral staircase that winds around the outside. The

The Great Mosque of Djenné, Mali. This unique mosque is the largest mud-brick structure in the world.

minaret resembles the ziggurats built in the region by pre-Islamic Mesopotamian civilizations, creating an architectural and cultural link between Islam and the cultures that preceded it. In 2005 the top of the minaret was damaged during fighting between U.S. forces and militant groups.

Great Mosque of Djenné, Djenné, Mali

The Great Mosque of Djenné is the largest mud-brick structure in the world. Because the bricks are continuously eroded by wind and rain, such structures require yearly maintenance, and the Great Mosque of Djenné is characterized by hundreds of wooden poles protruding from its external walls, which act as a sort of permanent scaffolding, allowing builders to apply new layers of mud in the spring. Although it looks dramatically different from mosques in other parts of the Muslim world, the Great Mosque of Djenné contains all the architectural features typical of a mosque, such as a minaret and mihrab.

Great Mosque of Xi'an, China

It is believed that there has been a mosque in Xi'an since the eighth century, when Persian traders settled in the area. The current building dates from the late 14th century and uses local architectural styles and methods of construction rather than imitating the mosques of the Arab world. Instead of the traditional minaret, for example, the mosque of Xi'an has a tall wooden pagoda.

Hazrat Ali Shrine, Mazar-e Sharif, Afghanistan
Shiite shrine

According to local tradition, the remains of the first Shiite imam, Ali ibn Abi Talib, were secretly brought to this isolated location by disciples worried that Ali's grave in Najaf was under threat. The first shrine on the site was erected in 1136 but was destroyed by invading Mongols around a century later. The shrine that stands on the site today was built in 1480. The exterior walls, minarets, and domes are completely covered with blue and turquoise tiles decorated with geometric patterns, abstract forms, and calligraphic inscriptions.

Huaisheng Mosque, Guangzhou, China

Local tradition asserts that the first mosque on this site was built in the 630s by Muhammad's uncle Abi Waqqas, who was sent to China on a trade mission. The mosque was rebuilt in 1350 and again in 1695 after being destroyed by a fire. The freestanding minaret—the first known to have been built in China—is based on the architecture of mosques in the Arab world but uses local construction techniques, creating a building that is a mixture of Eastern and Western styles.

Imam Ali Holy Shrine, Najaf, Iraq
Shiite shrine

The shrine of Imam Ali, cousin and son-in-law of the prophet Muhammad, is the third holiest place in Shia Islam after the mosques of Mecca and Medina. It is traditionally believed that the remains of Noah and Adam are also buried within the shrine. The shrine and its associated mosque were built in the 10th century by the Persian ruler Adud al-Dawla but have been rebuilt twice—once after a fire in the 11th century and once by the ruler of the Persian Empire in the 16th century. The outside of the mosque is decorated with gold leaf, colored tiles, and calligraphy. The mosque is built over the spot where Imam Ali was killed during the power struggles that followed the death of Muhammad. In the 20th century, the mosque became a center for militant Shiite groups and clerics, including Ayatollah Khomeini, leader of the Iranian revolution. In 1991, the mosque became the headquarters for the failed Shiite rebellion against Saddam Hussein, whose army attacked the mosque with chemical weapons, killing the fighters and Shiite families sheltered inside. In 2004, the mosque functioned as the base of operations for armed groups associated with radical Shia cleric Muqtada al-Sadr.

Imam Reza Shrine, Mashhad, Iran
Shiite shrine

Buried within this vast mosque complex are the seventh and eighth imams descended from the prophet Muhammad, both venerated as saints in the Shiite Twelver tradition. The complex is a popular pilgrimage site, visited by between 15 and 20 million Shiites every year. In addition to the shrine, the complex contains a museum, numerous educational institutions, an important library, and the Goharshad Mosque, a large and highly ornate 15th-century mosque. The earliest shrine on the site was a simple structure built soon after the martyrdom of Imam Reza, the eighth Imam, in 818. The shrine was demolished by the Sunni ruler Saboktakin in the late 10th century but was subsequently rebuilt and expanded by his successors. Accounts of miracles linked to the shrine caused its popularity to grow rapidly. With the construction of the Goharshad Mosque in the 15th century, the Imam Reza Shrine had become a major center for Shia Islamic scholarship and culture. The complex is run by an organization called Astan Quds Razavi, which has existed for almost as long as the shrine itself, and runs a number of cultural and social programs in Iran.

Imam Zadeh Saleh Shrine, Tehran, Iran
Shiite shrine

This small shrine in central Tehran, containing the tombs of family members of the 12 Imams, is popular with

local citizens who go there to pray and to break their fast in the evenings during Ramadan. The outside of the building is largely unadorned, but the interior is decorated with gold, marble, and multifaceted reflective tiles.

Jamkaran Mosque, Iran
Shiite shrine

This popular destination for Shiite pilgrims lies 9 miles (15 km) outside the city of Qom. Unlike other Iranian shrines, the mosque has no historical connection with the family of Muhammad or the twelve imams of Shia tradition. It is believed by many, however, that the Jamkaran Mosque is where the "hidden" twelfth imam, a messianic figure in Shiite tradition, will reappear. This belief is based on a local legend—claimed to date from the 10th century—that tells of a farmer who was visited by the twelve imams in a dream and told of his village's importance. Until the mid-1990s this was only a local tradition, and the mosque at Jamkaran was small and simple. In the early 21st century, however, the mosque's popularity grew, particularly after the election of Iranian president Mahmoud Ahmadinejad in 2005, who gave $17 million to pay for the construction of a more impressive mosque on the site. The Jamkaran Mosque has three domes and two minarets decorated with ornate blue tiles in the style of the shrines at Mashhad and Qom.

Jannat al-Baqi, Medina, Saudi Arabia
Cemetery shrine

The cemetery of Jannat al-Baqi contains the graves of many members of Muhammad's family and important figures from early Islam. Jannat al-Baqi is an important pilgrimage site for Shiite Muslims as it contains the graves of Hasan ibn Ali, the second Shiite imam; Ali ibn Husayn, the fourth Shiite imam; Muhammad al-Baqir, the fifth Shiite imam; and Jafar Sadiq, the sixth Shiite imam. Before the 20th century, many of the graves were marked with small shrines or domed buildings and attracted many thousands of pilgrims every year. In 1925 the forces of King Abdul Aziz al-Saud took control of the city and demolished all grave markers and buildings in the cemetery, following the Wahhabi interpretation of a Koranic verse concerning graves and shrines. Today the Jannat al-Baqi is bare land, with small markers on a few graves.

Jerusalem, Israel

Jerusalem is the third most important city in the Muslim world after Mecca and Medina. Its significance for Muslims primarily derives from the Koran's description of the Night Journey of Muhammad, which tells of Muhammad's trip on a flying horse to Temple Mount in the heart of Jerusalem. Jerusalem was brought under the rule of the Umayyad Caliphate in 639 and for the next four centuries was a prosperous provincial city and stopping point for pilgrims making the hajj from the Umayyad capital, Damascus. In 1099 Jerusalem was captured by a crusader army, which massacred the Muslim and Jewish population. Over the next 89 years of Christian rule, many Islamic monuments, including the Dome of the Rock and the Al-Aqsa mosque, were converted into churches or palaces. After Jerusalem was recaptured by Saladin's Muslim army in 1188, there was a prolonged period of instability in which the city was occupied by Christians, rival Muslim leaders, and Mongols, who looted the city and left it in ruins. From 1517 to 1917 Jerusalem was part of the Ottoman Empire, which set out to restore the city to its former glory. Jerusalem was ruled by the British between 1917 and 1946, when the Jewish population increased dramatically as many Jews fled persecution in Europe and the Soviet Union. In 1946 the UN declared that Jerusalem should be under international control, but after the creation of the State of Israel in 1948, Israel and neighboring Jordan fought over the city. Since 1967 Jerusalem has been entirely controlled by Israel, with the exception of the al-Haram as-Sharif (the noble sanctuary; a site also known as the Temple Mount)—including the Al-Aqsa Mosque and the Dome of the Rock—which is governed by an organization called the Supreme Muslim Council.

Kaaba

The Kaaba is a cube—around 42 feet tall (13 m) and 36 feet (11 m) on each side—located in the center of the Great Mosque of al-Haram in Mecca. The Kaaba is the most sacred site in Islam and the place that all Muslims face during prayer. The Kaaba is believed to have been first built by the prophet Ibrahim (Abraham) and his son Ismail (Ishmael) and is known to have existed as a holy site long before the rise of Islam. The current structure was built in 1629 from large black granite blocks and is decorated inside and outside with gold geometric patterns and inscribed with Koranic verses, including the declaration of faith. On the eastern corner of the structure is the Black Stone, a large rock that Islamic tradition asserts was part of the first altar on Earth, built by Adam and Eve after they were banished from the Garden of Eden. The rock has never been scientifically analyzed but is believed to be either a piece of volcanic rock or a fragment of a meteorite. The black stone was broken into a number of smaller fragments during the medieval era, most likely during a raid on Mecca by Shiite fanatics in 930. Today the Black Stone is held together by a silver frame.

Kabul, Afghanistan

Kabul, the capital city of Afghanistan, is located in a high mountain valley on the banks of the Kabul River. Its easily defended position has made it an important city in the region for centuries. The city came under Islamic control in the ninth century, but its population remained predominantly non-Muslim for some time. Kabul was ruled by many different empires and dynasties over the next centuries, and constant conflict took its toll on the city. The Moroccan traveler, Ibn Battuta, who visited in the 1330s, described Kabul as a small bandit village on the site of a ruined city. Kabul recovered, however, and became the capital city of the early Mughal Empire. Although the capital moved to Agra and later Delhi in India, Kabul continued to prosper through the Mughal era and for some time after. Kabul suffered damaging attacks by British forces in the 19th and early 20th centuries but was extensively modernized and expanded during a period of peace and prosperity, which lasted until the Soviet invasion of Afghanistan in 1979. Kabul was the scene of vicious fighting between Afghans and the Soviet Army, as well as between competing Afghan factions. By the early 1990s, Kabul was in ruins, with no electricity or running water, and 90 percent of its buildings uninhabitable. Since the UN-backed invasion of 2001, the city has been the recipient of large amounts of international aid, which has enabled many areas to begin a process of reconstruction. Large parts of the city are still in ruins, however, and dangerous due to unexploded bombs and land mines.

Al-Kadhimiya Mosque, Baghdad, Iraq
Shiite shrine

Located in what is now a northern suburb of Baghdad, the Al-Kadhimiya Mosque was built over the cemetery that contained the tombs of the seventh and ninth Shiite imams, as well as the tombs of a number of important Shiite scholars. In the late-1970s Saddam Hussein's regime demolished whole neighborhoods in the streets around the mosque, destroying many ancient bazaars and houses. Since 2003 a number of international Islamic organizations, together with the Iraqi government, have funded an extensive renovation of the 500-year-old building and its surroundings.

Kampung Hulu Mosque, Malacca, Malaysia

The Kampung Hulu Mosque is the oldest surviving mosque in Malaysia, constructed in 1728. The building was commissioned by the Dutch East India Company for the Muslim population of the town. The previous colonial governors, the Portuguese, had demolished all traces of non-Christian religious worship and attempted to enforce Catholicism on the population. The Dutch, by contrast, followed a policy of religious tolerance, constructing houses of worship for the various religious communities of the region in exchange for social and economic cooperation. The mosque is similar to others in Southeast Asia, with a broad, shallow roof and a minaret constructed in a similar manner to a Chinese pagoda.

Ketchaoua Mosque, Algiers, Algeria

Located in the center of the casbah—the oldest part of the city—the Ketchaoua Mosque was originally built in 1612. Built when Algeria was part of the Ottoman Empire, the mosque combines Ottoman and North African architectural styles, decorated with black and white marble and painted tiles. In 1838, when Algiers became part of the French empire, the mosque was turned into a Christian cathedral and renamed the Cathedral of Saint Philippe. When the French pulled out of Algeria in 1962, the building was turned back into a mosque. It is now a popular tourist attraction, as well as the venue for regular prayer services. The mosque contains the bones of a Christian martyr known as San Geronimo—whose bones were interred there during its time as a cathedral.

Khamis Mosque, Manama, Bahrain

Although most estimates date the Khamis Mosque to the 11th century, some historians believe that there may have been a mosque on the site since the late seventh century, making it one of the oldest mosques in the Arab world. Two tall minarets were added in the 15th century. Most of the mosque is now a ruin, having fallen into disuse, but it remains a popular tourist attraction.

Kiliç Ali Pasha Mosque, Edirne, Turkey

The Kiliç Ali Pasha Mosque was one of the last great buildings of Ottoman architect Mimar Sinan (1489–1588), built in the 1580s when Sinan was over 90 years old. The mosque was commissioned by the commander of the Ottoman navy, Kiliç Ali Pasha, and built on land reclaimed from the sea. The walls are inscribed with verses from the Koran, and the interior contains many features that allude to the occupation and status of its patron, such as the large ship's lamp that hangs from the central dome.

Madrassa al-Zahiriyya, Damascus, Syria

The Madrassa al-Zahiriyya in Damascus is a 13th-century madrassa that houses the tomb of the Mamluk sultan Baibars (1223–1277). Originally a private residence, the building was altered considerably to suit

its new purpose. A domed mausoleum was constructed at one end, and the interior spaces were richly adorned with mosaics depicting castles, plants, and landscapes, and calligraphic inscriptions. Today the madrassa holds an important collection of medieval manuscripts by Muslim scholars.

Al-Masjid al-Haram, Mecca, Saudi Arabia
Mosque

The Great Mosque of al-Haram, which encloses the Kaaba, is the largest and most important mosque in the Muslim world, as well as being one of the oldest. The first mosque on the site was a walled enclosure that surrounded the Kaaba, built in 638 to accommodate the increasing numbers of pilgrims who wished to perform the hajj. In 692 a minaret and prayer hall were added to the existing structure. The mosque has been rebuilt and expanded many times since, however, and the oldest parts of the current building date from 1570, when the mosque was rebuilt under the orders of the Ottoman sultan Selim II. Today, the Mosque of al-Haram occupies around 3,840,000 square feet (356,800 sq. m) in the heart of Mecca and can accommodate over 800,000 worshippers during the hajj.

Mecca, Saudi Arabia

Mecca is the most important city in Islam and a central location in early Muslim history. The city was the birthplace of Muhammad and his home for most of his life. Mecca was originally constructed around an oasis at a crossroads of several caravan routes that carried merchants and their goods across the Arabian Peninsula. The city has been ruled by Muslims since 628, when the Muslim community returned from their exile in Medina. Mecca contains the most important pilgrimage sites for Sunni and Shiite Muslims, including the Kaaba, the Zamzam Well, Mount Arafat, and the Jamarat Bridge. The city has been controlled by many different Muslim rulers who have used control of Mecca as a means to gain their empire religious legitimacy. Today Mecca is part of the Kingdom of Saudi Arabia and has a resident population of 1.7 million. Non-Muslims are not permitted to travel within the city limits.

Medina, Saudi Arabia

After Mecca, Medina is the second most important city in the Muslim world. The city was home to the earliest Muslim community and the first mosque, and it is the location of Muhammad's tomb. Before the migration of the Muslim community to Medina in 622, the city was already well established—it is believed to have been first settled at least 1,000 years earlier—although not as prosperous as its southern neighbor, Mecca. In the pre-Islamic period, Medina was split into ethnic areas, each with its own well and defensive structures. The Muslim community left the increasingly hostile environment of Mecca and traveled to Medina in 622, building the first mosque in their quarter of the city. The Muslim community fought several battles against the tribes of Mecca around or near Medina. When Muhammad died in 632, two years after the capture of Mecca, his remains were buried outside the home of his wife, Aisha. After Muhammad's death, Medina continued to be the Muslim community's most politically important city, serving as the capital of the Rashidun Caliphate. The tomb of Muhammad, located in the Mosque of the Prophet, is an important pilgrimage site, traditionally visited by hajj pilgrims returning from Mecca.

Mihrimah Mosque, Istanbul, Turkey

Built by Ottoman architect Mimar Sinan (1489–1588), the Mihrimah Mosque is located near the highest point of Istanbul. Although it is not the tallest or largest mosque in the city, its elevated location and tall single minaret make it a prominent landmark. The mosque and surrounding complex of public buildings were commissioned by Sultan Suleiman I in honor of his favorite daughter, Princess Mihrimah.

Mosque and Madrassa of Sultan Hassan, Cairo, Egypt

This large mosque and madrassa complex in the center of Cairo was built in the mid-14th century by Sultan Hassan, using funds gathered from the sale of properties belonging to families who died during an outbreak of plague in the city. The complex consists of a large and imposing mosque with a madrassa attached to each of the building's four sides. The layout enabled each of the four schools of Islamic jurisprudence to have its own separate teaching area. The complex also contains a grand mausoleum that the sultan intended for himself; he was assassinated before its completion, however, and his body was never found. The remains of his two sons occupy the space instead.

Mosque of the Prophet, Medina, Saudi Arabia

The first mosque to occupy this site was built in 622, soon after the migration of the Muslim community from Mecca to Medina. It occupied a site next to the home of the Prophet Muhammad. The mosque was first expanded by Muhammad, who ordered that the size of the prayer hall be doubled to accommodate the increasing number of Muslims and that the *qibla* be moved to face the Kaaba rather than Jerusalem. Muhammad's remains were interred at the mosque soon after his death, and the mosque became a popular

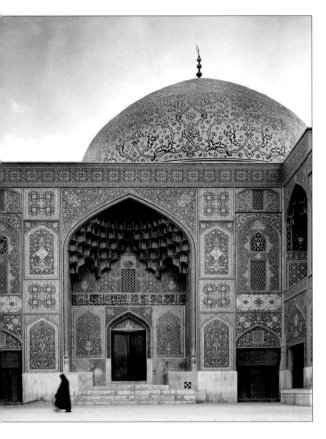

The courtyard of the Sheikh Lotf Allah Mosque, located on the east side of the Naghsh-e Jahan Square in Isfahan, Iran.

destination with pilgrims. The building itself has been rebuilt numerous times, and the current complex, with the exception of the area around Muhammad's tomb, is mostly less than 100 years old. The current mosque is capable of accommodating around 500,000 worshippers. Wahhabis—followers of a fundamental form of Sunni Islam—have often expressed concerns that the veneration of the Prophet's tomb constitutes idolatry. Although Wahhabi groups have destroyed many sites in Medina associated with early Islamic figures—including members of Muhammad's family venerated by Shiite Muslims—the Mosque of the Prophet has escaped harm.

Mughal Empire

Between 1526 and the mid-18th century, the Mughal dynasty ruled over an empire that covered most of India, Afghanistan, Pakistan, and Bangladesh. At its height, the empire encompassed most of the Indian subcontinent and was probably the richest and largest empire in the world. Because Muslims were a minority in many parts of the Mughal Empire, the attitude of the empire's Muslim rulers toward other religious groups was more tolerant than in other Muslim empires. Continuing the policies of the smaller sultanates they conquered, the Mughal Emperors abolished the *jizya*—a tax that the Koran states should be extracted from all non-Muslims living in areas under Muslim control. The Mughal emperors were strongly influenced by the culture of Persia, as well as Indian culture, and spent large sums of money constructing monuments and commissioning works of art. It is these monuments, such as the Taj Mahal in Agra, that constitute probably the most enduring legacy of the empire.

Naghsh-e Jahan Square, Isfahan, Iran

During the 16th and 17th centuries, the ancient city of Isfahan was the capital of the Persian Safavid Empire, and many grand mosques and monuments were built in the city. The most impressive were the buildings that surround the vast Naghsh-e Jahan Square (Image of the World Square), properly known today as Imam Square. On the south side stands the 17th-century Shah Mosque, considered one of the finest surviving examples of Persian architecture. The large dome and entrance arch are decorated with calligraphic inscriptions and complex abstract designs in carved stone and painted tile. The west side of the square is dominated by the Ali Qapu palace, an imposing and lavishly decorated residence designed for Shah Abbas in 1597. To the east is the Sheikh Lotf Allah Mosque, a smaller structure than the Shah Mosque but equally impressively decorated. Around the rest of the square is a terrace of shops and cafés, and the north side opens into the Isfahan bazaar and the old town. The square itself was originally used for polo matches.

Niujie Mosque, Beijing, China

The Niujie Mosque was first built in 996 but was expanded in the 15th century to accommodate the many thousands of Muslims living in the city of Beijing. The first Muslims in the area were Arab and Persian merchants who settled there as a result of their travels along the Silk Route through Central Asia. The Muslims mixed with the local population and formed a sizable community that still exists in the area today.

Qubbah Mosque, Medina, Saudi Arabia

This mosque is built on the site of what is traditionally thought to have been the first ever mosque, built by Muhammad and his followers shortly after their arrival in Medina. The mosque has been rebuilt and extended several times. In the 1980s the site was leveled and an

entirely new mosque built, designed in the style of other mosques in Medina.

Rashidun Caliphate

The Rashidun Caliphate is the name given to the Islamic empire during the first 30 years of its existence. In this period it was ruled by the so-called "rightly guided caliphs"—the first four rulers to succeed Muhammad as leader of the Muslim world. Unlike other subsequent caliphates, the Rashidun Caliphate was not ruled by a royal family, rather each caliph's successor was either chosen by the serving caliph or by prominent members of the Muslim community. Under the first caliph, Abu Bakr, the caliphate only covered the states of the Arabian Peninsula. Within 20 years, however, the caliphate had expanded to cover the North African coast as far as Morocco in the west, Persia in the east, and reached Armenia and the Black Sea in the north. Although these regions were brought under Muslim control during this time, many of them were still primarily non-Muslim.

Rukn-e-Alam Mausoleum, Multan, Pakistan

This 14th-century mausoleum is a renowned example of pre-Mughal Islamic architecture in South Asia. Originally constructed for a sultan, the mausoleum now holds the remains of Rukn-e-Alam, a Sufi saint. This monumental structure is octagonal in plan and

stands around 100 feet (30 m) tall. The lower walls were built 13 feet (4 m) thick in order to support the balcony, which surrounds the upper half of the building and the 58-foot (18 m) diameter dome at the top. The outside of the mausoleum is decorated with courses of colored bricks and tiles. The mausoleum is a common destination for pilgrims, and there is a small mosque nearby for their use.

Samarkand, Uzbekistan

The city of Samarkand, in modern Uzbekistan, was once an important economic, political, and cultural center. Samarkand's importance was a result of its location near the middle of the Silk Road, a network of trade routes that carried goods, people, and ideas between China, India, Central and western Asia, and Europe. The city was captured by Muslim rulers in the eighth century and prospered on trade from the Silk Road. This first period of prosperity ended abruptly when the city was almost completely destroyed by the Mongol army of Genghis Khan in 1220. The golden age of Samarkand's history began in 1370, when the Turko-Mongol Muslim ruler Timur established the city as the capital of an empire that stretched from the Mediterranean to northern India. Under Timur, the city became a center of scholarship and culture, as well as a trade hub. During this time a number of great mosques were built, surrounded by religious schools,

*The **interior of the central dome of the Selimiye Mosque in Edirne, Turkey.** This combination of abstract forms, vibrant colors, and complex calligraphic inscriptions is typical of 16th- and 17th-century Ottoman mosques.*

libraries, and funerary monuments. One, the Bibi Khanum Mosque, was one of the largest structures in the Muslim world. With the development of faster ships and better navigational techniques in the 15th and 16th centuries, the Silk Road lost much traffic and the city went into decline. Of the great mosques and madrassas, which were described by European travelers as being as large and impressive as the pyramids of Egypt, only scattered ruins and modern reconstructions remain. Today the city is the industrial and cultural center of Uzbekistan.

Sehzade Mosque, Istanbul, Turkey

The Sehzade Mosque was the first major project undertaken by Ottoman architect Mimar Sinan (1489–1588). The construction began in 1543 and was completed five years later. The mosque was dedicated to the memory of Sehzade, eldest son of Sultan Suleiman I, who had died of smallpox at the age of 21. Like contemporary Ottoman mosques, the building is constructed from a series of domes and half domes, with tall minarets placed at the corners of the structure. The interior is brightly lit by many high windows and decorated with colored stonework, calligraphic inscriptions, and abstract patterns of paint and tilework. The large central dome is supported by four pillars, which occupy more space than in later Sinan mosques, where the mihrab is typically visible from everywhere in the prayer hall.

Selimiye Mosque, Edirne, Turkey

The construction of the Selimiye Mosque began in 1568 and was completed in 1574. Like other Ottoman mosques from this period, the building is constructed from a series of domes and half domes, with tall minarets placed at the corners of the structure. The interior is brightly lit by many high windows and decorated with colored stonework, calligraphic inscriptions, and abstract patterns of paint and tile.

Shah Abdol Azam Shrine, Rayy, Iran
Shiite shrine

This Shiite shrine is the location of the tombs of various descendants of Muhammad and companions of the 12 imams. The shrine and mosque complex is located in Rayy, a town that is now part of the city of Tehran. The building itself dates back to the 15th century and has been added to and improved many times since then. The penultimate monarch of Iran, Reza Shah, was buried in a tomb nearby, but this tomb was demolished during the Iranian revolution.

Shah Cheragh Mosque, Shiraz, Iran
Shiite shrine

A large mosque built around the tombs of Ahmad and Muhammad, brothers of the seventh Shiite imam. At the time of their deaths, Shiraz was an important refuge for Shiites fleeing persecution by the ruling Abbasid family. The shrine became a common destination for pilgrims during the 14th century, when the mosque and an important madrassa were built in the city. The mosque has been extensively rebuilt because of the earthquakes that periodically strike the city. As it attracted more visitors and powerful patrons, the reconstructions became more and more ornate. The interior of the mosque is decorated with an elaborate mosaic of tinted mirror-glass tiles, which reflect the light from windows and chandeliers.

Shah-do Shamsira Mosque, Kabul, Afghanistan

This 19th-century mosque stands on the edge of the Kabul River that winds through the Afghan capital. It occupies the site of one of the earliest mosques in the city, built over the site of a seventh-century battle between local tribes and Arab Muslims. The tomb of the commander of the Arab forces is nearby. The building was damaged during fighting between militant groups in the 1990s but has remained open.

Shrine of Husayn ibn Ali, Karbala, Iraq
Shiite shrine

This shrine contains the tomb of Husayn ibn Ali, grandson of the Prophet Muhammad, and the second Shiite imam. This shrine, together with the adjacent shrine of Abbas, Husayn's companion and half brother, make Karbala the fourth most important pilgrimage destination in the Shiite tradition. Imam Husayn was killed at the battle of Karbala in 680 CE, and the first shrine was built over his tomb around five years later. The mosque as it currently stands was built in the 11th century and extended in the 14th century. Like the Imam Ali Mosque in Najaf, the exterior is decorated with golden tiles, while the inside is covered with calligraphic inscriptions and mirrored glass tiles, which reflect the light of chandeliers and windows. The mosque is a popular destination with pilgrims all year round, but many choose to travel there during the festival of Ashura, which is traditionally associated with the death of Hussein in the Shiite calendar.

Stari Most, Mostar, Bosnia

The Stari Most (Old Bridge) was constructed in 1557 by the Ottoman architect Mimar Hayruddin, a pupil of Mimar Sinan (1499–1598). The bridge is a spectacular single arch that crosses between two high cliffs over the Neretva River. In order to span the distance between

The Umayyad Mosque in Damascus, Syria— the first mosque to be designed and built on a monumental scale. The raised structure in the foreground is the domed treasury.

the two banks and support the weight of traffic, Hayruddin was forced to use an innovative design and untested construction methods. The resulting bridge was celebrated for its beauty and became a symbol of the multiculturalism of the Balkans, spanning the divide between the Muslim and Christian communities who lived on opposite sides of the river in Mostar. In 1993, during the Bosnian civil war, Bosnian Croat forces, aware of the bridge's symbolic significance, blew it up. Following the end of the war, several international organizations helped raise the funds necessary to rebuild the bridge. After 10 years of construction, the new Stari Most was completed in 2004, made from local stone and pieces of the old bridge that were recovered from the river.

Suleimaniye Mosque, Istanbul, Turkey

Built as a mausoleum complex for Ottoman sultan Suleiman I in 1557, the Suleimaniye Mosque dominates the skyline of central Istanbul on the other side of the city from the Hagia Sophia. The mosque is located within a large garden, surrounded by the schools, hospitals, and hospices that were typically built to accompany major mosques. Sultan Suleiman and his wife Hurren Sultan, known in the West as Roxelana,

are buried in mausoleums to the south of the mosque, which is one of the finest creations of the Ottoman architect Mimar Sinan (1489–1588), and had the highest and widest dome of any Ottoman mosque. The interior is decorated with colored masonry, geometric mosaics, and calligraphic inscriptions, which have been restored several times after the mosque has been damaged by fire or earthquakes.

Sultan Ahmed Mosque, Istanbul, Turkey

The Sultan Ahmed Mosque, also known as the Blue Mosque for its interior decorated with blue tiles, is the national mosque of Turkey. The mosque was commissioned by Sultan Ahmed I in 1609 and designed by a student of the architect Mimar Sinan. The Sultan Ahmed Mosque is generally considered to be the last monumental mosque built by the Ottoman Empire, as declining economic and military power made it impossible for subsequent generations to build such ambitious structures. The building's patron died before construction was completed and was buried in a domed tomb on the northeast corner of the mosque grounds. Controversially, the mosque had six minarets, a number matched at the time only by the Al-Haram Mosque in Mecca. To placate critics,

Ottoman sultans later paid to add a seventh minaret to the Al-Haram Mosque. In recent years the Sultan Ahmed Mosque has become a symbolic point of entry for Western public figures who wish to engage with the Muslim world. In 2006 Pope Benedict XVI prayed there and spoke of the need for greater religious tolerance.

Tekkiye Mosque, Damascus, Syria

The construction of this mosque was ordered by Ottoman sultan Suleiman I in 1560 and designed by the Ottoman architect Mimar Sinan (1489–1588). Like many Ottoman mosques, the building is surrounded by gardens and public buildings such as madrassas, public baths, libraries, and hospices. The mosque has a single central dome and two tall cylindrical minarets on either side of the covered entrance area. Both the interior and exterior of the mosque, as well as the other buildings in the complex, are decorated with painted tiles and ornamental calligraphy.

Ulugh Beg Observatory, Samarkand, Uzbekistan
Cultural site

A short distance northeast of Samarkand lie the ruins of the Ulugh Beg Observatory. Ulugh Beg was a 15th-century Timurid sultan, renowned for scholarship, who wrote influential texts on mathematics and astronomy. In 1402 Ulugh Beg commissioned the construction of an observatory to assist with his astronomical research. All that remains today is a deep curved channel excavated into the bedrock to house a giant sextant, but contemporary accounts describe a complex of buildings surrounding a three-story high observatory. With these resources, Ulugh Beg and astronomers working under his patronage were able to ascertain the precise locations of hundreds of stars, compiling a list that was later used by Muslim and Western astronomers. The observatory was destroyed after Ulugh Beg's assassination in 1449.

Umayyad Caliphate

The Umayyad Caliphate, which succeeded the Rashidun Caliphate, further expanded the Muslim empire across North Africa and Asia. The position of caliph became a hereditary one during this time, passed down through successive generations of the Umayyad dynasty. Under the Umayyads, who ruled from the city of Damascus in Syria, the Islamic state extended from northern Spain to the edges of India. Some Islamic scholars of the time were critical of the policies of the Umayyads, and many complained that their extravagant lifestyles were unfitting in a Muslim leader. Several important mosques and institutions were founded during the reign of the Umayyads, such as the

Umayyad Mosque in Damascus and the Dome of the Rock in Jerusalem.

Umayyad Mosque (Great Mosque of Damascus), Damascus, Syria

The Umayyad Mosque is the first great work of Islamic religious architecture. By the time of its construction, from 709 to 715, the Islamic empire had spread as far as North Africa and Persia. The site of the present-day mosque has been occupied by religious structures for thousands of years; archaeological investigations have revealed the remains of an ancient Aramaic temple, a Roman temple dedicated to the god Jupiter, and a Christian cathedral. These earlier structures were largely destroyed before the construction of the mosque began, however, allowing the architects to create a new building, designed according to Islamic principles, which would become the model for many mosques throughout the Muslim world. Although the mosque has been damaged over time by earthquakes and fires, the original design remains essentially unchanged.

The structure is rectangular, with a large courtyard occupying most of the area within the walls. The prayer halls and libraries were once decorated with marble panels of gold, colored glass, and mother-of-pearl, and retain some elements of this rich ornamentation. The mosque is thought to contain the remains of many Shiite Muslims who were killed at the Battle of Karbala in 680, which makes it a minor pilgrimage site for Shiite Muslims. The tomb of Saladin, the famed Islamic ruler and military commander, lies within a garden on the north side of the mosque.

University of Al-Karaouine, Fez, Morocco

Founded in 859, the University of al-Karaouine in Fez is arguably the oldest university in the world. Although it started with courses on Islamic law and theology, the university became a center for scholars studying logic, philosophy, natural sciences, astronomy, and mathematics. During the Islamic golden age of the early medieval era, the university accepted non-Muslim students and scholars such as the influential Jewish philosopher and scholar Maimonides. The university had close links with religious and political leaders in Islamic Spain, and the exchange of ideas between the scholars of Al-Karaouine and European visitors may have led to the introduction of many innovations and inventions from the Islamic world to Christian centers of learning. These included astronomical instruments, translations of ancient Greek and Roman texts, and, most importantly, the number zero. The architecture of the university and its mosque share many features with the mosques and palaces of Islamic Spain.

FACT FILES OF NATIONS WITH LARGE MUSLIM POPULATIONS

AFGHANISTAN

GEOGRAPHY

Location	Southern Asia, between Iran and Pakistan
Area	250,000 sq. miles (647,500 sq. km)
Natural resources	Natural gas, petroleum, copper, coal, chromite, precious and semiprecious stones
Land use	
Arable land	12.1 percent
Permanent crops	0.2 percent
Other	87.7 percent

GOVERNMENT

Official country name	Islamic Republic of Afghanistan
Conventional short form	Afghanistan
Nationality noun and adjective	Afghan
Official languages	Pashto, Dari
Currency	Afghani (AFA)
Capital city	Kabul
Type of government	Islamic Republic
Voting rights	18 years and over, universal
National anthem	"So Che Da Mezaka Wee" (So long as there is the earth and the heavens)
National day	Independence Day, August 19, 1919

POPULATION PROFILE, 2000 ESTIMATES

Population	21,800,000 (2002 Afghan government estimate)
Ethnic groups	
Pashtun	44.0 percent
Tajik	25.0 percent
Hazara	10.0 percent
Uzbek	8.0 percent
Turkmen, Aimak, Baluchi, and others	13.0 percent
Religions	
Sunni Muslim	84.0 percent
Shia Muslim	15.0 percent
Other	1.0 percent
Languages	
Dari (Afghan Farsi)	50.0 percent
Pashto	35.0 percent
Uzbek and Turkmen	11.0 percent
Other	4.0 percent
Adult literacy	87.9 percent

ALGERIA

GEOGRAPHY

Location	Coastal North Africa, between Morocco and Tunisia
Area	919,595 sq. miles (2,381,741 sq. km)
Natural resources	Petroleum, natural gas, iron ore, phosphates, uraniumm, lead, zinc
Land use	
Arable land	3.2 percent
Permanent crops	nearly 0.2 percent
Other	96.6 percent

GOVERNMENT

Official country name	People's Democratic Republic of Algeria
Conventional short form	Algeria
Nationality noun and adjective	Algerian
Official languages	Arabic, Tamazight (Berber)
Currency	Algerian dinar (DZD)
Capital city	Algiers
Type of government	Republic
Voting rights	18 years and over, universal
National anthem	"Qassamanbin Nazilat il-Mahiqat" (We swear by the lightning that destroys)
National day	Revolution Day, November 1, 1954

POPULATION PROFILE, 2000 ESTIMATES

Population	31,540,000 (2003 Algerian government estimate)
Ethnic groups	
Arab-Berber	99 percent
Europeans	under 1 percent
Religions	
Sunni Muslim	99 percent
Others	1 percent
Languages	
Arabic	nearly 100 percent
Tamazight	percentage disputed
Adult literacy	70 percent

AZERBAIJAN

GEOGRAPHY

Location	Southwestern Asia, between Russia, Georgia, Armenia, and Iran
Area	33,436 sq. miles (86,600 sq. km)
Natural resources	Petroleum, natural gas, iron ore
Land use	
Arable land	19.3 percent
Permanent crops	3.0 percent
Other	77.7 percent

GOVERNMENT

Official country name	Republic of Azerbaijan
Conventional short form	Azerbaijan
Nationality noun and adjective	Azeri or Azerbaijani
Official language	Azeri
Currency	Manat (AZM)
Capital city	Baku
Type of government	Republic
Voting rights	18 years and over, universal
National anthem	"Azerbaijan! Azerbaijan!" (So long as there is the earth and the heavens)
National day	Founding of the Azerbaijan Republic, May 28, 1918

POPULATION PROFILE, 2000 ESTIMATES

Population	8,203,000 (2003 Azeri government estimate)
Ethnic groups	
Azeri	90.0 percent
Dagestani	3.0 percent
Russian	2.5 percent
Armenian	2.0 percent
Others	2.5 percent
Religions	
Shia Muslim	65.0 percent
	(30 percent practicing)
Sunni Muslim	25.0 percent
	(few practicing)
Nonreligious	60.0 percent
Christian minorities	4.0 percent
Others	2.5 percent
Languages	
Azeri	89.0 percent
Russian	3.0 percent
Armenian	2.0 percent
Others	6.0 percent
Adult literacy	98.8 percent

BAHRAIN

GEOGRAPHY

Location	Western Asia, two main island groups in the Persian Gulf off the coast of Saudi Arabia
Area	253 sq. miles (655 sq. km)
Natural resources	Petroleum, natural gas, fish
Land use	
Arable land	4.4 percent
Permanent crops	4.4 percent
Other	91.2 percent

GOVERNMENT

Official country name	Kingdom of Bahrain
Conventional short form	Bahrain
Nationality noun and adjective	Bahraini
Official language	Arabic
Currency	Bahraini dinar (BHD)
Capital city	Manama
Type of government	Monarchy
Voting rights	20 years and over, universal
National anthem	"Bahrainona" (Our Bahrain)
National day	National Day, December 16, 1971 (end of British protectorate)

POPULATION PROFILE, 2000 ESTIMATES

Population	651,000 (2001 census)
Ethnic groups	
Bahraini Arab	63 percent
South Asian	19 percent
Other Arab	10 percent
Iranian	8 percent
Religions	
Shia Muslim	70 percent
Sunni Muslim	29 percent
Hindu and Christian minorities	1 percent
Languages	
Arabic	73 percent
Languages of Southern Asia	19 percent
Farsi	8 percent
Adult literacy	89 percent

BANGLADESH

GEOGRAPHY

Location	Southern Asia, between Myanmar (Burma) and India
Area	56,977 sq. miles (147,570 sq. km)
Natural resources	Natural gas (largely offshore), timber
Land use	
Arable land	55.4 percent
Permanent crops	3.1 percent
Other	41.5 percent

GOVERNMENT

Official country name	People's Republic of Bangladesh
Conventional short form	Bangladesh
Nationality noun and adjective	Bangladeshi
Official language	Bengali (also known as Bangla)
Currency	Taka (BDT)
Capital city	Dhaka
Type of government	Parliamentary Republic
Voting rights	18 years and over, universal
National anthem	"Amar Sonar Bangla" (My golden Bengal)
National day	Independence Day, March 26, 1971

POPULATION PROFILE, 2005 ESTIMATES

Population	129,247,000 (2001 census)
Ethnic groups	
Bengali	98 percent
Others	2 percent
Religions	
Sunni Muslim	83 percent
Hindu	16 percent
Christian and others	1 percent
Languages	
Bengali (Bangla)	99 percent
Tribal languages, English, and others	1 percent
Adult literacy	43 percent

BRUNEI

GEOGRAPHY

Location	Southeastern Asia in northern Borneo
Area	2,226 sq. miles (5,765 sq. km)
Natural resources	Petroleum, natural gas, timber
Land use	
Arable land	0.6 percent
Permanent crops	0.8 percent
Other	98.6 percent

GOVERNMENT

Official country name	Sultanate of Brunei Land of Peace
Conventional short form	Brunei
Nationality noun and adjective	Bruneian
Official language	Malay
Currency	Bruneian dollar (BND)
Capital city	Bandar Seri Begawan
Type of government	Absolute Monarchy
Voting rights	18 years and over, universal (Local elections only)
National anthem	"Allah Pelihakaran Sultan" (God bless the sultan)
National day	National Day, February 23, 1984 (end of British protectorate)

POPULATION PROFILE, 2005 ESTIMATES

Population	333,000 (2001 census)
Ethnic groups	
Malayan	67 percent
Chinese	15 percent
Borneo ethnic groups	6 percent
Indians, Eurasians, Europeans, and others	12 percent
Religions	
Sunni Muslim	67 percent
Buddhist	13 percent
Protestant Christians and Roman Catholics	10 percent
Chinese folk religions (including Taoism), Hindu, traditional religions, and nonreligious	10 percent
Languages	
Malay	67 percent
Chinese	15 percent
Languages of the Indian subcontinent and other minorities	11 percent
Languages of Borneo	6 percent

English is spoken by under 1 percent of the population as a first language but is understood by the majority.

Adult literacy	94 percent

CHAD

GEOGRAPHY

Location	Sahelian West Africa, between Sudan and Niger
Area	495,750 sq. miles (1,284,000 sq. km)
Natural resources	Petroleum, uraniumm, natron, kaolin
Land use	
Arable land	2.9 percent
Permanent crops	Virtually none
Other	97.1 percent

GOVERNMENT

Official country name	Republic of Chad
Conventional short form	Chad
Nationality noun and adjective	Chadian
Official languages	French, Arabic
Currency	CFA franc/franc of the African Financial Community (XOF)
Capital city	N'Djamena
Type of government	Republic
Voting rights	18 years and over, universal
National anthem	"Peuple tchadien, debout et à l'ouvrage" (People of Chad, arise and to your work)
National day	Independence Day, August 11, 1960

POPULATION PROFILE, 2000 ESTIMATES

Population	9,254,000 (2003 Chadian government estimate)

Ethnic groups
There are some 200 ethnic groups including Arabs, Gorane, Zaghawa, and others in the north and the center; and Sara, Moundang, Moussei, and others in the south. No figures for the breakdown are available.

Religions	
Sunni Muslim	51.0 percent
Roman Catholic	20.0 percent
Protestant	14.0 percent
Traditional and other religions	15.0 percent
Languages	
French	understood by 13.0 percent
Arabic	26.0 percent
Sara (and related languages)	31.0 percent
Teda	7.0 percent
Mbum	6.0 percent
Masalit	6.0 percent
Tama	6.0 percent
Other	5.0 percent
Adult literacy	47.5 percent

EGYPT

GEOGRAPHY

Location	Coastal North Africa, between Libya and Israel
Area	386,660 sq. miles (1,001,450 sq. km)
Natural resources	Petroleum, natural gas, iron ore, phosphates, manganese, lead, zinc
Land use	
Arable land	2.9 percent
Permanent crops	0.5 percent
Other	96.6 percent

GOVERNMENT

Official country name	Arab Republic of Egypt
Conventional short form	Egypt
Nationality noun and adjective	Egyptian
Official languages	Arabic
Currency	Egyptian pound (EGP)
Capital city	Cairo
Type of government	Republic
Voting rights	18 years and over, universal
National anthem	"Misr Ya Umm al-Bilad" (Egypt, mother of all lands)
National day	Revolution Day, July 23, 1952

POPULATION PROFILE, 2000 ESTIMATES

Population	68,649,000 (2004 Egyptian government estimate)

Ethnic groups	
Arab (including Berbers and Bedouins)	99 percent
Europeans, Nubians, and Beja	under 1 percent
Religions	
Sunni Muslim	94 percent
Coptic Christian	5 percent
Other	1 percent
Languages	
Arabic	nearly 100 percent
Adult literacy	58 percent

GAMBIA

GEOGRAPHY

Location	Coastal West Africa, surrounded by Senegal
Area	4,361 sq. miles (11,295 sq. km)
Natural resources	Fish, titanium, tin, zircon, silica sand, clay, petroleum
Land use	
Arable land	27.9 percent
Permanent crops	0.4 percent
Other	71.7 percent

GOVERNMENT

Official country name	Republic of The Gambia
Conventional short form	Gambia
Nationality noun and adjective	Gambian
Official language	English
Currency	Gambian dalasi (GMD)
Capital city	Banjul
Type of government	Republic
Voting rights	18 years and over, universal
National anthem	"For the Gambia Our Homeland"
National day	Independence Day, February 18, 1965

POPULATION PROFILE, 2003 CENSUS

Population	1,783,000 (2009 estimate)
Ethnic groups	
Mandinka	42 percent
Fula	18 percent
Wolof	16 percent
Jola	10 percent
Serahuli	9 percent
Other	5 percent
Religions	
Muslim	90 percent
Christian	8 percent
Traditional religions	2 percent
Languages	
Mandinka	32 percent
Fula	20 percent
Wolof	12 percent
Soninke	10 percent
Jola	4 percent
Mandjak	2 percent
Other	20 percent
Adult literacy	40 percent

INDIA

GEOGRAPHY

Location	South Asia, between the Bay of Bengal and the Arabian Sea
Area	1,269,212 sq. miles (3,287,263 sq. km)
Natural resources	Coal, iron ore, manganese, mica, bauxite, natural gas, chromite, molybdenum, titanium ore, diamonds, petroleum
Land use	
Arable land	48.8 percent
Permanent crops	2.8 percent
Other	48.4 percent

GOVERNMENT

Official country name	Republic of India
Conventional short form	India
Nationality noun and adjective	Indian
Official languages	Hindi (official language), English (associate official language)
Currency	Indian rupee (INR)
Capital city	New Delhi (part of the Delhi metropolitan area)
Type of government	Federal Republic
Voting rights	18 years and over, universal
National anthem	"Jana-Gana-Mana" (Thou art the ruler of the minds of all people)
National day	Republic Day, January 26, 1950

POPULATION PROFILE, 2005 ESTIMATES

Population	1,027,015,000 (2001 census)
Ethnic groups	
Indo-Aryan	72 percent
Dravidian	25 percent
Mongoloid and others	3 percent
Religions	
Hindu	80 percent
Sunni Muslim	13 percent
Christian	2 percent
Sikh	2 percent
Other	3 percent
Languages	
Hindi	33 percent
Bengali	7 percent
Telugu	6 percent
Marathi	6 percent
Tamil	5 percent
Urdu	4 percent

Gujarati	4 percent
Kannada	4 percent
Malayalam	3 percent
Angika	3 percent
Oriya	3 percent
Punjabi	2 percent
Bhojpuri	2 percent
Tulu	2 percent
Assamese	1 percent
Marwari	1 percent
Chhattisgarhi	1 percent
Magadhi	1 percent
Maithili	1 percent
Others	11 percent
Adult literacy	60 percent

INDONESIA

GEOGRAPHY

Location	Southeastern Asia, an archipelago between the Indian and the Pacific Oceans
Area	734,294 sq. miles (1,904,414 sq. km)
Natural resources	Petroleum, natural gas, tin, nickel, timber, bauxite, copper, gold, silver
Land use	
Arable land	11.3 percent
Permanent crops	7.2 percent
Other	81.5 percent

GOVERNMENT

Official country name	Republic of Indonesia
Conventional short form	Indonesia
Nationality noun and adjective	Indonesian
Official language	Bahasa Indonesia
Currency	Rupiah (IDR)
Capital city	Jakarta
Type of government	Republic
Voting rights	17 years and over, universal; younger married persons receive the right to vote
National anthem	"Indonesia Raya" (Great Indonesia)
National day	Independence Day, August 17, 1945

POPULATION PROFILE, 2004 ESTIMATES

Population	206,265,000 (2000 census)
Ethnic groups	
Javanese	45 percent
Sundanese	14 percent
Madurese	8 percent
Coastal Malays	8 percent
Others, including Dyaks, Bataks, and Minangkabau	25 percent
Religions	
Sunni Muslim	88 percent
Protestant Christian	5 percent
Roman Catholic	3 percent
Hindu	2 percent
Others, including Buddhist, and Traditional religions	2 percent
Languages	
Javanese	45 percent
Sundanese	14 percent
Bahasa Indonesia	12 percent
Madurese	8 percent
Minang	2 percent
Batak	2 percent
Buginese	2 percent
Others	15 percent

Most speakers of Bahasa Indonesia also speak at least one other language.

Adult literacy	87.9 percent

IRAN

GEOGRAPHY

Location	Western Asia, between Iraq and Pakistan
Area	636,368 sq. miles (1,648,195 sq. km)
Natural resources	Petroleum, natural gas, coal, chromium, copper, iron ore, lead, manganese, zinc, sulfur
Land use	
Arable land	10 percent
Permanent crops	1 percent
Other	89 percent

GOVERNMENT

Official country name	Islamic Republic of Iran
Conventional short form	Iran
Nationality noun and adjective	Iranian
Official language	Farsi (Persian)
Currency	Rial (IRR)
Capital city	Tehran
Type of government	Theocratic republic
Voting rights	18 years and over, universal
National anthem	"Sorood-e Jomhoori-e Eslami-e Iran" (The national song of Iran)
National day	Republic Day, April 1, 1979

POPULATION PROFILE, 1996 CENSUS

Population	68,920,000 (2003 UN estimate)
Ethnic groups	
Persian	51.0 percent
Azerbaijani	24.0 percent
Gilaki and	
Mazandarani	8.0 percent
Kurd	7.0 percent
Arab	3.0 percent
Lur	2.0 percent
Baluchi	2.0 percent
Turkmen	2.0 percent
Other	1.0 percent
Religions	
Shia Muslim	89.0 percent
Sunni Muslim	10.0 percent
Other	1.0 percent
Languages	
Farsi (Persian and	
Persian dialects)	58.0 percent
Turkic and Turkic	
dialects	26.0 percent
Kurdish	9.0 percent
Luri	2.0 percent
Baluchi	1.0 percent
Arabic	1.0 percent
Turkish	1.0 percent
Other	2.0 percent
Adult literacy	79.4 percent

IRAQ
GEOGRAPHY

Location	Southwestern Asia, between Iran, Syria, and Saudi Arabia
Area	168,754 sq. miles (437,072 sq. km)
Natural resources	Petroleum, natural gas, phosphates, sulfur
Land use	
Arable land	13.1 percent
Permanent crops	0.6 percent
Other	86.3 percent

GOVERNMENT

Official country name	Republic of Iraq
Conventional short form	Iraq
Nationality noun and adjective	Iraqi
Official languages	Arabic, Kurdish
Currency	Iraqi dinar (IRR)
Capital city	Baghdad
Type of government	Parliamentary republic

Voting rights	18 years and over, universal
National anthem	"Mawtini" (My homeland)
National day	Republic Day, July 14, 1958

POPULATION PROFILE, 2000 ESTIMATES

Population	28,945,657 (2009 estimate)
Ethnic groups	
Arab	75–80 percent
Kurdish	15–20 percent
Other	5 percent
Religions	
Shia Muslim	60–65 percent
Sunni Muslim	32–37 percent
Christian or other	3 percent
Languages	
Arabic	75–80 percent
Kurdish	15–20 percent
Other	5 percent
Adult literacy	40 percent

JORDAN
GEOGRAPHY

Location	Southwestern Asia, between Iraq, Saudi Arabia, and Israel
Area	34,865 sq. miles (92,300 sq. km)
Natural resources	Phosphates, potash
Land use	
Arable land	2.7 percent
Permanent crops	1.8 percent
Other	95.5 percent

GOVERNMENT

Official country name	Hashemite Kingdom of Jordan
Conventional short form	Jordan
Nationality noun and adjective	Jordanian
Official language	Arabic
Currency	Jordanian dinar (JOD)
Capital city	Amman
Type of government	Constitutional monarchy
Voting rights	18 years and over, universal
National anthem	"As-salam al-malaki al-urdoni" (Long live the king of Jordan)
National day	Independence Day, May 25, 1946

POPULATION PROFILE, 2004 ESTIMATES

Population	5,101,000 (2004 census)
Ethnic groups	
Arab	98 percent
Circassians, Armenians, and others	2 percent

Religions	
Sunni Muslim	92.0 percent
Christian minorities	6.0 percent
Shia Muslim	2.0 percent
Languages	
Arabic	nearly 100 percent
Armenian and other minorities	under 1.0 percent
Adult literacy	91.3 percent

KAZAKHSTAN

GEOGRAPHY

Location	Central Asia, between Russia, Uzbekistan, and China
Area	1,049,150 sq. miles (2,717,300 sq. km)
Natural resources	Petroleum, natrual gas, coal, iron ore, manganese, chrome ore, nickel
Land use	
Arable land	8.0 percent
Permanent crops	0.1 percent
Other	nearly 92.0 percent

GOVERNMENT

Official country name	Republic of Kazakhstan
Conventional short form	Kazakhstan
Nationality noun and adjective	Kazakh
Official languages	Kazakh, Russian
Currency	Tenge (KZT)
Capital city	Astana
Type of government	Republic
Voting rights	18 years and over, universal
National anthem	"Erkindik kyrany, sharykta" (Soar up in the sky, eagle of freedom)
National day	Republic Day, October 25, 1990

POPULATION PROFILE, 1999 CENSUS

Population	14,952,000 (1999 census)
Ethnic groups	
Kazakh	53.4 percent
Russian	30.0 percent
Ukranian	3.7 percent
Uzbek	2.5 percent
German	2.4 percent
Uighur	1.4 percent
Other	6.6 percent
Religions	
Sunni Muslim	47.0 percent
Russian Orthodox	23.0 percent
Nonreligious	27.0 percent
Protestant	2.0 percent
Other	1 percent
Languages	
Russian	95 percent
Kazakh	64 percent
Adult literacy	98.4 percent

KUWAIT

GEOGRAPHY

Location	Southwestern Asia, between Iraq and Saudi Arabia
Area	6,880 sq. miles (17,820 sq. km)
Natural resources	Petroleum, natural gas,
Land use	
Arable land	0.7 percent
Permanent crops	0.1 percent
Other	99.2 percent

GOVERNMENT

Official country name	State of Kuwait
Conventional short form	Kuwait
Nationalitynoun and adjective	Kuwaiti
Official language	Arabic
Currency	Kuwaiti dinar (KD)
Capital city	Kuwait City
Type of government	Monarchy
Voting rights	21 years and over, limited to descendants of those living in Kuwait in 1920 and citizens naturalized for at least 30 years
National anthem	"Watanil Kuwait" (Kuwait, my country)
National day	National Day, February 25, 1950

POPULATION PROFILE, 2000 ESTIMATES

Population	2,243,000 (2001 estimate)
Ethnic groups	
Kuwaiti	45 percent
Other Arabs	35 percent
South Asian	9 percent
Iranian	4 percent
Others	7 percent
Religions	
Sunni Muslim	60 percent
Shia Muslim	25 percent
Others, mainly Christian and Hindu	15 percent
Languages	
Arabic	80 percent
Languages of South Asia	9 percent
Farsi (Persian)	4.0 percent
Others (including English)	7.0 percent
Adult literacy	83.5 percent

KYRGYZSTAN

GEOGRAPHY

Location	Central Asia, between Kazakhstan and China
Area	76,640 sq. miles (198,500 sq. km)
Natural resources	Hydropower, gold, coal
Land use	
Arable land	7.0 percent
Permanent crops	0.4 percent
Other	nearly 92.0 percent

GOVERNMENT

Official country name	Kyrgyz Republic
Conventional short form	Kyrgyzstan
Nationality	
noun and adjective	Kyrgyz
Official languages	Kyrgyz, Russian
Currency	Som (KGS)
Capital city	Bishkek
Type of government	Republic
Voting rights	18 years and over, universal
National anthem	"Algaí ber, Kyrgyz el" (Come on, Kyrgyz people)
National day	Independence Day, August 31, 1991

POPULATION PROFILE, 1999 CENSUS

Population	4,822,000 (1999 Kyrgyz government estimate)
Ethnic groups	
Kyrgyz	64.9 percent
Uzbek	13.8 percent
Russian	12.5 percent
German	2.4 percent
Dungun	1.1 percent
Ukranian	1.0 percent
Other	4.3 percent
Religions	
Sunni Muslim	70.0 percent
Russian Orthodox	6.0 percent
Nonreligious	24.0 percent
Languages	
Kyrgyz	64.7 percent
Uzbek	13.6 percent
Russian	12.5 percent
Dungun	1.0 percent
Other	8.2 percent
Adult literacy	99.0 percent

LEBANON

GEOGRAPHY

Location	Southwestern Asia, between Syria and Israel
Area	4,015 sq. miles (10,400 sq. km)
Natural resources	Limestone, iron ore
Land use	
Arable land	16.6 percent
Permanent crops	14.0 percent
Other	69.4 percent

GOVERNMENT

Official country name	Lebanese Republic
Conventional short form	Lebanon
Nationality	
noun and adjective	Lebanese
Official language	Arabic
Currency	Lebanese pound (LBP)
Capital city	Beirut
Type of government	Republic
Voting rights	18 years and over, universal
National anthem	"Koullouna lilouatann lil oula lil alam" (For all of us! For our country, for our flag and glory)
National day	Independence Day, November 22, 1943

POPULATION PROFILE, 2000 ESTIMATES

Population	3,282,000 (2000 United Nations estimate)
Ethnic groups	
Arab	95 percent
Armenians	4 percent
Others	1 percent
Religions	
Muslim	60 percent
Christian	39 percent
Other	1 percent
Languages	
Arabic	nearly 100 percent
Armenian and other minorities	under 1 percent
Adult literacy	87 percent

LIBYA

GEOGRAPHY

Location	Coastal North Africa, between Egypt and Tunisia
Area	679,360 sq. miles (1,179,540 sq. km)
Natural resources	Petroleum, natural gas, gypsum
Land use	
Arable land	1.0 percent
Permanent crops	nearly 0.2 percent
Other	98.8 percent

GOVERNMENT

Official country name	Great Socialist People's Libyan Arab Jamahiriya (Jamahiriya means "state of the masses")
Conventional short form	Libya
Nationality noun and adjective	Libyan
Official language	Arabic
Currency	Libyan dinar (LYD)
Capital city	Tripoli, Surt (administrative capital)
Type of government	Republic
Voting rights	18 years and over, universal and compulsory
National anthem	"Allah Akbar" (God is great)
National day	Revolution Day, September 1, 1969

POPULATION PROFILE, 2000 ESTIMATES

Population	5,679,000 (2003 Libyan government estimate)
Ethnic groups	
Arab–Berber	97.0 percent
Other (including foreign oil industry workers)	3.0 percent
Religions	
Sunni Muslim	97.0 percent
Roman Catholic and Protestant churches	2.0 percent
Other	1 percent
Languages	
Arabic	97.0 percent
European languages and languages of South Asia	3.0 percent
Adult literacy	82.6 percent

MALAYSIA

GEOGRAPHY

Location	Southeastern Asia on a peninsula south of Thailand, plus the northern third of the island of Borneo
Area	127,320 sq. miles (329,758 sq. km)
Natural resources	Tin, petroleum, natural gas, iron ore, bauxite, timber
Land use	
Arable land	5.5 percent
Permanent crops	17.6 percent
Other	76.9 percent

GOVERNMENT

Official country name	Federation of Malaysia
Conventional short form	Malaysia
Nationality noun and adjective	Malaysian
Official languages	Malay (Bahasa Melayu)
Currency	Ringgit (MYR)
Capital city	Kuala Lumpur, Putrajaya (administrative capital)
Type of government	Federal constitutional monarchy
Voting rights	21 years and over, universal
National anthem	"Negera Ku" (My country)
National day	Independence Day, August 31, 1957

POPULATION PROFILE, 2005 ESTIMATES

Population	23,275,000 (2000 census)
Ethnic groups	
Malayan	50 percent
Chinese	24 percent
Sabah and Sarawak	11 percent
Indian	7 percent
Others	8 percent
Religions	
Sunni Muslim	53 percent
Buddhist	17 percent
Chinese folk religions	12 percent
Christians	10 percent
Others	8 percent
Languages	
Malay (Bahasa Melayu)	58 percent
Chinese	24 percent
Tamil	4 percent
Iban	3 percent
Other	11 percent

English is spoken by under 1 percent of the population as a first language but is understood by 31 percent.

Adult literacy	88.7 percent

MALI

GEOGRAPHY

Location	Sahelian West Africa, between Niger and Mauritania
Area	482,077 sq. miles (1,248,574 sq. km)
Natural resources	Gold, phosphates, kaolin (china clay), salt, limestone, uranium
Land use	
Arable land	3.8 percent
Permanent crops	Virtually none
Other	96.2 percent

GOVERNMENT

Official country name	Republic of Mali
Conventional short form	Mali
Nationality noun and adjective	Malian
Official language	French
Currency	CFA franc (XOF)
Capital city	Bamako
Type of government	Republic
Voting rights	18 years and over, universal
National anthem	"A ton appel, Mali" (At your call, Mali)
National day	Independence Day, September 22, 1960

POPULATION PROFILE, 2000 ESTIMATES

Population	11,234,000 (2000 UN estimate)
Ethnic groups	
Mande/Manding (Bambara, Malinke, Soninke)	50 percent
Peul	17 percent
Voltaic peoples	12 percent
Tuareg and Moor	10 percent
Songhai	6 percent
Other	5 percent
Religions	
Sunni Muslim	90 percent
Traditional religions	10 percent
Languages	
French	understood by 8 percent
Bambara	spoken by 32 percent as a first language, understood by 80 percent
Fulani	14 percent
Senufo	12 percent
Soninke	9 percent
Tuareg	7 percent
Songhai	7 percent
Malinke	7 percent
Adult literacy	46 percent

MAURITANIA

GEOGRAPHY

Location	On the Sahelian West African coast, between Western Sahara and Senegal
Area	398,000 sq. miles (1,030,700 sq. km)
Natural resources	Iron ore, gypsum, copper, phosphates, rich coastal fishing grounds
Land use	
Arable land	0.5 percent
Permanent crops	Virtually none
Other	99.5 percent

GOVERNMENT

Official country name	Islamic Republic of Mauritania
Conventional short form	Mauritania
Nationality noun and adjective	Mauritanian
Official languages	Arabic, Wolof
Currency	Ouguiya (MRO)
Capital city	Bamako
Type of government	Republic
Voting rights	18 years and over, universal
National anthem	The anthem has no name and no words: it is officially known as the National Anthem of the Islamic Republic of Mauritania
National day	Independence Day, November 28, 1960

POPULATION PROFILE, 2000 ESTIMATES

Population	2,508,000 (2000 census)
Ethnic groups	
Mixed Moors (Maurs)/black Africans	40.0 percent
Moors (Maurs)	30.0 percent
Black Africans	30.0 percent
Religions	
Sunni Muslim	nearly 100.0 percent
Christians	under 1.0 percent
Languages	
Arabic	understood by 81.0 percent
Wolof	7.0 percent
Tukulor	5.0 percent
Soninke	3.0 percent
Other	4.0 percent
Adult literacy	41.7 percent

MOROCCO

GEOGRAPHY

Location	Northwestern Africa, with coasts on the Mediterranean Sea and the Atlantic Ocean
Area	172,413 sq. miles (446,550 sq. km) excluding the disputed territory of Western Sahara; de facto 275,115 sq. miles (712, 550 sq. km)
Natural resources	Phosphates (most in Western Sahara), iron ore, manganese, salt, zinc, lead, Atlantic fishing grounds
Land use (excluding Western Sahara)	
Arable land	19.6 percent
Permanent crops	nearly 2.2 percent
Other	78.2 percent

GOVERNMENT

Official country name	Kingdom of Morocco
Conventional short form	Morocco
Nationality noun and adjective	Moroccan
Official language	Arabic
Currency	Moroccan dirham (MAD)
Capital city	Rabat
Type of government	Monarchy
Voting rights	18 years and over, universal
National anthem	"Manbit al Ahrah, Mashriq al Anwar" (Fountain of freedom, source of light)
National day	Throne Day (accession of the present monarch), July 30, 1999

POPULATION PROFILE, 2000 ESTIMATES

Population	29,475,000 (2004 census), excluding Western Sahara; 29,892,000 (2004 census) de facto
Ethnic groups	
Arab–Berber	99 percent
Europeans	under 1 percent
Religions	
Sunni Muslim	nearly 99 percent
Others	1 percent
Languages	
Arabic	nearly 100 percent
Tamazight (Berber)	30 percent (percentage disputed)
French	widely understood
Adult literacy	52 percent

NIGER

GEOGRAPHY

Location	Sahelian West Africa, between Nigeria and Algeria
Area	489,190 sq. miles (1,267,000 sq. km)
Natural resources	Uranium, coal, tin, iron ore, gold
Land use	
Arable land	3.5 percent
Permanent crops	Virtually none
Other	96.5 percent

GOVERNMENT

Official country name	Republic of Niger
Conventional short form	Niger
Nationality noun and adjective	None in English
Official language	French
Currency	CFA franc (XOF)
Capital city	Niamey
Type of government	Republic
Voting rights	18 years and over, universal
National anthem	"Aupres du grand Niger puissant" (By the banks of the mighty Niger River)
National day	Republic Day, December 18, 1958

POPULATION PROFILE, 2000 ESTIMATES

Population	10,790,000 (2001 census)
Ethnic groups	
Hausa	56.0 percent
Djerma	22.0 percent
Fula	8.5 percent
Tuareg	8.0 percent
Beri Beri (Kanouri)	4.3 percent
Other	1.2 percent
Religions	
Sunni Muslim	89.0 percent
Traditional religions	10.0 percent
Christian	1.0 percent
Languages	
French	understood by 15.0 percent
Hausa	56.0 percent
Djerma-Songhai	22.0 percent
Fulani	8.5 percent
Tuareg	8.0 percent
Adult literacy	17.6 percent

OMAN

GEOGRAPHY

Location	Western Asia, between Yemen and the United Arab Emirates. Oman includes the Musandam Peninsula, north of the United Arab Emirates, and a small enclave within the United Arab Emirates
Area	82,030 sq. miles (212,460 sq. km)
Natural resources	Petroleum, natural gas, copper, asbestos, marble
Land use	
Arable land	0.1 percent
Permanent crops	0.2 percent
Other	97.7 percent

GOVERNMENT

Official country name	Sultanate of Oman
Conventional short form	Oman
Nationality noun and adjective	Omani
Official language	Arabic
Currency	Omani rial (OMR)
Capital city	Muscat
Type of government	Monarchy
Voting rights	21 years and over, universal
National anthem	"Ya Rabbana Ehfid Lana Jalalat Al Sultan" (The sultan's anthem)
National day	Birthday of Sultan Qaboos, November 18, 1940

POPULATION PROFILE, 2000 ESTIMATES

Population	2,331,000 (2003 census)
Ethnic groups	
Arab	nearly 75 percent
South Asian	about 25 percent
Baluchi, African, and European minorities	under 1 percent
Religions	
Ibadi Muslim	75 percent
Hindu	20 percent
Sunni and Shia Muslim and other minorities	5 percent
Languages	
Arabic	75 percent
Languages of Southern Asia	about 25 percent
Baluchi and other minorities	1 percent
Adult literacy	76 percent

PAKISTAN

GEOGRAPHY

Location	Southern Asia, between India and Iran
Area	310,403 sq. miles (803,940 sq. km), excluding the disputed regions of Azad Kashmir and the Northern Areas; 342,897 sq. miles (888,099 sq. km) with these regions included
Natural resources	Natural gas, iron ore, coal, copper, salt
Land use	
Arable land	27.8 percent
Permanent crops	0.9 percent
Other	71.3 percent

GOVERNMENT

Official country name	Islamic Republic of Pakistan
Conventional short form	Pakistan
Nationality noun and adjective	Pakistani
Official languages	Urdu and English
Currency	Pakistani rupee (PKR)
Capital city	Islamabad
Type of government	Federal republic
Voting rights	18 years and over, universal
National anthem	"Pak sarzamin shad bad" (Blessed be the sacred land)
National day	Republic Day, March 23, 1956

POPULATION PROFILE, 2000 ESTIMATES

Population	156,483,000 (2004 UN estimate, excluding Azad Kashmir and the Northern Areas) or 160,600,000 (2000 estimate, including Azad Kashmir and the Northern Areas)
Ethnic groups	
Punjabi	58 percent
Sindhi	12 percent
Pashtun	8 percent
Baluchi	3 percent
Muhajir, Kashmiris, Hunzukats, and others	19 percent
Religions	
Sunni Muslim	77 percent
Shia Muslim	20 percent
Christian, Hindu, and others	3 percent
Languages	
Punjabi	48 percent
Sindhi	12 percent
Siraki	10.0 percent

Pashto	8.0 percent
Urdu	8.0 percent
Baluchi	3.0 percent
Others	11.0 percent
Adult literacy	45.7 percent

QATAR

GEOGRAPHY

Location	Western Asia, a peninsula north of Saudi Arabia on the Persian Gulf
Area	4,416 sq. miles (11,437 sq. km)
Natural resources	Petroleum, natural gas, fish
Land use	
Arable land	1.3 percent
Permanent crops	0.3 percent
Other	98.4 percent

GOVERNMENT

Official country name	State of Qatar
Conventional short form	Qatar
Nationality noun and adjective	Qatari
Official language	Arabic
Currency	Qatari rial (QAR)
Capital city	Doha
Type of government	Monarchy
Voting rights	18 years and over, universal
National anthem	"Al-Salam al-Amiri" (The peace of Amiri anthem)
National day	Independence Day, September 3, 1971

POPULATION PROFILE, 2000 ESTIMATES

Population	744,000 (2004 census)
Ethnic groups	
Qatari Arab	40.0 percent
South Asian	36.0 percent
Iranian	10.0 percent
Other (including non–Qatari Arabs)	14.0 percent
Religions	
Sunni Muslim	85.0 percent
Shia Muslim	10.0 percent
Other	5.0 percent
Languages	
Arabic	over 50.0 percent
Languages of Southern Asia	36.0 percent
Farsi	10.0 percent
English and other languages	4.0 percent
Adult literacy	82.5 percent

SAUDI ARABIA

GEOGRAPHY

Location	Western Asia, between the Persian Gulf and the Red Sea
Area	756,890 sq. miles (1,960,582 sq. km)
Natural resources	Petroleum, natural gas, iron ore, gold
Land use	
Arable land	1.7 percent
Permanent crops	0.1 percent
Other	98.2 percent

GOVERNMENT

Official country name	Kingdom of Saudi Arabia
Conventional short form	Saudi Arabia
Nationality noun and adjective	Saudi
Official language	Arabic
Currency	Saudi riyal (QAR)
Capital city	Riyadh
Type of government	Monarchy
Voting rights (for municipal elections only)	21 years and over, male
National anthem	"Sarei Lil Majd Walaya" (Hasten to glory and supremacy)
National day	Unification of the Kingdom Day, September 23, 1932

POPULATION PROFILE, 2000 ESTIMATES

Population	22,674,000 (2004 census)
Ethnic groups	
Arab	90.0 percent
African, Southern and Eastern Asian, and European minorities	10.0 percent
Religions	
Sunni Muslim	nearly 95.0 percent
Shia Muslim	5.0 percent
Hindu and Christian minorities	under 1.0 percent
Languages	
Arabic	nearly 100.0 percent
Adult literacy	78.8 percent

SENEGAL

GEOGRAPHY

Location	Coastal West Africa, between Guinea-Bissau and Mauritania
Area	75,955 sq. miles (196,722 sq. km)
Natural resources	Fish, phosphates, iron ore
Land use	
Arable land	12.5 percent
Permanent crops	0.2 percent
Other	87.3 percent

GOVERNMENT

Official country name	Republic of Senegal
Conventional short form	Senegal
Nationality noun and adjective	Senegalese
Official language	French
Currency	CFA franc (XOF)
Capital city	Dakar
Type of government	Republic
Voting rights	18 years and over, universal
National anthem	"Un peuple, un but, une foi badiane" (One people, one goal, one faith)
National day	Independence Day, April 4, 1960

POPULATION PROFILE, 2002 ESTIMATES

Population	13,712,000 (2009 estimate)
Ethnic groups	
Wolof	43.0 percent
Pular	24.0 percent
Serer	15.0 percent
Jola	4.0 percent
Mandinka	3.0 percent
Soninke	1.0 percent
Others (including Europeans)	10.0 percent
Religions	
Muslim	94.0 percent
Christian	5.0 percent
Traditional religions	1.0 percent
Languages	
Wolof	33.4 percent
Pulaar	23.3 percent
Serer	9.6 percent
Jola	3.3 percent
Mandinka	5.7 percent
Malinke	3.6 percent
Soninke	2.1 percent
Other	19.0 percent
Adult literacy	39.0 percent

SOMALIA

GEOGRAPHY

Location	Coastal East Africa, between Kenya and Djibouti
Area	75,955 sq. miles (196,722 sq. km)
Natural resources	Uranium, iron ore, tin, gypsum, bauxite, copper, salt, natural gas
Land use	
Arable land	1.7 percent
Permanent crops	Virtually none
Other	98.3 percent

GOVERNMENT

Official country name	Somalia
Conventional short form	Somalia
Nationality noun and adjective	Somalian
Official language	Somali
Currency	Somali shilling (SOS); the United States dollar and other foreign currencies are also widely used
Capital city	Mogadishu
Type of government	No functioning national government
Voting rights	18 years and over, universal (in the areas controlled by the transitional government), no voting rights in areas outside government control
National anthem	"Soomaaliyeey toosoo" (Somalia, wake up)
National day	Independence Day, July 1, 1960.

POPULATION PROFILE

The last census conducted in Somalia was completed in 1975. Since then, decades of war and famine have displaced or killed millions, and it is not known how many refugees have fled to other countries. It has been estimated that Somalia currently has a population of around 10 million, but a detailed demographic breakdown cannot be given with any reasonable degree of accuracy.

SUDAN

GEOGRAPHY

Location	Sahelian eastern Africa, between Egypt and Ethiopia
Area	967,495 sq. miles (2,505,810 sq. km)
Natural resources	Petroleum, iron ore, zinc, copper, chromium, tungsten, silver, mica
Land use	
Arable land	6.8 percent
Permanent crops	0.2 percent
Other	93.0 percent

GOVERNMENT

Official country name	Republic of the Sudan
Conventional short form	Sudan
Nationality noun and adjective	Sudanese
Official language	Arabic
Currency	Sudanese dinar (SDD)
Capital city	Khartoum
Type of government	Republic
Voting rights	18 years and over, universal
National anthem	"Nahnu Jundullah, Jundu al-Wattan" (We fight for our homeland, blessed by Allah)
National day	Independence Day, January 1, 1956

POPULATION PROFILE, 2000 ESTIMATES

Population	31,801,000 (2000 official estimate)
Ethnic groups	
Southern African peoples	52 percent
Arab	39 percent
Beja	6 percent
Other	3 percent
Religions	
Sunni Muslim	72 percent
Traditional religions	17 percent
Christian	9 percent
Other	2 percent
Languages	
Arabic	49 percent
Dinka	12 percent
Nubian languages	8 percent
Beja	6 percent
Nuer	5 percent
Other	20 percent
Adult literacy	61 percent

SYRIA

GEOGRAPHY

Location	Southwestern Asia, along the Mediterranean Sea between Turkey and Lebanon
Area	71,498 sq. miles (185,180 sq. km), of which 436 sq. miles (1,130 sq. km) is currently occupied by Israel
Natural resources	Petroleum, phosphates, chrome, manganese, asphalt
Land use	
Arable land	25.2 percent
Permanent crops	4.4 percent
Other	70.4 percent

GOVERNMENT

Official country name	Syrian Arab Republic
Conventional short form	Syria
Nationality noun and adjective	Syrian
Official language	Arabic
Currency	Syrian pound (SYP)
Capital city	Damascus
Type of government	Republic
Voting rights	18 years and over, universal
National anthem	"Homat el Diyar" (Guardians of the homeland)
National day	Independence Day, April 17, 1946

POPULATION PROFILE, 2000 ESTIMATES

Population	16,720,000 (2001 official estimate)
Ethnic groups	
Arab	90.0 percent
Kurds, Armenians, and others	10.0 percent
Religions	
Sunni Muslim	74.0 percent
Alawite, Druze, and other Muslims	16.0 percent
Christian	10.0 percent
Languages	
Arabic	90.0 percent
Kurdish, Armenian, Aramaic, Circassian, and other	10.0 percent
Adult literacy	76.9 percent

TAJIKISTAN

GEOGRAPHY

Location	Central Asia, between Afghanistan and China
Area	55,300 sq. miles (143,100 sq. km)
Natural resources	Hydropower, petroleum, uranium, mercury, brown coal
Land use	
Arable land	6.6 percent
Permanent crops	under 1 percent
Other	93.5 percent

GOVERNMENT

Official country name	Republic of Tajikistan
Conventional short form	Tajikistan
Nationality noun and adjective	Tajik
Official language	Tajik
Currency	Somoni (TJS)
Capital city	Dushanbe
Type of government	Republic
Voting rights	18 years and over, universal
National anthem	"Suudi Mellii" (Happiness of the nation)
National day	Independence Day, September 11, 1991

POPULATION PROFILE, 2000 CENSUS

Population	14,952,000 (2000 census)
Ethnic groups	
Tajik	79.9 percent
Uzbek	15.3 percent
Russian	1.1 percent
Other	3.7 percent
Religions	
Sunni Muslim	80.0 percent
Shia Muslim	5.0 percent
Nonreligious	over 10.0 percent
Russian Orthodox	2.0 percent
Languages	
Tajik	65.0 percent
Uzbek	25.0 percent
Russian	4.0 percent
Other	6.0 percent
Adult literacy	99.4 percent

TANZANIA

GEOGRAPHY

Location	Coastal East Africa, between Kenya and Mozambique
Area	365,754 sq. miles (947,300 sq. km)
Natural resources	Hydropower, tin, phosphates, iron ore, coal, diamonds, gemstones, gold, natural gas, nickel
Land use	
Arable land	4.2 percent
Permanent crops	1.2 percent
Other	94.6 percent

GOVERNMENT

Official country name	United Republic of Tanzania
Conventional short form	Tanzania
Nationality noun and adjective	Tanzanian
Official languages	Swahili, English
Currency	Tanzanian shilling (TZS)
Capital city	Dar es Salaam
Type of government	Republic
Voting rights	18 years and over, universal
National anthem	"Mungu ibariki Afrika" (God bless Africa)
National day	Union Day, April 26, 1964

POPULATION PROFILE, 2002 CENSUS

Population	41,050,000 (2009 estimate)
Ethnic groups	
Bantu	94 percent
Arab	3 percent
Other	3 percent
Religions	
Muslim	37 percent
Christian	29 percent
Traditional religions	34 percent

Languages

There are more than 120 languages spoken by the people of Tanzania. Most of the population speak variants of the Bantu languages, including Swahili, but Arabic is widely used on the island of Zanzibar and in some coastal communities. English is used within universities and by some government agencies.

Adult literacy	69 percent

TUNISIA

GEOGRAPHY

Location	Coastal North Africa, between Libya and Algeria
Area	63,170 sq. miles (163,610 sq. km)
Natural resources	Petroleum, phosphates, iron ore, zinc, salt, lead
Land use	
Arable land	17.9 percent
Permanent crops	13.7 percent
Other	68.4 percent

GOVERNMENT

Official country name	The Tunisian Republic
Conventional short form	Tunisia
Nationality noun and adjective	Tunisian
Official language	Arabic
Currency	Tunisian dinar (TND)
Capital city	Tunis
Type of government	Republic
Voting rights	20 years and over, universal
National anthem	"Humata al Hima" (Defenders of the homeland)
National day	Independence Day, March 20, 1956

POPULATION PROFILE, 2000 ESTIMATES

Population	9,911,000 (2004 Tunisian national census)
Ethnic groups	
Arab-Berber	98.0 percent
Europeans and others	2.0 percent
Religions	
Sunni Muslim	98.0 percent
Roman Catholic and others	2.0 percent
Languages	
Arabic	almost 100.0 percent
Adult literacy	74.2 percent

TURKEY

GEOGRAPHY

Location	Southwestern Asia and Southeastern Europe
Area	301,382 sq. miles (780,580 sq. km)
Natural resources	Coal, iron ore, copper, hydroelectric power potential, chromium, antimony, mercury
Land use	
Arable land	30.9 percent
Permanent crops	3.4 percent
Other	65.7 percent

GOVERNMENT

Official country name	Republic of Turkey
Conventional short form	Turkey
Nationality noun and adjective	Turkish
Official language	Turkish
Currency	New Turkish lira (YTL)
Capital city	Ankara
Type of government	Republic
Voting rights	18 years and over, universal
National anthem	"Korkma! Sönmez bu safaklarda yüzen al sancak" (Do not be afraid! Our flag will never fade)
National day	Republic Day, October 26, 1923

POPULATION PROFILE, 2000 ESTIMATES

Population	67,804,000 (2000 census)
Ethnic groups	
Turkish	80.0 percent
Kurdish	20 percent (percentage disputed)
Religions	
Muslim (Sunni, small Shia minority)	over 99.0 percent
Christian (Greek Orthodox, Armenian Apostolic, and other minorities) and Jewish	0.2 percent
Languages	
Turkish	80.0 percent
Kurdish	20.0 percent (percentage disputed)
Armenian, Arabic, and Greek	under 1.0 percent
Adult literacy	86.5 percent

TURKMENISTAN

GEOGRAPHY

Location	Central Asia, between Iran and Kazakhstan
Area	188,500 sq. miles (488,100 sq. km)
Natural resources	Petroleum, natural gas, coal, sulfur
Land use	
Arable land	3.7 percent
Permanent crops	under 0.2 percent
Other	96.1 percent

GOVERNMENT

Official country name	Turkmenistan
Conventional short form	Turkmenistan
Nationality noun and adjective	Turkmen
Official language	Turkmen
Currency	Manat (TMM)
Capital city	Ashgabat
Type of government	Republic
Voting rights	18 years and over, universal
National anthem	"Garasyz, Bitarap, Türkmenostanyn Döwlet Gimni"(Independent, neutral Turkmenistan state anthem)
National day	Independence Day, October 27, 1991

POPULATION PROFILE, 1999 CENSUS

Population	14,952,000 (1999 census)
Ethnic groups	
Turkmen	77.0 percent
Uzbek	9.2 percent
Russian	6.7 percent
Kazakh	2.0 percent
Other	5.1 percent
Religions	
Sunni Muslim	87.0 percent
Nonreligious	11.0 percent
Russian Orthodox	2.0 percent
Languages	
Turkmen	72.0 percent
Russian	12.0 percent
Uzbek	9.0 percent
Other	7.0 percent
Adult literacy	98.0 percent

UNITED ARAB EMIRATES

GEOGRAPHY

Location	Western Asia, bordering the Persian Gulf and the Gulf of Oman
Area	32,000 sq. miles (82,880 sq. km)
Natural resources	Petroleum, natural gas
Land use	
Arable land	0 percent
Permanent crops	1.0 percent
Other	99.0 percent

GOVERNMENT

Official country name	United Arab Emirates
Conventional short form	None
Nationality noun and adjective	Emirati
Official language	Arabic
Currency	Qatari rial (QAR)
Capital city	Abu Dhabi
Type of government	Confederation of monarchies
Voting rights	None
National anthem	"Emirati Tahiat Alalam" (The emirati anthem)
National day	National Day, December 2, 1971

POPULATION PROFILE, 2000 ESTIMATES

Population	4,041,000 (2003 census department estimate)
Ethnic groups	
Emirati Arab	19.0 percent
South Asian	50.0 percent
Non-Emirati Arab and Iranian	23.0 percent
Other (mainly Europeans and East Asians)	8.0 percent
Religions	
Sunni Muslim	80.0 percent
Shia Muslim	16.0 percent
Hindu and Christian minorities	4.0 percent
Languages	
Arabic	over 40.0 percent
Languages of Southern Asia	50.0 percent
Farsi, English, and other languages	under 10.0 percent
Adult literacy	77.9 percent

UZBEKISTAN

GEOGRAPHY

Location	Central Asia, between Turkmenistan and Kazakhstan
Area	172,700 sq. miles (447,400 sq. km)
Natural resources	Natural gas, petroleum, coal, gold, uranium, silver
Land use	
Arable land	10.8 percent
Permanent crops	0.9 percent
Other	88.3 percent

GOVERNMENT

Official country name	Republic of Uzbekistan
Conventional short form	Uzbekistan
Nationality	
noun and adjective	Uzbek
Official language	Uzbek
Currency	Sum (UZS)
Capital city	Tashkent
Type of government	Republic
Voting rights	18 years and over, universal
National anthem	"Altin bu vadiylar, jan Ozbekistan"(These valleys are golden, my dear Uzbekistan)
National day	Independence Day, September 1, 1991

POPULATION PROFILE, 1996 ESTIMATES

Population	27,606,007 (2009 estimate)
Ethnic groups	
Uzbek	80.0 percent
Russian	5.5 percent
Tajik	5.0 percent
Kazakh	3.0 percent
Karakalpak	2.5 percent
Tatar and other	4.0 percent
Religions	
Sunni Muslim	88.0 percent
Russian Orthodox	6.0 percent
Nonreligious	6.0 percent
Languages	
Uzbek	74.3 percent
Russian	14.2 percent
Tajik	4.4 percent
Other	7.1 percent
Adult literacy	99.3 percent

WEST BANK AND GAZA

GEOGRAPHY

Location	**West Bank** southwestern Asia, between Israel and Jordan **Gaza:** southwestern Asia, between Israel and Egypt
Area	**West Bank:** 2,263 sq. miles (5,860 sq. km), includes East Jerusalem, which has been annexed by Israel, an action that has not been recognized by the UN **Gaza:** 139 sq. miles (360 sq. km)
Natural resources	**West Bank:** none **Gaza:** natural gas

Land use	West Bank	Gaza
Arable land	16.9 percent	29.0 percent
Permanent crops	19.0 percent	21.0 percent
Other	64.1 percent	50.0 percent

GOVERNMENT

Official country name	None
Conventional short form	West Bank and Gaza
Nationality	
noun and adjective	Palestinian
Official language	Arabic
Currency	Israeli new shekel (ILS)
Capital city	none (the administration is divided between Ramallah and Gaza City)
Type of government	Republic
Voting rights	18 years and over, universal
National anthem	None
National day	None

POPULATION PROFILE, 2000 ESTIMATES

Population	**West Bank:** 2,305,000 (2003 census) **Gaza:** 1,330,000 (2003 census) **Total:** 3,635,000 (2003 census)
Ethnic groups	
West Bank	
Arab	83 percent
Israeli	17 percent
Gaza	
Arab	nearly 100 percent
Religions	
West Bank	
Sunni Muslim	75 percent
Jewish	17 percent
Christian	8 percent
Gaza	
Sunni Muslim	99 percent
Christian	nearly 1 percent

Languages

West Bank

Arabic	83 percent
Hebrew	17 percent

Gaza

Arabic	nearly 100 percent

Adult literacy

West Bank	91 percent
Gaza	92 percent

WESTERN SAHARA

GEOGRAPHY

Location	On the Atlantic coast of North Africa, between Mauritania and Morocco
Area	102,700 sq. miles (266,000 sq. km)
Natural resources	Phosphates, iron ore
Land use	
Arable land	Virtually none
Permanent crops	Virtually none
Other	100 percent

GOVERNMENT

Official country name	The Sahrawi Arab Democratic Republic
Conventional short form	Western Sahara
Nationality noun and adjective	Western Saharan or Sahrawi
Official language	Arabic
Currency	Moroccan dinar (MAD)
Capital city	The government-in-exile is based near the Algerian city of Tindouf. It claims el Aaiun (Laayoune to Moroccans) as the national capital.
Type of government	Not applicable
Voting rights	None
National anthem	None
National day	None

POPULATION PROFILE, 2000 ESTIMATES

Population	19,722,000 (2004 census)
Ethnic groups	
Arab	virtually 100 percent
Religions	
Sunni Muslim	virtually 100 percent
Languages	
Arabic	virtually 100 percent
Adult literacy	No figure available

YEMEN

GEOGRAPHY

Location	Western Asia, bordering the Arabian Sea and the Red Sea, south of Saudi Arabia
Area	203,850 sq. miles (527,970 sq. km)
Natural resources	Petroleum, salt, marble, fish
Land use	
Arable land	2.8 percent
Permanent crops	0.2 percent
Other	97.0 percent

GOVERNMENT

Official country name	Republic of Yemen
Conventional short form	Yemen
Nationality noun and adjective	Yemeni
Official language	Arabic
Currency	Yemeni rial (YER)
Capital city	Sanaa
Type of government	Republic
Voting rights	18 years and over, universal
National anthem	"Raddidi Ayyatuha D-dunya Nashidi" (Repeat, O world, my song)
National day	Unification Day, May 22, 1990

POPULATION PROFILE, 2000 ESTIMATES

Population	19,722,000 (2004 census)
Ethnic groups	
Arab	about 98.0 percent
African, South Asian, and other minorities	2.0 percent
Religions	
Sunni Muslim	about 75.0 percent
Zaydi Shia Muslim	about 25.0 percent
Hindu Jewish, and Christian minorities	under 1.0 percent
Languages	
Arabic	nearly 100.0 percent
Adult literacy	50.2 percent

FURTHER READING AND RESEARCH

Reference

Armstrong, Karen. *Islam: A Short History*. New York: Mordern Library, 2002.

Calvert, John. *Islamism: A Documentary and Reference Guide*. Westport, CT: Greenwood Press, 2008.

Esposito, John L. *What Everyone Needs to Know about Islam*. New York: Oxford University Press, 2002.

Esposito, John L. (ed.). *The Oxford Encyclopedia of the Islamic World*. New York: Oxford University Press, 2009.

Grieve, Paul. *A Brief Guide to Islam: History, Faith, and Politics: The Complete Introduction*. New York: Carroll and Graf, 2006.

Lewis, Bernard, and Buntzie Churchill. *Islam: The Religion and the People*. Indianapolis, IN: Wharton Press, 2009.

Martin, Richard C. (ed.). *Encyclopedia of Islam and the Muslim World*. New York: Macmillan Reference USA, 2004.

Nagy, Luqman. *The Book of Islamic Dynasties: A Celebration of Islamic History and Culture*. London: Ta-Ha Publications, 2008.

Nasr, Seyyed Hossein. *Islam: Religion, History, and Civilization*. San Francisco: Harper, 2003.

Robinson, Francis (ed.). *The Cambridge Illustrated History of the Islamic World*. New York: Cambridge University Press, 1996.

Ruthven, Malise. *Islam in the World*. New York: Oxford University Press, 2006.

Shepard, William E. *Introducing Islam*. New York: Routledge, 2009.

Turner, C. *Islam: The Basics*. New York: Routledge, 2006.

Ünal, Ali. *An Introduction to Islamic Faith and Thought*. Somerset, NJ: Tughra Books, 2009.

Zepp, Ira. *A Muslim Primer: Beginner's Guide to Islam*. Fayetteville: University of Arkansas Press, 2000.

History

Abisaab, Rula Jurdi. *Converting Persia: Religion and Power in the Safavid Empire*. New York: I. B. Tauris, 2004.

Ansary, Mir Tamim. *Destiny Disrupted: A History of the World through Islamic Eyes*. New York: PublicAffairs, 2009.

Babaie, Sussan. *Slaves of the Shah: New Elites of Safavid Iran*. New York: I. B. Tauris, 2004.

Berinstain, Valerie. *India and the Mughal Dynasty*. New York: Abrams, 1998.

Brett, Michael. *The Berbers*. Cambridge, MA: Blackwell, 1996.

Casale, Giancarlo. *The Ottoman Age of Exploration*. New York: Oxford University Press, 2010.

Cribb, Joe, and Georgina Herrmann (eds). *After Alexander: Central Asia before Islam*. New York: Oxford University Press, 2007.

Crone, Patricia. *From Arabian Tribes to Islamic Empire: Army, State, and Society in the Near East 600–850*. Burlington, VT: Ashgate, 2008.

Eaton, Richard M. *India's Islamic Traditions, 711–1750.* New Delhi, India: Oxford University Press, 2003.

El-Hibri, Tayeb. *Reinterpreting Islamic Historiography: Harun al-Rashid and the Narrative of the Abbasid Caliphate.* New York: Cambridge University Press, 1999.

Floor, Willem M. *The Economy of Safavid Persia.* Wiesbaden, Germany: Reichert, 2000.

Goldschmidt, Arthur. *A Brief History of Egypt.* New York: Facts On File, 2008.

Gordon, Matthew. *The Rise of Islam.* Indianapolis, IN: Hackett Publishing, 2008.

Haider, A. F. *The Administrative Structure of the Safavid Empire.* Patna, India: Khuda Bakhsh Oriental Public Library, 2000.

Hawting, G. R. *The First Dynasty of Islam: The Umayyad Caliphate, AD 661–750.* New York: Routledge, 2000.

January, Brendan. *Arab Conquests of the Middle East.* Minneapolis, MN: Twenty-First Century Books, 2009.

Kennedy, Hugh. *The Prophet and the Age of the Caliphates: The Islamic Near East from the Sixth to the Eleventh Century.* New York: Longman, 1986.

Khattak, Shahin Kuli Khan. *Islam and the Victorians: Nineteenth-Century Perceptions of Muslim Practices and Beliefs.* New York: Tauris Academic Studies, 2008.

Le Strange, G. *Baghdad during the Abbasid Caliphate: From Contemporary Arabic and Persian Sources.* New York: Barnes and Noble, 1972.

Le Tourneau, Roger. *The Almohad Movement in North Africa in the Twelfth and Thirteenth Centuries.* Princeton, NJ: Princeton University Press, 1969.

Lewis, David Levering. *God's Crucible: Islam and the Making of Europe, 570 to 1215.* New York: W. W. Norton, 2008.

Madden, Thomas F. *The New Concise History of the Crusades.* Lanham, MD: Rowman and Littlefield, 2006.

Marozzi, Justin. *Tamerlane: Sword of Islam, Conqueror of the World.* London: HarperCollins, 2004.

Matthee, Rudolph P. *The Politics of Trade in Safavid Iran: Silk for Silver, 1600–1730.* New York: Cambridge University Press, 1999.

Meserve, Margaret. *Empires of Islam in Renaissance Historical Thought.* Cambridge, MA: Harvard University Press, 2008.

Moczar, Diane. *Islam at the Gates: How Christendom Defeated the Ottoman Turks.* Manchester, NH: Sophia Institute Press, 2008.

Mukhia, Harbans. *The Mughals of India.* Malden, MA: Blackwell, 2004.

Newman, Andrew J. *Society and Culture in the Early Modern Middle East: Studies on Iran in the Safavid Period.* Boston: Brill, 2003.

Nicolle, David. *Yarmuk, AD 636: The Muslim Conquest of Syria.* Westport, CT: Praeger, 2005.

O'Callaghan, Joseph F. *Reconquest and Crusade in Medieval Spain.* Philadelphia: University of Pennsylvania Press, 2003.

Ohlig, Karl-Heinz, and Gerd-R. Puin (eds.). *The Hidden Origins of Islam: New Research into its Early History.* Amherst, NY: Prometheus Books, 2008.

Powers, David Stephan. *Muhammad Is Not the Father of Any of Your Men: The Making of the Last Prophet.* Philadelphia: University of Pennsylvania Press, 2009.

Quigley, Mary. *Ancient West African Kingdoms: Ghana, Mali, and Songhai.* Chicago: Heinemann Library, 2002.

Schimmel, Annemarie. *The Empire of the Great Mughals: History, Art, and Culture.* New Delhi, India: Oxford University Press, 2005.

Sharma, Gauri. *Prime Ministers under the Mughals, 1526–1707.* New Delhi, India: Kanishka Publishers, 2006.

Smith, Richard L. *Ahmad al-Mansur: Islamic Visionary.* New York: Pearson Longman, 2006.

Sonn, Tamara. *A Brief History of Islam.* Malden, MA: Blackwell, 2004.

Walker, Paul E. *Exploring an Islamic Empire: Fatimid History and its Sources.* London: I. B. Tauris, 2002.

Walker, Paul E. *Fatimid History and Ismaili Doctrine.* Burlington, VT: Ashgate, 2008.

Wheatcroft, Andrew. *The Enemy at the Gate: Habsburgs, Ottomans, and the Battle for Europe.* New York: Basic Books, 2009.

Beliefs and Practices

Bravmann, M. M. *The Spiritual Background of Early Islam: Studies in Ancient Arab Concepts.* Boston: Brill, 2008.

Caner, Emir Fethi. *More than a Prophet: An Insider's Response to Muslim Beliefs about Jesus and Christianity.* Grand Rapids, MI: Kregel Publications, 2003.

Caner, Ergun Mehmet. *Unveiling Islam: An Insider's Look at Muslim Life and Beliefs.* Grand Rapids, MI: Kregel Publications, 2002.

Dakake, Maria Massi. *The Charismatic Community: Shi'ite Identity in Early Islam.* Albany: State University of New York Press, 2007.

Dawood, N. J. (trans.). *The Koran.* New York: Penguin Books, 1990.

Drummond, Richard Henry. *Islam for the Western Mind: Understanding Muhammad and the Koran.* Charlottesville, VA: Hampton Roads Publishing, 2005.

Farah, Caesar E. *Islam: Beliefs and Observances.* Hauppauge, NY: Barron's, 2003.

Gordon, Matthew. *Understanding Islam: Origins, Beliefs, Practices, Holy Texts, Sacred Places.* London: Duncan Baird, 2002.

Gulevich, Tanya. *Understanding Islam and Muslim Traditions: An Introduction to the Religious Practices, Celebrations, Festivals, Observances, Beliefs, Folklore, Customs, and Calendar System of the World's Muslim Communities, including an Overview of Islamic History and Geography.* Detroit, MI: Omnigraphics, 2004.

Hazleton, Lesley. *After the Prophet: The Epic Story of the Shia-Sunni Split in Islam.* New York: Doubleday, 2009.

Kabbani, Muhammad Hisham. *Encyclopedia of Islamic Doctrine.* Mountainview, CA: As-Sunna Foundation of America, 1998.

Khan, Ruqayya Yasmine. *Self and Secrecy in Early Islam.* Columbia, SC: University of South Carolina Press, 2008.

Lane, Jan-Erik. *Religion and Politics: Islam and Muslim Civilization.* Burlington, VT: Ashgate, 2009.

McCullar, Michael D. *A Christian's Guide to Islam.* Macon, GA: Smyth and Helwys, 2008.

Marranci, Gabriele. *The Anthropology of Islam.* New York: Berg, 2008.

Marshall, Paul A. *Islam at the Crossroads: Understanding Its Beliefs, History, and Conflicts.* Grand Rapids, MI: Baker Books, 2002.

Paas, Steven. *Beliefs and Practices of Muslims: The Religion of Our Neighbours.* Zomba, Malawi: Good Messenger Publications, 2006.

Ramadan, Tariq. *The Messenger: The Meanings of the Life of Muhammad.* New York: Penguin Books, 2008.

Rippin, Andrew. *Muslims: Their Religious Beliefs and Practices.* New York: Routledge, 2005.

Safran, Janina M. *The Second Umayyad Caliphate: The Articulation of Caliphal Legitimacy in al-Andalus.* Cambridge, MA: Harvard University Press, 2000.

Schwartz, Stephen. *The Other Islam: Sufism and the Road to Global Harmony.* New York: Doubleday, 2008.

Sherwani, Muhammad Habibur Rahman Khan (translated by Syed Moinul Haq). *Hazrat Abu Bakr: The First Caliph of Islam.* Lahore, Pakistan: Muhammad Ashraf, 1963.

Swarup, Ram. *Understanding the Hadith: The Sacred Traditions of Islam.* Amherst, NY: Prometheus Books, 2002.

Walker, Paul E. *Fatimid History and Ismaili Doctrine.* Burlington, VT: Ashgate, 2008.

Culture

Adeney, Miriam. *Daughters of Islam: Building Bridges with Muslim Women.* Downers Grove, IL: InterVarsity Press, 2002.

Behrens-Abouseif, Doris, and Stephen Vernoit. *Islamic Art in the 19th Century: Tradition, Innovation, and Eclecticism.* Boston: Brill, 2006.

Blair, Sheila, and Jonathan Bloom. *Rivers of Paradise: Water in Islamic Art and Culture.* New Haven: Yale University Press, 2009.

Broug, Eric. *Islamic Geometric Patterns.* New York: Thames and Hudson, 2008.

Burckhardt, Titus. *Art of Islam: Language and Meaning.* Bloomington, IN: World Wisdom, 2009.

Clot, André (translated by John Howe). *Harun al-Rashid and the World of the Thousand and One Nights.* New York: New Amsterdam, 1989.

Curatola, Giovanni, and Gianroberto Scarcia (translated by Marguerite Shore). *The Art and Architecture of Persia.* New York: Abbeville Press, 2007.

Fakhry, Majid. *Averroës, Aquinas, and the Rediscovery of Aristotle in Western Europe.* Washington, D.C.: Georgetown University Press, 1997.

Goodman, Lenn Evan. *Avicenna.* Ithaca, NY: Cornell University Press, 2006.

Grabar, Oleg. *Islamic Visual Culture, 1100–1800.* Burlington, VT: Ashgate, 2006.

Grabar, Oleg. *Masterpieces of Islamic Art: The Decorated Page from the 8th to the 17th Century.* New York: Prestel, 2009.

Gruendler, Beatrice, and Louise Marlow (eds). *Writers and Rulers: Perspectives on Their Relationship from Abbasid to Safavid Times.* Wiesbaden, Germany: Reichert, 2004.

Husain, Salma. *The Emperor's Table: The Art of Mughal Cuisine.* New Delhi, India: Lustre Press, 2008.

Jones, Owen. *Ornament and Design of the Alhambra.* Mineola, NY: Dover Publications, 2008.

Kellner-Heinkele, Barbara, Joachim Gierlichs, and Brigitte Heuer (eds.). *Islamic Art and Architecture in the European Periphery: Crimea, Caucasus, and the Volga-Ural Region.* Wiesbaden, Germany: Harrassowitz, 2008.

Khalili, Nasser D. *Visions of Splendour in Islamic Art and Culture.* London: Worth Press, 2008.

McCaughrean, Geraldine (ed.). *One Thousand and One Arabian Nights.* New York: Oxford University Press, 1999.

Michell, George. *The Majesty of Mughal Decoration: The Art and Architecture of Islamic India.* New York: Thames and Hudson, 2007.

O'Kane, Bernard. *The Treasures of Islamic Art in the Museums of Cairo.* New York: The American University in Cairo Press, 2006.

Rogers, J. M. *The Arts of Islam: Treasures from the Nasser D. Khalili Collection.* Sydney, Australia: Art Gallery of New South Wales Press, 2007.

Ruggles, D. Fairchild. *Islamic Gardens and Landscapes.* Philadelphia: University of Pennsylvania Press, 2008.

Welzbacher, Christian. *Euro Islam Architecture: New Mosques in the West.* Amsterdam, Netherlands: SUN, 2008.

Modern Society

Ageron, Charles Robert (translated and edited by Michael Brett). *Modern Algeria: A History from 1830 to the Present.* Trenton, NJ: Africa World Press, 1991.

Ahmed, Akbar S. *Journey into Islam: The Crisis of Globalization.* Washington, DC: Brookings Institution Press, 2007.

Aslan, Reza. *No God but God: The Origins, Evolution, and Future of Islam.* New York: Random House, 2006.

Ayoob, Mohammed. *The Many Faces of Political Islam: Religion and Politics in the Muslim World.* Ann Arbor: University of Michigan Press, 2008.

Bhutto, Benazir. *Reconciliation: Islam, Democracy, and the West.* New York: Harper, 2008.

Blauer, Ettagale. *Mauritania.* New York: Marshall Cavendish Benchmark, 2009.

Braswell, George W. *Islam and America: Answers to the 31 Most-Asked Questions.* Nashville, TN: Broadman and Holman, 2005.

Cesari, Jocelyne (ed.). *Encyclopedia of Islam in the United States.* Westport, CT: Greenwood Press, 2007.

Collins, Robert O. (ed.). *Civil Wars and Revolution in the Sudan: Essays on the Sudan, Southern Sudan, and Darfur, 1962–2004.* Hollywood, CA: Tsehai Publishers, 2005.

Coughlin, Con. *Khomeini's Ghost: The Iranian Revolution and the Rise of Militant Islam.* New York: Ecco, 2009.

Delgado, Kevin. *Morocco.* Detroit, MI: Lucent Books, 2006.

Dresch, Paul. *A History of Modern Yemen.* New York: Cambridge University Press, 2000.

Farmer, Brian R. *Understanding Radical Islam: Medieval Ideology in the Twenty-First Century.* New York: Peter Lang, 2007.

Gelletly, LeeAnne. *Somalia.* Broomall, PA: Mason Crest Publishers, 2008.

Gerges, Fawaz A. *America and Political Islam: Clash of Cultures or Clash of Interests?* New York: Cambridge University Press, 1999.

Gershoni, Israel, Hakan Erdem, and Ursula Woköck (eds.). *Histories of the Modern Middle East: New Directions*. Boulder, CO: Lynne Rienner Publishers, 2002.

Gillespie, Carol Ann. *Bahrain*. Philadelphia: Chelsea House Publishers, 2002.

Hunter, Shireen T. (ed.). *Reformist Voices of Islam: Mediating Islam and Modernity*. Armonk, NY: M. E. Sharpe, 2009.

Jensen, Erik. *Western Sahara: Anatomy of a Stalemate*. Boulder, CO: Lynne Rienner Publishers, 2005.

Jinju, Muhammadu Hambali. *Islam in Africa: Historico-Philosophical Perspectives and Current Problems*. Zaria, Nigeria: Bello University Press, 2001.

Kramer, Martin S. *Arab Awakening and Islamic Revival: The Politics of Ideas in the Middle East*. Piscataway, NJ: Transaction Publishers, 2008.

McAmis, Robert Day. *Malay Muslims: The History and Challenge of Resurgent Islam in Southeast Asia*. Grand Rapids, MI: W. B. Eerdmans, 2002.

Mackintosh-Smith, Tim. *Yemen: The Unknown Arabia*. New York: Overlook Press, 2000.

Marcovitz, Hal. *Islam in Africa*. Philadelphia: Mason Crest Publishers, 2007.

Marr, Phebe. *The Modern History of Iraq*. Boulder, CO: Westview Press, 2004.

Miller, Debra A. *Kuwait*. Farmington Hills, MI: Lucent Books, 2005.

Morrison, John, with additional text by Adam Woog. *Syria*. New York: Chelsea House, 2009.

Nydell, Margaret K. *Understanding Arabs: A Guide for Modern Times*. Yarmouth, ME: Intercultural Press, 2006.

O'Kane, David, and Tricia Redeker. *Biopolitics, Militarism, and Development: Eritrea in the Twenty-first Century*. New York: Berghahn Books, 2009.

Owtram, Francis. *A Modern History of Oman: Formation of the State since 1920*. New York: I. B. Tauris, 2004.

Polonskaya, Ludmila, and Alexei Malashenko (eds.). *Islam in Central Asia*. Reading, England: Ithaca Press, 1994.

Radu, Michael. *Islam in Europe*. Broomall, PA: Mason Crest Publishers, 2006.

Rashid, Ahmed. *Jihad: The Rise of Militant Islam in Central Asia*. New Haven: Yale University Press, 2002.

Salibi, Kamal S. *The Modern History of Jordan*. New York: I. B. Tauris, 1993.

Shelley, Toby. *Endgame in the Western Sahara: What Future for Africa's Last Colony?* New York: Zed Books, 2004.

Tanner, Stephen. *Afghanistan: A Military History from Alexander the Great to the Fall of the Taliban*. Karachi, Pakistan: Oxford University Press, 2003.

Tomohiko, Uyama (ed.). *Empire, Islam, and Politics in Central Eurasia*. Sapporo, Japan: Hokkaido University Press, 2007.

Turner, Richard Brent. *Islam in the African-American Experience*. Bloomington: Indiana University Press, 2003.

Vandewalle, Dirk (ed.). *Libya since 1969: Qadhafi's Revolution Revisited*. New York: Palgrave Macmillan, 2008.

Young, Mitchell (ed.). *Islam*. Farmington Hills, MI: Greenhaven Press, 2006.

Islamic World

Bowen, Wayne H. *The History of Saudi Arabia*. Westport, CT: Greenwood Press, 2008.

Caner, Ergun Mehmet. *Unveiling Islam: An Insider's Look at Muslim Life and Beliefs*. Grand Rapids, MI: Kregel Publications, 2002.

Chinyong Liow, Joseph, and Nadirsyah Hosen (eds.). *Islam in Southeast Asia*. New York: Routledge, 2009.

Corrigan, Jim. *Kazakhstan*. Philadelphia: Mason Crest, 2005.

Engineer, Asgharali. *Islam in Post-Modern World: Prospects and Problems*. Gurgaon, India: Hope India Publications, 2008.

Esposito, John L. *The Future of Islam*. New York: Oxford University Press, 2010.

Esposito, John L., and Dalia Mogahed. *Who Speaks for Islam? What a Billion Muslims Really Think*. New York: Gallup Press, 2007.

Gordon, Alijah. *The Propagation of Islam in the Indonesian-Malay Archipelago*. Kuala Lumpur, Malaysia: Malaysian Sociological Research Institute, 2001.

Habeeb, William Mark. *Turkmenistan*. Philadelphia: Mason Crest, 2005.

Harmon, Daniel E. *Kyrgyzstan*. Philadelphia: Mason Crest, 2005.

Israeli, Raphael. *Islam in China: Religion, Ethnicity, Culture, and Politics*. Lanham, MD: Lexington Books, 2002.

Losleben, Elizabeth. *The Bedouin of the Middle East*. Minneapolis, MN: Lerner Publications, 2003.

Nomachi, Kazuyoshi. *Mecca the Blessed, Medina the Radiant: The Holiest Cities of Islam*. New York: Aperture, 1997.

Rashid, Ahmed. *Jihad: The Rise of Militant Islam in Central Asia*. New York: Penguin Books, 2003.

Sagdeev, Roald, and Susan Eisenhower (eds.). *Islam and Central Asia: An Enduring Legacy or an Evolving Threat?* Washington, DC: Center for Political and Strategic Studies, 2000.

Tyler, Aaron. *Islam, the West, and Tolerance: Conceiving Coexistence*. New York: Palgrave Macmillan, 2008.

WEBSITES

Abbasids
i-cias.com/e.o/abbasids.htm
Article about the family that formed the last Arab caliphates; includes dates for the various caliphs.

Abu Bakr
www.sunnah.org/publication/khulafa_rashideen/caliph1.htm
An account of the life and work of the prophet Muhammad's close adviser.

Aga Khan Archnet
www.archnet.org
Website that provides profiles of all sites of architectural interest in the Muslim world, along with numerous diagrams, photographs, and academic papers.

Averroës
www.muslimphilosophy.com/ir
Biography of the influential Islamic philosopher;
includes extensive links to other resources.

Babur
*www.bbc.co.uk/religion/religions/islam/history/
mughalempire_2.shtml*
Website that is devoted to the life and times of the
first Mughal emperor.

Bedouin
www.geographia.com/egypt/sinai/bedouin.htm
Website that covers all aspects of the culture
and history of the desert-dwelling people.

Berbers
i-cias.com/e.o/berbers.htm
Website that gives an accessible introduction to the
history and significance of these peoples who lived
in northern Africa before the arrival of Islam.

Comparative Islamic Studies
www.equinoxjournals.com/ojs/index.php/CIS/index
The website of an academic journal dedicated
to the study of Islam.

Exploring Religions—Islam
uwacadweb.uwyo.edu/religionet/er/islam/index.htm
A website about different aspects of Islam from the
University of Wyoming.

Islam
www.bbc.co.uk/religion/religions/islam
Website that provides a comprehensive outline
of Muslim beliefs as well as an account of the
religion's historical development.

Islamic–American Zakat Foundation
www.iazf.org
Information about an organization that provides
food, shelter, clothing, and transportation to
the needy.

Islamic Calligraphy
www.islamicity.com/culture/Calligraphy/default.HTM
Website dedicated to the intricate art of Islamic
calligraphy.

Islamic Finder
www.islamicfinder.org/Hcal/index.php
Website showing the Muslim calendar; converts
Gregorian dates into *hijri* dates and vice versa.

Islamic Philosophy Online
www.muslimphilosophy.com
A site covering the history of Muslim thought.

Islamic Relief USA
www.irw.org
The website of a nonprofit, humanitarian
organization based in California that is working
to alleviate poverty.

Mecca
i-cias.com/e.o/mecca.htm
Description of the city; includes a list of key dates
in the history of the city.

Mughals
www.wsu.edu/~dee/mughal/contents.htm
Website about the dynasty that ruled India in the
16th and 17th centuries CE.

Muslim Students Association National
www.msanational.org
A website dedicated to the needs of Muslim
students in North America.

One Thousand and One Nights
www.al-bab.com/arab/literature/nights.htm
Website that contextualizes the celebrated Arabic
story collection and provides a link to the famous
English translation of the work by Richard Burton.

Online Hadith Collection
www.hadithcollection.com
Website providing translations of the full text of
all the major collections of Hadith; also includes
introductions that explain the origins of each
collection and its author.

Online Koran Project
www.al-quran.info
Website that provides searchable translations
of the Koran in many languages.

Ottomans

www.wsu.edu/~dee/ottoman/ottoman1.htm
Website that details the history of the Ottomans from their rise in the 13th century CE to their ultimate downfall almost 700 years later.

Oxford Islamic Studies Online

wwww.oxfordislamicstudies.com
Comprehensive resource comprising nearly four thousand entries, primary documents, and curriculum resources.

Persian Empire

www.crystalinks.com/persia.html
Detailed description of the civilization; includes useful maps and time lines.

The Reconquista

www.ucalgary.ca/applied_history/tutor/eurvoya/timeline.html
Time line that charts the Christian reclamation of the Iberian Peninsula.

Tariq Ramadan

www.tariqramadan.com
Website of Swiss-Muslim intellectual Tariq Ramadan; includes lectures, debates, and essays by Ramadan and other Muslim intellectuals.

Umayyads

www.princeton.edu/~batke/itl/denise/umayyads.htm
Short account of the first Muslim dynasty; includes suggestions for further reading.

Academic Institutions Teaching Islamic Studies

Abbasi Program in Islamic Studies at Stanford University

www.stanford.edu/dept/islamic_studies/index.html
Find out about undergraduate and postgraduate courses on Islamic subjects.

Arabic and Islamic Studies, Georgetown University, Washington

arabic.georgetown.edu
Learn about Georgetown's Arabic and Islamic program for students.

Arabic and Islamic Studies Program, University of Washington

depts.washington.edu/arabiyya
Visit this site to find out about courses that aim to give students a broad understanding of the Islamic world.

Carolina Duke Emory Institute for the Study of Islam

www.unc.edu/depts/cdeisi
Information about Islamic studies offered at this consortium of departments of religion from three colleges: University of North Carolina at Chapel Hill, Duke University (North Carolina), and Emory University (Atlanta).

Center for Arab and Islamic Studies, Villanova University, Pennsylvania

www.villanova.edu/artsci/arabislamic
Learn about the center's outreach program and its conferences and courses on Islamic studies.

Center for Islamic Studies, Youngstown State University, Ohio

class.ysu.edu/~islamst/index.html
Information about courses on Islamic culture, history, and religion.

Center for Middle Eastern and North African Studies, University of Michigan

www.ii.umich.edu/cmenas
Learn about the courses at this center on the peoples, cultures, and religions of northern Africa and western Asia.

Center for Middle Eastern Studies, Harvard University

cmes.hmdc.harvard.edu
Information about Harvard's courses aimed at increasing awareness and understanding of the cultures and politics of western Asia.

Center for Middle Eastern Studies, University of California at Berkeley

cmes.berkeley.edu/Programs/grants_alfalah.html
Find out about the center's program to promote better understanding of Islam in the United States.

Center for Middle Eastern Studies, University of Chicago

www.cmes.uchicago.edu/index.html
Learn about the courses available in the languages and civilizations of western Asia.

Department of Near Eastern Languages and Cultures, Indiana University
www.indiana.edu/~nelc
Discover Indiana University's range of programs dedicated to western Asian culture, religion, and history.

Department of Near Eastern Studies, Cornell University
www.arts.cornell.edu/nes/index.html
Learn about courses in western Asian archaeology, history, religion, and literature.

Department of Near Eastern Studies, Princeton University
www.princeton.edu/~nes
Visit this website to find out about Princeton's program of Islamic studies.

Department of Near Eastern Studies, University of California, Berkeley
neareastern.berkeley.edu
Find out about Berkeley's courses that cover Islamic culture, history, and politics.

Institute of Islamic Studies, McGill University, Montreal
www.mcgill.ca/islamicstudies
Information about this Canadian university's program of courses on the Muslim world.

Islamic Legal Studies at Harvard Law School
www.law.harvard.edu/programs/ilsp
Find out about Harvard Law School's research program to advance understanding of Islamic law.

Islamic Studies Program, University of Michigan
www.ii.umich.edu/ii/aboutus/specialinit/isi
Information on the university's program, which has more than 50 faculty members.

Islamic Studies Program, University of South Carolina
www.cas.sc.edu/Iis/ISLM
The Islamic studies program at this university focuses on Islamic cultures throughout the world.

Jewish, Islamic, and Near Eastern Studies Program, Washington University in Saint Louis
artsci.wustl.edu/~jines/undergrad.htm
Information about an interdisciplinary program exploring history, religion, culture, and politics.

King Fahd Center for Middle East and Islamic Studies, University of Arkansas
www.uark.edu/depts/mesp
An educational resource center on western Asia and northern Africa.

Middle East Center, University of Pennsylvania
mec.sas.upenn.edu
Learn about the courses centering on raising awareness of the circumstances in present-day western Asia.

Middle Eastern and Islamic Studies, New York University
www.nyu.edu/gsas/dept/mideast/
Information on the long-established studies on western Asian culture and languages in New York.

Middle East Studies Association (MESA), University of Arizona
mesa.wns.ccit.arizona.edu
A nonprofit, nonpolitical association that fosters the study of western Asia.

Middle East Studies, Brown University, Rhode Island
www.watsoninstitute.org/middleeast
Learn about the courses, including Arabic and Islamic history, offered at Brown University.

Middle East Studies Program, University of Wisconsin-Madison
mideast.wisc.edu/index.htm
Visit this website to find out information on courses covering western Asian culture and religion.

Middle Eastern Studies, University of Texas
www.utexas.edu/cola/depts/mes
Information on the college's western Asian program that has been running for five decades.

Religious Studies, Yale University
yale.edu/religiousstudies/fields/islamic.html
A website outlining Yale's program of Islamic studies.

Zwemer Center for Muslim Studies, Columbia International University, South Carolina
www.ciu.edu/muslimstudies
Learn more about this center dedicated to fostering Christian-Muslim relations.